18 Practice Sets for

EPFO

Social Security Assistant

Preliminary Exam 2019

with 3 Online Tests

- **Corporate Office :** 45, 2nd Floor, Maharishi Dayanand Marg, Corner Market, Malviya Nagar, New Delhi-110017

  Tel. : 011-49842349 / 49842350

Get free access to Online Test(s)?
INSTRUCTIONS

1. You can access your test on any Window based Desktop, android tablets or ipads and mobile phones absolutely free.
2. Visit the link below or scan the QR code:

3 Mock Tests - EPFO SSA Prelims Exam

http://bit.ly/EPFO3

3. Click on **"Attempt Free Mock Tests"**, a Registration window pops up, enter all the details in the form & click "Sign UP".
4. User is now logged in the account & all the Mock Tests appears in the grid. User can attempt the Free Mock Test(s) by clicking the **"Start"** button.
5. Contact us at support@mylearninggraph.com for any support.

Typeset by Disha DTP Team

Compiled and Edited by Disha Expert Team

DISHA PUBLICATION

For further information about the books from DISHA,

Log on to **www.dishapublication.com** or email to **info@dishapublication.com**

CONTENTS

ONLINE 3 PRACTICE SETS

PRACTICE SET (1)

Time : 60 Minutes **Max. Marks : 100**

NUMERICAL ABILITY

DIRECTIONS (Qs. 1-10) : *What should come in place of the question mark (?) in the following questions?*

1. $16\% \text{ of } 450 \div ?\% \text{ of } 250 = 4.8$
   - (a) 12
   - (b) 6
   - (c) 4
   - (d) 10
   - (e) None of these

2. $\sqrt{?} - 11 = \sqrt{1521}$
   - (a) $\sqrt{2500}$
   - (b) $(28)^2$
   - (c) $\sqrt{28}$
   - (d) 50
   - (e) None of these

3. $700 \div 70 \div 0.5 = ?$
   - (a) 10
   - (b) 2.5
   - (c) 1.5
   - (d) 20
   - (e) None of these

4. $12.8 \times 4.5 \times 2.2 = ?$
   - (a) 168.72
   - (b) 126.72
   - (c) 128.27
   - (d) 162.72
   - (e) None of these

5. $\left(5\times5\times5\times5\times5\times5\right)^4 \times \left(5\times5\right)^6 \div \left(5\right)^2 = \left(25\right)^?$
   - (a) 10
   - (b) 17
   - (c) 19
   - (d) 12
   - (e) None of these

6. $4 \times ? = 4062 \div 5$
   - (a) 203.1
   - (b) 213.1
   - (c) 205.1
   - (d) 215.1
   - (e) None of these

7. $5\dfrac{1}{5} + 2\dfrac{3}{5} + 1\dfrac{2}{5} = ?$
   - (a) $7\dfrac{4}{5}$
   - (b) $8\dfrac{3}{5}$
   - (c) $6\dfrac{2}{5}$
   - (d) $9\dfrac{1}{5}$
   - (e) None of these

8. $13\% \text{ of } 258 - ? = 10$
   - (a) 23.45
   - (b) 24.53
   - (c) 23.54
   - (d) 24.35
   - (e) None of these

9. $\dfrac{4}{5} \times 2\dfrac{3}{4} \div \dfrac{5}{8} = ?$
   - (a) $4\dfrac{12}{35}$
   - (b) $1\dfrac{12}{35}$
   - (c) $2\dfrac{11}{35}$
   - (d) $3\dfrac{13}{25}$
   - (e) None of these

10. $5437 - 3153 + 2284 = ? \times 50$
   - (a) 96.66
   - (b) 91.36
   - (c) 96.13
   - (d) 93.16
   - (e) None of these

DIRECTIONS (Qs. 11-15) : *What should come in place of the question mark (?) in the following number series?*

11. 2 16 112 672 3360 13440 ?
   - (a) 3430
   - (b) 3340
   - (c) 40320
   - (d) 43240
   - (e) None of these

12. 4   9   19   ?   79   159   319
    (a) 59   (b) 39
    (c) 49   (d) 29
    (e) None of these

13. 4000 2000 1000 500   250   125   ?
    (a) 80   (b) 65
    (c) 62.5   (d) 83.5
    (e) None of these

14. 588 563   540   519   ?   483   468
    (a) 500   (b) 496
    (c) 494   (d) 490
    (e) None of these

15. 121 ? 81 64 49 36 25
    (a) 92   (b) 114
    (c) 98   (d) 100
    (e) None of these

16. The sum of 15% of a positive number and 10% of the same number is 70. What is twice of that number?
    (a) 440   (b) 280
    (c) 560   (d) 140
    (e) None of these

17. Vikram scored 72 per cent marks in five subjects together, viz. Hindi, Science, Maths, English and Sanskrit together, where in the maximum marks of each subject were 100. How many marks did Vikram score in Science if he scored 80 marks in Hindi, 70 marks in Sanskrit, 76 marks in Maths and 65 marks in English?
    (a) 72   (b) 69
    (c) 59   (d) 71
    (e) None of these

18. The respective ratio between Pooja's, Prarthana's and Falguni's monthly income is 53:70: 57. If Prarthana's annual income is ₹4,20,000, what is the sum of Pooja's and Falguni's annual incomes? (In some cases monthly income and in some cases annual income is used.)
    (a) ₹ 5,92,500   (b) ₹ 6,83,500
    (c) ₹ 6,60,000   (d) ₹ 7,79,200
    (e) None of these

19. Manhar sold an item for ₹ 8,400 and incurred a loss of 25%. At what price should he have sold the item to have gained a profit of 40%?
    (a) ₹ 15,680
    (b) ₹ 16,220
    (c) ₹ 14,540
    (d) Cannot be determined
    (e) None of these

20. What will come in place of both the question marks (?) in the following question?

$$\frac{(?)^{2.3}}{8} = \frac{2}{(?)^{1.7}}$$

    (a) 8   (b) 1
    (c) 4   (d) 16
    (e) 2

21. A box contains 4 blue, 6 green and 5 red balls. If two balls are drawn at random, what is the probability that no ball is red in color?
    (a) $\dfrac{3}{10}$ (b) $\dfrac{1}{5}$
    (c) $\dfrac{3}{7}$ (d) $\dfrac{4}{11}$
    (e) $\dfrac{2}{9}$

22. A truck covers a distance of 360 km in 8 hours. A car covers the same distance in 6 hours. What is the respective ratio between the speed of the truck and the car?
    (a) 3 : 5   (b) 3 : 4
    (c) 1 : 2   (d) 4 : 5
    (e) None of these

23. In order to pass in an exam a student is required to get 975 marks out of the aggregate marks. Priya got 870 marks and was declared failed by 7 per cent. What are the maximum aggregate marks a student can get in the examination?
    (a) 1500   (b) 1000
    (c) 1200   (d) Cannot be determined
    (e) None of these

24. A group of men were assigned a work. After half of the work completed, double the number of men joined the original group. Now the work gets completed 6 days earlier than the scheduled number of days. What is the total number of days the initial group of men would have taken to complete the work?
    (a) 18 days   (b) 16 days
    (c) 12 days   (d) 15 days
    (e) None of these

25. A person travels from A to B at 30 km/hr and back from B to A at 34 km/hr. If the total time taken for the journey is 48 minutes, find the total distance travelled by the man.
    (a) 27.5 km   (b) 25.5 km
    (c) 20 km   (d) 30.25 km
    (e) 36 km

26. On children's day sweets were to be equally distributed amongst 200 children. But on that particular day 40 children remained absent; hence each child got 2 sweets extra. How many sweets were distributed?
    (a) 3000   (b) 1500
    (c) 2000   (d) 1600
    (e) Cannot be determined

27. The sum of the present ages of A and B is 66. The ratio of ages of A after 4 years and B 6 years ago is 5 : 3. What is B's present age(in years)?
    (a) 32   (b) 37
    (c) 42   (d) 30
    (e) 36

28. What is the difference between the compound interest and simple interest accrued on an amount of ₹12,000 at the end of three years at the rate of 12%?
    (a) ₹ 539.136   (b) ₹ 602.242
    (c) ₹ 495.248   (d) ₹ 488.322
    (e) None of these

29. The area of a rectangle is equal to the area of a circle with circumference equal to 220 metres. What is the length of the rectangle if its breadth is 50 metres?
    (a) 56 metres   (b) 83 metres
    (c) 77 metres   (d) 69 metres
    (e) None of these

30. Radhika got two successive discounts of 20% each on article marked at ₹ 30,000. She spent ₹ 2,800 on its repairs and then sold the same for ₹ 26,000. What is her profit percent in the whole transaction?
    (a) 103/10%   (b) 82/5%
    (c) 10%   (d) 5%
    (e) 200/11%

DIRECTIONS (Qs. 31-35) : *Study the following graph carefully and answer the questions that follow.*

Three different products (in Thousands) produced by a company in five different years

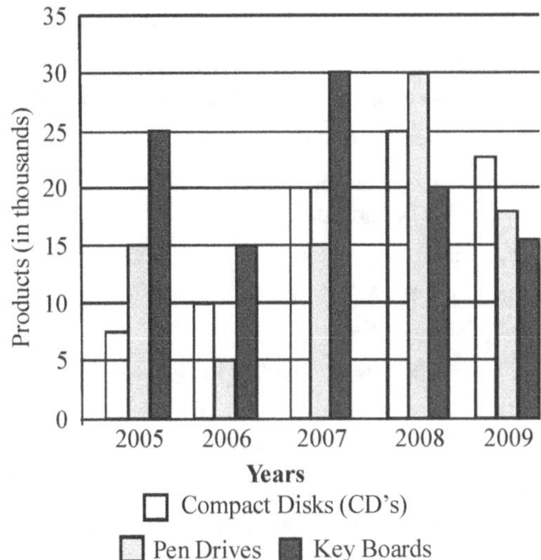

31. What was the total number of all the products produced by the company in the year 2006 and 2008 together ?
    (a) 105000   (b) 107 lacs
    (c) 105700   (d) 10570
    (e) None of these

32. What was the average number of Pen-drives produced by the company over all the years together ?
    (a) 1700   (b) 16500
    (c) 17000   (d) 85000
    (e) None of these

33. What is the difference between the total number of Pen-drives and CDs produced by the company together in the year 2008 and the number of Key boards produced by the company in the year 2006 ?
    (a) 40000   (b) 4000
    (c) 35000   (d) 3500
    (e) None of these

34. What was the respective ratio between the number of Key boards produced by the company in the year 2006, 2007 and 2009 ?
    (a) 1 : 2 : 3   (b) 1 : 2 : 2
    (c) 2 : 1 : 3   (d) 1 : 2 : 1
    (e) None of these

35. What was the respective ratio between the number of CDs produced by the company in the year 2009 and the number of Keyboards produced by the company in the year 2005 ?
    (a) 9 : 10   (b) 11 : 10
    (c) 10 : 9   (d) 10 : 11
    (e) None of these

REASONING ABILITY

36. Nishu starting from a fixed point goes 15 km towards North and then after turning to his right he goes 15 km. Then he goes 10, 15 and 15 metres after turning to his left each time. How far is he from his starting point?
    (a) 5 metres   (b) 10 metres
    (c) 20 metres   (d) 15 metres
    (e) Can not be determined

37. In a class of 90, where girls are twice that of boys, Shridar ranked fourteenth from the top, if there are 10 girls ahead of Shridar, how many boys are after him in rank?
    (a) 23   (b) 26
    (c) 25   (d) 22
    (e) None of the above

DIRECTIONS (Qs. 38-39) : *These questions are based on the following information.*

Six students P, Q, R, S, T and V are the top six rankers of the class. No two persons got the same rank. The student who got the highest marks is given rank 1 and the student who got the least marks is given rank 6. Q got less marks than both R and U. P got more marks than T but less than S. Q got the second least rank and U got the second highest rank, R got less marks than P.

38. _______ got the 3rd rank.
    (a) S   (b) P
    (c) R   (d) T
    (e) Cannot be determined

39. _______ got the 6th rank.
    (a) T   (b) P
    (c) R   (d) S
    (e) Cannot be determined

40. In a certain code, a number 13479 is written as AQFJL and 2568 is written as DMPN. How is 396824 written in that code?
    (a) QLPNMJ   (b) QLPNMF
    (c) QLPMNF   (d) QLPNDE
    (e) None of these

41. Ashok started walking towards South. Afterwalking 50 metres he took a right turn and walked 30 metres. He then took a right turn and walked 100 metres. He again took a right turn and walked 30 metres and stopped. How far and in which direction was he from the starting point?
    (a) 50 metres South   (b) 150 metres North
    (c) 180 metres East   (d) 50 metres North
    (e) None of these

42. How many such pairs of letters are there in the word 'VIRTUAL', each of which has as many letters between them in the word (in both forward and backward direction) as they have between them in the English alphabetical series ?
    (a) None   (b) One
    (c) Two   (d) Three
    (e) More than three

43. Town D is towards East of town F. Town B is towards North of town D. Town H is towards South of town B. Towards which direction is town H from town F?
    (a) East
    (b) South-East
    (c) North-East
    (d) Data inadequate
    (e) None of these

DIRECTIONS (Qs. 44-48) : *In each of the following questions there are three items. These three items may or may not be related with one another. Each group of items may fit into one of the diagrams (a), (b), (c), (d) and (e). You have to decide in which of the following diagrams and groups of items may fit. The number of that diagram is the answer.*

> **Give answer (a)** if only conclusion I follows.
> **Give answer (b)** if only conclusion II follows.
> **Give answer (c)** if either I or II follows.
> **Give answer (d)** if neither I nor II follows.
> **Give answer (e)** if both I and II follow.

44. **Statements:**
    All leaders are good team workers.
    All good team workers are good orators.
    Conclusions:
    I. Some good team workers are leaders.
    II. All good orators are leaders.

45. **Statements:**
    All terrorists are human.
    All humans are bad.
    Conclusions:
    I. All terrorists are bad.
    II. No human can be a terrorist.

46. **Statements:**
    Some teachers are followers.
    Some followers are famous.
    Conclusions:
    I. Some teachers are famous.
    II. Some followers are teachers.

47. **Statements:**
    Some books are pens.
    No pen is pencil.
    Conclusions:
    I. Some books are pencils.
    II. No book is pencil.

48. **Statements:**
    Some dedicated souls are angles
    All social workers are angles.
    Conclusions:
    I. Some dedicated souls are social workers
    II. Some social workers are dedicated souls

DIRECTIONS (Qs. 49-50) : *Study the information given below and answer the questions following it:*

Mohan is son of Arun's father's sister. Prakash is son of Reva, who is mother of Vikash and grandmother of Arun. Pranab is father of Neela and grandfather of Mohan. Reva is wife of Pranab.

49. How is Mohan related to Reva ?
    (a) Grandson
    (b) Son
    (c) Nephew
    (d) Data inadaequate
    (e) None of these

50. How is Vikash's wife related to Neela ?
    (a) Sister
    (b) Niece
    (c) Sister-in-law
    (d) Data inadaequate
    (e) None of these

DIRECTIONS (Qs. 51-55) : *Read the following information carefully to answer the questions that follow.*

There are six teachers A, B, C, D, E and F in a school. Each of the teachers teaches two subjects, one compulsory subject and the other optional subject. D's optional subject is History while three others have it as compulsory subject. E and F have Physics as one of their subjects. F's compulsory subject is Mathematics which is an optional subject of both C and E. History and English are A's subjects but in terms of compulsory and optional subjects, they are reverse of those of D's. Chemistry is an optional subject of any one of them. There is only one female teacher in the school who has English as her compulsory subject.

51. What is C's compulsory subject ?
    (a) History
    (b) Physics
    (c) Chemistry
    (d) English
    (e) None of these

52. Who is a female member in the group ?
    (a) A
    (b) B
    (c) C
    (d) D
    (e) None of these

53. Who among the following has same optional subjects as that of the compulsory subject of F ?
    (a) D
    (b) B
    (c) A
    (d) C
    (e) None of these

54. Disregarding which is compulsory and which is the optional subject, who has the same two subjects combination as F ?
    (a) A
    (b) B
    (c) E
    (d) D
    (e) None of these

55. Which of the following groups of teachers has History as the compulsory subject ?
    (a) A, C and D
    (b) B, C and D
    (c) C and D
    (d) A, B and C
    (e) None of these

DIRECTIONS (Qs. 56-60) : *Study the following information to answer the given questions.*

Seven friends - L, M, N, O, P, Q and R are sitting in a straight line facing North, not necessarily in the same order. M sits fifth to the right of O. P sits third to the right of L. Both L and P do not sit at the extreme ends of the line. Q and R are immediate neighbours of each other. N sits third to the left of Q.

56. What is O's position with respect of R ?
    (a) Second to the right   (b) Third to the left
    (c) Second to the left   (d) Third to the right
    (e) None of these
57. Which of the following represents the friends sitting at the extreme ends of the line?
    (a) O, M   (b) Q, O
    (c) N, M   (d) Q, N
    (e) None of these
58. If all the seven friends are made to sit in alphabetical order from **left to right,** the positions of how many will remain unchanged ?
    (a) Four   (b) Three
    (c) One   (d) Two
    (e) None of these
59. Who sits exactly in the middle of the row ?
    (a) P   (b) L
    (c) Q   (d) R
    (e) None of these
60. Four of the following five are alike in a certain way based on their seating positions in the above arrangement and so form a group. Which is the one that **does not** belong to the group ?
    (a) MP   (b) RQ
    (c) ON   (d) LN
    (e) QL

DIRECTIONS (Qs. 61-65) : *Study the following information carefully and answer the given questions.*

A, B, C, D, E, F and G are sitting in around a circle and are facing the centre. G is the second to the left of C, who is to the immediate left of F. A is third to the left of E. B is between D and E.

61. Which of the following is false?
    (a) A is fourth to the right of E.
    (b) G is to immediate right of D
    (c) F is third to the right of D
    (d) B is to immediate left of D
    (e) None of these
62. Which of the following is true?
    (a) C is fourth to the left of B
    (b) A is to immediate right of G
    (c) D is second to the left of E
    (d) B is second to the right of G
    (e) None of these
63. Which of the following pair has the first person sitting to the immediate left of the second person?
    (a) BE   (b) C A
    (c) GD   (d) DG
    (e) None of these
64. Which of the following has the middle person sitting between the remaining two ?
    (a) FCE   (b) EFB
    (c) DEB   (d) GDA
    (e) None of these

65. Which of the following is the position of F?
    (a) Fourth to the right of D
    (b) To the immediate left of C
    (c) Between A and E
    (d) To the immediate right of A
    (e) None of these

DIRECTIONS (Qs. 66-70): *Study the following arrangement carefully and answer the questions given below:*

F 4 @ H 2 E % M P 5 W 9 @ I Q R 6 U H 3 Z 7 A T B 8 V # G $ Y D

66. How many such consonants are there in the above arrangement, each of the which is immediately preceded by a number but not immediately followed by a number?
    (a) None   (b) One
    (c) Two   (d) Three
    (e) More than three
67. Which of the following is the 10th to the right of the 19th from the right end of the above arrangement?
    (a) M   (b) T
    (c) #   (d) 2
    (e) None of these
68. If all the symbols are dropped from the above arrangement, which of the following will be the 14th from the left end?
    (a) R   (b) Q
    (c) U   (d) 3
    (e) None of these
69. What should come in place of the question mark (?) in the following series based on the above arrangement?
    HEM, 59I, RU3, ?
    (a) 7AB   (b) 7AT
    (c) ★78   (d) ABV
    (e) None of these
70. How many such symbols are there in the above arrangment, each of which is immediately preceded by a number and immediately followed by a letter?
    (a) None   (b) One
    (c) Two   (d) Three
    (e) More than three

ENGLISH LANGUAGE

DIRECTIONS (Qs. 71-80): *Read the following passage carefully and answer the questions given below it. Certain words are printed in bold to help you locate them while answering some of the questions.*

The Emperor had inherited a peaceful and prosperous kingdom at a young age after the **untimely** death of his father. A few months later a man arrived at court. He stated that he was from a far off land and had the gift of foresight. He impressed the Emperor with his witty remarks and was appointed a courtier. The Emperor and those at court all enjoyed hearing accounts of his travels. One day the newly appointed minister said, "Your Majesty, you are destined for great things. It is written in the stars. I have learnt the art of fortune telling. Do not be content with your kingdom alone. Travel, see the world and conquer.

There are many who are oppressed. They will bless you for rescuing them from the tyranny of their rulers." The Emperor was **stunned** to hear this but he refused to discuss the matter at the time. The courtiers too were astonished to hear this and began debating among themselves. "It is true," they said, "Our Emperor's father was a great warrior and he ruled wisely. Perhaps there is truth in this." So the newly appointed courtier shrewdly planted the idea of waging war against other kingdoms at court. After hearing several repeated arguments in **favour** of this idea the Emperor finally agreed. He was a young man and a battle seemed to be exciting and an adventure. So the newly appointed minister planned the first campaign against a smaller neighbouring kingdom.

The Emperor knew the ruler was cruel and felt justified in waging war against him. Having the superior army he easily defeated the king. Everyone celebrated. But the campaign did not stop there. With every victory the new minister would **urge** the Emperor on to the next battle. The soldiers grew tired after over two years at war but did not complain out of respect and loyalty to their ruler. Meanwhile the situation in his kingdom began to deteriorate. With no one to look after the daily administration and to resolve disputes, signs of neglect began to be seen. The Emperor was no longer **bothered** if he was freeing the oppressed when he attacked a kingdom. He would plunder their riches to fund his wars. The new minister who was in charge of these funds kept a large part for himself and grew richer.

An old man who had been a minister in the Emperor's father's court grew worried and decided to do something about this situation. A few days later when the Emperor was out riding in the forest he suddenly saw the old man. He greeted him like an old friend and inquired what he was doing there. The man pointed to two owls in the trees. "I am listening to their conversation". "What are they saying?" the Emperor asked unbelievingly. "They are negotiating the marriage of their children. The first owl wants to know whether the other will be gifting his daughter fifty villages on her wedding day. To which the second one replied that he would have to gift her one hundred and fifty as the villages were in ruins and as such were worthless but with the Emperor as ruler there would be many such villages." When the Emperor heard this he realised the error of his ways. He returned home immediately, rewarded the old minister putting him in charge of reconstructing the ruined villages and dismissed the fortune teller from his court.

71. Which of the following is TRUE in the context of the passage?

(a) The Emperor's father inherited his kingdom at a very young age.

(b) The soldiers followed the Emperor only because they were afraid of him.

(c) It took time at first to convince the Emperor to conquer other kingdoms.

(d) The Emperor was afraid to wage war against the neighbouring kingdom because its ruler was cruel.

(e) After his father's death the Emperor had to wage many wars to ensure his kingdom remained peaceful.

72. What was the Emperor's reaction when he saw the old minister?

(a) He was ashamed to see him because he had replaced him with a new minister.

(b) He was relieved to see him because he wanted his advice.

(c) He felt sorry for the old man because he was talking to birds.

(d) He was pleased to see him.

(e) None of these

73. What justification did the courtier give for attacking the neighbouring kingdom?

(a) The Emperor needed the money to maintain his army.

(b) The money was needed for the benefit of the Emperor's subjects and to ensure the kingdom did not fall into debt.

(c) To better the condition of its people who were being unjustly treated by their ruler.

(d) It was his father's last wish.

(e) Its ruler had attacked the Emperor's kingdom during his father's reign.

74. Why did the Emperor reward the old man?

(a) For his talent of talking to birds

(b) He was successful at reconstructing the destroyed villages.

(c) He felt sorry for his plight in his old age and wanted to do something to help.

(d) For narrating an imaginative story to the Emperor

(e) For showing the Emperor where his duty lay

75. Under what circumstances did the Emperor inherit his kingdom?

(a) His father was suddenly killed in battle.

(b) His courtiers requested him to become the king.

(c) He inherited the kingdom on reaching a particular age.

(d) His father had died after an illness.

(e) None of these

DIRECTIONS (76-78): *Choose the word which is most nearly the SAME in meaning to the word given in bold as used in the passage.*

76. **Urge**

(a) advice   (b) need

(c) prey   (d) encourage

(e) praise

77. **Untimely**

(a) early   (b) rapid

(c) punctual   (d) late

(e) gradual

78. **Stunned**

    (a) fainted   (b) surprised

    (c) pleased   (d) unconscious

    (e) injured

DIRECTIONS (79-80): *Choose the word which is most OPPOSITE in meaning of the word given in bold as used in the passage.*

79. **Favour**

    (a) mistake   (b) bias

    (c) appeal   (d) punishment

    (e) against

80. **Bothered**

    (a) calm   (b) uninterested

    (c) focused   (d) distracted

    (e) sure

DIRECTIONS (Qs. 81-90): *In the following passage there are blanks, each of which has been numbered. These numbers are printed below the passage and against each, five words are suggested, one of which fills the blanks appropriately. Find out the appropriate word in each case.*

One of the most brutal features of gender inequality takes the form of physical violence against women. The ..(81).. of such violence is remarkably high, not in poorer and less developed economies but also in wealthy and modern societies. Indeed the ..(82).. of battering women even in the richest and most developed economies is ..(83).. high. Turing to India, it must be ..(84).. first that the frequency of assaults on women is high in the country. To that ..(85).. general recognition has to be added the special role of violence connected with particular ..(86).. features, such as dowry and economic settlements. Even though the numbers involved with in violent deaths are ..(87).. by the larger numbers that ..(88).. from ..(89).. of healthcare, the crude and brutal nature of this from gender inequality makes it a particularly severe ..(90).. of the deprivation of women.

81.   (a) expectations   (b) counting

    (c) incidence   (d) acceptance

    (e) responses

82.   (a) frequency   (b) occurrence

    (c) event   (d) chance

    (e) blocking

83.   (a) relatively   (b) clearly

    (c) surely   (d) undoubtedly

    (e) astonishingly

84.   (a) accomplished   (b) acknowledged

    (c) cleared   (d) understand

    (e) assured

85.   (a) anxiety   (b) terrible

    (c) surprise   (d) power

    (e) form

86.   (a) national   (b) visible

    (c) social   (d) category

    (e) personal

87.   (a) fewer   (b) outshine

    (c) lean   (d) dwarfed

    (e) horrible

88.   (a) perish   (b) develop

    (c) spoil   (d) incline

    (e) direct

89.   (a) omission   (b) attention

    (c) care   (d) effort

    (e) neglect

90.   (a) remark   (b) indication

    (c) happening   (d) manifestation

    (e) rise

DIRECTIONS (Qs. 91-100): *In each of the questions given belows, a sentence is given which is divided into 5 parts. It is then followed by 5 options which give the sequence of the correct parts. Choose the option which gives the correct sequence of the grammatically correct parts. If all the parts are grammatically correct or if the correct sequence is not given in the options choose option (e) as the correct choice.*

91. Time magazine dedicated(A)/ its person of the year(B)/ cover to women who broke the silence surrounding(C)/ the pervasiveness of sexually harassment and violence(D), especially in the workplace(E).

    (a) ABCD   (b) ACDE

    (c) CBDE   (d) ABCE

    (e) None of these

92. These experiences have(A)/ an insidious effect on women's lives(B)/ and ability to participation(C)/ in educational, work and(D)/ social activities(E).

    (a) ABDE   (b) ACDE

    (c) ABDE   (d) BCDE

    (e) None of these

93. What mattered to them was that(A)/ Lenin had inspired the(B)/ Communist Party of India(C)/ (Marxist)-led government in that northeastern State, which(D)/ have un-seated after an un-broken 25 years of 'red rule'(E).

    (a) ABCD   (b) BCDE

    (c) ACDE   (d) ABDE

    (e) None of these

94. The new Chief Minister, too,(A)/ deserves appreciation for his expression of disapproval(B)./ Those who said things that seemed to explain(C)/ away the dhakka will be hopefully be sobered(D)/ by the Prime Minister's admonition(E).

    (a) ACDE   (b) BCDE

    (c) ABCD   (d) ABDE

    (e) None of these

95. It says to Presidents and Governors(A)/ what they should or should not do(B)/, how they should and should not act(C)/ when scrutinised results to see(D)/ who should be called to form governments(E).
    (a) ABDE
    (b) ABCD
    (c) ABCE
    (d) ACDE
    (e) None of these

96. The beauty of what Ghosh discovers(A)/ is that these villagers have been(B)/ following such sane ecological practices for many(C) decades without any help from the State,(D) and well beyond the gaze of the media(E).
    (a) ABCD
    (b) BCDE
    (c) ACDE
    (d) ABDE
    (e) None of these

97. Today's appliances can communicate(A)/ with each other, interacted(B)/ with people, and even(C)/ to a degree act out compelling(D)/ stories by themselves(E).
    (a) ABCE
    (b) ACDE
    (c) ABCD
    (d) BCDE
    (e) None of these

98. A few thousand sensors, systematically(A)/ placed all around a city,(B)/ might accurately track(C)/ traffic rule violations, mob violence,(D)/ or other irregularities(E).
    (a) ABCD
    (b) ACDE
    (c) BCDE
    (d) ABDE
    (e) None of these

99. A lot of our personal and lifestyle data are(A)/ shared through 'smart' objects, and we don't even understand that(B)./ Your breakfast time, TV watching schedule, and even when your house remained(C)/ empty are pieces of information sure to get exposed through the IoT(D)/, posing a serious security and privacy threat(E).
    (a) ABCD
    (b) ABDE
    (c) ACDE
    (d) BCDE
    (e) None of these

100. The arrival of a new toy, "Buzz Lightyear"(A)/, creates a sense of insecurity between(B)/ the older toys, with the current leader(C)/, "Woody", even feeling that(D)/ this leadership is under threat(E).
    (a) ACDE
    (b) ABCD
    (c) BCDE
    (d) ABDE
    (e) None of these

Answer Key

1	(b)	11	(c)	21	(c)	31	(a)	41	(d)	51	(a)	61	(c)	71	(c)	81	(c)	91	(d)
2	(e)	12	(b)	22	(b)	32	(b)	42	(b)	52	(d)	62	(b)	72	(d)	82	(a)	92	(c)
3	(d)	13	(c)	23	(a)	33	(a)	43	(b)	53	(d)	63	(d)	73	(c)	83	(e)	93	(a)
4	(b)	14	(a)	24	(a)	34	(d)	44	(a)	54	(c)	64	(e)	74	(e)	84	(b)	94	(e)
5	(b)	15	(d)	25	(b)	35	(a)	45	(a)	55	(d)	65	(a)	75	(e)	85	(e)	95	(c)
6	(a)	16	(c)	26	(d)	36	(b)	46	(b)	56	(b)	66	(b)	76	(d)	86	(c)	96	(b)
7	(d)	17	(b)	27	(d)	37	(b)	47	(c)	57	(c)	67	(b)	77	(a)	87	(a)	97	(b)
8	(c)	18	(c)	28	(a)	38	(c)	48	(d)	58	(e)	68	(e)	78	(b)	88	(a)	98	(e)
9	(d)	19	(a)	29	(c)	39	(a)	49	(a)	59	(c)	69	(a)	79	(e)	89	(e)	99	(b)
10	(b)	20	(e)	30	(b)	40	(b)	50	(c)	60	(d)	70	(d)	80	(b)	90	(d)	100	(a)

HINTS & EXPLANATIONS

1. (b) 16% of $450 \div ?\%$ of $250 = 4.8$

    $\Rightarrow \quad 450 \times \dfrac{16}{100} \div 250 \times \dfrac{?}{100} = 4.8$

    $\Rightarrow \quad 72 \div 2.5 \times ? = 4.8$

    $\Rightarrow \quad 2.5 \times ? = \dfrac{72}{4.8}$

    $\therefore \quad ? = \dfrac{72}{4.8 \times 2.5} = 6$

2. (e) $\sqrt{?} - 11 = \sqrt{1521}$

    $\Rightarrow \sqrt{?} - 11 = 39$

    $\Rightarrow \sqrt{?} = 39 + 11 = 50$

    $\therefore \ ? = (50)^2 = 2500$

3. (d) $? = 700 \div 70 \div 0.5 = 700 \times \dfrac{1}{70} \times \dfrac{1}{0.5} = 20$

4. (b) $? = 12.8 \times 4.5 \times 2.2 = 126.72$

5. (b) $(25)^? = (5 \times 5 \times 5 \times 5 \times 5 \times 5)^4 \times (5 \times 5)^6 \div (5)^2$

$= (25 \times 25 \times 25)^4 \times (25)^6 \div (25)^1$

$= (25^3)^4 \times (25)^6 \div 25^1 = (25)^{12} \times (25)^6 \div (25)^1$

$= (25)^{12+6-1} = (25)^{17}$

$\therefore \quad ? = 17$

6. (a) $4 \times ? = 4062 \div 5 = 4062 \times \dfrac{1}{5} = 812.4$

$\therefore \quad ? = \dfrac{812.4}{4} = 203.1$

7. (d) $? = 5\dfrac{1}{5} + 2\dfrac{3}{5} + 1\dfrac{2}{5} = \dfrac{26}{5} + \dfrac{13}{5} + \dfrac{7}{5}$

$= \dfrac{26 + 13 + 7}{5} = \dfrac{46}{5} = 9\dfrac{1}{5}$

8. (c) 13% of $258 - ? = 10$

$\therefore \quad ? = 13\%$ of $258 - 10$

$= 258 \times \dfrac{13}{100} - 10 = 33.54 - 10 = 23.54$

9. (d) $? = \dfrac{4}{5} \times 2\dfrac{3}{4} \div \dfrac{5}{8} = \dfrac{4}{5} \times \dfrac{11}{4} \div \dfrac{5}{8}$

$= \dfrac{4}{5} \times \dfrac{11}{4} \times \dfrac{8}{5} = \dfrac{88}{25} = 3\dfrac{13}{25}$

10. (b) $? \times 50 = 5437 - 3153 + 2284 = 7721 - 3153 = 4568$

$\therefore \quad ? = \dfrac{4568}{50} = 91.36$

11. (c) Given series.

2   16   112   672   3360   13440   40320

$\times 8 \quad \times 7 \quad \times 6 \quad \times 5 \quad \times 4 \quad \times 3$

$\therefore \quad ? = 40320$

12. (b) Given series.

4   9   19   39   79   159   319

$\times 2+1 \quad \times 2+1 \quad \times 2+1 \quad \times 2+1 \quad \times 2+1 \quad \times 2+1$

$\therefore \quad ? = 39$

13. (c) Given series

4000   2000   1000   500   250   125   62.5

$\div 2 \quad \div 2 \quad \div 2 \quad \div 2 \quad \div 2 \quad \div 2$

$\therefore \quad ? = 62.5$

14. (a) Given series.

588   563   540   519   500   483   468

$-25 \quad -23 \quad -21 \quad -19 \quad -17 \quad -15$

$\therefore \quad ? = 500$

15. (d) Given series.

121   100   81   64   49   36   25

$(11)^2 \quad (10)^2 \quad (9)^2 \quad (8)^2 \quad (7)^2 \quad (6)^2 \quad (5)^2$

$\therefore \quad ? = 100$

16. (c) Let the positive no. be x.

According to question, 15% of x + 10% of $x = 70$

$\Rightarrow \quad x \times \dfrac{15}{100} + x \times \dfrac{10}{100} = 70$

$\Rightarrow \quad \dfrac{15x}{100} + \dfrac{10x}{100} = 70$

$\Rightarrow \quad \dfrac{25x}{100} = 70$

$\therefore \quad x = \dfrac{70 \times 100}{25} = 280$

$\therefore \quad$ Double of given no. $= 280 \times 2 = 560$

17. (b) Total number obtained by Vikram

$= (100 \times 5) \times \dfrac{72}{100} = 500 \times \dfrac{72}{100} = 360$

$\therefore \quad$ Number in science

$= 360 - (80 + 70 + 76 + 65) = 360 - 291 = 69$

18. (c) Monthly income of Prarthana $= \dfrac{4,20,000}{12} = ₹\, 35,000$

Monthly income of Pooja and Falguni

$= 35,000 \times \dfrac{53 + 57}{70} = 35,000 \times \dfrac{110}{70} = ₹\, 55,000$

$\therefore \quad$ Annual income of Pooja and Falguni

$= 55,000 \times 12 = ₹\, 6,60,000$

19. (a) Cost price of item $= 8400 \times \dfrac{100}{100 - 25}$

$= 8400 \times \dfrac{100}{75} = ₹\, 11200$

SP of item

$= 11200 \times \dfrac{100 + 40}{100} = 11200 \times \dfrac{140}{100} = ₹\, 15680$

20. (e) $\dfrac{(?)^{2.3}}{8} = \dfrac{2}{(?)^{1.7}}$

$\Rightarrow (?)^{2.3 + 1.7} = 16 \Rightarrow (?)^4 = 16 = (2)^4$

$\therefore \quad ? = 2$

21. (c) Total balls $= 15$

Not red ball means 2 balls from blue or green color i.e. any of $(4 + 6) = 10$ balls

So required probability $= {}^{10}C_2 / {}^{15}C_2 = 3/7$

22. (b) Speed of truck $= \dfrac{\text{distance}}{\text{time}} = \dfrac{360}{8} = 45\,\text{km/hr}$

Speed of car $= \dfrac{\text{distance}}{\text{time}} = \dfrac{360}{6} = 60\,\text{km/hr}$

$\therefore$ Required Ratio $= 45 : 60 = 3 : 4$

23. (a) Minimum marks to pass $= 975$

Priya failed by $975 - 870 = 105$ marks

$\therefore$ Maximum marks $= \dfrac{105}{7} \times 100 = 1500$

24. (a) Let initially x men are there to complete work in 2y days.

Now after half of work completed, i.e. after 'y' days, double men as before joined the group.

This means now there are 3x men working.

So after y days

$M1 \times D1 = M2 \times D2$

$x \times y = 3x \times (y - 6) \Rightarrow y = 9$

So total days x men would have taken $= 2y = 18$ days

25. (b) When we are given total time for 2 journeys of equal distance,

One way distance $=$ (multiplication of speeds/addition of speeds) $\times$ total time

So here distance from A to B

$= [(30 \times 34)/(30 + 34)] \times 48/60 = 51/4$

So total distance travelled $= 2 \times (51/4) = 51/2 = 25.5$ km

26. (d) Let x sweets is distributed to each children

According to question,

$(200 - 40) \times (x + 2) = 200 \times x$

$\Rightarrow (160) \times (x + 2) = 200x \Rightarrow 160x + 320 = 200x$

$\Rightarrow 200x - 160x = 320 \Rightarrow 40x = 320$

$\therefore \quad x = \dfrac{320}{40} = 8$

$\therefore$ Total no. of sweets $= 200 \times x = 200 \times 8 = 1600$

27. (d) Let the present ages of A & B be x years and y years respectively.

$x + y = 66$ ...(i)

$(x + 4)/(y - 6) = 5/3$ ...(ii)

Solving equations (i) and (ii), we get $x = 36$, $y = 30$

So, the present age of B is 30 years.

28. (a) $\text{S.I.} = \dfrac{\text{principal} \times \text{time} \times \text{rate}}{100}$

$= \dfrac{12000 \times 3 \times 12}{100} = ₹\,4320$

$\text{C.I.} = P\left[\left(1 + \dfrac{\text{rate}}{100}\right)^{\text{time}} - 1\right]$

$= 12000\left[\left(1 + \dfrac{12}{100}\right)^{3} - 1\right]$

$= 12000\left[\left(\dfrac{28}{25}\right)^{3} - 1\right]$

$= 12000\left[\dfrac{21952}{15625} - 1\right] = 12000 \times \dfrac{6327}{15625}$

$= ₹\,4859.136$

$\therefore$ Required difference $= 4859.136 - 4320 = ₹\,539.136$

29. (c) Radius of circle (r) $= \dfrac{\text{circumference}}{2\pi} = \dfrac{220 \times 7}{2 \times 22} = 35$ m.

area of circle $= \pi r^2 = \dfrac{22}{7} \times (35)^2 = \dfrac{22}{7} \times 35 \times 35$

$= 3850\,\text{m}^2 = $ area of rectangle

$\therefore$ Length of rectangle $= \dfrac{\text{area of rectangle}}{\text{width}}$

$= \dfrac{3850}{50} = 77\,\text{m}$

30. (e) Successive discounts of 20% and 20% makes overall discount of

$(-20) + (-20) + (-20)(-20)/100 = -40 + 4 = -36\%$

So she buys the article for

$[(100-36)/100] \times 30000 = ₹\,19,200$

Radhika spends 2800 on repairs, so total CP

$= 2800 + 19200 = ₹\,22,000$

$SP = ₹\,26,000$

So profit% $= (4000/22000) \times 100 = 200/11\,\%$

31. (a) Required number of all products

$= (10 + 5 + 15 + 25 + 30 + 20)$ thousand

$= 105000$

32. (b) Average number of produced pen-drives

$= \left(\dfrac{15 + 5 + 15 + 30 + 17.5}{5}\right)$ thousand $= 16500$

33. (a) Required difference

$= (30 + 25 - 15)$ thousand $= 40000$

34. (d) Required ratio $= 15 : 30 : 15 = 1 : 2 : 1$

35. (a) Required ratio $= 22.5 : 25 = 225 : 250 = 9 : 10$

36. (b)

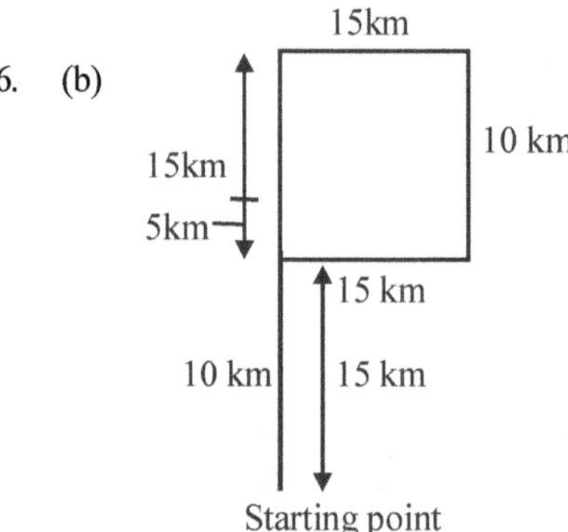

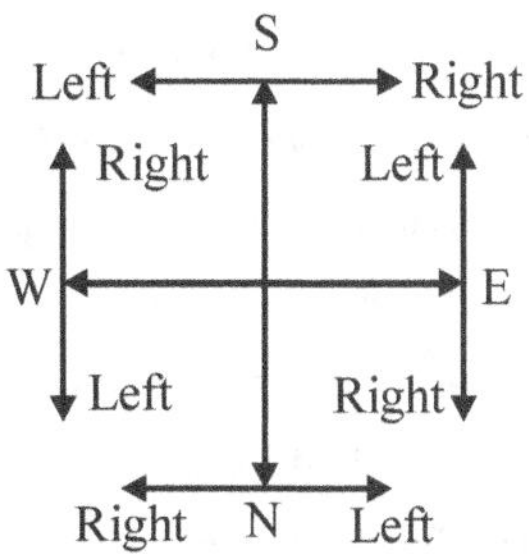

So, he is 10 metres from his starting point.

37. (b) No of boys = x; No of girls = 2x;
$x + 2x = 90 \Rightarrow 3x = 90$
x (Boys) = 30 ; 2x (Girls) = 60
Number of student behind Shridar = 90 – 14 = 76
No of girls behind Shridar = 60 – 10 = 50
No of boys behind Shridar = 76 – 50 = 26

38. (b) Given that,
$Q < R$ and U
also $T > P > S$ and $R > P$
Q got the second least rank and U got the second highest rank.
So, T shohan should have got least and S should have got the highest ranks.

T Q _ _ U S

Since $R > P$ the final arrangement is as follows.

Student	T	Q	R	P	U	S
Rank	6	5	4	3	2	1

39. (a) T

40. (b)

41. (d)

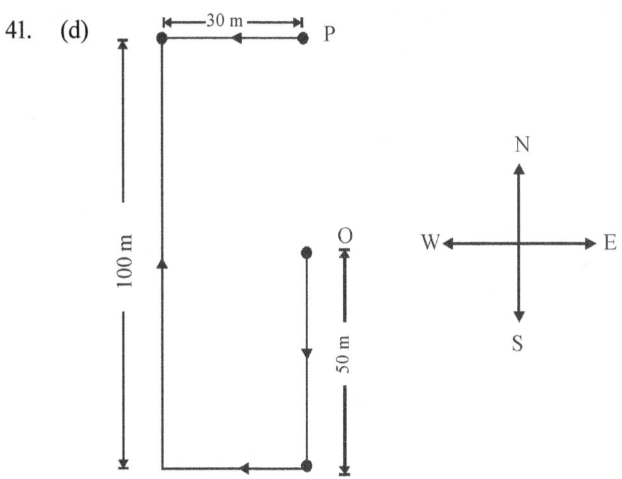

OP = 100 m – 50 m = 50 m
Besides, P is north of O.

42. (b)
2 9 18 20 21 I 12
V I R T U A L

43. (d)

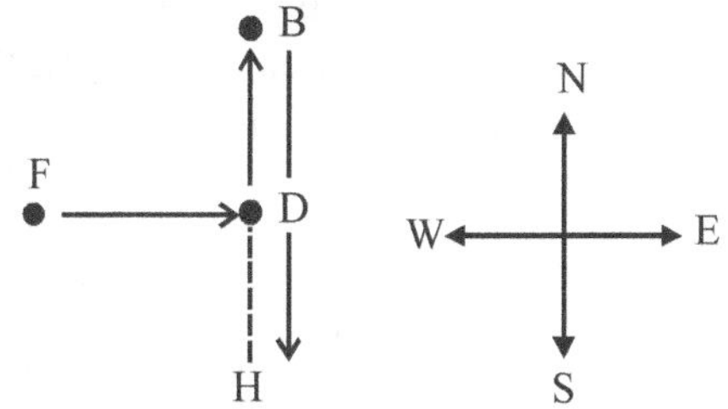

The position of town H is not specifically mentioned.

44. (a) Conclusion I is the conversion of first statement, hence I follows. But II does not follow because A + A = A i.e. All leaders are good orators but not *vice versa*.

45. (a) A + A = A; i.e. All terrorists are human.

46. (b) I does not follow. But II follows because it is conversion of the first statement.

47 (c)   48. (d)

Sol. (49-50) :

Pranab ⇔ Reva
(+)   (–)
↓   ↓   ↓
Neela Prakash Vikash
(–)   (+)
↓
Mohan Arun
(+)

49. (a)   50. (c)

Sol. (51 -55)

The given information is summarised in a table as follows :

Teachers	Subjects	
	Compulsory	Optional
A	History	English
B	History	Chemistry
C	History	Mathematics
D	(Female) English	History
E	Physics	Mathematics
F	Mathematics	Physics

51. (a) History is the compulsory subject of C.

52. (d) D is a female member in the group.

53. (d) The compulsory subject of F (Mathematics) is the optional subject of C.

54. (c) E has physics and Mathematics as his two subjects.

65. (d) A, B and C all have History as the compulsory subjects.

Sol. (56-60) :

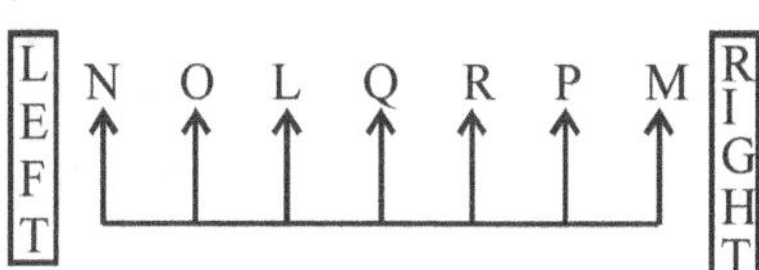

56. (b) O is third to the left of R.

57. (c) N and M are sitting at the extreme ends of the line.

58. (e)

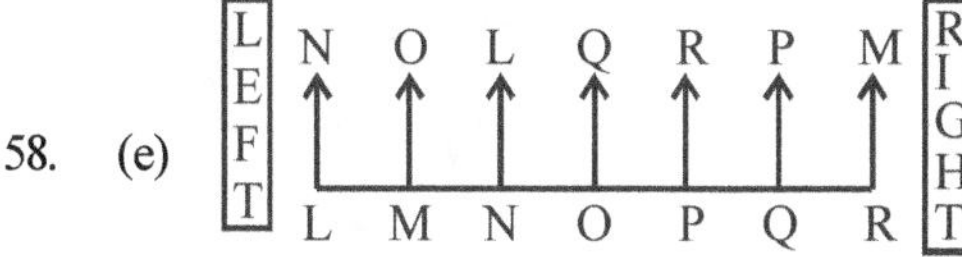

59. (c) Q is sitting exactly in the middle of the row.

60. (d) Except LN, in all others the first person is to immediate right of the second person. L is second to the right of N.

61. (c) F is third to the right of D.

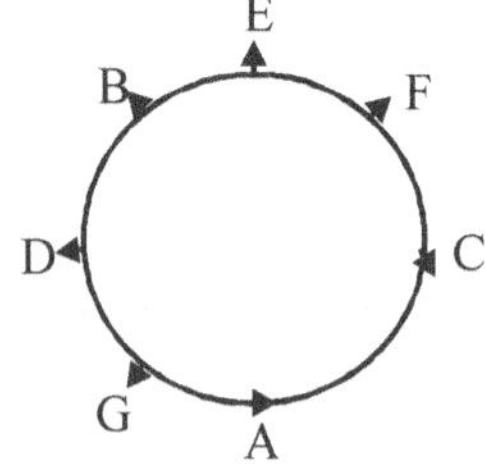

62. (b) A is to immediate right of G

63. (d) DG

64. (e) None of these

65. (a) Fourth to the right of D

66. (b) Required consonant in the arrangement = 8 ∨ #

67. (b) From right 19th element is Q and from Q, rightward 10th element is T.

68. (e) After eliminating all symbols arrangement will be F 4 H 2 E M P 5 W 9 I Q R 6 U H 3 Z 7 A T B 8 V G Y D. 14th element from leftward is '6'.

69. (a)
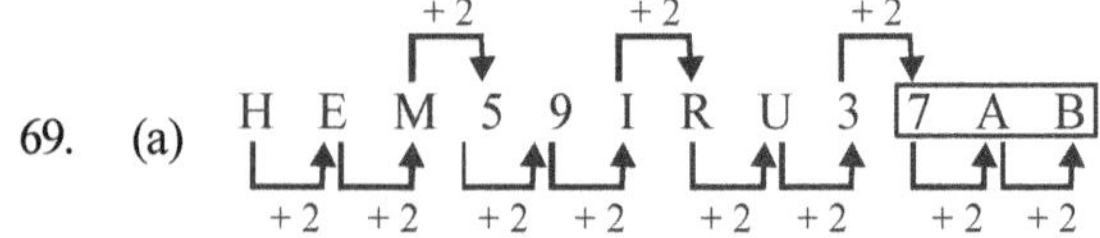

70. (d) Required symbol in the arrangement = 4 @ H, 9 @ 1, 7 ★ A

81. (c) (incidence -the occurrence, rate, or frequency of a disease, crime, or other undesirable things.)

82. (a) (frequency correctly fits in the context)

83. (e) (astonishing-extremely surprising or impressive; amazing.)

84. (b) (acknowledged-recognized as being good or important.)

85. (e) ('form' is appropriate word here)

86. (c) ('social' is appropriate word here)

87. (a) (we use fewer for numbers in comparative degree)

88. (a) (perish- die, especially in a violent or sudden way.)

89. (e) (neglect- fail to care for properly.)

90. (d) (manifestation-an event, action, or object that clearly shows or embodies something abstract or theoretical.)

91. (d) The error lies in the part (d) as the word 'sexual harassment' is the correct usage instead of 'sexually harassment'.

92. (c) The correct usage is 'participate' instead of 'participation' as there should be use of Ist form of verb after 'to'.

93. (a) The error lies in the part (E) as 'have' should be replace with 'had been' because the sentence is in the past tense.

94. (e) The given sentence is grammatically correct.

95. (c) The error lies in part (D) as 'scrutinising' will be used in place of 'scrutinised'.

96. (b) The error is in part (A) as 'discovered' will come in place of 'discovers'.

97. (b) The error is in statement (B) as the word 'interacted' is grammatically incorrect. The correct usage is 'interact'.

98. (e) There is no error in this statement as the sentence is grammatically correct.

99. (b) The error lies in part (C) of the statement as 'remains' will be used in place of 'remained'.

100. (a) Part (B) is incorrect of the given sentence as the followed noun is in plural form i.e. 'the older toys'. Therefore, 'among' will come in place of 'between'.

PRACTICE SET 2

INSTRUCTIONS

- This Preliminary Exam practice set consists of three sections. Numerical Ability (Qs. 1-35), Reasoning (Qs. 36-70) and English Language (Qs. 71-100).
- All the questions are compulsory.
- Each question has five options, of which only one is correct. The candidates are advised to read all the options thoroughly.
- There is negative marking equivalent to 1/4th of the mark allotted to the specific question for wrong answer.

Time : 60 Minutes   **Max. Marks : 100**

NUMERICAL ABILITY

DIRECTIONS (Qs. 1-10) : *What will come in place of question mark (?) in the following questions?*

1. 48% of 525 + ?% of 350 = 399
   - (a) 42
   - (b) 46
   - (c) 28
   - (d) 26
   - (e) None of these

2. $\frac{3}{7}$ of $\frac{4}{5}$ of $\frac{5}{8}$ of 490 = ?
   - (a) 115
   - (b) 105
   - (c) 108
   - (d) 116
   - (e) None of these

3. $\sqrt{?} + 17^2 = 335$
   - (a) 46
   - (b) 42
   - (c) 1764
   - (d) 2116
   - (e) None of these

4. 125% of 560 + 22% of 450 = ?
   - (a) 799
   - (b) 700
   - (c) 782
   - (d) 749
   - (e) None of these

5. $\dfrac{28 \times 5 - 15 \times 6}{7^2 + \sqrt{256} + (13)^2} = ?$
   - (a) $\dfrac{27}{115}$
   - (b) $\dfrac{22}{117}$
   - (c) $\dfrac{25}{117}$
   - (d) $\dfrac{22}{115}$
   - (e) None of these

6. 18.76 + 222.24 + 3242.15 = ?
   - (a) 3384.15
   - (b) 3483.15
   - (c) 3283.25
   - (d) 3383.25
   - (e) None of these

7. 784 ÷ 16 ÷ 7 = ?
   - (a) 49
   - (b) 14
   - (c) 21
   - (d) 7
   - (e) None of these

8. $\frac{3}{2}$ of 455 + $\frac{5}{8}$ of 456 = ?
   - (a) 448
   - (b) 476
   - (c) 480
   - (d) 464
   - (e) None of these

9. 1.05% of 2500 + 2.5% of 440 = ?
   - (a) 37.50
   - (b) 37.25
   - (c) 370.25
   - (d) 372.50
   - (e) None of these

10. 4900 ÷ 28 × 444 ÷ 12 = ?
    - (a) 6575
    - (b) 6475
    - (c) 6455
    - (d) 6745
    - (e) None of these

11. A and B started a business by investing ₹10,000 and ₹ 12,000 respectively. After 4 months they withdrew their half money and after another 4 months they again withdrew their half of money of previous investment. If at the end of year, A got ₹ 10,500 as share of his profit, then what is the total profit made at the end of year?
    - (a) ₹ 23,800
    - (b) ₹ 22,600
    - (c) ₹ 22,000
    - (d) ₹ 23,100
    - (e) None of these

12. A train running at the speed of 60 km/hr crosses a 200 m long platform in 27 s. What is the length of the train?
    - (a) 250 m
    - (b) 200 m
    - (c) 240 m
    - (d) 450 m
    - (e) None of these

13. 10 men can complete a piece of work in 8 days. In how many days can 16 men complete that work?
    - (a) 4 days
    - (b) 5 days
    - (c) 6 days
    - (d) 3 days
    - (e) None of these

14. If the numerator of a certain fraction is increased by 100% and the denominator is increased by 200%; the new fraction thus formed is $\frac{4}{21}$. What is the original fraction?

(a) $\dfrac{2}{7}$ (b) $\dfrac{3}{7}$ (c) $\dfrac{2}{5}$

(d) $\dfrac{4}{7}$ (e) None of these

15. The ratio of the ages of A and B seven years ago was 3 : 4 respectively. The ratio of their ages nine years from now will be 7 : 8 respectively. What is B's age at present?

(a) 16 years (b) 19 years (c) 28 years
(d) 23 years (e) None of these

16. The perimeter of a square is thrice the perimeter of a rectangle. If the perimeter of the square is 84 cm and the length of the rectangle is 8 cm, what is the difference between the breadth of the rectangle and the side of the square?

(a) 15 cm (b) 19 cm (c) 10 cm
(d) 8 cm (e) None of these

17. The sum of money invested at compound interest amounts to ₹ 4680 in 2 years and to ₹ 5616 in 3 years. What was the amount of sum invested?

(a) ₹ 3450 (b) ₹ 3000
(c) ₹ 3250 (d) ₹ 4100
(e) ₹ 3500

18. A committee of 4 members is to be made from 5 men and 5 women. What is the probability that the committee will contain more men than women?

(a) 22/49 (b) 11/42
(c) 11/34 (d) 5/42
(e) 6/13

19. How many kg of wheat costing ₹ 10 per kg must be mixed with 16 kg of wheat costing ₹ 15 per kg, so that there may be gain of 30% by selling the mixture at ₹ 15.6 per kg?

(a) 28 (b) 25
(c) 24 (d) 18
(e) 20

20. In a class of 96 students, ratio of number of boys to girls is 5 : 3. Among the boys, ratio of number of sports persons to non-sports persons is 7 : 5. If the ratio of total sports persons to total non-sports persons in class is 2 : 1, find the ratio of number of girls of sports persons to non-sports persons.

(a) 22 : 13 (b) 13 : 5
(c) 21 : 10 (d) 14 : 9
(e) 29 : 7

21. Find the HCF of $\dfrac{2}{3}, \dfrac{6}{15}, \dfrac{4}{5}, \dfrac{8}{21}$

(a) $\dfrac{2}{105}$ (b) $\dfrac{6}{121}$

(c) $\dfrac{5}{123}$ (d) $\dfrac{1}{210}$

(e) None of these

22. Find the least number which when divided by 3, 5, 10 and 12 leaves a remainder 4 but leaves no remainder when same number is divided by 23.

(a) 188 (b) 184
(c) 160 (d) 163
(e) 124

23. An article is sold at a discount of 4% making a profit of 20%. What would have been the profit percent if the article was sold without discount?

(a) 22% (b) 25%
(c) 28% (d) 20%
(e) 32%

24. A truck covers a distance of 256 km at the speed of 32 km/hr. What is the average speed of a car which travels a distance of 160 km more than the truck in the same time?

(a) 46 km/hr (b) 52 km/hr (c) 49 km/hr
(d) 64 km/hr (e) None of these

25. In an examination, the maximum aggregate marks is 1020. In order to pass the exam a student is required to obtain 663 marks out of the aggregate marks. Shreya obtained 612 marks. By what percent did Shreya fail the exam?

(a) 5% (b) 8% (c) 7%
(d) Can't be determined
(e) None of these

DIRECTIONS (Qs. 26-30) : *What should come in place of question mark (?) in the following number series?*

26. 8 52 ? 1287 4504.5 11261.25 16891.875
(a) 462 (b) 286 (c) 194
(d) 328 (e) None of these

27. 3 42 504 ? 40320 241920 967680
(a) 6048 (b) 5544 (c) 4536
(d) 5040 (e) None of these

28. 403 400 394 382 358 310 ?
(a) 244 (b) 210 (c) 214
(d) 256 (e) None of these

29. 7 8 4 13 –3 22 ?
(a) –7 (b) –10 (c) –12
(d) –14 (e) None of these

30. 250000 62500 12500 3125 625 ? 31.25
(a) 156.25 (b) 172.25 (c) 125
(d) 150 (e) None of these

DIRECTIONS (Qs. 31-35) : *Study the table carefully and answer the given questions.*

Number of Pages Printed by 6 Printers in 5 Different Weeks

Week \ Printer	A	B	C	D	E	F
1st	664	618	628	552	638	419
2nd	569	441	519	438	621	537
3rd	440	614	503	527	541	742
4th	256	563	347	651	412	321
5th	717	429	598	582	519	693

31. What is the respective ratio between the number of pages printed by Printer B in 2nd week and the number of pages printed by Printer F in 5th week?
(a) 4 : 9 (b) 11 : 13
(c) 9 : 13 (d) 7 : 11
(e) 9 : 11

32. What is the average number of pages printed by all the given printers in 4th week?
(a) 375 (b) 425
(c) 415 (d) 430
(e) 390

33. Which of the following printer printed maximum number of pages in all the given weeks together?
    (a) Printer A   (b) Printer E
    (c) Printer D   (d) Printer C
    (e) Printer F
34. Number of pages printed by Printer A in 3rd week is what per cent of the total number of pages printed by Printed D in all the given weeks?
    (a) 22   (b) 18
    (c) 12   (d) 14
    (e) 16
35. What is the difference between the total number of pages printed by Printer E in 1st, 2nd and 4th week together and total number of pages printed by Printer C in all the given weeks together?
    (a) 952   (b) 878
    (c) 924   (d) 934
    (e) 918

REASONING ABILITY

DIRECTIONS (Qs. 36-37) : *Read the following information carefully to answer the following questions.*

'A $ B' means 'A is mother of B'
'A # B' means 'A is father of B'
'A @ B' means 'A is husband of B'
'A % B' means 'A is daughter of B'

36. S @ Q $ P # W indicates what relationship of S with W?
    (a) Paternal Grandmother   (b) Maternal Grandmother
    (c) Paternal Grandfather   (d) Maternal Grandfather
    (e) None of these
37. Which of the following expression indicates 'J is the sister of H'?
    (a) H $ A @ P # J   (b) J % A @ P $ H
    (c) J $ A @ P # H   (d) H % A @ P $ J
    (e) None of these
38. How many pairs of letters are there in the word METALCASTING, each of which have as many letters between then in the word as they have between then in the English alphabet?
    (a) None   (b) One
    (c) Two   (d) Three
    (e) More than three
39. In a row of 40 girls, when Komal was shifted to her left by 4 places her number from the left end of the row became 10. What was the number of Swati from the right end of the row of Swati was three places to the right of Komal's original position?
    (a) 22   (b) 23
    (c) 24   (d) 25
    (e) 26
40. A man starts from point P and goes 5 km east, then he turns to his left and goes 5 km, next he turns to his right and walks 9 km, next to his left and goes 2 km. now he takes a left turn and finally stops at point Q after moving 13 km. Find the distance between P and Q (in km), and the direction he is now as seen from point P.

    (a) $\sqrt{20}$, South-West   (b) 7, North
    (c) $\sqrt{50}$, North-East   (d) $\sqrt{80}$, North
    (e) None of these

DIRECTIONS (Qs. 41-43): *Study the following information carefully to answer the questions that follow*

There are six people - A, B, C, D, E and F, each of them are having different weights. A is heavier than F but lighter than B. E is heavier than C but lighter than A. B is lighter than D, and C is not the lightest. The second lightest person weighs 64 kilograms while the second heaviest person weighs 82 kilograms.

41. Who among the following may be of 70 kilograms?
    (a) D   (b) A
    (c) E   (d) F
    (e) A or E
42. How many persons are heavier than C?
    (a) None   (b) One
    (c) Two   (d) Three
    (e) More than three
43. Which of the following may represent the weight of D?
    (a) 72 kg   (b) 80 kg
    (c) 74 kg   (d) 84 kg
    (e) 75 kg

DIRECTIONS (Qs. 44-48): *Study the information given below and answer the given questions:*

There are five friends - A, B, C, D, and E. Two of them like sitting on sofa, while the other three like sitting on chair, table and bed. The one who like sitting on sofa and who like sitting on bed like the color green. The other three like the colors red, blue and black. Two of these five persons like Pepsi as soft drink while the remaining three like the soft drinks Fanta, Limca and Sprite.
The one who likes sitting on bed is the oldest in age while the one who likes sitting on double seated sofa is the youngest, the other who likes sitting on sofa likes sitting on a single seat sofa and lies between the one who like sitting on chair and the one who likes sitting on bed age wise. D likes sitting on single seat sofa and likes color green while E likes drinking Fanta and likes color black. The one who likes sitting on chair likes drinking Limca and likes color red. B likes Sprite while A likes Pepsi and likes sitting on double seated sofa.

44. On which of the following does B like to sit?
    (a) Sofa   (b) Chair
    (c) Table   (d) Bed
    (e) Data inadequate
45. On which of the following does E like to sit?
    (a) Sofa   (b) Chair
    (c) Table   (d) Bed
    (e) Data inadequate
46. Age wise, who among the following lies between E and D?
    (a) The one who likes sitting on sofa
    (b) The one who likes drinking Fanta
    (c) The one who like color green
    (d) A
    (e) None of these

47. Which of the following statements is true based on the given information?
    - (a) E likes the color red
    - (b) C likes sitting on bed
    - (c) D likes the color red
    - (d) D likes drinking Pepsi
    - (e) All of the above are false
48. Which of the following combinations is correct?
    - (a) Fanta-Black-E-Chair
    - (b) Pepsi-Blue-B-Bed
    - (c) Sprite-Red-E-Bed
    - (d) Limca-Red-A-Chair
    - (e) Pepsi-Green-D-Single Sofa
49. In a certain code language 'how many goals scored' is written as '5 3 9 7'; 'many more matches' is written as '9 8 2'; and 'he scored five' is written as '1 6 3'. How is 'goals' written in that code language?
    - (a) 5
    - (2) 7
    - (c) 5 or 7
    - (4) Data inadequate
    - (e) None of these
50. Pointing to a girl, Mr. Arun said. "She is the daughter of my mother's only child". How is the girl related to Mr. Arun ?
    - (a) Sister
    - (b) Mother
    - (c) Cousin
    - (d) Daughter
    - (e) Cannot be determined
51. Read the following information carefully and answer the question which follows:
    'A × B' means 'A is the father of B'.
    'A + B' means 'A is the daughter of B'.
    'A ÷ B' means 'A is the son of B'.
    'A – B' means 'A is the sister of B'.
    What will come in place of question mark to establish that P is the son-in-law of S in the following expression?
    P × Q + R – T ? S
    - (a) +
    - (b) ×
    - (c) –
    - (d) ÷
    - (e) Either + or ÷

DIRECTIONS (Qs. 52-56) : *In each of the questions below are given four statements followed by three conclusions numbered I, II and III. You have to take the given statements to be true even if they seem to be at variance from commonly known facts. Read all the conclusions and then decide which of the given conclusions logically follows from the given statements disregarding commonly known facts.*

---

52. **Statements:** All petals are flowers. Some flowers are buds. Some buds are leaves. All leaves are plants.
    Conclusions: I. Some petals are not buds.
    II. Some flowers are plants.
    III. No flower is plant.
    - (a) Only I follows
    - (b) Either II or III follows
    - (c) I and II follow
    - (d) Only III follows
    - (e) None of the above
53. **Statements:** Some pens are keys. Some keys are locks. All locks are cards. No card is paper
    Conclusions:
    I. No lock is paper.
    II. Some cards are keys.
    III. Some keys are not paper.

- (a) I and II follow
- (b) Only I follows
- (c) Only II follows
- (d) All follows
- (e) None follows

54. **Statements:** Some pearls are gems. All gems are diamonds. No diamond is stone. Some stones are corals.
    Conclusions:
    I. Some stones are pearls.
    II. Some corals being diamond is a possibility.
    III. No stone is pearl.
    - (a) Only I follows
    - (b) Only II follows
    - (c) Either I or III follows
    - (d) I and II follow
    - (e) None of these
55. **Statements:** Some apartments are flats. Some flats are buildings. All buildings are bungalows. All bungalows are gardens.
    Conclusions:
    I. All apartments being building is a possibility
    II. All bungalows are not buildings.
    III. No flat is garden.
    - (a) None follows
    - (b) Only I follows
    - (c) Either I or III follows
    - (d) II and III follow
    - (e) Only II follows
56. **Statements:** All chairs are tables. All tables are bottles. Some bottles are jars. No jar is bucket.
    Conclusions:
    I. Some tables being jar is a possibility.
    II. Some bottles are chairs.
    III. Some bottles are not bucket.
    - (a) Only I follows
    - (b) I and II follow
    - (c) All follow
    - (d) Only II follows
    - (e) None of these

DIRECTIONS (Qs. 57-61): *In these questions the symbols @. #, $, % and ★ are used with different meanings as follow.*

'A @ B ' means 'A is not smaller then B'.
'A # B ' means 'A is neither smaller than nor equal to B'.
'A $ B ' means 'A is neither greater than nor smaller than B'.
'A % B' means 'A is not greater than B'.
'A ★ B' means 'A is neither greater than nor equal to B'.
In each questions, four statements showing relationships have been given, which are followed by three conclusions I, II and III. Assuming that the given statements are true, find out which conclusion (s) is/are definitely true?

57. **Statements:** V $ Y, Y @ Z, Z % X, X # T
    Conclusions:
    I. T # Z
    II. X # Y
    III. Z ★ Y
    - (a) None follows
    - (b) Only I follows
    - (c) II and III follow
    - (d) I and III follow
    - (e) Only III follows
58. **Statements:** R @ J, J % F, F ★ E, E % M
    Conclusions:
    I. M # J
    II. F % M
    III. M ★ R
    - (a) Only I follows
    - (b) Only II follows
    - (c) Only III follows
    - (d) I and II follow
    - (e) All follow

59. **Statements:** H#R, R@L, L ★ W, W%F
Conclusions:
I.   H # J   II.   F # L
III. H $ F
(a) Only I follows   (b) I and II follow
(c) II and III follow   (d) Either I or II follows
(e) All follow

60. **Statements:** M # K, M $ F, F % Q, Q ★ H
Conclusions:
I.   H # K
II. Q # K
III. Q @ M
(a) I and II follow   (b) Either I or II follows
(c) All follow   (d) II and III follow
(e) None of the above

61. **Statements:** D ★ Q, Q $ L, L # T, T % H
Conclusions:
I.   D ★ L
II. L @ H
III. H # L
(a) Only I follows   (b) I and II follow
(c) Either II or III follows (d) All follow
(e) None follow

DIRECTIONS (Qs. 62-66) : *Read the following information carefully and answer the following questions.*

P,Q,R,S,T,U and V are sitting on a wall facing East.R is on the immediate right of S.Q is at an extreme end and has T as his neighbour. V is between T and U.S is sitting between R and U.S is sitting third from the south end.

62. Who is sitting to the right of T ?
(a) P   (b) R
(c) S   (d) U
(e) V

63. Which of the following pairs of people are sitting at the extreme ends ?
(a) PQ   (b) PT
(c) RQ   (d) UQ
(e) None of these

64. Name the person who should change place with R such that he gets the third place from the North end ?
(a) T   (b) U
(c) V   (d) S
(e) None of these

65. Immediately between which of the following pairs of people is S sitting ?
(a) PR   (b) PU
(c) RT   (d) RU
(e) None of these

66. Who is sitting between S and P ?
(a) V   (b) Q
(c) R   (d) S
(e) U

DIRECTIONS(Qs. 67-70) *Read the following information carefully and answer the following questions.*

A ,B ,C ,D ,E ,F ,G and H are sitting around a circular table with equal distance between them, facing the centre but not necessarily in the same order. A sits second to the right of G. Only 2 persons sitting between A and H.C sit second to the left of H. Only 3 persons sit between H and F.B sits on the immediate left of D.

67. Who among the following sits second to the right of F ?
(a) B   (b) C
(c) D   (d) G
(e) None of these

68. If all the persons are made to sit in alphabetical order in clockwise direction, starting from A , the positions of how many, excluding A would remain unchanged ?
(a) One   (b) Two
(c) Three   (d) Four
(e) None of these

69. Which of the following statement is true with respect to E ?
(a) E is an immediate neighbour of B
(b) Only one person sitting between E and F
(c) Only 3 persons sitting between E and G
(d) A sits third to the right of E
(e) All the given statements are true

70. Who among the following represent the immediate neighbour of G ?
(a) E, D   (b) H, C
(c) H, D   (d) D, F
(e) None of these

ENGLISH LANGUAGE

DIRECTIONS (Qs. 71-80): *Read the following passage carefully and answer the questions given after the passage Certain words/ phrases have been printed in bold to help you locate them while answering some of the questions.*

The tech-savy state of Karnataka will **incubate** about 20,000 start-ups by 2020 to create six lakh direct and 12 lakh indirect jobs, Chief Minister Siddaramaiah said on Tuesday.

"We are setting up a start-up cell as a one-stop-shop to help young entrepreneurs float start-ups and guide them in launching their **ventures** as they will have little knowledge of corporate affairs," Siddaramaiah said, flagging off the 18th edition of Bangalore ITE.biz 2015 here.

The Karnataka government has recently unveiled a start-up policy 2015-2020 to promote entrepreneurship, set up incubation centres, **foster** partnerships between research and development (R&D) and industry and provide early stage funding to start-ups.

"With hundreds of entrepreneurs with creative ideas setting up start-ups here, Bengaluru is emerging also as the country's start-up capital over a decade after it became IT capital," the chief minister asserted.

Noting that the start-up policy covered information technology, biotechnology and manufacturing sectors, Siddaramaiah said a start-up council under his chairmanship would review implementation of the policy on a regular basis for feedback and suggestions.

The start-up policy is the outcome of the state government's 'Karnataka I-4' initiative launched in 2014, spanning IT, IT-**enabled** services (back office and business process outsourcing), innovation and incentives.

The three-day annual event showcases the state's prowess in the knowledge sector, with over 2,000 firms, including 500 global

IT majors, multinationals and offshore software development centres for services and products, operating from in and around this tech hub, providing 1.5 million direct jobs and 2.5 million indirect jobs.

"Bengaluru has the distinction of being the country's largest IT cluster, with 350 of the Fortune 500 firms locating their R&D and offshore development operations, thanks to its talent pool, research and academic institutions in the government and private sectors and best higher education system, including universities," the chief minister told about 500 delegates at the inaugural event. The country's first electronic city, which was set up in the 1980s on the outskirts of southern Bengaluru across 400 acres of land, has become a major hub for about 200 software and hardware firms, including home-grown Indian IT **bellwethers** like Infosys and Wipro.

71. According to the passage, which of the following is not true?
    (a) Bangalure is a talent pool.
    (b) Recently, Bangalore flaged off 18th edition of Bagaluru ITE biz 2015.
    (c) Siddaramaiah made a committee to startup which gives a unique idea how to start business.
    (d) Karnataka will create 6 lakh direct and 12 lakh indirect job.
    (e) None of these

72. According to the passage, which of the following is true?
    (a) Tech Savy of Karnataka will incubate about 20,000 start-up by 2030.
    (b) The start-up policy is the outcome of the state government Karnatak I-4 intitative lauched in 2014.
    (c) Bengalure has distinction of being the Country's largest I.T Cluster with 350 of fortune 600 firm.
    (d) Country's first electronic city was setup 1990.
    (e) None of these

73. Which of the following would be the suitable title?
    (a) Bangaluru intiative in providing job
    (b) Tech-Savy Karnataka
    (c) Karnataka is best in start-up policy.
    (d) Karnataka's intiative to incubate entrepreneurs.
    (e) No business in karnataka

74. According to author, what we can say about Karnataka?
    (a) Karnataka is growing fast and implementing new policies day by day.
    (b) Karnataka chief minister is very knowledgeable and loyal towards his constituency.
    (c) Karnataka wants to promote entrepreneurship with creative idea including manufacturing, I.T. and biotechnology all together.
    (d) Karnataka is best place startup policy which is outcome of state government 1-4 intiative
    (e) None of these

DIRECTIONS (Qs. 75-77): *Choose the word which is most* **OPPOSITE** *in meaning to the word printed in bold as used in the passage.*

75. **Ventures**
    (a) jeopard   (b) proceed
    (c) peril   (d) gamble
    (e) shield

76. **Bellwethers**
    (a) leader   (b) pacer
    (c) pacemaker   (d) trend setter
    (e) followers

77. **Incubate**
    (a) endorse   (b) uphold
    (c) patronize   (d) underwrite
    (e) hinder

DIRECTIONS (Qs. 78-80): Choose the word which is most **SIMILAR** in meaning to the word printed in bold as used in the passage

78. **Innovation**
    (a) clone   (b) copy
    (c) novelty   (d) replica
    (e) facsimile

79. **Foster**
    (a) forbid   (b) snuff
    (c) suppress   (d) oppose
    (e) boost

80. **Enable**
    (a) disenfranchise   (b) impede
    (c) preclude   (d) let
    (e) veto

DIRECTIONS (Qs. 81-90): *In the following passage, some of the words have been left out, each of which is indicated by a number. Find the suitable word from the options given against each number and fill up the blanks with appropriate words to make the paragraph meaningfully complete.*

If the phone is (81) in India today, it is largely due to the amazing (82) of one man - Satyanarayan (abbreviated to 'Sam' by an HR clerk who couldn't get her tongue around the name) Pitroda (a Gujarati community of metal-workers who traditionally used pitr or brass), the son of an (83) labourer. Pitroda's drive and vision not only (84) him a 100 patents and millions of (85) in America, but the role of a change agent and (86) in his home country. Pitroda believes his (87) was shaped by his parent's decision to send him away, at the age of eight, from their (88) home in Orissa to a school in Gujarat. The Gandhian values (89) there, followed by a Baroda college, which honed his interest in physics and (90) his entrepreneurial instincts, provided the platform for a master's degree in electrical engineering from Illinois Institute of Technology and entry into the field of telecommunications.

81. (a) scarce   (b) flimsy
    (c) unwanted   (d) ubiquitous
    (d) ramshackle

82. (a) journey   (b) inaction
    (c) retrogress   (d) tardiness
    (e) scurry

83. (a) educated   (b) unschooled
    (c) schooled   (d) graduate
    (e) organised

84. (a) earned   (b) spend
    (c) loosed   (d) gained
    (e) moved

85. (a) capital   (b) rupees
    (c) wealth   (d) money
    (e) dollars

86. (a) safe-breaker   (b) law-breaker
    (c) path-breaker   (d) breaker
    (e) vision

87. (a) adversity   (b) fortuity
    (c) complex   (d) catastrophe
    (e) destiny

88. (a) arrant   (b) meagre
    (c) bursting   (d) chubby
    (e) aplenty

89. (a) ignited   (b) instilled
    (c) doused   (d) afire
    (e) blazing

90. (a) ensconced   (b) imperceptive
    (c) dissimulated   (d) camouflaged
    (e) revealed

DIRECTIONS (Qs. 91-100): *In each of the questions given below, a sentence is given which is divided into 5 parts. Out of the given 5 parts, one is grammatically correct and the rest are not. It is then followed by 5 options which give one of the options as a correct on(e) Choose the option which is grammatically correct. If all the parts are grammatically correct then answer according to the options given below.*

---

91. They are complicited in this(A)/ violent by their deliberate negligence,(B)/ to saying the least, if not(C)/ active support, by not come(D)/ to the rescue of Muslims in a timely manner(E).
    (a) A   (b) B
    (c) C   (d) D
    (e) E

92. We kept spoken to all the(A)/ responsible officers, they kept(B)/ reassure us that there was nothing(C)/ to worrying about and that(D)/ they would taken care(E).
    (a) B   (b) C
    (c) D   (d) E
    (e) A

93. They should have been preparing(A)/ to such a calamity(B)/. It looks like callous(C)/ disregarding for the safety of(D)/ the student minority in that country(E).
    (a) A   (b) E
    (c) B   (d) D
    (e) C

94. A company may be opening(A)/ a significant number of new stores(B)/ almost every year, which in turn(C)/ could cause its total revenue(D)/ to increase year after year(E).
    (a) D   (b) B
    (c) All are correct   (d) A
    (e) C

95. This shows the government's arrogant(A)/ and unilateral move to bulldozer(B)/ all the financing business(C)/ without discuss them on(D)/ the floor of the House(E).
    (a) E   (b) A
    (c) C   (d) D
    (e) B

96. Though they might not be debarred(A)/ from conducting arbitration in India arised out(B)/ of international commercial arbitration, they will be(C)/ governed by the code of conducting applicable(D)/ of the legal profession in India(E).
    (a) B   (b) A
    (c) D   (d) E
    (e) C

97. The Secretary have every(A)/ intention of staying(B)/ because the critical(C)/ progress making(D)/ of national security(E).
    (a) B   (b) A
    (c) C   (d) E
    (e) D

98. The two poisonings, just over a(A)/ decade apart, has raised serious(B)/ questions domestically on Britain's ability(C)/ to protecting those seeking(D)/ politically asylum on its shores(E).
    (a) B   (b) D
    (c) A   (d) B
    (e) E

99. On Tuesday, airport operations returning(A)/ to normally, while the wreckage of the(B)/ crashed aircraft laid near(C)/ the runway, guarding(D)/ by security personnel(E).
    (a) D   (b) E
    (c) B   (d) A
    (e) C

100. A separate security source of(A)/ Gaza said the convoy is(B)/ also fire on(C)/ by unknown gunmen at the(D)/ time of the exploding(E).
    (a) A   (b) B
    (c) C   (d) D
    (e) E

Answer Key

1	(a)	11	(d)	21	(a)	31	(d)	41	(e)	51	(e)	61	(e)	71	(c)	81	(d)	91	(e)
2	(b)	12	(a)	22	(b)	32	(b)	42	(e)	52	(b)	62	(a)	72	(b)	82	(a)	92	(a)
3	(d)	13	(b)	23	(b)	33	(c)	43	(d)	53	(d)	63	(a)	73	(d)	83	(b)	93	(e)
4	(a)	14	(a)	24	(b)	34	(e)	44	(d)	54	(e)	64	(c)	74	(c)	84	(a)	94	(c)
5	(c)	15	(d)	25	(a)	35	(c)	45	(c)	55	(a)	65	(d)	75	(e)	85	(e)	95	(a)
6	(b)	16	(a)	26	(b)	36	(c)	46	(e)	56	(c)	66	(c)	76	(e)	86	(c)	96	(b)
7	(d)	17	(c)	27	(d)	37	(b)	47	(e)	57	(a)	67	(b)	77	(e)	87	(e)	97	(a)
8	(c)	18	(b)	28	(c)	38	(c)	48	(e)	58	(a)	68	(a)	78	(c)	88	(b)	98	(c)
9	(b)	19	(c)	29	(d)	39	(c)	49	(c)	59	(b)	69	(c)	79	(e)	89	(b)	99	(b)
10	(b)	20	(e)	30	(a)	40	(c)	50	(d)	60	(e)	70	(d)	80	(d)	90	(e)	100	(d)

HINTS & EXPLANATIONS

1. (a) 48% of $525 + ?\%$ of $350 = 399$

$\Rightarrow \quad \dfrac{48}{100} \times 525 + \dfrac{?}{100} \times 350 = 399$

$\Rightarrow \quad 25200 + ? \times 350 = 399 \times 100$

$\Rightarrow \quad ? \times 350 = 39900 - 25200 = 14700$

$\Rightarrow \quad ? = \dfrac{14700}{350} = 42$

2. (b) $? = \dfrac{3}{7}$ of $\dfrac{4}{5}$ of $\dfrac{5}{8}$ of 490

$\Rightarrow \quad ? = \dfrac{3}{7} \times \dfrac{4}{5} \times \dfrac{5}{8} \times 490$

$\Rightarrow \quad ? = 35 \times 3 = 105$

3. (d) $\sqrt{?} + 17^2 = 335$

$\Rightarrow \quad \sqrt{?} + 289 = 335$

$\Rightarrow \quad \sqrt{?} = 335 - 289 = 46$

$\Rightarrow \quad ? = 46 \times 46 = 2116$

4. (a) $? = 125\%$ of $560 + 22\%$ of 450

$\Rightarrow \quad ? = \dfrac{125}{100} \times 560 + \dfrac{22}{100} \times 450$

$\Rightarrow \quad ? = \dfrac{70000}{100} + \dfrac{9900}{100}$

$\Rightarrow \quad ? = 700 + 99 = 799$

5. (c) $? = \dfrac{28 \times 5 - 15 \times 6}{7^2 + \sqrt{256} + (13)^2}$

$\Rightarrow \quad ? = \dfrac{140 - 90}{49 + 16 + 169}$

$\Rightarrow \quad ? = \dfrac{50}{234} = \dfrac{25}{117}$

6. (b) $? = 18.76 + 222.24 + 3242.15$

$\Rightarrow \quad ? = 3483.15$

7. (d) $? = 784 \div 16 \div 7$

$\Rightarrow \quad ? = \dfrac{784}{16} \div 7$

$\Rightarrow \quad ? = 49 \div 7 = 7$

8. (c) $? = \dfrac{3}{7}$ of $455 + \dfrac{5}{8}$ of 456

$\Rightarrow \quad ? = \dfrac{3}{7} \times 455 + \dfrac{5}{8} \times 456$

$\Rightarrow \quad ? = 195 + 285$

$\Rightarrow \quad ? = 480$

9. (b) $? = 1.05\%$ of $2500 + 2.5\%$ of 440

$\Rightarrow \quad ? = \dfrac{1.05}{100} \times 2500 + \dfrac{2.5}{100} \times 440$

$\Rightarrow \quad ? = \dfrac{2625}{100} + \dfrac{1100}{100}$

$\Rightarrow \quad ? = \dfrac{3725}{100} = 37.25$

10. (b) $? = 4900 \div 28 \times 444 \div 12$

$\Rightarrow \quad ? = 175 \times 37$

$\Rightarrow \quad ? = 6475$

11. (d)   A's investment : B's investment = $(10{,}000 \times 4 + 5{,}000 \times 4 + 2{,}500 \times 4) : (12{,}000 \times 4 + 6{,}000 \times 4 + 3{,}000 \times 4)$

$100 + 50 + 25 : 120 + 60 + 30$

$20 + 10 + 5 : 24 + 12 + 6$

$35 : 42$

Let the total profit made be ₹ x.

So $(35/77) \times x = ₹\ 10{,}500$

Therefore, $x = 23{,}100$

12. (a)   Let length of the train be x m

Speed of the train be 60 km/h $= 60 \times \dfrac{5}{18} = \dfrac{50}{3}$ m/s

Then, $\dfrac{x + 200}{\dfrac{50}{3}} = 27$

$$\Rightarrow \quad \frac{3(x+200)}{50} = 27$$

$$\Rightarrow \quad 3x + 600 = 1350$$

$$\Rightarrow \quad 3x = 1350 - 600$$

$$\Rightarrow \quad 3x = 750$$

$$\Rightarrow \quad x = \frac{750}{3} = 250 \text{ m}$$

13. **(b)** Suppose 16 men can complete the same work in x days

Then,   Men   days

$$\begin{array}{cc} 10\uparrow & 8\downarrow \\ 16 & x \end{array}$$

$$16 : 10 :: 8 : x$$

$$\Rightarrow \quad 16 \times x = 10 \times 8$$

$$\Rightarrow \quad x = \frac{10 \times 8}{16} = 5 \text{ days}$$

14. **(a)** Let the original fraction $= \dfrac{x}{y}$

$$\therefore \quad \frac{x \times 200}{y \times 300} = \frac{4}{21} \Rightarrow \frac{x}{y} = \frac{4}{21} \times \frac{3}{2} = \frac{2}{7}$$

15. **(d)** Let the present age of A $= x$ and B $= y$ years

According to first condition

$$\frac{x-7}{y-7} = \frac{3}{4} \Rightarrow 4x - 28 = 3y - 21 \Rightarrow 4x - 3y = 7 \quad \text{......... (i)}$$

According to second condition

$$\frac{x+9}{y+9} = \frac{7}{8} \Rightarrow 8x + 72 = 7y + 63$$

$$\Rightarrow 7y - 8x = 9 \quad \text{......... (ii)}$$

Solving (i) and (ii), we get

$x = 19$ years, $y = 23$ years

16. **(a)** Perimeter of the square $= 84$ cm

Perimeter of the rectangle $= 28$ cm

Perimeter of the rectangle $= 2(1 + b)$

or, $2(8 + b) = 28$ cm

or, $b = 14 - 8 = 6$ cm

$\therefore$ Breadth of the rectangle $= 6$ cm

$$\text{Side of the square} = \frac{84}{4} = 21 \text{ cm}$$

Difference $= 21 - 6 = 15$ cm

17. **(c)** SI on 3380 for 1 yr $= 5616 - 4680 = 936$

So rate $= (100 \times 936 / 4680 \times 1) = 20$

So, $P(1 + 20/100)^2 = 4680$

Therefore, $P = ₹ 3250$

18. **(b)** Case 1: all 4 men, no woman

Probability $= {}^5C_4 / {}^{10}C_4 = 1/42$

Case 2: 3 men, 1 woman

Probability $= {}^5C_3 \times {}^5C_1 / {}^{10}C_4 = 5/21$

Adding both the cases, required probability

$= 1/42 + 5/21 = 11/42$

19. **(c)** With 30% gain,

SP $= ₹ 15.6$, CP $= (100/130) \times 15.6 = ₹ 12$

By rule of alligation:

1st wheat (x kg)..............2nd wheat (16 kg)

10...................15

,..............12

3...............2

$3 : 2$

So $x/16 = 3/2$

So $x = 24$ kg

20. **(e)** Boys in class $= (5/8) \times 96 = 60$,

So girls $= 96 - 60 = 36$

Sports persons among boys $= (7/12) \times 60 = 35$,

So non-sports persons $= 60 - 35 = 25$

Total sports person in class $= 2/(2 + 1) \times 96 = 64$,

So non-sports persons $= 96 - 64 = 32$

So Sports persons among girls $= 64 - 35 = 29$, non-sports $= 32 - 25 = 7$

Therefore, ratio $= 29 : 7$

21. **(a)** HCF = HCF of numerators/LCM of denominators

So HCF = (HCF of 2,6,4,8)/(LCM of 3, 15, 5, 21) = 2/105

22. **(b)** LCM(3, 5, 10, 12) = 60

So the number $= 60x + 4$, where x is any integer

This number leaves no remainder when divided by 23, so $x = 3$ to get $(60x + 4)$ fully divided by 23

So number $= 60 \times 3 + 4 = 184$

23. **(b)** Let MP $= ₹ 100$

At 4% discount SP $= ₹ 96$

Now profit $= 20\%$

So CP $= (100/120) \times 96 = 80$

No discount given means SP = MP = 100

So Profit% when no discount

$= [(100 - 80)/80] \times 100 = 25\%$

24. **(b)** Time taken by the truck $= \dfrac{256}{32} = 8$ hr

Distance covered by the car $= (256 + 160) = 416$ km

Time $= 8$ hr

$$\therefore \text{ Speed of the car} = \frac{416}{8} = 52 \text{ km / hr}$$

25. **(a)** Required percentage $= \dfrac{663 - 612}{1020} \times 100 = 5\%$

26. **(b)** $8 \times 6.5 = 52$

$52 \times 5.5 = \boxed{286}$

$286 \times 4.5 = 1287.$

27. **(d)** $3 \times 14 = 42$

$42 \times 12 = 504$

$504 \times 10 = \boxed{5040}$

$5040 \times 8 = 40320.$

28. **(c)** $403 - 3 = 400$

$400 - 6 = 394$

$394 - 12 = 382$

$382 - 24 = 358$

$358 - 48 = 310$

$310 - 96 = \boxed{214}$.

29. (d) 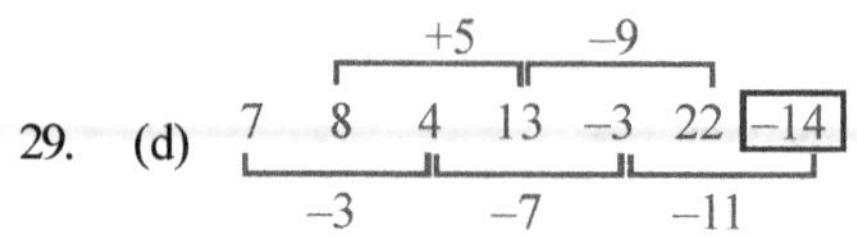

30. (a) $250000 \div 4 = 62500$

$62500 \div 5 = 12500$

$12500 \div 4 = 3125$

$3125 \div 5 = 625$

$625 \div 4 = \boxed{156.25}$

$156.25 \div 5 = 31.25.$

31. (d) Ratio

$$= \frac{\text{number of pages printed by printer B in 2nd week}}{\text{number of pages printed by printer F in } 5^{th}\text{ week}}$$

32. (b) Average number of pages printed by all the printer =

$$= \frac{256 + 563 + 347 + 651 + 412 + 321}{6} = 425$$

33. (c)

Week \ Printer	A	B	C	D	E	F
1st	664	618	628	552	638	419
2nd	569	441	519	438	621	537
3rd	440	614	503	527	541	742
4th	256	263	347	651	412	321
5th	717	429	598	582	519	693
Total up to 5th week	2646	2365	2595	2750	2731	2712

Printer D printed maximum pages.

34. (e) Required percentage (%) =

$$= \frac{\text{Pages printed by A in 3rd week}}{\text{Total page printed by D from 1st to 5th weeks}} \times 100$$

$$= \frac{440}{2750} \times 100 = 16\%$$

35. (c) Required difference = Total no. of pages printed by printer C in all given weeks – Total no. of pages by E in 1st, 2nd, 4th week

$$= 2595 - (638 + 621 + 412) = 924$$

36. (c) S and Q are husband wife. Q is the mother of P and P is the father of W.

So, S is father of P and P is father of W. Hence, S - paternal grandfather of W

37. (b) J and H are children of A and P, and J being the daughter is a female, so J is sister of H.

38. (e) 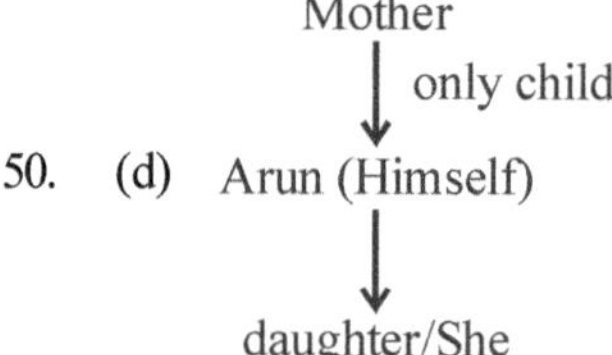

39. (c) When Komal place is changed to 4 places to her left, her position is 10 from the left end, this means that Komal original position should be 14 from the left. So

this means Swati position from left is 17. After Swati there are 40–17 = 23 girls are sitting in the row.

So when we see from right side, Swati is sitting after 23 girls, i.e. at number 24 from the right

40. (c) 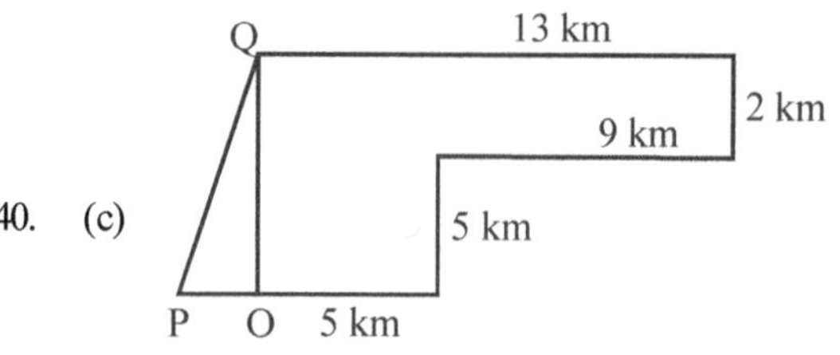

$$PQ = \sqrt{OP^2 + QO^2}$$

$$= \sqrt{7^2 + 12}$$

$$= \sqrt{50} \text{ km}$$

41. (e) The order from heaviest to lightest is – D, B, A, E, C, F
B is 82 kgs, C is 64 kgs.
So in between 64 and 82, A or E lies

42. (e) E, A, B, and D

43. (d) D is heavier than B, and B is 82, so D's weight should be greater than 82 kg. Only 84 > 82

(44 -48)

44. (d)

Drinks	Colors	Person	Furniture
Sprite	Green	B	Bed
Pepsi	Green	D	Single Sofa
Limca	Red	C	Chair
Fanta	Black	E	Table
Pepsi	Blue	A	Double Sofa

45. (d)   46. (e)   47. (d)   48. (e)

49. (c) How many goals scored = 5 3 9 7 (i)
many more matches = 9 8 2 (ii)
he scored five = 1 6 3 (iii)
From (i) and (ii), many = 9   (iv)
From (i) and (iii), scored = 3 (v)
Using (iv) and (v) in (i), we get
goals = 5 or 7

50. (d)

Mother
↓ only child
Arun (Himself)
↓
daughter/She

Therefore, the girl is the daughter of Arun.

51. (e) P × Q means P is a father of Q.

Q + P means Q is daughter of R

R – T means R is sister of T.

It is clear that P is husband of R. If he establish that T is either son or daughter of S, then P would be son-in-law of S.

T + S means T is daughter of S.

T ÷ S means T is son of S.

52. (b)   According to question,

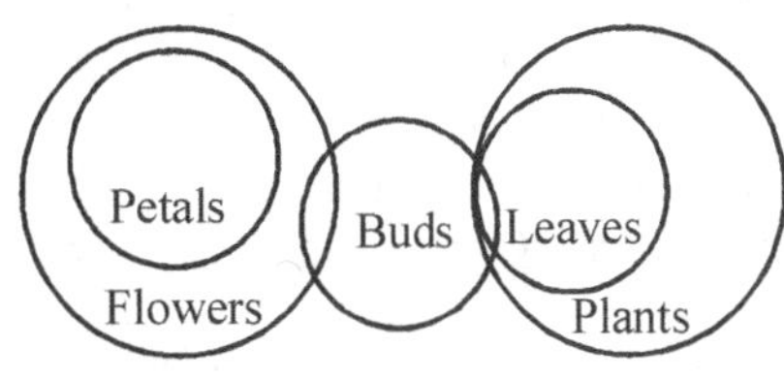

OR

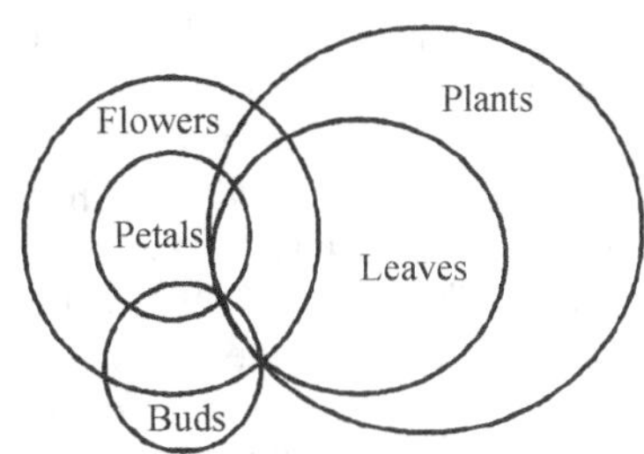

Conclusions I. false

II. false ⎤
III. false ⎦ or

Hence, only either II or III follows.

53. (d)   According to question

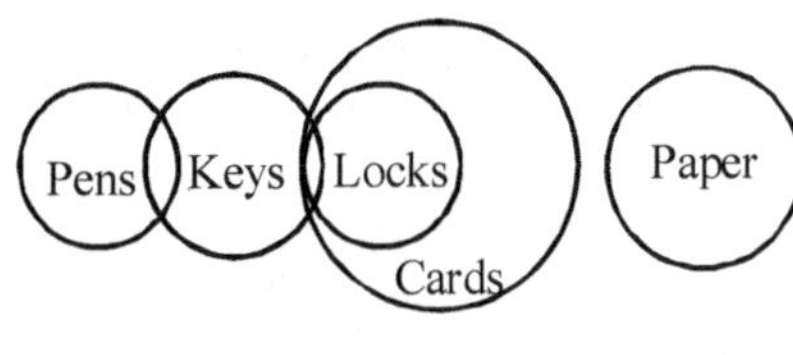

OR

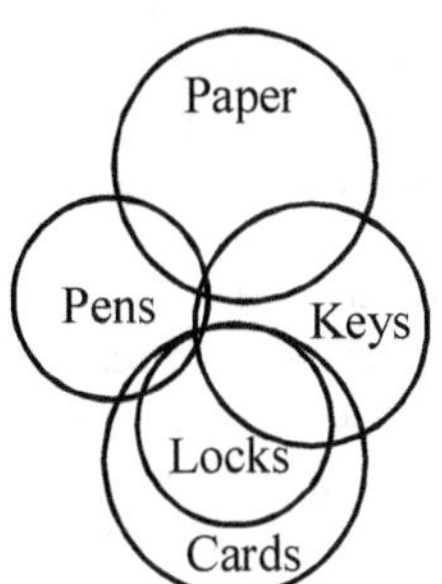

Conclusions I. True
II. True
III. True

Hence, All conclusions follow.

54. (e)   According to question,

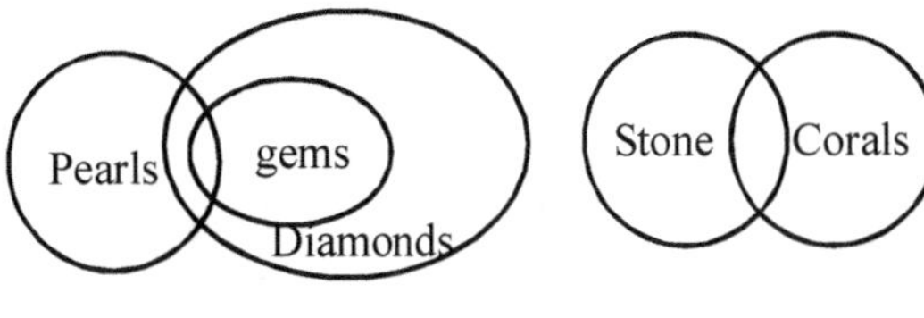

OR

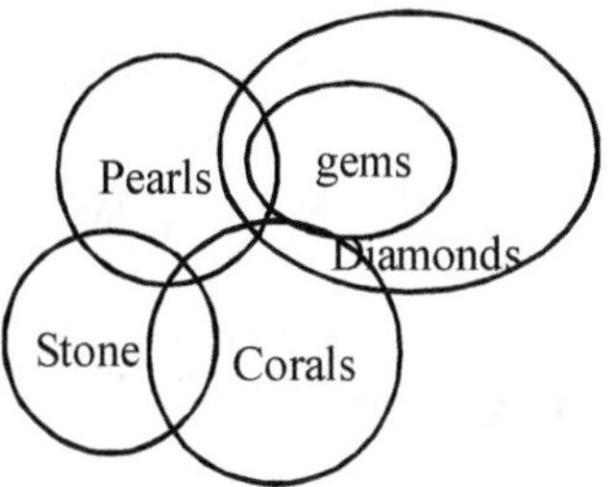

I. False ⎤
Conclusion II. True ⎟ or
III. False ⎦

Hence, only conclusions II and either I or III follow.

55. (a)   According to question,

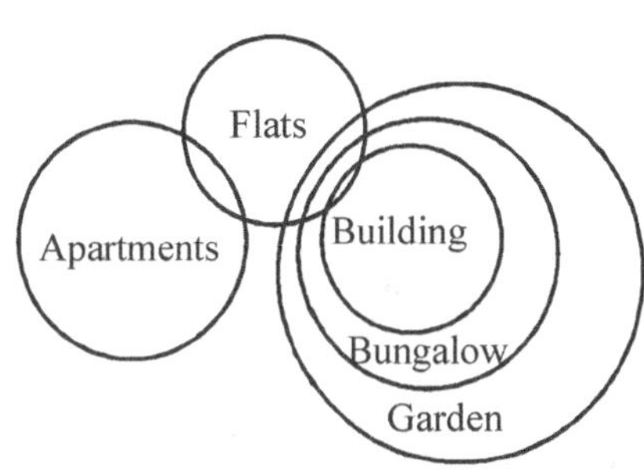

OR

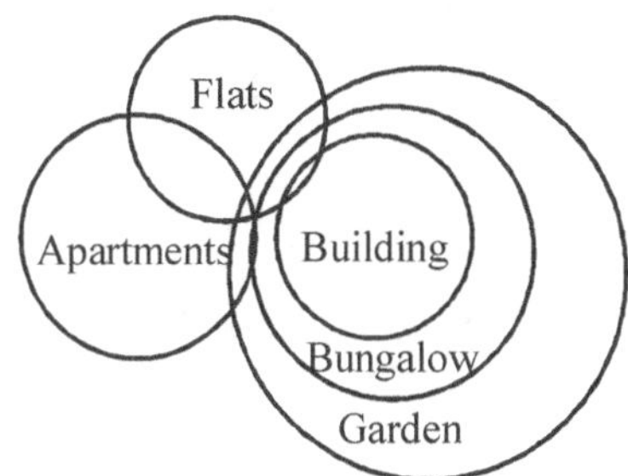

Conclusions I. True, II. False, III. False

Hence, only conclusion I follows.

56. (c)   According to question,

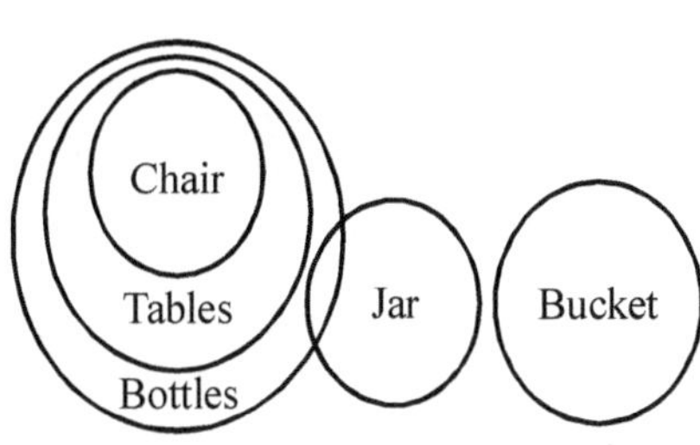

OR

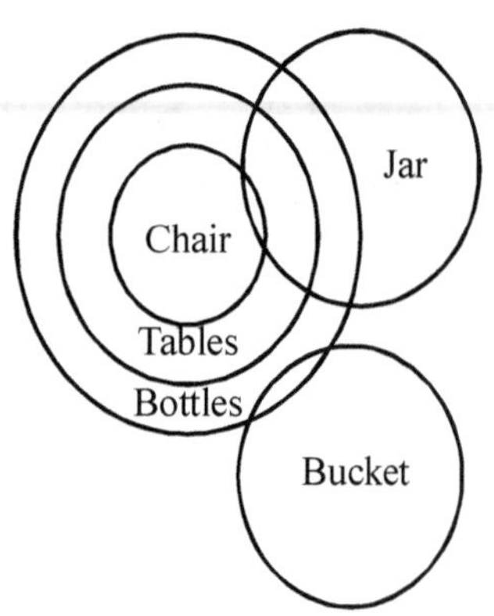

Conclusions, I. True, II. True, III. True.
Hence, All I, II and III follow.

| 57. | (a) | 58. | (a) | 59. | (b) | 60. | (e) |

61. (e)

(62 - 66) :

62. (a)

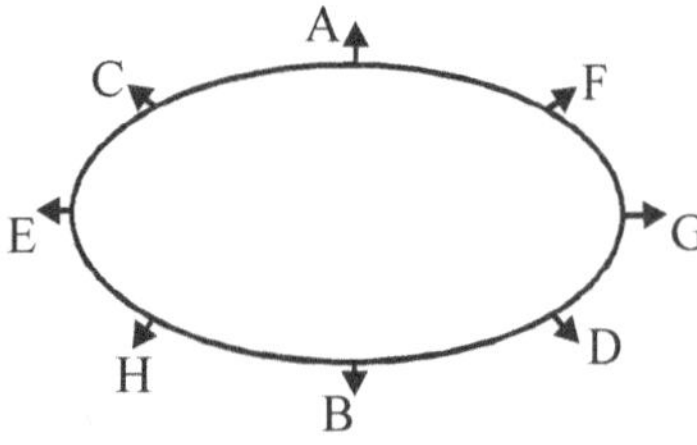

63. (a) PQ
64. (c) V
65. (d) RU
66. (c) R

(67 - 70) :

67. (b) C
68. (a) one
69. (c) Only 3 persons sitting between E and G
70. (d) D, F

81. (d) (ubiquitous-present, appearing, or found everywhere.)
82. (a) (journey fits correctly in the context)
83. (b) (unschooled-not educated or trained.)
84. (a) (earned-fits correctly in the context)
85. (e) (dollars-fits correctly in the context)
86. (c) (path-breaker-One that is original or innovative; a pioneer.)
87. (e) (destiny-fits correctly in the context)
88. (b) {meagre-(of something provided or available) lacking in quantity or quality.}
89. (b) (instilled-gradually but firmly establish (an idea or attitude) in a person's mind.}
90. (e) (revealed-fits correctly in the context)
91. (e) They are complicit in this violence by their deliberate negligence, to say the least, if not active support, by not coming to the rescue of Muslims in a timely manner.
92. (a) We kept speaking to all the responsible officers, they kept reassuring us that there was nothing to worry about and that they would take care.
93. (e) They should have been prepared for such a calamity. It looks like callous disregard for the safety of the student minority in this country.
94. (c) A company may be opening a significant number of new stores almost every year, which in turn could cause its total revenue to increase year after year.
95. (a) This shows the government's arrogance and unilateral move to bulldoze all the financial business without discussing them on the floor of the Hous(e)
96. (b) Though they might not be debarred from conducting arbitration in India arising out of international commercial arbitration, they would be governed by the code of conduct applicable to the legal profession in India.
97. (a) The Secretary had every intention of staying because of the critical progress made in national security.
98. (c) The two poisonings, just over a decade apart, have raised serious questions domestically about Britain's ability to protect those seeking political asylum on its shores.
99. (b) On Tuesday, airport operations returned to normal, while the wreckage of the crashed aircraft lay near the runway, guarded by security personnel.
100. (d) A separate security source in Gaza said the convoy was also fired on by unknown gunmen at the time of the explosion.

PRACTICE SET 3

Time : 60 Minutes **Max. Marks : 100**

NUMERICAL ABILITY

DIRECTIONS (Qs. 1-5) : *What will come in place of the question mark (?) in the following equations?*

1. $\dfrac{117 \times 117 \times 117 - 98 \times 98 \times 98}{117 \times 117 + 117 \times 98 + 98 \times 98} = ?$

   (a) 215 (b) 311 (c) 19 (d) 29
   (e) None of these

2. If $\dfrac{a}{b} = \dfrac{4}{3}$, then $\dfrac{3a+2b}{3a-2b} = ?$

   (a) 6 (b) 3 (c) 5 (d) –1
   (e) None of these

3. $\sqrt{\dfrac{?}{196}} = \dfrac{72}{56}$

   (a) 18 (b) 14 (c) 324 (d) 212
   (e) None of these

4. $\dfrac{17.28 \div ?}{3.6 \times 0.2} = 200$

   (a) 120 (b) 1.20 (c) 12 (d) 0.12
   (e) None of these

5. $\dfrac{(3.537 - 0.948)^2 + (3.537 + 0.948)^2}{(3.537)^2 + (0.948)^2} = ?$

   (a) 4.485 (b) 2.589 (c) 4 (d) 2
   (e) None of these

DIRECTIONS (Qs. 6-10): *Find out the approximate value which should come in place of the question mark in the following questions. (You are not expected to find the exact value.)*

6. $\sqrt{45689} = ?$

   (a) 180 (b) 415 (c) 150 (d) 210
   (e) 300

7. $\dfrac{(10008.99)^2}{10009.001} \times \sqrt{3589} \times 0.4987 = ?$

   (a) 3000 (b) 300000
   (c) 3000000 (d) 5000
   (e) 9000000

8. $399.9 + 206 \times 11.009 = ?$

   (a) 2800 (b) 6666
   (c) 4666 (d) 2400
   (e) 2670

9. $\dfrac{2}{5} + \dfrac{7}{8} \times \dfrac{17}{19} \div \dfrac{6}{5} = ?$

   (a) 1 (b) $\dfrac{1}{2}$

   (c) $2\dfrac{1}{2}$ (d) $\dfrac{3}{4}$

   (e) $\dfrac{9}{11}$

10. $(299.99999)^3 = ?$

    (a) 27000000 (b) 9000000000
    (c) 180000 (d) 2.7×10^9
    (e) 2700000

11. Ram went to a shop to buy 50 kg of rice. He bought two varieties of rice which cost him ₹ 4.50 per kg and ₹ 5 per kg. He spent a total of ₹ 240. What was the quantity of the cheaper rice purchased by him ?

    (a) 20 kg (b) 25 kg
    (c) 30 kg (d) 40 kg
    (e) None of these

12. A man has ₹ 640 in the denominations of one rupee, five rupee and ten rupee notes. The number of each type of notes are equal. What is the total number of notes he has ?
   (a) 60   (b) 150
   (c) 90   (d) 120
   (e) None of these

13. How many 3 digits numbers are there which end with digit 6 (repetition not allowed)?
   (a) 72   (b) 52
   (c) 80   (d) 64
   (e) 66

14. A, B and C invested ₹ 3000, ₹ 3500 and ₹ 4000 in a business. After 8 months they all added ₹ 500 to their investments. In what respective ratio they will get the profits after a year?
   (a) $7:10:15$ (b) $14:23:12$
   (c) $18:22:25$ (d) $11:2:7$
   (e) $8:13:15$

15. The speed of the stream is 6 km/hr and speed of the boat in still water is 9 km/hr. If a boat takes 70 hrs to travel downstream from point A to B and coming back to point C midway between A and B, the what is the total distance travelled by the boat?
   (a) 550 km   (b) 300 km
   (c) 450 km   (d) 480 km
   (e) 420 km

16. The total surface area of a cylinder is 748 cm². Find the volume of this cylinder if the height of cylinder and radius of its base are in the ratio 10 : 7.
   (a) 1390 cm³   (b) 1290 cm³
   (c) 1250 cm³   (d) 1540 cm³
   (e) 1680 cm³

17. If the sum of a few numbers is 450 and their mean is 50 and if another number 100 is included, the mean would become
   (a) 55   (b) 60
   (c) 75   (d) 150
   (e) None of these

18. In a mixture of 60 litres, the ratio of milk and water is 2 : 1. What amount of water must be added to make the ratio of milk and water as 1 : 2?
   (a) 42 Litres   (b) 56 Litres
   (c) 60 Litres   (d) 77 Litres
   (e) None of these

19. 19 persons went to a hotel for a combined dinner party. 13 of them spent ₹ 79 each on their dinner and the rest spent ₹ 4 more than the average expenditure of all the 19. What was the total money spent by them?
   (a) 1878   (b) 1760
   (c) 1536   (d) 1492
   (e) None of these

20. 20 men when work for 20 days and 6 hours a day complete three-fifth of a work. For the remaining work they are replaced by some number of women who complete the remaining work in 10 days working 8 hours each day. Find the number of women required to complete remaining work if efficiency of a man is twice that of woman.

   (a) 20   (b) 12
   (c) 35   (d) 25
   (e) 30

21. In an examination a candidate has to get 35% of total marks to pass. In one paper he gets 62 out of 150 and in the second 35 out of 150. How many marks should he get out of 200 marks in the third paper to pass ?
   (a) 61   (b) 68
   (c) 70   (d) 78
   (e) None of these

22. The difference between the simple interest and compund interest obtained on a principal amount at 5% per annum after 2 yrs is ₹35. What is the principal amount?
   (a) ₹ 41,000/-   (b) ₹ 13,000/-
   (c) ₹ 31,000/-   (d) ₹ 14,000/-
   (e) None of these

23. Two-third of a consignment was sold at a profit of 5% and the remainder at a loss of 2% if the total profit was ₹400, what was the value of the consignment ?
   (a) ₹13,000/-   (b) ₹17,000/-
   (c) ₹15,000/-   (d) ₹40,000/-
   (e) None of these

24. The sum of the number of boys and girls in a school is 150. If the number of boys is x, then the number of girls becomes x% of the total number of students. How many boys are there in the school ?
   (a) 51   (b) 65
   (c) 60   (d) 95
   (e) None of these

25. The ratio of B's present age and A's age 2 years hence is 5 : 6. If twice B's present age is 10 more than A's age 8 years after, what is the ratio of present ages of A and B?
   (a) $11:7$ (b) $20:17$
   (c) $10:7$ (d) $11:10$
   (e) $12:7$

DIRECTIONS (Qs. 26-30): *In each of these questions, a number series is given. In each series, only one number is wrong. Find out the wrong number.*

26. 3601 3602 1803 604 154 36 12
   (a) 3602   (b) 1803   (c) 604   (d) 154
   (e) 36

27. 4 12 42 196 1005 6066 42511
   (a) 12   (b) 42   (c) 1005   (d) 196
   (e) 6066

28. 2 8 12 20 30 42 56
   (a) 8   (b) 42   (c) 30   (d) 20
   (e) 12

29. 32 16 24 65 210 945 5197.5
   (a) 945   (b) 16   (c) 24   (d) 210
   (e) 65

30. 7 13 25 49 97 194 385
   (a) 13   (b) 49   (c) 97   (d) 194
   (e) 25

DIRECTIONS (Qs. 31-35): *Study the following table carefully and answer the questions given below.*

Number (in thousands) of Workers in the Given Six Shifts of Various Factories

Factories→ Shifts↓	L	M	N	O	P
7:00 am-11 : 00 am	7.5	8.0	7.8	7.59	8.32
11:00 am-3 : 00 pm	6.38	7.0	7.16	6.5	7.5
3:00 pm-7 : 00 am	6.5	7.28	6.35	6.15	7.24
7:00 pm-11 : 00 pm	7.8	5.25	6.0	6.0	6.5
11:00 pm-3 : 00 am	5.5	5.0	5.10	5.5	5.7
3:00 am-11 : 00 am	4.2	3.0	4.12	3.5	2.15

31. The total number of workers from Factory 0 is approximately what percent of the total number of workers from Factory L?
    - (a) 89
    - (b) 80
    - (c) 96
    - (d) 78
    - (e) 93

32. What is the average number of workers working in various shifts in Factory P?
    - (a) 6045
    - (b) 6200
    - (c) 6235
    - (d) 6150
    - (e) None of these

33. What is the difference in the total number of workers working in various shifts in Factory M and the total number of workers working in various shifts in Factory 0?
    - (a) 290
    - (b) 275
    - (c) 295
    - (d) 270
    - (e) None of these

34. What is the ratio of the total number of workers from factories L and M working in the shift of 11:00 pm-3:00 am and the total number of workers working in the same shifts in Factories 0 and P?
    - (a) 13 : 14
    - (b) 15 : 16
    - (c) 13 : 15
    - (d) 15 : 17
    - (e) None of these

35. What is the total of the average number of workers working in the shift of 7 : 00 am - 11 : 00 am in all the factories and the average number of workers working in the shift of 7 : 00 pm - 11 : 00 pm in all the factories ?
    - (a) 11502
    - (b) 15142
    - (c) 14520
    - (d) 14152
    - (e) None of these

REASONING ABILITY

DIRECTIONS (Qs. 36-40): *In each question below are given two/three statements followed by two conclusions numbered I and II. You have to take the given statements to be true even if they seem to be at variance with commonly known facts. Read all the conclusions and then decide which of the given conclusions logically follows from the given statements, disregarding commonly known facts. Give answer*

- *(a) if only conclusion I follows.*
- *(b) if only conclusion II follows.*
- *(c) if either conclusion I or conclusion II follows.*
- *(d) if neither conclusion I nor conclusion II follows.*
- *(e) if both conclusion I and conclusion II follow.*

36. **Statements** : No house is an apartment.
    Some bungalows are apartments.
    Conclusions : **I.** No house is a bungalow.
    II. All bungalows are houses.

37. **Statements** : Some gases are liquids.
    All liquids are water.
    Conclusions : **I.** All gases being water is a possibility.
    II. All such gases which are not water can never be liquids.

38. **Statements** : All minutes are seconds.
    All seconds are hours.
    No second is a day.
    Conclusions : **I.** No day is an hour.
    II. At least some hours are minutes.

(39-40): **Statements** : Some teachers are professors.
    Some lecturers are teachers.

39. **Conclusions** : **I.** All teachers as well as professors being lecturers is a possibility.
    II. All those teachers who are lecturers are also professors.

40. **Conclusions** : **I.** No professor is a lecturer.
    II. All lecturers being professors is a possibility.

DIRECTIONS (Qs. 41-45) : *Study the following information carefully and answer the given questions :*

A, B, C, D, E, F, G and H are sitting around a circle facing the centre but not necessarily in the same order.

- B sits second to left of H's husband. No female is an immediate neighbour of B.
- D's daughter sits second to right of F. F is the sister of G. F is not an immediate neighbour of H's husband.
- Only one person sits between A and F. A is the father of G. H's brother D sits to the immediate left of H's mother. Only one person sits between H's mother and E.
- Only one person sits between H and G. G is the mother of C. G is not an immediate neighbour of E.

41. What is position of A with respect to his mother-in-law ?
    - (a) Immediate left
    - (b) Third to the right
    - (c) Third to the left
    - (d) Second to the right
    - (e) Fourth to the left

42. Who amongst the following is D's daughter ?
    - (a) B
    - (b) C
    - (c) E
    - (d) G
    - (e) H

43. What is the position of A with respect to his grandchild ?
    - (a) Immediate right
    - (b) Third to the right
    - (c) Third to the left
    - (d) Second to the left
    - (e) Fourth to the left

44. How many people sit between G and her uncle ?
    - (a) One
    - (b) Two
    - (c) Three
    - (d) Four
    - (e) More than four

45. Four of the following five are alike in a certain way based on the given information and so form a group. Which is the one that does not belong to that group ?
    (a) F   (b) C
    (c) E   (d) H
    (e) G

46. A school bus driver starts from the school, drives 2 km towards North, takes a left turn and drives for 5 km. He then takes a left turn and drives for 8 km before taking a left turn again and driving for 5 km. The driver finally takes a left turn and drives 1 km before stopping. How far and towards which direction should the driver drive to reach the school again?
    (a) 3 km towards North   (b) 7 km towards East
    (c) 6 km towards South   (d) 6 km towards West
    (e) 5 km towards North

DIRECTIONS (Qs. 47-49) : *These questions are based on the following information.*

Six persons A, B, C, D, E and F are comparing their weights and each of them is having a different weight. D is heavier than only two persons. E is the only person heavier than F and lighter than D. C's weight is less than only B's weight. The third heaviest weight is 100kgs and the fifth heaviest weight is 60kgs.

47. What is the possible weight of D?
    (a) 60 kgs   (b) 100 kgs
    (c) 105 kgs   (d) 4 : 75 kgs
    (e) Data inadequate

48. Who is the third heaviest?
    (a) D   (b) E
    (c) A   (d) B
    (e) Data inadequate

49. If the heaviest weight is 30kgs more than A's weight, then what is the possible weight of C?
    (a) 130   (b) 100
    (c) 115   (d) 90
    (e) Data inadequate

DIRECTIONS (Qs. 50-51) : *Read the followinginformation carefully and answer the questions which follow:*

If 'A × B' means 'A is son of B'.
If 'A + B' means 'A is daughter of B'.
If 'A ÷ B' means 'A is wife of B'.
If 'A – B' means 'A is father of B'.

50. What will come in place of the questionmark, to establish that Q is mother of N in the following expression? 'N + O – P ? Q'
    (a) +   (b) ×
    (c) –   (d) ÷
    (e) Either (a) or (b)

51. Which of the following relations are true based upon the relations given in the equation:
    'S ÷ T × V – W + Y' ?
    (a) T is brother of Y.
    (b) S is daughter-in-law of W.
    (c) S is daughter-in-law of Y.
    (d) Y is daughter of V.
    (e) None is true

DIRECTIONS (Qs. 52-53) : *Each of the following questions is based on the following information:*

A # B means B is at 1 metre to the right of A.
A $ B means B is at 1 metre to the North of A.
A * B means B is at 1 metre to the left of A.
A @ B means B is at 1 metre to the south of A.
In each question first person from the left is facing North.

52. According to X @ B * P, P is in which direction with respect to X?
    (a) North   (b) South
    (c) North-East   (d) South-West
    (e) None is these

53. According to M # N $ T, T is in which direction with respect to M?
    (a) North-West   (b) North-East
    (c) South-West   (d) South-East
    (e) None of these

DIRECTIONS (Qs. 54-58): *Read the following carefully and answer the given questions:*

10 friends (5 boys P, Q, R, S and T and 5 girls A, E, I, O and U) are playing a game and they are sitting in a circle. The distance between every two friends is equal. Two boys and two girls are facing opposite to the centre of the circle and other 6 friends are facing towards the centre of the circle. A is the fourth to the left of O, who is third to the right of P. R is second to the right of T, who is not near to E. There are three friends between I and R. S is second to the left of U and facing the centre of the circle. P and E are sitting opposite and facing each other. I is second to the left of Q. A is facing opposite to the centre of the circle. More than three boys or girls are not sitting together. Not more than two friends who are facing opposite to the centre ofthe circle are sitting together.

54. Which two girls are sitting facing opposite to the centre of the circle?
    (a) I and U   (b) O and A
    (c) E and I   (d) O and E
    (e) O and I

55. Which of the following boys is not sitting between two girls?
    (a) P   (b) Q
    (c) R   (d) S
    (e) Both P and S

56. What is the position of I vis-a-vis A?
    (a) Immediate left   (b) Immediate right
    (c) Opposite   (d) (a) and (b)
    (e) None of these

57. Which two boys are facing opposite to thecentre of the circle?
    (a) R and Q   (b) Q and P
    (c) R and T   (b) Can't be determined
    (e) All of the above are possible

58. How many persons are sitting between S and Q?
    (a) Four   (b) Three
    (c) Two   (d) One
    (e) Either (a) or (c)

59. Pointing to a man in a photograph, Reena said, "His brother's father is the only son of my grandfather." How is Reena related to the man in photograph?
    - (a) Mother
    - (b) Grand Daughter
    - (c) Sister
    - (d) Daughter
    - (e) None of these

DIRECTIONS (Qs. 60-64): *Study the following information to answer the given questions:*

Twelve people are sitting in two parallel rows containing six people each such that they are equidistant from each other. In row 1: P, Q, R, S, T and V are seated and all of them are facing South. In row 2: A, B, C, D, E and F are seated and all of them are facing North. Therefore, in the given seating arrangement, each member seated in a row faces another member of the other row.

   S sits third to the right of Q. Either S or Q sits at an extreme end of the line. The one who faces Q sits second to the right of E. Two people sit between B and F. Neither B nor F sits at an extreme end of the line. The immediate neighbour of B faces the person who sits third to the left of P. R and T are immediate neighbours. C sits second to the left of A. T does not face the immediate neighbour of D.

60. Who amongst the following sit at the extreme ends of the rows?
    - (a) S, D
    - (b) Q, A
    - (c) V, C
    - (d) P, D
    - (e) Q, F
61. Who amongst the following faces S?
    - (a) A
    - (b) B
    - (c) C
    - (d) D
    - (e) F
62. How many persons are seated between V and R?
    - (a) One
    - (b) Two
    - (c) Three
    - (d) Four
    - (e) None of these
63. P is related to A in the same way as S is related to B based on the given arrangement. Which of the following is T related to, following the same pattern?
    - (a) C
    - (b) D
    - (c) E
    - (d) F
    - (e) Cannot be determined
64. Which of the following is true regarding T?
    - (a) F faces T.
    - (b) V is an immediate neighbour of T.
    - (c) F faces the one who is second to the right of T.
    - (d) T sits at one of the extreme ends of the line.
    - (e) Q sits second to the right of T.

DIRECTIONS (Qs. 65-69): *Read below information and answer these questions on the basic of following set of numbers.*

937   483   465   572   684

65. If in each number the order of digits is reversed and then the numbers are arranged in descending order, which number will be second?
    - (a) 937
    - (b) 483
    - (c) 765
    - (d) 572
    - (e) 684
66. If in each number '1' is added to the last digit and then the position of second and the third digits are interchanged which number will be the largest?
    - (a) 483
    - (b) 937
    - (c) 572
    - (d) 765
    - (e) 684
67. If in each number the first two digits are replaced by their sum, which number will be the largest?
    - (a) 937
    - (b) 483
    - (c) 765
    - (d) 572
    - (e) 684
68. If in each number the positions of first and the second digits are interchanged, which number will be the smallest?
    - (a) 937
    - (b) 483
    - (c) 765
    - (d) 572
    - (e) 684
69. If 'I' is added to the second digit and then the first and second digits are interchanged which number will be third?
    - (a) 937
    - (b) 483
    - (c) 765
    - (d) 572
    - (e) 684
70. In a row of 16 persons, position of A from left side of the row is 12th. Find the position of A from right side of the row
    - (a) 6th
    - (b) 5th
    - (c) 8th
    - (d) 9th
    - (e) 10th

ENGLISH LANGUAGE

DIRECTIONS (Qs. 71-80): *Read the following passage carefully and answer the questions given below it. Certain words are given in bold to help you locate them while answering some of the questions.*

The government has no business to be in the business of owning airports, running hotels, making bread - and owning banks. When the government stepped into these sectors in the first flush of Independence, it was with a view to creating basic capacities. With the passage of time, it became clear that **overwhelming** government presence was doing no good to anyone. Today, the benefits of the government stepping back in sectors like telecom and aviation are evident. Till as recently as the early 90s, a landline was a status symbol because it was **accessible** to just 2 per cent of the population. Today, the mobile phone is a **ubiquitous** feature of rural and urban India. Indian Airlines and Air-India had reduced air travel to a privilege; with competition, rates have fallen to a third of levels that obtained a decade ago, despite little change in input costs. The time is **ripe** for the government to ease itself out of banking as well.

The recent strike by State Bank of India employees will result in higher pension outgo in the entire banking sector. This will further **consolidate** the organised labour aristocracy and its tendency to act as a law unto itself. Bank nationalisation was seen as a necessity in 1969, in order to direct credit to Green Revolution areas. Today, that system has outlived its utility, as agriculture is a transformed occupation with new risks and opportunities. Green Revolution is in the grip of diminishing returns, and prosperous farmers of yesteryears are fast moving out of agriculture. Small farmers all over the country are in distress, as rural banks lend to moneylenders instead of dealing directly with them. New forms of production based on contract farming do not really need the sarkari banking network.

Private players have made lending more competitive and customer-friendly. A small-scale entrepreneur need not suffer for lack of working capital, nor does he have to bow and scrape before a bank manager. Credit is **readily** available to business, in varying packages to suit different needs. It is not hard to visualise a replication of this situation in rural areas. With a number of players in rural credit, entrepreneurs who come forward with proposals for food processing and cold storage would benefit. Farmers seeking to add value to their produce will encounter fewer hindrances in a competitive situation. A spirit of enterprise in rural banking can transform rural India. Gramin banking, or microcredit, has worked wonders in Bangladesh. Given the chance, it could do the same here.

71. That the mobile phone is a ubiquitous feature of rural and urban India today shows that
    (a) people have no interest in landline phone these days.
    (b) telephone is easily available everywhere now.
    (c) technology can invade all the barriers.
    (d) telephone has become affordable for all now.
    (e) mobile phone has taken the place of landline phone everywhere.

72. Which of the following seems to be false in the context of the passage?
    (a) Agriculture sector has witnessed much change over the years.
    (b) Green Revolution has lost its charm with the farmers.
    (c) The government is facing competition in telecom, aviation, banking etc.
    (d) Agriculture is no more a lucrative area for the wealthy farmers now.
    (e) None of these

73. Which of the following is 'true' in the context of the passage?
    (a) Getting loans from private banks is easier than the nationalised banks.
    (b) Credit through banks is readily available for even small farmers these days.
    (c) Landline phone is considered a status symbol.
    (d) Gramin Banking has failed in India.
    (e) None of these

74. What message does the author want to convey to the government through this passage?
    (a) Govt should compete with private players in telecom, aviation, banking etc.
    (b) Govt should withdraw from telecom, aviations banking etc.
    (c) Govt should allow private players in all the areas of business.
    (d) Govt should provide credit to the farmers on simpler terms.
    (e) None of these

DIRECTIONS (Qs. 75-77): *Choose the word which is the SAME in meaning as the word given in bold as used in the passage.*

75. **OVERWHELMING**
    (a) large   (b) majority
    (c) feasible   (d) vigilant
    (e) viable

76. **ACCESSIBLE**
    (a) convincing   (b) deliberate
    (c) targeted   (d) approachable
    (e) distributed

77. **UBIQUITOUS**
    (a) unique   (b) modern
    (c) omnipresent   (d) enormous
    (e) stylish

DIRECTIONS (Qs. 78-80): *Choose the word which is the OPPOSITE in meaning of the word given in bold as used in the passage.*

78. **RIPE**
    (a) lengthy   (b) inappropriate
    (c) rare   (d) hard
    (e) umpteen

79. **CONSOLIDATE**
    (a) deviate   (b) strike
    (c) drag   (d) weaken
    (e) instigate

80. **READILY**
    (a) deliberately   (b) strictly
    (c) strangely   (d) supposedly
    (e) hardly

DIRECTIONS (Qs. 81-90): *In the following passage, some of the words have been left out. First read the passage over and try to understand what it is about. Then fill in the blanks with the help of the alternatives given.*

Civilisation, like (81), fall, not so much because of (82) of the enemy outside, as through the weakness and (83) within. Rome fell not because of the (84), they merely knocked (85) something that was already dead. The heart of Rome had (86) beating when the arms and legs were cut (87) we see something of this (88) in India and China and in the case of the Arabs. The (89) of Arabian civilisation was sudden even as their rise had been. In India and China, the process is long-drawn (90) and it is not easy to spot it.

81. (a) states   (b) kingdom
    (c) empires   (d) buildings
    (e) house

82. (a) weakness   (b) strength
    (c) power   (d) tenacity
    (e) symptom

83. (a) disease   (b) decease
    (c) decay   (d) fortitude
    (e) fortune

84. (a) barbarity   (b) barbarous
    (c) barbarians   (d) romans
    (e) barbaric

85. (a) off   (b) on
    (c) down   (d) no word
    (e) without

86. (a) seized   (b) rotated
    (c) ceased   (d) started
    (e) startled

87. (a) down   (b) off
    (c) up   (d) without
    (e) like

88. (a) process   (b) procedure
    (c) spectacle   (d) scene
    (e) drama

89. (a) downfall   (b) death
    (c) collapse   (d) dismemberment
    (e) collage

90. (a) out   (b) up
    (c) upon   (d) no word
    (e) by

DIRECTIONS (Qs. 91-100): *In each of the questions given below, a sentence is given in which some parts are given in bold which are grammatically correct. The other three parts of the sentence may or may not be grammatically correct. The sentence is then followed by three alternatives for the parts of the sentence which is not given in bold which may replace the incorrect portion. Choose the alternative(s) which will replace the incorrect part in the sentence to make it grammatically and contextually correct.*

91. In the end of the Rigvedic period(A)/, the Aryan society began to(B)/ expand of the northwestern region(C)/ of the Indian subcontinent(D)/, into the western Ganges plain(E).
    (I)   At the end of the Rigvedic period
    (II) expand from the northwestern region
    (III) onto the western Ganges plain
    (a) Only (I)   (b) Only (II)
    (c) Both (I) & (II)   (d) Only (III)
    (e) All of the above

92. Many smaller clans mentioned(A)/ within early literature seems(B)/ to has been(C)/ present across the(D)/ rest of the subcontinent(E).
    (I)   within early literature seem
    (II) to have been
    (III) rest in the subcontinent
    (a) Only (I)
    (b) Only (II)
    (c) Only (III)
    (d) Both (I)&(II)
    (e) No replacement required

93. On the same time it(A)/ must be note that overwhelming(B)/ majority of Muslims in(C)/ India of Indian natives(D)/ converted to Islam(E).
    (I)   At the same time it
    (II) must be noted that overwhelming
    (III) India are Indian natives
    (a) Only (III)
    (b) Both (I) & (II)
    (c) All (I),(II) & (III)
    (d) No replacement required
    (e) Only (II)

94. The spark that lead to the(A)/ mutiny was the issue of new(B)/ gunpowder cartridges for the(C)/ Enfield rifle, which was insensitive(D)/ to local religious prohibition(E).
    (I)   The spark that led to the
    (II) Mutiny were the issue of new
    (III) Enfield Rifle, which is insensitive
    (a) Only (I)
    (b) Only (II)
    (c) Only (III)
    (d) Both (I) & (III)
    (e) No correction required

95. Bengal witnesses(A)/ an intellectual awakening(B)/ that was in(C)/ some way similar(D)/ to the Renaissance(E).
    (I)   Bengal witnessed
    (II) of intellectual awakening
    (III) that is in
    (a) Both (I) & (II)
    (b) Both (I) & (III)

(c) Only (II)
(d) Only (III)
(e) All of the above

96. The burning of coal and wood(A)/, and the presence of many houses(B)/ in concentrated areas(C)/ making the cities the primary(D)/ sources of pollution(E).
    (I)   of concentrated areas
    (II) makes the cities the primary
    (III) sourced on pollution
    (a) Only (III)   (b) Only (I)
    (c) No correction required (d) Only (II)
    (e) All (I),(II)&(III)

97. In addition, many states have(A)/ the authority to immediately(B)/ embargo adulterated(C)/ food and to(D)/ impose civil fines(E).
    (I)   the authority of immediately
    (II) embargo adulteration
    (III) imposing civil fines
    (a) Only (I)   (b) Only (II)
    (c) Only (III)   (d) Both (I) & (III)
    (e) No correction required

98. Monalisa is a half-length portrait painted by the Italian Renaissance (A)/ artist Leonardo Da Vinci that has been described(B)/ as "the best known, the most visited(C)/, the most written about, the most sang about, the most(D)/ parodied work of art in the world(E).
    (I)   Monalisa is a half-length portrait painting by the Italian Renaissance
    (II) the most written about, the most sung about, the most
    (a) Only (I)
    (b) Only (II)
    (c) Both (I)&(II)
    (d) All of the above
    (e) No correction required

99. The Miami Police Department state that(A)/ they believe they have recovered(B)/ the last of the(C)/ victims killed in(D)/ the bridge's collapse(E).
    (I)   The Miami Police Department states that
    (II) they believe they had recovered
    (III) victims killed by
    (a) Both (I)&(III)
    (b) Only (I)
    (c) Only (III)
    (d) Only (II)
    (e) No correction required

100. Foreign financial institutions are now(A)/ on notice that gone forward they(B)/ can choose to do business with the(C)/ United States or North Korea(D)/, but both(E).
    (I)   on notice that going forward they
    (II) United States or North Korea
    (III) but not both
    (a) Only (III)
    (b) Only (I)
    (c) Only (II)
    (d) Both (I)&(III)
    (e) All of the above

Answer Key

1	(c)	11	(a)	21	(d)	31	(e)	41	(d)	51	(c)	61	(a)	71	(c)	81	(c)	91	(c)
2	(b)	12	(d)	22	(d)	32	(c)	42	(c)	52	(d)	62	(b)	72	(e)	82	(c)	92	(d)
3	(c)	13	(d)	23	(c)	33	(a)	43	(b)	53	(b)	63	(b)	73	(a)	83	(c)	93	(c)
4	(d)	14	(c)	24	(c)	34	(b)	44	(a)	54	(a)	64	(c)	74	(c)	84	(c)	94	(a)
5	(d)	15	(c)	25	(d)	35	(d)	45	(b)	55	(e)	65	(c)	75	(a)	85	(c)	95	(b)
6	(d)	16	(d)	26	(d)	36	(d)	46	(e)	56	(b)	66	(b)	76	(d)	86	(c)	96	(d)
7	(b)	17	(a)	27	(b)	37	(a)	47	(d)	57	(a)	67	(e)	77	(c)	87	(b)	97	(e)
8	(e)	18	(c)	28	(a)	38	(b)	48	(a)	58	(e)	68	(a)	78	(b)	88	(c)	98	(c)
9	(a)	19	(c)	29	(e)	39	(a)	49	(c)	59	(c)	69	(d)	79	(d)	89	(c)	99	(a)
10	(a)	20	(a)	30	(d)	40	(b)	50	(e)	60	(d)	70	(b)	80	(e)	90	(a)	100	(d)

HINTS & EXPLANATIONS

1. (c) Given Expression $= \dfrac{(a^3 - b^3)}{(a^2 + ab + b^2)}$,

   where $a = 117, b = 98$

   $= \dfrac{(a-b)(a^2 + ab + b^2)}{(a^2 + ab + b^2)} = (a-b) = (117-98) = 19.$

2. (b) Dividing numerator as well as denominator by b, we get:

   $$\dfrac{3a + 2b}{3a - 2b} = \dfrac{3 \times \dfrac{a}{b} + 2}{3 \times \dfrac{a}{b} - 2} = \dfrac{3 \times \dfrac{4}{3} + 2}{3 \times \dfrac{4}{3} - 2} = \dfrac{4+2}{4-2} = 3$$

3. (c) Let $\sqrt{\dfrac{x}{196}} = \dfrac{72}{56} = \dfrac{9}{7}$

   Then, $\dfrac{x}{196} = \dfrac{9}{7} \times \dfrac{9}{7} = \dfrac{81}{49}$. So, $x = \dfrac{81 \times 196}{49} = 324.$

4. (d) Let $\dfrac{17.28 \div x}{3.6 \times 0.2} = 200$. Then, $\dfrac{17.28}{x} = 200 \times 3.6 \times 0.2$

   $\therefore x = \dfrac{17.28}{200 \times 3.6 \times 0.2} = \dfrac{1728}{200 \times 36 \times 2} = 0.12$

5. (d) Given Expression $=$

   $$\dfrac{(a-b)^2 + (a+b)^2}{(a^2 + b^2)} = \dfrac{2(a^2 + b^2)}{(a^2 + b^2)} = 2$$

6. (d) $? = \sqrt{45689} = 213.75 \approx 210$

7. (b) $? = \dfrac{(10008.99)^2}{10009.001} \times \sqrt{3589} \times 0.4987$

   $= (10009)^2 \times \sqrt{3600} = 0.50$

   $= 10009 \times 60 \times 0.50 \approx 300000$

8. (e) $? = 399.9 + 206 \times 11.009$

   $= 400 + (200 + 6) \times 11 = 400 + 2200 + 66 = 2670$

9. (a) $? = \dfrac{2}{5} + \dfrac{7}{8} \times \dfrac{17}{19} \div \dfrac{6}{5} = \dfrac{2}{5} + \dfrac{7}{8} \times \dfrac{17}{19} \times \dfrac{5}{6}$

   $= \dfrac{2}{5} + \dfrac{595}{912} = 0.40 + 0.65 \approx 1.05 \approx 1$

10. (a) $? = (299.99999)^3 \approx (300)^3 = 27000000$

11. (a) Let one variety of rice be x kg.

    Another quantity $= (50 - x)$ kg

    According to question $x \times 4.50 + (50 - x) \, 5 = 240$

    $4.5x + 250 - 5x = 240$

    $0.5x = 10$

    $x = 20$

    Hence, the quantity of cheaper rice was 20 kg.

12. (d) Let the number of each type of notes be x. According to question $1 \times x + 5 \times x + 10 \times x = 640$

    $16x = 640$

    $x = 40$

    Total number of notes $= 40 + 40 + 40 = 120$

13. (d) Repetition not allowed:

    For a number to be a 3 digit number, 1st digit should be from 1 to 9, excluding 6 which is at the 3rd digit's place. For 2nd digit, there are only 8 choices after including 0 and excluding the digit taken as the 1st digit and 6 at the 3rd digit's place.

    For 3rd digit, only 1 choice is there which is 6.

    So total 3 digit numbers that can be formed which end with digit $6 = 8 \times 8 \times 1 = 64$

14. (c) $A : B : C$

    $3000 \times 8 + 3500 \times 4 : 3500 \times 8 + 4000 \times 4 : 4000 \times 8 + 4500 \times 4$

    $30 \times 8 + 35 \times 4 : 35 \times 8 + 40 \times 4 : 40 \times 8 + 45 \times 4$

    $30 \times 2 + 35 : 35 \times 2 + 40 : 40 \times 2 + 45$

    $6 \times 2 + 6 : 7 \times 2 + 8 : 8 \times 2 + 9$

    $12 + 6 : 14 + 8 : 16 + 9$

    $18 : 22 : 25$

15. (c) Downstream speed $= 9 + 6 = 15$ km/hr

    Upstream speed $= 9\text{-}6 = 3$ km/hr

    Let the distance from A to B is x km.

    downstream distance $=$ x, upstream distance is half of x because boat goes half way upstream, then

    x/15 + (x/2)/3 = 70

    So x = 300

    Therefore, distance covered by boat $= 300 + 300/2 = 300 + 150 = 450$ km

16. (d) Height = 10x, radius = 7x
Total surface area = $2 \times (22/7) \times (7x) \times (7x+10x) = 748$
So x = 1
Height = 10 cm, radius = 7 cm
Volume = $(22/7) \times (7)2 \times 10 = 1540\,\text{cm}^3$

17. (a) $50 = \dfrac{\text{Sum of all numbers}}{\text{number of observations}}$

$50 = \dfrac{450}{\text{Number of observations}}$

Number of observations $= \dfrac{450}{50} = 9$

New mean $= \dfrac{450+100}{10} = \dfrac{550}{10} = 55$

18. (c) Milk $= \dfrac{2}{3} \times 60 = 40l$

Water $= \dfrac{1}{3} \times 60 = 20l$

Let 'x' be the amount to be added to milk and water.

$\dfrac{40+x}{20+x} = \dfrac{1}{2}$

$80 + 2x = 20 + x$
$60 = x$

19. (c) Let average of all persons = x
$\therefore$ $(13 \times 79) + 6(x+4) = 19 \times x$
$13 \times 79 + 6x + 24 = 19x$
$13 \times 79 + 24 = 13x$

$x = \dfrac{13 \times 79 + 24}{13} = 80.85$

Total money spent = 1536

20. (a) 1 man = 2 women
Let x men have to complete remaining (2/5th) work in 10 days working 8 hrs each day.
So, M1 × D1 × H1 × W2 = M2 × D2 × H2 × W1
$20 \times 10 \times 6 \times (2/5) = x \times 10 \times 8 \times (3/5)$
So, x = 10 men
Since, 1 man = 2 women, so 10 men = 20 women

21. (d) Total marks = 150 + 150 + 200 = 500
35% of 500 = 175
175 = 62 + 35 + x
x = 78

22. (d) Principal $= \dfrac{\text{difference} \times (100)^2}{r^2}$

$= \dfrac{35 \times 100 \times 100}{25}$

$= ₹\,14000$

23. (c) Let value of consignment was ₹ x

$\left(\dfrac{2}{3}\right)^{rd}$ consignment costs $\dfrac{2x}{3}$

Selling price of $\left(\dfrac{2}{3}\right)^{rd}$ consignment

$= \dfrac{2x}{3} + \dfrac{5}{100} \times \dfrac{2x}{3} = \dfrac{7}{10}x$

S.P of $\left(\dfrac{1}{3}\right)^{rd}$ consignment $= \dfrac{x}{3} - \dfrac{2}{100} \times \dfrac{x}{3} = \dfrac{49}{150}x$

Total S.P $= \dfrac{49x}{150} + \dfrac{7x}{10} = \dfrac{49x+105x}{150} = \dfrac{154x}{150}$

Profit = S.P – C.P

$400 = \dfrac{154x}{150} - x = \dfrac{4x}{150}$

$x = \dfrac{400 \times 150}{4} = 15000$

Value of consignment was ₹ 15,000

24. (c) If number of boys is x, then number of girls is (150–x)
$(150 - x) = x\,\%$ of 150

$150 - x = \dfrac{x}{100} \times 150 = \dfrac{3x}{2}$

$\Rightarrow \dfrac{5x}{2} = 150$

$\Rightarrow x = \dfrac{150 \times 2}{5} = 60$

Number of boys is 60

25. (d) Let A and B be the present ages of A and B respectively.
B/(A+2) = 5/6, so 6B - 5A = 10   ...(i)
Also 2B = (A+8) +10, so 2B – A = 18   ...(ii)
Solving equations (i) and (ii), we get A = 22, B = 20
Hence, the required ratio is 22/20 or 11:10.

26. (d)

| 3601 | 3602 | 1803 | 604 | 155 → 154 | 36 | 12 |

÷ 1 + 1   ÷ 2 + 2   ÷ 3 + 3   ÷ 4 + 4   ÷ 5 + 5   ÷ 6 + 6

154 is written in place of 155.

27. (b)

| 4 | 12 | 45 → 42 | 196 | 1005 | 6066 | 42511 |

$\times 2 + (2)^2$ $\times 3 + (3)^2$ $\times 4 + (4)^2$ $\times 5 + (5)^2$ $\times 6 + (6)^2$ $\times 7 + (7)^2$

42 is written in place of 45.

28. (a)

| 2 | 6 → 8 | 12 | 20 | 30 | 42 | 56 |

+ 4   + 6   + 8   + 10   + 12   + 14

8 is written in place of 6.

29. (e)

| 32 | 16 | 24 | 60 → 65 | 210 | 945 | 5197.5 |

$\times\,0.5$ $\times\,1.5$ $\times\,2.5$ $\times\,3.5$ $\times\,4.5$ $\times\,5.5$

65 is written in place of 60.

30. (d)

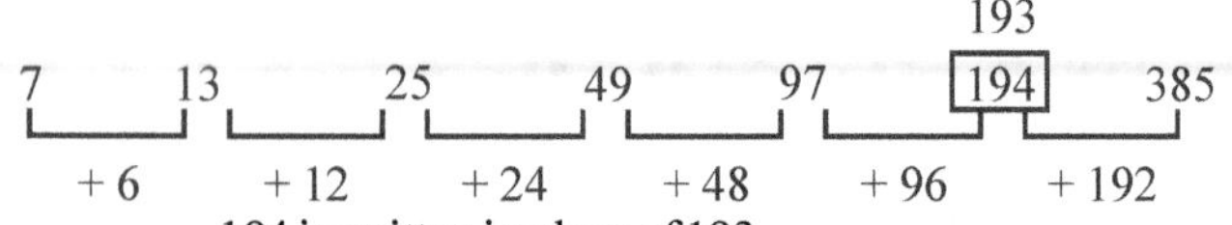

194 is written in place of 193

31. (e) Required percent

$$= \frac{(7.59 + 6.5 + 6.15 + 6.0 + 5.5 + 3.5)}{(7.5 + 6.38 + 6.5 + 7.8 + 5.5 + 4.2)}$$

$$= \frac{35.24}{37.88} \times 100 = 93.03\% \approx 93\%$$

32. (c) Required average

$$\frac{(8.32 + 7.5 + +7.24 + 6.5 + 5.7 + 2.15)}{6}$$

$$= \frac{37.41}{6} = 6.235 \text{ thousand} = 6235$$

33. (a) Required difference (in thousand)
$$= (8.0 + 7.0 + 7.28 + 5.25 + 5 + 3)$$
$$- (7.59 + 6.5 + 6.15 + 6 + 5.5 + 3.5)$$
$$= 35.53 - 35.24 = 0.29 \text{ thousand} = 290$$

34. (b) Required ratio

$$= \frac{(5.5 + 5)}{(5.5 + 5.7)} = \frac{10.5}{11.2} = \frac{15}{16} = 15:16$$

35. (d) Required total

$$= \frac{(7.5 + 8 + 7.8 + 7.59 + 8.32)}{5} + \frac{(7.8 + 5.25 + 6 + 6 + 6.5)}{5}$$

$$= \frac{(39.21 + 31.55)}{5} = 14.152 \text{ thousand}$$

$$= 14152$$

36. (d) 

OR

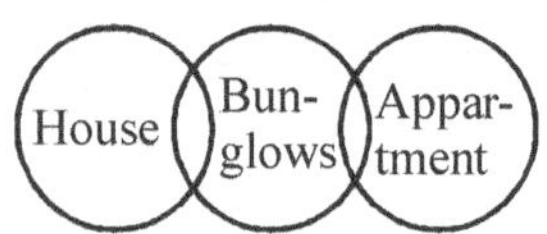

Conclusion I : False
Conclusion II : False

37. (a) 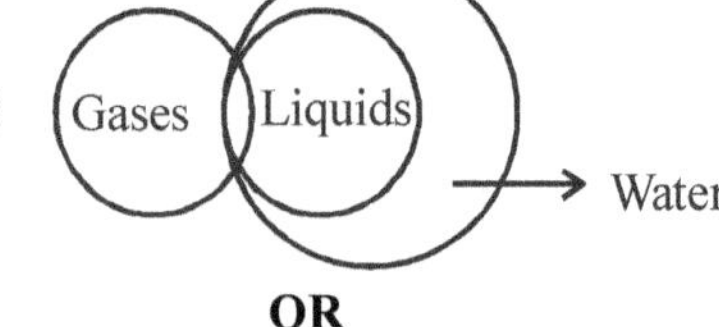

OR

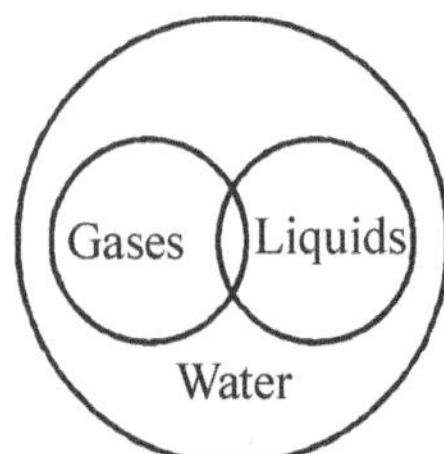

Conclusion I : True
Conclusion II : False

38. (b) 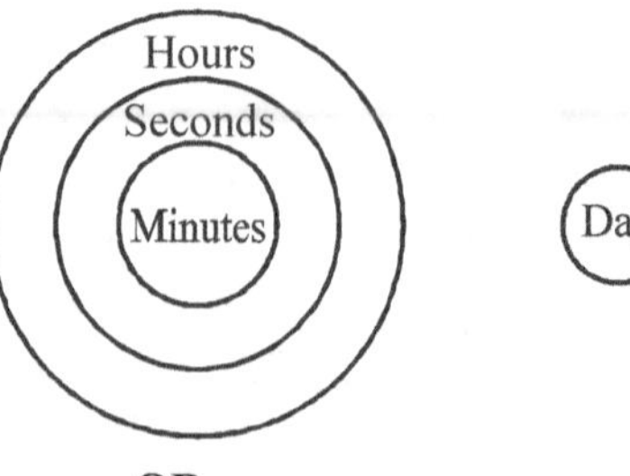

OR

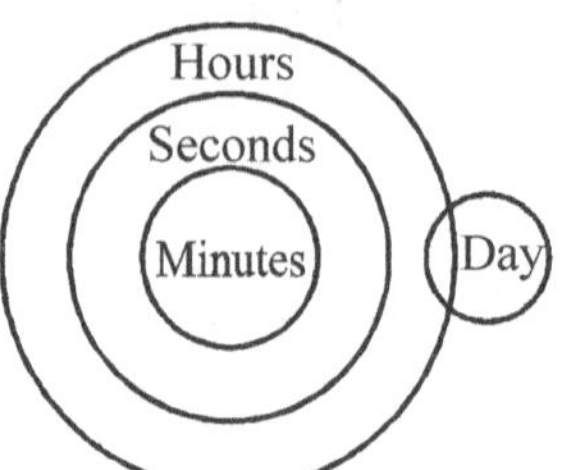

Conclusion I : False
Conclusion II : True

Sol. (39-40):

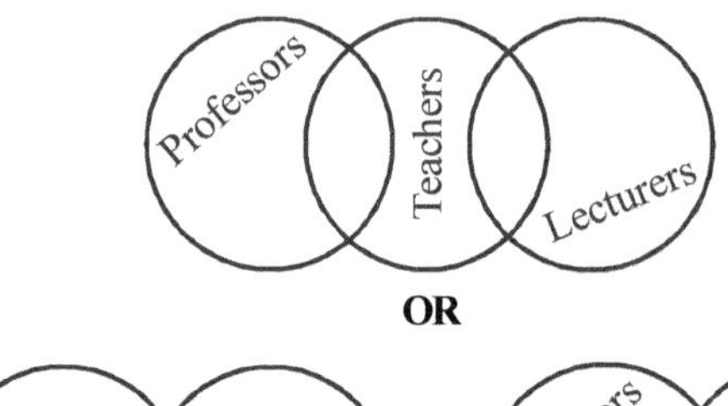

OR

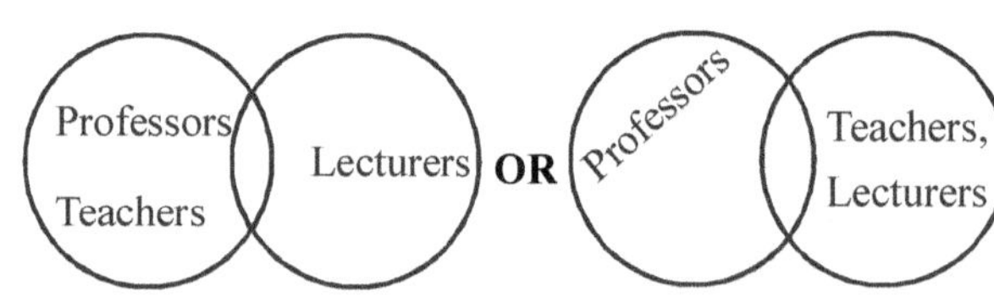

39. (a) Conclusion I : True
Conclusion II : False
40. (b) Conclusion I : False
Conclusion II : True.

Sol. (41-45) :

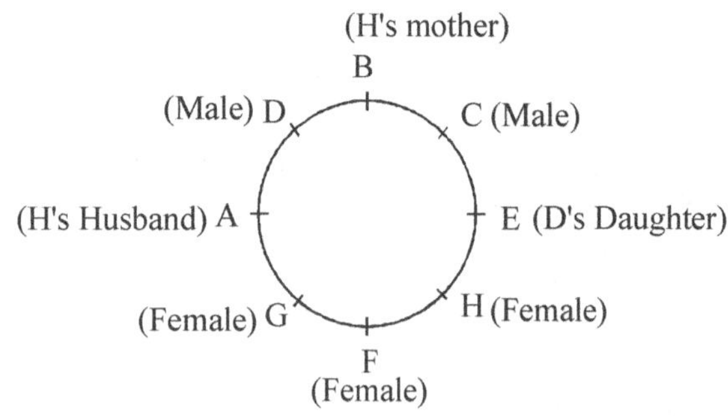

41. (d) A's wife is H. H's mother is B. Therefore, B is the mother-in-law of A, A is second to the right of B.
42. (c) E is the daughter of D.
43. (b) A is the father of F and G. G is the mother of C. Therefore, C is the grandchild of A. A is third to the right of C.
44. (a) D is brother-in-law of A. A is father of F and G. Therefore, D is material uncle of G. There is only one person between G and D is clockwise direction.
45. (b) Except C, all others are females.

46. (e) According to questions.
AB = 2 km; BC = 5 km; CD = 8 km
DE = 5 km; EF = 1 km; BC = DE = 5 km
CD = BE = 8 km
BE = EF + AF + AB

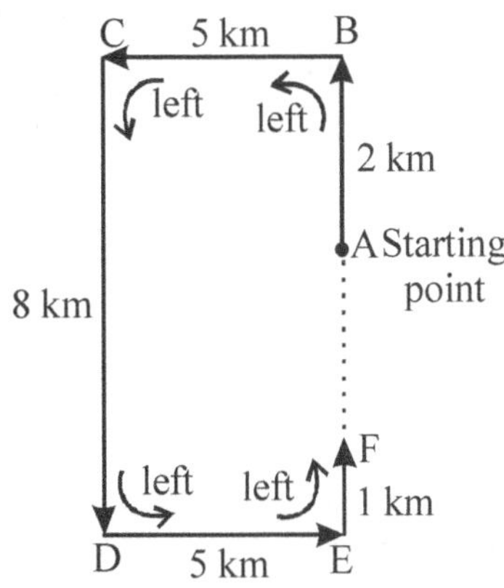

∴   AF = BE − (EF + AB)
= 8 − (1 + 2) = 8 − 3 = 5 km
∴   Required distance = AF = 5 km and required direction is North

Sol. (47-50) :

47. (d) From the information, D is heavier than only two persons and E is the only person taller than F and shorter than D. So we can say that D is the fourth heaviest, E is the fifth heaviest and F is the sixth heaviest. Also it is given that C's weight is less than only B's weight. So we can say that B is the heaviest and C is the second heaviest, then A is the third heaviest.

∴ The final arrangement is as follows:

Heaviest	2nd heaviest	3rd heaviest	4th heaviest	5th heaviest	6th heaviest
B	C	A	D	E	F
		100 kg		60 kg	

The possible weight of D is > 60 and < 100 i.e; 75 kgs.

48. (c) 3rd heaviest is 'A', 100 kg
49. (c)
50. (e) O (+) ⇔ Q(−)
N (−) P

Hence P is either son or daughter of Q.

51. (c)   V (+) ⇔ Y(−)
(−)S ⇔ T(+)   W(−)

52. (d) According to X @ B * P

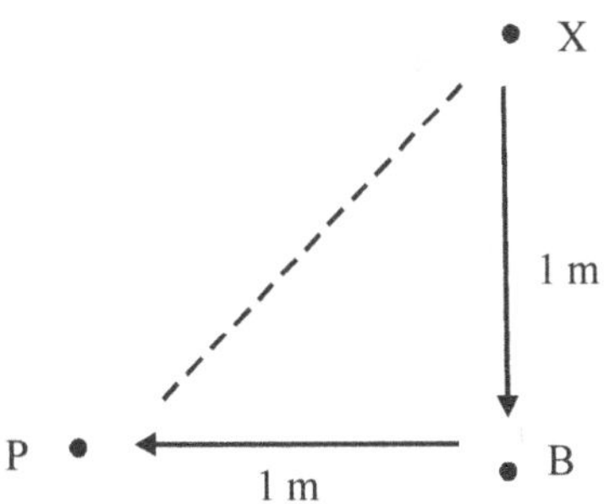

Hence P is in South-West of X.

53. (b) According to M # N $ T

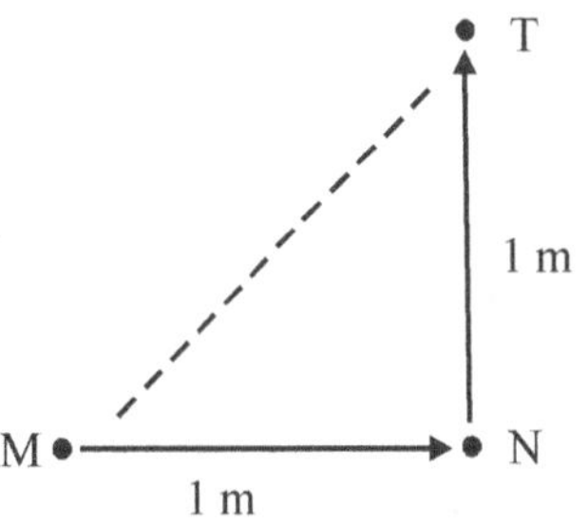

Hence T is in the North-East of M.

Sol. (54-58):

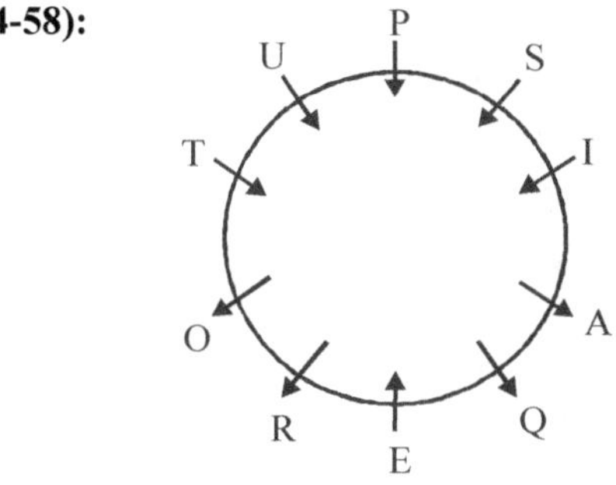

54 (a)   **55** (e)   **56** (b)   **57** (a)   **58** (e)

59. (c)   Grand Father
↓ only son
Reena's Father
↓
Reena

Man's Father
↓
Man — Brother

From above two diagram, it is clearly under stood that Reena's father and Man's father is the same. And Reena is sister to that man.

Sol. (60-64) :
Row 1. ↓ P V S T R Q
Row 2. ↑ C F A E B D

60. (d) **61.** (a) **62.** (b) **63.** (b) **64.** (c)

65. (c) 937 ⇒ 739, 483 ⇒ 384,
765 ⇒ 567, 572 ⇒ 275,
684 ⇒ 486
739 > 567 > 486 765

66. (b) 937 ⇒ 738 ⇒ 983
483 ⇒ 484 ⇒ 448
765 ⇒ 766 ⇒ 766
572 ⇒ 573 ⇒ 537
684 ⇒ 685 ⇒ 658
Largest number ⇒ 983 ⇒ 937

67. (e) 937 ⇒ 127, 483 ⇒ 123,
765 ⇒ 135
572 ⇒ 122, 684 ⇒ 144
Highest number ⇒ 144 ⇒ 684

68. (a) $937 \Rightarrow 397, 483 \Rightarrow 843,$
$765 \Rightarrow 675, 572 \Rightarrow 752$
$684 \Rightarrow 864$
Smallest number $\Rightarrow 397 \Rightarrow 937$
Trick : Smallest number will have the least middle digit.

69. (d) $937 \Rightarrow 947 \Rightarrow 497$
$483 \Rightarrow 493 \Rightarrow 943$
$765 \Rightarrow 775 \Rightarrow 775$
$572 \Rightarrow 582 \Rightarrow 852$
$684 \Rightarrow 694 \Rightarrow 964$
Third number $\Rightarrow 852 \Rightarrow 572$

70. (b) Position of A from right side $= (16-12) + 1 = 5^{th}$

81. (c) (empires -an extensive group of states or countries ruled over by a single monarch, an oligarchy, or a sovereign state.)

82. (c) (Strength ' fits in the context correctly)

83. (c) ('decay' fits in the context correctly)

84. (c) (Barbarians -(in ancient times) a member of a people not belonging to one of the great civilizations (Greek, Roman, Christian).)

85. (c) ('down' is correct preposition)

86. (c) ('Ceased ' come or bring to an end.)

87. (b) ('off' is correct preposition)

88. (c) (spectacle - a visually striking performance or display.)

89. (c) (collapse - (of a structure) suddenly fall down or give way.)

90. (a) ('out' is correct preposition)

91. (c) The Correct Sentence is : At the end of the Rigvedic period, the Aryan society began to expand from the northwestern region of the Indian subcontinent, into the western Ganges plain. When we talk about any period of time it should be started with 'at' as we are talking about the end of the era so 'in' should be replaced by 'at'. Moreover, expansion of the region has been mentioned. Therefore, there should be 'expand from' in place of 'expand of'.

92. (d) The Correct Sentence is: Many smaller clans mentioned within early literature seem to have been present across the rest of the subcontinent. Here, 'clans' is a plural form, therefore plural form of verb should be placed .i.e. 'seem' instead of 'seems'. Furthermore, according to the rule, 'to' always takes 'have' with it so it 'has' should be replaced by 'have'.

93. (c) The Correct Sentence is: At the same time it must be noted that overwhelming majority of Muslims in India are Indian natives converted to Islam. The same thing which we discussed in the solution of the Q1 is repeated here i.e. 'at the same time' should come here. Moreover,

'must' is followed by 'be', therefore third form of verb .i.e. 'noted' should replace 'note'. Furthermore, the context of the passage says that the majority of the Muslims are the natives are the natives of India, thus ....'India are Indian natives' is the correct formation.

94. (a) The Correct Sentence is: The spark that led to the mutiny was the issue of new gunpowder cartridges for the Enfield rifle, which was insensitive to local religious prohibition. As the sentence is in the past tense, therefore the error is only in the first part .i.e. 'lead' should be replaced by 'led'.

95. (b) The Correct Sentence is: Bengal witnessed an intellectual awakening that is in some way similar to the Renaissance. The given sentence is the present form of tense but the context of the passage talks about the awakening which is witnessed by the Bengal due to intellectual awakening. Thus, 'Bengal witnessed' is the correct usage, and accordingly 'that in some way similar to' will come further.

96. (d) The Correct Sentence is: The burning of coal and wood, and the presence of many horses in concentrated areas made the cities the primary sources of pollution. 'making' will be replaced by 'makes'.

97. (e) No correction required as the sentence is grammatically correct.

98. (c) The Correct Sentence is: Monalisa is a half-length portrait painting by Italian Renaissance artist Leonardo Da Vinci that has been described as "the best known, the most visited, the most written about, the most sung about, the most parodied work of art in the world. Here, the mentioned thing is the painting of Monalisa and the description of the same is given. Thus, 'Monalisa is half-length portrait painting' is the correct usage. Moreover, in the followed part of the sentence, the phrase 'most sang about' should be replaced with 'most sung' about as the verb of sentence says.

99. (a) The Correct Sentence is: The Miami Police Department states that they believe they have recovered the last of the victims killed by the bridge's collapse. Here, Police department is a singular object, hence, states will come instead of state. Moreover, 'victims killed by' should be used in place of 'victims killed in'.

100. (d) The Correct Sentence is: Foreign financial institutions are now on notice that going forward they can choose to do business with the United States or North Korea, but not both. The given sentence is in present form of tense so....'are now on notice that going'......is the correct usage.

PRACTICE SET   4

INSTRUCTIONS

- This Preliminary Exam practice set consists of three sections. Numerical Ability (Qs. 1-35), Reasoning (Qs. 36-70) and English Language (Qs. 71-100).
- All the questions are compulsory.
- Each question has five options, of which only one is correct. The candidates are advised to read all the options thoroughly.
- There is negative marking equivalent to $1/4^{th}$ of the mark allotted to the specific question for wrong answer.

Time : 60 Minutes　　　　　　**Max. Marks : 100**

NUMERICAL ABILITY

DIRECTIONS (Qs. 1-5): *What will come in place of question mark (?) in the following questions?*

1. $\dfrac{137\times137+137\times133+133\times133}{137\times137\times137-133\times133\times133}=?$
   - (a) 4
   - (b) 270
   - (c) $\dfrac{1}{4}$
   - (d) $\dfrac{1}{270}$
   - (e) None of these

2. If $\sqrt{3^n}=81$, then $n=?$
   - (a) 2
   - (b) 4
   - (c) 6
   - (d) 8
   - (e) None of these

3. $\left[\left(5\sqrt{7}+\sqrt{7}\right)+\left(4\sqrt{7}+8\sqrt{7}\right)\right]-(19)^2=?$
   - (a) 143
   - (b) $72\sqrt{7}$
   - (c) 134
   - (d) $70\sqrt{7}$
   - (e) None of these

4. $(4444\div40)+(645\div25)+(3991\div26)=?$
   - (a) 280.4
   - (b) 290.4
   - (c) 295.4
   - (d) 285.4
   - (e) None of these

5. $\dfrac{.23-.023}{.0023\div23}=?$
   - (a) 0.207
   - (b) 207
   - (c) 2070
   - (d) 0.0207
   - (e) None of these

DIRECTIONS (Qs. 6-10): *Find out the approximate value which should replace the question mark (?) in the following questions. (You are not expected to find out the exact value).*

6. $196.1\times196.1\times196.1\times4.01\times4.01\times4.001\times4.999\times4.999$
   $=196.1^3\times4\times?$
   - (a) 100
   - (b) 16
   - (c) 10
   - (d) 64
   - (e) 32

7. $\dfrac{2}{7}\times\dfrac{1}{8}+\dfrac{3}{7}\div\dfrac{6}{14}=?$
   - (a) $\dfrac{2}{56}$
   - (b) $\dfrac{3}{56}$
   - (c) 1
   - (d) 2.5
   - (e) $\dfrac{50}{60}$

8. $10.1^{2.01}+2.9^{3.001}=?$
   - (a) 130
   - (b) 160
   - (c) 115
   - (d) 147
   - (e) None of these

9. $\sqrt{1999.9997}=4.76\times?$
   - (a) 11
   - (b) 45
   - (c) 49
   - (d) 6
   - (e) 9

10. $23\%\ of\ 4011+\dfrac{1}{7}\ of\ 5555=?$
    - (a) 7000
    - (b) 1900
    - (c) 9022
    - (d) 1700
    - (e) 1450

11. In a 225 meter long yard 26 trees are planted at equal distance, one tree being at each end of the yard.

    What is the distance between two consecutive trees ?
    (a) 10 meters   (b) 8 meters
    (c) 12 meters   (d) 9 meters
    (e) None of these

12. A rectangular park has dimensions 100 m × 40 m. A circular lawn is in the middle of park. If the area of rectangular park leaving the circular lawn is $1536\,m^2$, what is the circumference of the circular lawn?
    (a) 182 m   (b) 140 m
    (c) 176 m   (d) 148 m
    (e) 132 m

13. The number whose square is equal to the difference of the squares of 40 and 32 is
    (a) 45.09   (b) 24
    (c) 25   (d) 28
    (e) None of these

14. In a fort there was sufficient food for 200 soldiers for 31 days. After 27 days, 120 soldiers left the fort. For how many extra days will the rest of the food last for the remaining soldiers ?
    (a) 12 days   (b) 10 days
    (c) 8 days   (d) 6 days
    (e) None of these

15. 7 is added to a certain number, the sum is multiplied by 5; the product is divided by 9 and 3 is subtracted from the quotient. The remainder left is 12. What is the number ?
    (a) 20   (b) 30
    (c) 40   (d) 5
    (e) None of these

16. If the selling price of an article is $4/3^{rd}$ of its cost price, the profit in transaction is
    (a) 16.75%   (b) 20.50%
    (c) 25.50%   (d) 33.33%
    (e) None of these

17. In an election between two candidates, 70% of the voters cast their votes, out of which 2% of the votes were declared invalid. A candidate got 7203 votes which was 60% of the total valid votes. Find the total number of voters enrolled in that election.
    (a) 18050   (b) 17500
    (c) 17000   (d) 7203
    (e) None of these

18. A sum of rupees is divided between three people A, B and C in such a way that after 2 years, 3 years and 4 years respectively the amount they get is equal. If the rate of interest is 5 percent, what is the ratio in which the amount is divided?
    (a) 276 : 264 : 253   (b) 264 : 256 : 243
    (c) 276 : 264 : 233   (d) 243 : 255 : 253
    (e) None of these

19. A vessel is full of milk. 10 litres of milk is taken out and replaced by water. Again the process is followed and now 15 litres of the mixture is replaced by water. After this the final ratio of milk to water becomes 4 : 5. What is the capacity of vessel in litres?
    (a) 65   (b) 45   (c) 40
    (d) 30   (e) Cannot be determined

20. A's salary is 20% lower than B's salary, which is 15% lower than C's salary. By how much percent is C's salary more than A's salary?
    (a) 44.05%   (b) 45.05%
    (c) 46.05%   (d) 47.05%
    (e) None of these

21. 'A' and 'B' can do a piece of work in 30 days while 'B' and 'C' can do the same work in 24 days and 'C' and 'A' in 20 days. They all work for 10 days and 'B' and 'C' leave. How many days more will 'A' take to finish the work ?
    (a) 12 days   (b) 18 days
    (c) 20 days   (d) 22 days
    (e) None of these

22. A man can row $9\dfrac{1}{3}$ kmph in still water and finds that it takes him thrice as much time to row up than as to row down the same distance in the river. The speed of the current is
    (a) $3\dfrac{1}{3}$ kmph   (b) $3\dfrac{1}{9}$ kmph
    (c) $4\dfrac{2}{3}$ kmph   (d) $4\dfrac{1}{3}$ kmph
    (e) None of these

23. A starts from point P at 20 km/hr towards point Q. After 2 hours B starts from point Q at some speed towards A. They both meet when they reach half the distance between points P and Q. If A covered one-fourth of total distance in 2 hours, what is the speed of B?
    (a) 40 km/hr   (b) 45 km/hr
    (c) 48 km/hr   (d) 38 km/hr
    (e) 42 km/hr

24. On a shelf there are four books on History, three on Engineering and four on Statistics. In how many different ways can the books be arranged, so that the books on History are kept together?
    (a) 967680   (b) 120960
    (c) 5040   (d) 40320
    (e) None of these

25. Ram borrows ₹ 8000 at 12% p.a. simple interest and Mohan borrows ₹ 9100 at 10% p.a. simple interest. In how many years will their borrowed amounts (debt) be equal ?
    (a) 18   (b) 20
    (c) 22   (d) 24
    (e) None of these

DIRECTIONS (Qs. 26-30) : *In the following number series, a wrong number is given. Find out the wrong number.*

26. 29, 37, 21, 43 ,13, 53, 5
    (a) 37   (b) 53   (c) 13
    (d) 21   (e) 43

27. 600, 125, 30, 13, 7.2, 6.44, 6.288
    (a) 6   (b) 10   (c) 15
    (d) 12   (e) None of these

28. 80, 42, 24, 13.5, 8.75, 6.375, 5.1875
    (a) 8.75   (b) 13.5   (c) 24
    (d) 6.375   (e) 42

29. 10, 8, 13, 35, 135, 671, 4007
    (a) 8   (b) 671   (c) 135
    (d) 13   (e) 35
30. 150, 290, 560, 1120, 2140, 4230, 8400
    (a) 2140   (b) 560   (c) 1120
    (d) 4230   (e) 290

DIRECTIONS (Qs. 31-35) : *Study the graph carefully to answer the following questions.*

Number of People Contributing Towards Helping Tsunami Victims from Different Cities

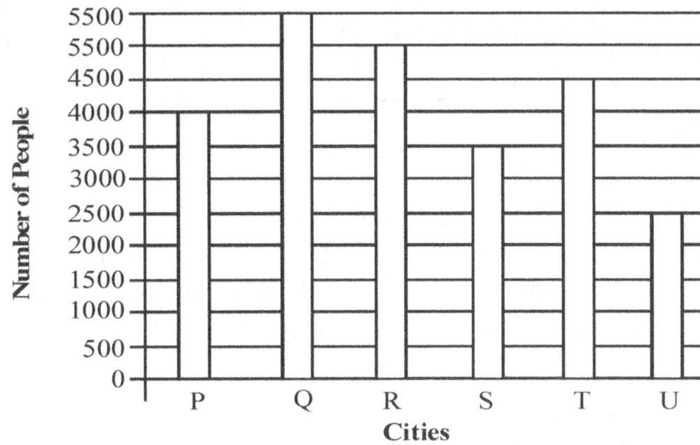

31. How, many more people form City S would have made the ratio 11 : 9 of the number of people contributing from City S to that from City T?
    (a) 1500   (b) 2000
    (c) 5500   (d) 3500
    (e) None of these
32. The number of people contributing from Cites Q and U together form what per cent of the total number of people contributing from all the given cities?
    (a) 30   (b) 36
    (c) 32   (d) 38
    (e) None of these
33. The number of people contributing from how many cities form less than 18% of the total number of people contributing from number form all cities together?
    (a) 3   (b) 4
    (c) 2   (d) 1
    (e) None of these
34. Approximately by what per cent is the number of people contributing from City T more in comparison to that form City S?
    (a) 38   (b) 18
    (c) 22   (d) 29
    (e) None of these
35. What is the ratio of the number of people contributing form City P to that form City R?
    (a) 5 : 4   (b) 4 : 7
    (c) 7 : 4   (d) 5 : 9
    (e) None of these

DIRECTIONS (Qs.36-40): *In each of the questions below, two/ three statements are given followed by conclusions/group of conclusions numbered I and II. You have to assume all the statements to be true even if they seem to be at variance from the commonly known facts and then decide which of the given two conclusions logically follows from the information given in the statements.*

Give answer (a) if **only** conclusion I follows
Give answer (b) if **only** conclusion II follows
Give answer (c) if **either** I or II follows
Give answer (d) if **neither** I or II follows
Give answer (e) if **both** I and II follow

(36-37). **Statements:** Some squares are circles.
               No circle is a triangle.
               No line is a square.
36. **Conclusions: I.** All squares can never be triangles.
          II. Some lines are circles.
37. **Conclusions: I.** No triangle is a square.
          II. No line is a circle.
(38-39): **Statements:** All songs are poems.
               All poems are rhymes.
               No rhymes is a paragraph.
38. **Conclusions: I.** No song is a paragraph.
          No poem is a paragraph.
39. **Conclusions: I.** All rhymes are poems.
          All songs are rhymes.
40. **Statements:** Some dews are drops. All drops are stones.
     Conclusions: I. Atleast some dews are stones.
                 II. Atleast some stones are drops.

DIRECTIONS (Qs. 41-45) : *Read the following information carefully and answer the given questions carefully.*

Seven people A,B,C,D,E,F and G are sitting in a straight line with equal distance between them, but not necessarily in the same order. Some of them are facing North and some are facing South. Only two people are sitting to the left of G. Only two people sit between G and B. A sits second to the left of B. The immediate neighbours of A face opposite directions. Only one person sits between A and C. F sits third to the left of C. D is not an immediate neighbour of B. Both the immediate neighbours of C face the same direction. A faces the same direction as that of C. E faces North. B sits to the immediate left of E.

41. Who among the following sits exactly between G and the one who is sitting to the immediate left of B ?
    (a) E   (b) A
    (c) C   (d) B
    (e) None of these
42. Who among the following sits exactly in the middle of the line ?
    (a) A   (b) C
    (c) D   (d) E
    (e) F

43. Which of the statement is true as per the given information ?
    (a) F sits to the immediate right of A
    (b) D sits exactly between A and C
    (c) G sits third to the left of B
    (d) S faces south.
    (e) None of these

44. Who is sitting second to the right of D ?
    (a) A   (b) B
    (c) F   (d) G
    (e) None of these

45. Which of the following pairs represents the immediate neighbour of B ?
    (a) AB   (b) AC
    (c) BG   (d) FG
    (e) EF

46. In a row of people A is 12th from the left end and B is 8th from the right end. When they exchange their position, A becomes 22th from the left end, What will be the B's position from the right end ?
    (a) 19   (b) 17
    (c) 16   (d) 18
    (e) None of these

DIRECTIONS (Qs. 47-51): *Study the given information to answer the question given below:*

Eight bikes A, B, C, D, E, F, G and H are parked around a circular ground(Facing the centre) with equal distance between each other, but not necessarily in the same order.

H is parked to the immediate left of C. Only one bike is parked between E and C. A is parked 3rd to the right of E. Only 3 bikes are parked between A and F. D is parked second to the left of F. G is not parked immediately next to A.

47. Which bike is parked fourth to the left of B ?
    (a) None   (b) One
    (c) Two   (d) Three
    (e) None of these

48. If all the bikes are parked in alphabetical order in anticlockwise direction starting from A, the position of how many bikes will remain unchanged ?
    (a) None   (b) One
    (c) Two   (d) Three
    (e) None of these

49. Which of the following pairs represents both bikes are parked immediately next to G ?
    (a) DF   (b) AB
    (c) BC   (d) DE
    (e) None of these

50. Four of the following five are alike in a certain way based on the given arrangement, which one of the following does not belong to that group ?
    (a) HA   (b) FH
    (c) BD   (d) GE
    (e) None of these

51. Which of the following statement is true with respect to the given arrangement?
    (a) D is parked second to the right of E
    (b) Only 2 cars are parked between G and C

(c) Only 3 cars are parked between G and H
(d) B is parked to the immediate left of D
(e) None of these

DIRECTIONS (Qs. 52-56) : *In each question a group of letters is given followed by four combinations of number/symbol numbered (a), (b), (c) and (d). Letters are to be coded as per the scheme and conditions given below. You have to find out the serial number of the combination, which represents the letter group. Serial number of that combination is your answer. If none of the combinations is correct, your answer is (e) i.e. None of these.*

Letters	Q	M	S	I	N	G	D	K	A	L	P	R	B	J	E
Number/Symbol	7	@	4	#	%	$	6	1	2	£	5	*	9	8	3

Conditions :

(i) If the first letter is a consonant and the last a vowel, both are to be coded as the code of the vowel.

(ii) If the first letter is vowel and the last a consonant, the codes for the first and the last are to be interchanged.

(iii) If no vowel is present in the group of letters, the second and the fifth letters are to be coded as ©.

52. **BARNIS**
    (a) 9 2 * % # 4   (b) 9 2 4 # * %
    (c) 9 2 * # % 9   (d) 4 2 * # % 4
    (e) None of these

53. **DMBNIA**
    (a) 6 @ 9 % # 2   (b) 2 @ 9 % # 6
    (c) 2 @ 9 % # 6   (d) 2 @ 9 % # 2
    (e) None of these

54. **IJBRLG**
    (a) # 8 9 * £ $ (b) # 8 9 * £ #
    (c) $ 8 9 * £ #   (d) $ 8 9 * £ $
    (e) None of these

55. **BKGQJN**
    (a) 9 © $ 7 © %   (b) © 9 $ 7 % ©
    (c) 9 1 $ 7 8 %   (d) % 1 $ 7 8 9
    (e) None of these

56. **EGAKRL**
    (a) # £ $ 2 1 *   (b) £ $ 2 1 * 3
    (c) £ $ 2 1 * #   (d) # £ $ 2 1 #
    (e) None of these

DIRECTIONS (Qs. 57-59): *Read the information carefully and answer the questions given below :*

(i) Seven students P, Q, R, S, T, U and V take a series of tests,
(ii) No two students get similar marks,
(iii) V always scores more than P.
(iv) P always scores more than Q.
(v) Each time either R scores the highest and T gets least, or alternatively S scores highest and U or Q scores least.

57. If S is ranked sixth and Q is ranked fifth, which of the following can be true ?
    (a) V is ranked first or fourth
    (b) R is ranked second or third
    (c) P is ranked second or fifth
    (d) U is ranked third or fourth
    (e) None of these

58. If R is ranked second and Q is ranked fifth, which of the following must be true ?
    (a) S is ranked third   (b) T is ranked sixth
    (c) P is ranked sixth   (d) V is ranked fourth
    (e) None of these

59. If S is ranked second, which of the following can be true ?
    (a) U gets more than V   (b) V gets more than S
    (c) P gets more than R   (d) P gets more than V
    (e) None of these

DIRECTIONS (Qs. 60-61) : *Study the following information to answer the given questions:*

Point P is 9 m towards the East of Point Q. Point R is 5 m towards the South of Point P. Point S is 3 m towards the West of Point R. Point T is 5 m towards the North of Point S. Point V is 7 m towards the South of Point S.

60. If a person walks in a straight line for 8 m towards West from Point R, which of the following points would he cross the first?
    (a) V   (b) Q
    (c) T   (d) S
    (e) Can't be determined.

61. Which of the following points are in a straight line?
    (a) P, R, V   (b) S, T, Q
    (c) P, T, V   (d) V, T, R
    (e) S, V, T

62. A man walks 1 km towards East and then turns towards South and walks 5 km. Again he turns to East and walks 2 km. After this he turns to North and walks 9 km. Now, how far is he from his starting point ?
    (a) 3 km   (b) 4 km
    (c) 5 km   (d) 7 km
    (e) None of these

63. A girl introduced a boy as the son of the daughter of the father of her uncle. The boy is girl's;
    (a) Cousin   (b) Son
    (c) Uncle   (d) Son-in-law
    (e) None of these

DIRECTIONS (Qs. 64-65): *Study the following information to answer the given questions:*

In a certain code, 'always to be right' is written as '4932', 'right is also just' is written as '9765', 'come to terms' is written as '138', 'terms are just' is written as '016', and 'always is' is written as '74'.

64. What is the code for 'come'?
    (a) 0   (b) 8
    (c) 1   (d) 3
    (e) either 1 or 8

65. What does '6' stand for?
    (a) terms   (b) also
    (c) are   (d) is
    (e) just

DIRECTIONS (Qs. 66-70) : *Study the following information carefully and answer the given questions.*

A, B, C, D, E, F, G and H are sitting around a square table facing the centre in such a way that four of them sit at four corners of the square while four sit in the middle of each of the four sides.
(i)   A sits second to right of F. F sits in the middle of one of the sides of the table.
(ii) G who does not sit at any of the corners of the table sits second to the right of D.
(iii) Only two people sit between D and B (taken from one side).
(iv) C is not an immediate neighbour of G.
(v)   H is sits second to left of B.
(vi) E is not an immediate neighbout of G or F.

66. Who sits exactly between F and A?
    (a) B   (b) C
    (c) E   (d) H
    (e) None of these

67. How many persons sit between A and H when counted in anti-clockwise direction from A?
    (a) None   (b) One
    (c) Two   (d) Three
    (e) Four

68. Four of the following five are alike in a certain way based on their seating positions in the above arrangement and so form a group. Which is the one that **does not** belong to that group?
    (a) D   (b) F
    (c) A   (d) E
    (e) G

69. What is the position of F with respect to C?
    (a) Third to the left   (b) Immediate to the right
    (c) Second to the left   (d) Third to the right
    (e) Immediate to the left

70. What will come in place of the question mark(?) based upon the given seating arrangement?
    AE, EH, HF, ?
    (a) FE   (b) HC
    (c) FD   (d) CB
    (e) FH

DIRECTIONS (Qs. 71-80): *Read the following passage carefully and answer the questions given after the passage. Certain words/ phrases have been printed in bold to help you locate them while answering some of the questions.*

The National Green Tribunal's decision to bar the registration of new and old diesel vehicles in Delhi till its next hearing on January 6 comes as a blow - though a temporary one for now - to passenger vehicle manufacturers. Automobile-makers have, in recent years, been building (from scratch, in a few cases) and scaling up their production capacities for diesel cars, driven by the **surge** in demand for diesel-powered vehicles as the fuel was subsidised and far cheaper than petrol. The differential between petrol and diesel prices has narrowed substantially since the government commenced the deregulation of diesel pricing in 2013, and diesel now is only 22 per cent cheaper than petrol. But diesel vehicles, including the sport utility vehicles, or SUVs, that are ubiquitous status symbols in the National Capital Region and beyond, now constitute 50 per cent of the auto industry's passenger car sales. That vehicular **exhaust** from diesel cars, SUVs and freight trucks has been identified as one of the major contributors to the alarming levels of particulate matter in Delhi's atmosphere is well-established. The tribunal has asked the Delhi and Central governments to decide whether a more permanent injunction prohibiting the registration of diesel vehicles in the NCR would be advisable, given the "serious contribution of vehicular pollution" to the city's air quality. Separately, the Supreme Court is set to hear on December 15 an independent plea to ban diesel vehicles in Delhi. Industry has reacted predictably, terming the move as unfair and discriminatory, and calling for a more holistic solution, while questioning the overall policy approach to diesel. With most of them investing to upgrade their technology to meet the more **stringent** BS-V (Bharat Stage-V) standards due in 2019, they suggest fleet modernisation to replace the older commercial transport vehicles, considered an equally major source of polluting exhaust emissions. Rating agency ICRA expects the share of diesel vehicles in annual auto sales to decline to 30-35 per cent by 2017 as the price difference between diesel and petrol narrows further. That may not help much in Delhi, the nation's largest urban market for cars and SUVs. By way of comparison, the U.S. has decided to **curb** emissions from vehicles by moving towards higher fuel efficiency standards for new cars, though economists say it may only encourage people to drive even more. India is pursuing similar goals, but as Volkswagen's 'defeat device' to rig emission tests for diesel vehicles shows, governments aren't capable of enforcing such norms efficiently. In the backdrop of the latest climate change commitments and the toxic air that hangs over Delhi, it could be an **opportune** moment for Indian policymakers to use the tools of behavioural economics to alter people's commuting preferences. Tax and other fiscal incentives to shift both freight haulage and public road transportation to cleaner CNG- and LPG-based technologies is one thing. But it's perhaps time to take a bolder step and levy a hefty green tax on diesel-fuelled private vehicles and SUVs.

71. What was the reason behind the deregulation of diesel prices in 2013?
    - (a) diesel vehicles have ubiquitous status symbol.
    - (b) NGT has advised the Delhi and central governments to prohibit the registration of diesel vehicles.
    - (c) diesel vehicles produce more pollution than petrol
    - (d) both (a) and (b)
    - (e) None of these

72. Why Indian policy makers using the tools of behavioural economics?
    - (a) To decrease the level of pollution.
    - (b) To change people's commuting choices.
    - (c) To shift to more clear LPG and CNG technologies.
    - (d) To reduce diesel cars, SUVs and fright trucks.
    - (e) None of the above

73. Which of the following would be the suitable title?
    - (a) Pollution free Delhi
    - (b) Get smart on diesel cars
    - (c) Powered vehicles
    - (d) Reducing diesel demand.
    - (e) NGT decision: A big relief

74. According to the passage Which of the following is true?
    - (a) ICRA expects increase in diesel vehicles by 2017.
    - (b) CNG and LPG are contributing in reducing Pollution.
    - (c) Diesel is 22 per cent heaper than petrol.
    - (d) All the above
    - (e) None of the above

75. According to the passage, Which of the following is not true?
    - (a) Industry is investing to upgrade their technology to meet the more stringent BS-V standards by 2017.
    - (b) SUVs are one of the major contributor to particulate matter in delhi's atmosphere.
    - (c) The U.S is moving towards higher fuel efficiency standards for new cars.
    - (d) Both A and C
    - (e) None of these

DIRECTIONS (Qs. 76 to 78): *Choose the word which is most SIMILAR in meaning to the word printed in bold as used in the passage.*

76. **Surge**
    - (a) decrease
    - (b) alleviate
    - (c) growth
    - (d) assugae
    - (e) decline

77. **Exhaust**
    - (a) weaken
    - (b) strengthen
    - (c) enable
    - (d) feeble
    - (e) aid

78. **Opportune**
    - (a) unhappy
    - (b) unsuitable
    - (c) convenient
    - (d) untimely
    - (d) disadvantage

DIRECTIONS (Qs. 79-80): *Choose the word which is most OPPOSITE in meaning to the word printed in bold as used in the passage.*

79. **Curb**
    - (a) deterrent
    - (b) hindrance
    - (c) freedom
    - (d) stop
    - (e) ledge

80. **Stringent**
    (a) amenable　　(b) infexible
    (c) acrimonious　　(d) callous
    (e) stiff

DIRECTIONS (81-90): *In the following passage there are blanks, each of which has been numbered. These numbers are again printed below the passage and against each, five words are suggested, one of which fits the blank appropriately. Find out the appropriate word in each case.*

Mr. Chamberlain had come to get gift to thirty-five million pounds from South Africa and to win the hearts of Englishmen and Boers. So he gave a ...(81)... shoulder to the Indian deputation. 'You know', he said, that the Imperial Government has little control over self-governing colonies. Your grievances seem to be genuine. I shall do what I can, but you must try your ...(82)... to placate the 'Europeans, if you wish to live in their midst'. The reply cast a chill over the members of the ...(83).... I was also disappointed.

It was an eye opener for us all, and I saw that we should start with our work de novo. I ...(84)... the situation to my colleagues. As a matter of fact there was nothing wrong about Mr. Chamberlain's reply. It was well that he did not mince ...(85).... He had brought home to us in a rather gentle way the rule of might being ...(86)..., or the law of the sword. But sword we had none. We ...(87)... had the nerve and the muscle even to receive sword-cuts. Mr. Chamberlain had given only a short time to the sub-continent. If Sri Nagar to Cape Comorin is 1,900 miles, Durban to Cape town is not less than 1,100 miles, and Mr. Chamberlain had to cover the long distance at hurricane speed. From Natal he hastened to the Transvaal. I had to prepare the case for the Indians there as well and ...(88)... it to him. But how was I to get to Pretoria? Our people there were not in a position to ...(89)... the necessary legal facilities for my getting to them in time. The war had reduced the Transvaal to a howling wilderness. There were neither provisions nor clothing available. Empty or closed shops were there, waiting to be ...(90)... or opened, but that was a matter of time.

81. (a) cold　　(b) cool
    (c) hot　　(d) warm
    (e) left
82. (a) hard　　(b) best
    (c) least　　(d) fate
    (e) hate
83. (a) reputation　　(b) crowd
    (c) delegate　　(d) leader
    (e) deputation
84. (a) expressed　　(b) said
    (c) explained　　(d) exclaimed
    (e) denied
85. (a) lectures　　(b) matter
    (c) topic　　(d) words
    (e) deals
86. (a) wrong　　(b) right
    (c) rite　　(d) bright
    (e) weak

87. (a) hardly　　(b) rare
    (c) might　　(d) do
    (e) scarce
88. (a) through　　(b) permit
    (c) submit　　(d) deposit
    (e) fill
89. (a) secure　　(b) procure
    (c) pull　　(d) fetch
    (e) buy
90. (a) replenished　　(b) fed
    (c) booked　　(d) filled
    (e) emptied

DIRECTIONS (Qs. 91-100): *In each of the questions given below, a sentence is given which is divided into 5 parts. It is then followed by 5 options one of which gives the sequence of the correct parts. Choose the option which gives the correct sequence of the grammatically correct parts. If all the parts are grammatically correct or if the correct sequence is not given in the option, choose option (e) as your answer.*

91. Egypt's endemic corruption and a sheer lack(A)/ of desire amongst government officials(B)/ to do an honest day's work is beautifully capturing(C)/ in The Nile Hilton Incident(D)/, by Tarik Saleh, a Swedish filmmaker of Egyptian origin(E).
    (a) ACDE　　(b) BCDE
    (c) ABDE　　(d) ABCD
    (e) No error
92. Consequent to the preliminary evaluation of the(A)/ impact of reportedly leaked(B)/ CBSE class 10 maths paper & keeping in mind the paramount interest(C)/ of students, CBSE have decided not(D)/ to conduct re-examination(E).
    (a) ABCD　　(b) ABCE
    (c) ABDE　　(d) ACDE
    (e) No error
93. The instructions issued by the Board to the centres included(A)/ identifying a safe and secure room for(B)/ installing of computers and(C)/ printers and ensuring high-speed(D)/ internet connection(E).
    (a) ABDE　　(b) ACDE
    (c) BCDE　　(d) ABCD
    (e) No error
94. If the Central government would have taken(A)/ steps after March 20 when we gave(B)/ them a memorandum to file a review(C)/ petition, there would(D)/ have been no loss of life and property(E).
    (a) ABCD　　(b) ACDE
    (c) ABCE　　(d) BCDE
    (e) No error
95. Contemporary Egyptian cinema has its own(A)/ style and the films that travel(B)/ wide are usually because(C)/ of their themes, and not(D)/ the filmmakers(E).
    (a) ABCE　　(b) ABCD
    (c) ACDE　　(d) BCDE
    (e) No error

96. The dam breached on Saturday and inundated(A)/ several areas. Over 50 families evacuation(B)/ by the district administration(C)/ are taking shelter in(D)/ community halls in the town(E).
    (a) ACDE   (b) ABDE
    (c) ABCD   (d) ABCE
    (e) No error

97. No major instance of violence was reported(A)/ from any part of the(B)/ State during the strike which(C)/ began at midnight on Sunday and(D)/ had ended at midnight on Monday(E).
    (a) ACDE   (b) ABCE
    (c) BCDE   (d) ABCD
    (e) No error

98. Government offices functioned(A)/ with minimal attendance(B) , but educational institutions(C)/ will not function(D)/ in most cases(E).
    (a) ABCE   (b) ACDE
    (c) ABCD   (d) BCDE
    (e) No error

99. The police tried to mitigating(A)/ the difficulties of the passengers by(B)/ pressing vans to(C)/ ferry the passengers(D)/ to central points(E).
    (a) ABCD   (b) ACDE
    (c) BCDE   (d) ABCE
    (e) No error

100. The relatives also staged a brief(A)/ dharna at the gate of the cargo terminal(B)/ when they were telling that(C)/ officials would not allow them(D)/ to see the remains of the men(E).
    (a) ABCD   (b) BCDE
    (c) ACDE   (d) ABDE
    (e) No error

Answer Key

1	(c)	11	(d)	21	(b)	31	(b)	41	(a)	51	(d)	61	(e)	71	(e)	81	(a)	91	(c)
2	(d)	12	(c)	22	(c)	32	(c)	42	(a)	52	(a)	62	(c)	72	(b)	82	(b)	92	(b)
3	(a)	13	(b)	23	(a)	33	(a)	43	(c)	53	(c)	63	(a)	73	(b)	83	(c)	93	(a)
4	(b)	14	(b)	24	(a)	34	(d)	44	(d)	54	(c)	64	(b)	74	(c)	84	(c)	94	(d)
5	(c)	15	(a)	25	(c)	35	(e)	45	(e)	55	(a)	65	(e)	75	(a)	85	(d)	95	(b)
6	(a)	16	(d)	26	(e)	36	(a)	46	(d)	56	(b)	66	(c)	76	(c)	86	(b)	96	(a)
7	(c)	17	(b)	27	(e)	37	(d)	47	(e)	57	(d)	67	(c)	77	(a)	87	(a)	97	(d)
8	(a)	18	(a)	28	(c)	38	(e)	48	(b)	58	(b)	68	(d)	78	(c)	88	(c)	98	(a)
9	(e)	19	(b)	29	(b)	39	(b)	49	(a)	59	(a)	69	(e)	79	(c)	89	(b)	99	(c)
10	(d)	20	(d)	30	(c)	40	(e)	50	(c)	60	(d)	70	(c)	80	(a)	90	(a)	100	(d)

HINTS & EXPLANATIONS

1. (c) Given Expression $= \dfrac{a^2 + ab + b^2}{a^3 - b^3}$, where $a = 137, b = 133$

$$= \frac{(a^2 + ab + b^2)}{(a-b)(a^2 + ab + b^2)} = \frac{1}{(a-b)} = \frac{1}{137 - 133} = \frac{1}{4}$$

2. (d) $\sqrt{3^n} = 81 \Rightarrow 3^{n/2} = 3^4 \Rightarrow \dfrac{n}{2} = 4 \Rightarrow n = 8$

3. (a) $\left[\left(5\sqrt{7} + \sqrt{7}\right) \times \left(4\sqrt{7} + 8\sqrt{7}\right)\right] - (19)^2 = ?$

$\Rightarrow (6\sqrt{7} \times 12\sqrt{7}) - (361) = ?$

$\Rightarrow 72 \times \sqrt{7} \times \sqrt{7} - 361 = ?$

$\therefore ? = 504 - 361 = 143$

4. (b) $(4444 \div 40) + (645 \div 25) + (3991 \div 26) = ?$
$\Rightarrow ? = (111.1) + (25.8) + (153.5) \Rightarrow ? = 290.4$

5. (c) Given Expression $= \dfrac{0.207}{\dfrac{0.0023}{23}} = \dfrac{0.207}{0.0001} = \dfrac{0.2070}{0.0001} = 2070.$

6. (a) $196.1 \times 196.1 \times 196.1 \times 4.01 \times 4.01 \times 4.001 \times 4.999 \times 4.999$
$= (196.1)^3 \times 4 \times ?$
or $4 \times ? = 4.01 \times 4.001 \times 4.999 \times 4.999$ or $? = 4 \times 5 \times 5 = 100$

7. (c) $? = \dfrac{2}{7} \times \dfrac{1}{8} + \dfrac{3}{7} \times \dfrac{14}{6} = \dfrac{1}{28} + 1 = 1\dfrac{1}{28} = 1$

8. (a) $? = (10.1)^{2.01} + (2.9)^{3.001} = (10)^2 + (3)^3 = 100 + 27 = 130$

9. (e) $4.76 \times ? = \sqrt{1999.9997}$
$4.76 \times ? = 44.72$ or $? = 9$

10. (d) $? = 23\%$ of $4011 + \dfrac{1}{7}$ of $5555 = 922.53 \div 79357 = 1700$

11. (d) Distance between two consecutive trees $= \dfrac{225}{25} = 9$ meters.

12. (c) Area of park $= 100 \times 40 = 4000\ \text{m}^2$
So area of circular lawn $= (4000 - 1536)\ \text{m}^2 = 2464\ \text{m}^2$
So $\pi r^2 = 2464$
We get, $r = 28$ m
So circumference $= 2\pi r = 2 \times (22/7) \times 28 = 176$ m

13. (b) $(40)^2 - (32)^2 = 1600 - 1024 = 576$
Hence, 24 is the required number.

14. (b) Let rest of the food last for the x days.
$\therefore\quad 200 \times 4 = (200 - 120) \times x$
$200 \times 4 = 80 \times x$

$x = \dfrac{800}{80} = 10$ days

15. (a) Let the number be x

$$\frac{5(7 + x)}{9} - 3 = 12$$

$$\frac{5(7 + x)}{9} = 15$$

$$7 + x = \frac{15 \times 9}{5} = 27$$

$$x = 27 - 7 = 20$$

16. (d) Let C. P. $= ₹\, x$, then S.P. $= ₹\, \dfrac{4x}{3}$

Gain $= ₹\left(\dfrac{4x}{3} - x\right) = ₹\, \dfrac{x}{3}$

$\therefore$ Gain % $\left(\dfrac{x}{3} \times \dfrac{1}{x} \times 100\right) = 33.33\%$

17. (b) Let the total number of votes enrolled be x. Then, number of votes cast $= 70\%$ of valid votes $= 98\%$ of $(70\%$ of x$)$
60% of $[98\%$ of 70% of x$] = 7203$

$$\frac{70}{100} \times \frac{98}{100} \times \frac{60}{100} \times x = 7203$$

$$x = \frac{7203 \times 100 \times 100 \times 100}{70 \times 98 \times 60}$$

$x = 17500$

18. (a) Shortcut when amounts are equal:
$1/(100 + 2 \times 5) : 1/(100 + 3 \times 5) : 1/(100 + 4 \times 5)$
$1/110 : 1/115 : 1/120$
$23 \times 12 : 22 \times 12 : 11 \times 23 = 276 : 264 : 253$

19. (b) Let x litres be the quantity of milk initially(or the capacity of the vessel).

After 2 steps , milk left $= x\,[1-(15/x)]^2$

We know that the total is x.

Now milk to water is 4 : 5, so milk to total becomes

$4:(4+5)=4:9$

So $[\,x\,[1-(15/x)]^2\,]\,/\,x = 4/9$

x got cancelled

So $[1-(15/x)]^2 = 4/9$

$[1-(15/x)] = 2/3$

Hence, x = 45 litres

20. (d) $A = B - 20\%$ of $B = 0.8\,B$

$B = C - 15\%$ of $C = 0.85\,C$

$A = 0.8 \times 0.85\,C = 0.68\,C$

$$\frac{C-A}{A}\times 100 = \frac{C-0.68C}{0.68C}\times 100 = \frac{32}{68}\times 100 = 47.05\%$$

21. (b) Let A, B and C individually complete the work in x,y and z days respectively.

$$\frac{1}{x}+\frac{1}{y}=\frac{1}{30} \qquad \qquad ...(1)$$

$$\frac{1}{y}+\frac{1}{z}=\frac{1}{24} \qquad \qquad ...(2)$$

$$\frac{1}{z}+\frac{1}{x}=\frac{1}{20} \qquad \qquad ...(3)$$

Adding equ (1) , (2) and (3)

$$2\left(\frac{1}{x}+\frac{1}{y}+\frac{1}{z}\right)=\frac{1}{8} \Rightarrow \frac{1}{x}+\frac{1}{y}+\frac{1}{z}=\frac{1}{16} \quad ...(4)$$

A,B and C together complete the work in 16 days.

In 10 days they completed $\dfrac{10}{16}=\dfrac{5}{8}$ Part

Remaining work $= 1-\dfrac{5}{8}=\dfrac{3}{8}$

Subtracting equ (2) from (4)

we get, $\dfrac{1}{x}=\dfrac{1}{48}$ or x = 48

A alone can finish the Remaining work in

$\dfrac{3}{8}\times 48 = 18$ days

22. (c) Distance covered by man = D km

Speed of man in still water = x kmph

Speed of current $= \dfrac{28}{3}$ kmph

According to question,

$$\frac{D}{\dfrac{28}{3}-x}=3\left(\frac{D}{\dfrac{28}{3}+x}\right)$$

$$\Rightarrow \frac{28}{3}+x=3\left(\frac{28}{3}-x\right) \Rightarrow 4x=2\times\frac{28}{3}$$

$$\Rightarrow x=\frac{14}{3} \text{ or } 4\frac{2}{3} \text{ Kmph}$$

23. (a) A covered one-fourth of total distance in 2 hours, so 1/2 distance in 4 hours

Now B has covered that same distance that A covered in $(4-2)=2$ hours $[\because$ B started after 2 hrs]

And since distances are same

So distance covered by A = distance covered by B

$\Rightarrow 20\times 4 = x\times 2$

Therefore, x = 40 km/hr

24. (a) The required number of ways

$= 8! \times 4! = 967680$

25. (c) Simple interest for Ram $= \dfrac{8000\times 12\times 1}{100}=₹960$

Simple interest for Mohan $= \dfrac{9100\times 10\times 1}{100}=₹910$

Let 'x' be the years when borrowed amount be equal.

$8000 + 960\,x = 9100 + 910\,x$

$50x = 9100 - 8000$

$50x = 1100$

$x = 22$ years

26. (e)

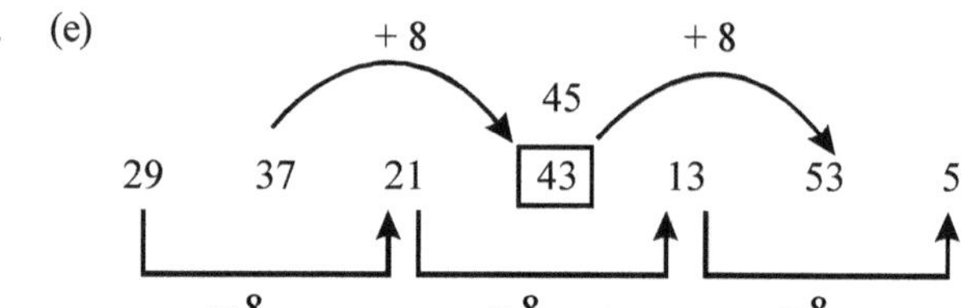

27. (e)

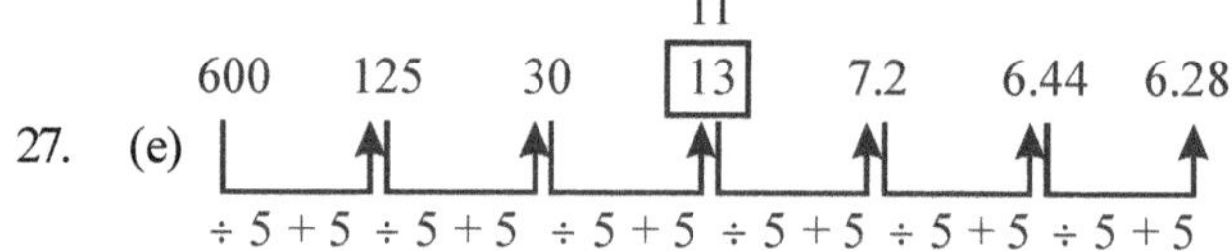

28. (c)

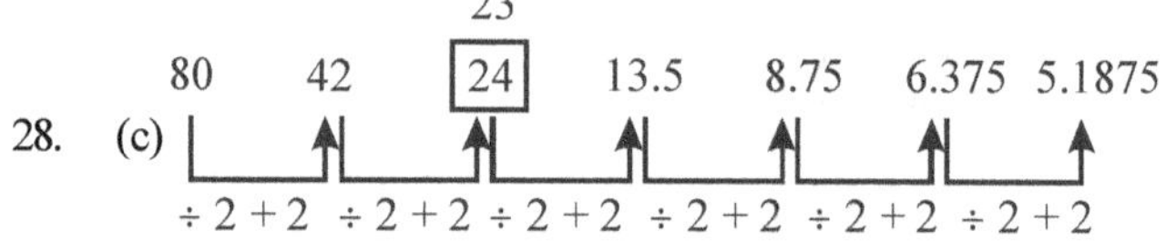

29. (b)

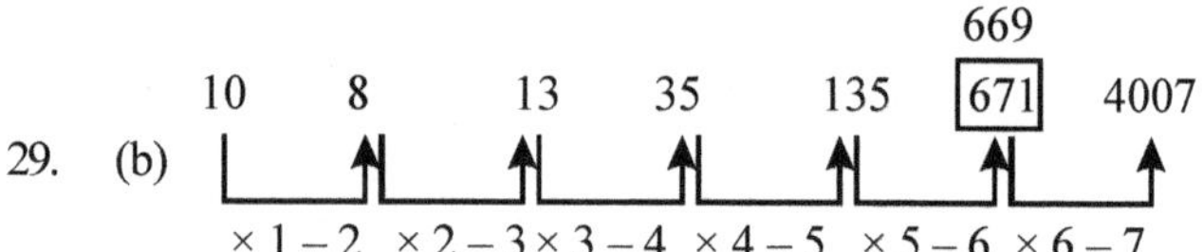

30. (c)

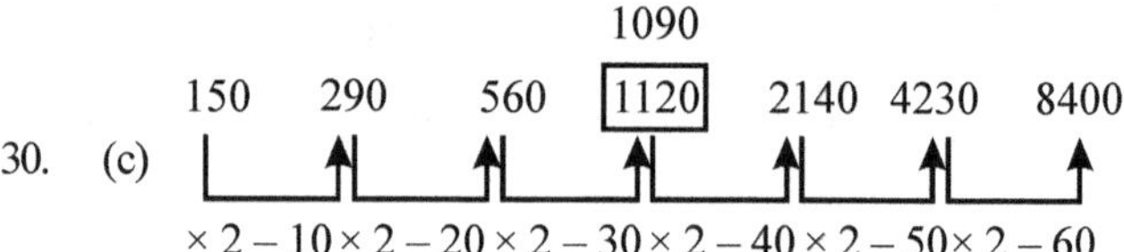

31. (b) From the given graph, we get

$$\frac{3500+x}{4500}=\frac{11}{9} \therefore x = 2000$$

32. (c) The required percent

$$=\frac{5500+2500}{4000+5500+5000+3500+4500+2500}\times 100$$

$$=\frac{8000}{25000}\times 100 = 32\%$$

33. (a) Total number of people contributing for all the given cities = 25000
For the three cities P, S and U the number of people contributing is less than 18% of 25000.

34. (d) The required per cent.
$$\frac{4500-3500}{3500}\times100 = \frac{1000}{35} \approx 28.57$$
$$\approx 29\%$$

35. (e) The required ratio
= 4000 : 5000 = 4000 : 5000 = 4 : 5

(36-37)

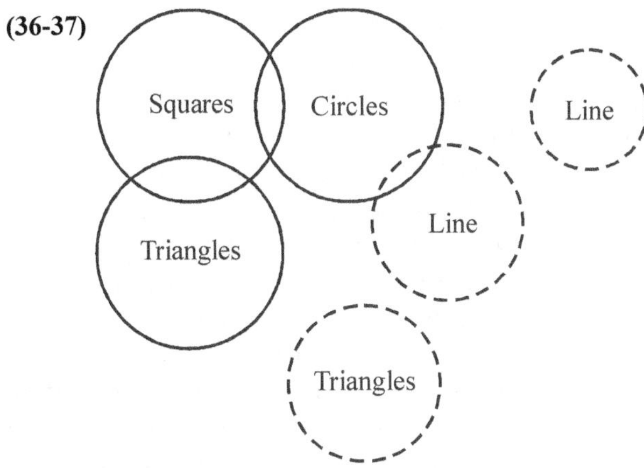

36. (a) Conclusion I - True
Conclusion II - False

37. (d) Conclusion I - False
Conclusion II - False

(38-39)

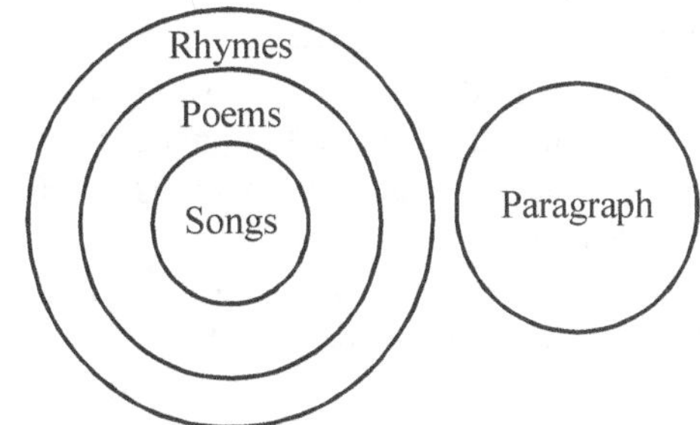

38. (e) Conclusion I - True
Conclusion II - True

39. (b) Conclusion I - False
Conclusion II - True

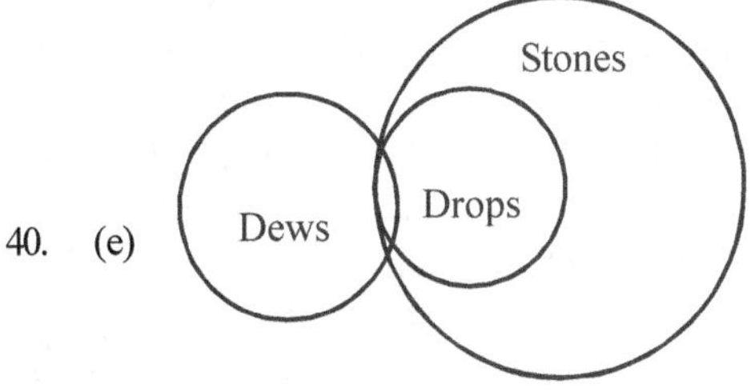

40. (e) Conclusion I - True
Conclusion II - True

(41-45) :

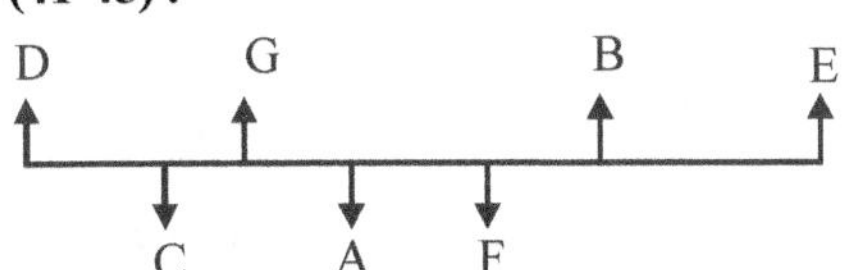

46. (d) No of people between both the position of
A = 22 – 12 – 1 = 9
B = 8 + 9 + 1 = 18

(47-51)

47. (e)
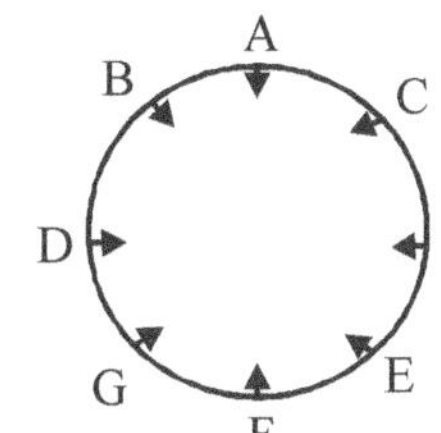

48. (b) One

49. (a) DF

50. (c) BD

51. (d) B is parked to the immediate left of D

52. (a) B → 9; A → 2; R → *; N → %; I → #; S → 4

53. (c) D → 2; M → @; B → 9; N → %; I → #; A → 2
Condition (i) is applied.

54. (c) I → $; J → 8; B → 9; R → *; L → £; G → #
Condition (ii) is applied.

55. (a) B → 9; K → ©; G → $; Q → 7; J → ©; N → %
Condition (iii) is applied.

56. (b) E → £; G → $; A → 2; K → 1; R → *; L → 3
Condition (ii) is applied.

57. (d) If S ranked sixth and Q ranked fifth we have the sequence ...... QS .... In this case R will be ranked highest and T the lowest, and we have the order R ...... QST. Also the order VPQ will stay. So V and P will have second, third or fourth place. So, the options *a*, *b* and *c* are wrong. Hence option (d) is correct answer.

58. (b) If R is second, S will rank first and Q and U lowest. But Q ranks fifth. So, U ranks least. Thus, in view of order VPQ, the arrangement will be SRVPQ – U. So, T will be ranked sixth.

59. (a) If S is second, R ranks first and T ranks least. So, the arrangement, in view of order VPQ, will be R, S, ... T. Thus, (b), (c) and (d) are not true. Hence, option (a) is correct.

(60-61) :

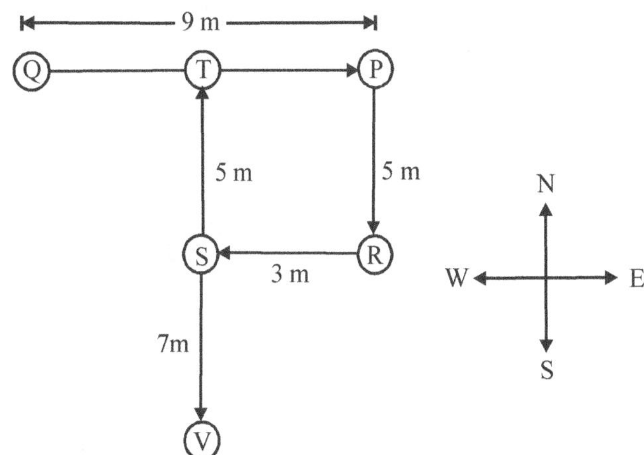

60. (d) If a person walks in a straight line for 8 m towards West from Point R, then he would be cross S.

61. (e) S, V and T are in straight line.

62. (c)

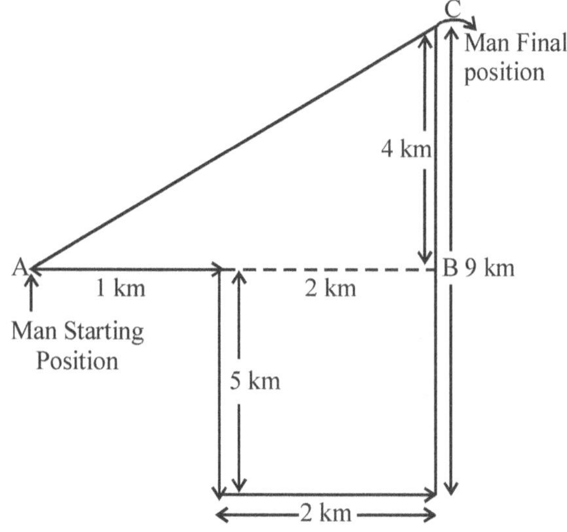

In $\triangle ABC$

$AC^2 = AB^2 + BC^2$

$AC^2 = 3^2 + 4^2 \Rightarrow AC = \sqrt{25} = 5$ km

63. (a) Cousin.

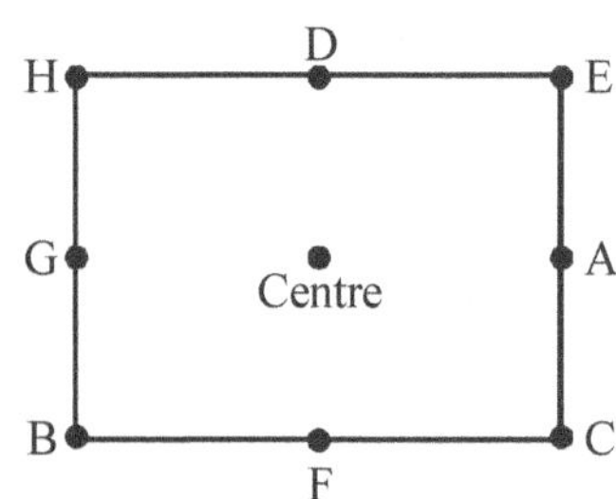

64. (b) 'come to terms' is written as '138' :
From 'always to be right' is written as '4932', to – 3
From 'terms are just' is written as '016', terms – 1
So come – 8

65. (e) 'right is also just' is written as '9765', 'terms are just' is written as '016'
Common : just – 6

Sol. (66-70) :

66. (b) C

67. (c) Two (E, D)

68. (d) E (All others sit middle of the each side)

69. (e) Immediate to the left

70. (c) One more person sits in each successive pair of person. Hence, three persons (C, A, E) are sitting between F and D.

81. (a) (cold -fits in the context correctly)

82. (b) (best -fits in the context correctly)

83. (c) (delegate -fits in the context correctly)

84. (c) (explained - fits in the context correctly)

85. (d) (words- fits in the context correctly)

86. (b) (right fits in the context correctly)

87. (a) (hardly fits in the context correctly)

88. (c) (submit fits in the context correctly)

89. (b) (obtain (something), especially with care or effort.)

90. (a) {replenished --fill (something) up again.}

91. (c) **ABDE-...'to do an honest day's work is beautifully captured'**....is the correct formation of sentence.

92. (b) **ABCE-....'of students, CBSE has decided not'**....as CBSE is an organisation which is a singular subject. Thus, singular form of verb will come here.

93. (a) **ABDE-....'installation of computers and'....'installation'** is a noun whereas **'installing'** is a verb. Thus, according to the structure of the sentence **'installation'** is the correct usage here.

94. (d) **BCDE- ...'If the Central government had taken'**...According to the conditional sentence agreement, the principal clause will always be in past perfect tense if the subordinate clause is in future perfect continuous or vice-versa.

95. (b) **ABCD-...'the filmmaking'**...Here, we are talking about the style and formation of a film, not of the persons who have made it. Thus, **'filmmaking'** is the most appropriate answer.

96. (a) **ACDE- 'Over 50 families evacuated'...'evacuation'** is a noun and **'evacuated'** is a verb. Hence, the structure of the sentence will take verb with it instead of noun.

97. (d) **ABCD- ....'ended at midnight on Monday'**...As the sentence is in simple past tense, hence the further part of the sentence will also be in simple past tense rather than past perfect tense.

98. (a) **ABCE- ...'did not function'**...The given statement is in simple past tensee. Therefore, **'will not'** will be replaced by the **'did not'**

99. (c) **BCDE-...'The police tried to mitigate'...'to'** is always followed by the first form of verb. So, **'mitigate'** will replace **'mitigating'**

100. (d) **ABDE- ...'when they were told that'**...In the given sentence, people are told/informed by the officials. Thus, **'telling'** doesn't fit here.

PRACTICE SET 5

NUMERICAL ABILITY

1. A trader mixes 26 kg of rice at ₹ 20 per kg with 30 kg rice of another variety costing ₹ 36 per kg. If he sells the mixture at ₹ 30 per kg his profit will be
   - (a) −7%
   - (b) 5%
   - (c) 8%
   - (d) 10%
   - (e) None of these

2. If a person repaid ₹ 22500 after 10 years of borrowing a loan, at 10% per annum simple interest find out what amount did he take as a loan?
   - (a) ₹ 11,225
   - (b) ₹ 11,250
   - (c) ₹ 10,000
   - (d) ₹ 7,500
   - (e) None of these

3. 6 women and 6 men together can complete a piece of work in 6 days. In how many days can 15 men alone complete the piece of work if 9 women alone can complete the work in 10 days?
   - (a) 7
   - (b) 5
   - (c) 4
   - (d) Data inadequate
   - (e) None of the above

4. A loss of 19% on a shirt gets converted into a profit of 17% when the selling price is increased by ₹ 162. What is the cost price of the shirt?
   - (a) ₹ 540
   - (b) ₹ 450
   - (c) ₹ 600
   - (d) ₹ 360
   - (e) None of these

5. A towel was 50 cm broad and 100 cm long. When bleached, it was found to have lost 20% of its length and 10% of its breadth. Find the percentage of decrease in area ?
   - (a) 32%
   - (b) 28%
   - (c) 33%
   - (d) 24%
   - (e) None of these

6. In an examination 75% of the total students passed in English and 65% passed in Mathematics, while 15% failed in English as well as Mathematics. If a total of 495 candidates passed in both exams. Find the total number of students who appeared in the exam.
   - (a) 850
   - (b) 900
   - (c) 1000
   - (d) 1050
   - (e) None of these

7. The present age of Ravi's father is 4 times of Ravi's present age. 5 years back, Ravi's father was seven times as old as Ravi was at that time. What is the present age of Ravi's father?
   - (a) 84 years
   - (b) 70 years
   - (c) 40 years
   - (d) 35 years
   - (e) None of these

8. Calculate the amount on ₹ 1250 for 2 years at 4% per annum. compounded yearly.
   - (a) ₹ 676
   - (b) ₹ 1352
   - (c) ₹ 1778
   - (d) ₹ 255
   - (e) None of these

9. M, N, O and P divided ₹44352 among themselves. M took $\frac{3}{8}$th of the money, N took $\frac{1}{6}$th of the remaining amount and rest was divided among O and P in the ratio of 3 : 4 respectively. How much did O get as his share?
   - (a) ₹ 9600
   - (b) ₹ 10600
   - (c) ₹ 10300
   - (d) ₹8700
   - (e) ₹ 9900

10. In how many different ways can the letters of the word BLOATING be arranged?
    (a) 20160   (b) 2520
    (c) 5040   (d) 40320
    (e) None of these

11. The price of sugar increases by 20% due to the festive season. By what percentage should a family reduce the consumption of sugar so that there is no change in the expenditure?
    (a) 20%   (b) $18\frac{1}{3}\%$
    (c) $16\frac{2}{3}\%$ (d) $16\frac{1}{3}\%$
    (e) None of these

12. The speed of three cars is in the ratio of 5 : 4 : 6. The ratio between the time taken by them to travel the same distance is
    (a) $5 : 4 : 6$ (b) $6 : 4 : 5$
    (c) $10 : 12 : 15$ (d) $12 : 15 : 10$
    (e) None of these

13. What is the least number to be added to 920 to make it is a perfect square?
    (a) 41   (b) 31
    (c) 21   (d) 51
    (e) None of these

14. The average of five consecutive odd numbers is 61. What is the difference between the highest and lowest number?
    (a) 2   (b) 5
    (c) 8   (d) 12
    (e) None of these

15. The ratio of three numbers is 3 : 4 : 5 and the sum of their squares is 1250. The sum of the three numbers is
    (a) 30   (b) 50
    (c) 60   (d) 90
    (e) None of these

DIRECTIONS (Qs. 16-20) : *What will come in place of the question mark (?) in the following questions ?*

16. $\sqrt{11449} \times \sqrt{6241} - \left(54\right)^2 = \sqrt{?} + \left(74\right)^2$
    (a) 384   (b) 3721
    (c) 381   (d) 3638
    (e) None of these

17. $\left[\left(3\sqrt{8} + \sqrt{8}\right) \times \left(8\sqrt{8} + 7\sqrt{8}\right)\right] - 98 = ?$
    (a) $2\sqrt{8}$ (b) $8\sqrt{8}$
    (c) 382   (d) 386
    (e) None of these

18. $3463 \times 295 - 18611 = ? + 5883$
    (a) 997091   (b) 997071
    (c) 997090   (d) 999070
    (e) None of these

19. $\frac{28}{65} \times \frac{195}{308} \div \frac{39}{44} + \frac{5}{26} = ?$
    (a) $\frac{1}{3}$ (b) 0.75   (c) $1\frac{1}{2}$
    (d) $\frac{1}{2}$ (e) None of these

20. $(23.1)^2 + (48.6)^2 - (39.8)^2 = ? + 1147.69$
    (a) $(13.6)^2$ (b) $\sqrt{12.8}$
    (c) 163.84   (d) 12.8
    (e) None of these

DIRECTIONS (Qs. 21-25): *What will come in place of question mark (?) in the following questions?*

21. $9845 - 3896 + 486 = ? - 1128$
    (a) 7365   (b) 7463
    (c) 7536   (d) 7653
    (e) None of these

22. $55\% \text{ of } 860 + ?\% \text{ of } 450 = 581$
    (a) 24   (b) 28
    (c) 32   (d) 36
    (e) None of these

23. $\frac{10}{11} = \frac{110}{?}$
    (a) 111   (b) 1100
    (c) 121   (d) 100
    (e) None of these

24. $\frac{20 + 8 \times 0.5}{20 - ?} = 12$
    (a) 8   (b) 18
    (c) 2   (d) 13
    (e) None of these

25. $16.45 \times 2.8 + 4.5 \times 1.6 = ?$
    (a) 56.23   (b) 56.32
    (c) 53.26   (d) 53.66
    (e) None of these

DIRECTIONS (Qs. 26-30) : *In the following number series only one number is wrong. Find out the wrong number.*

26. 9050   5675   3478   2147   1418   1077   950
    (a) 3478   (b) 1418
    (c) 5675   (d) 2147
    (e) 1077

27. 7   12   40   222   1742   17390   208608
    (a) 7   (b) 12
    (c) 40   (d) 1742
    (e) 208608

28. 6   91   584   2935   11756   35277   70558
    (a) 91   (b) 70558
    (c) 584   (d) 2935
    (e) 35277

29. 1   4   25   256   3125   46656   823543
    (a) 3125   (b) 823543
    (c) 46656   (d) 25
    (e) 256

30. 8424   4212   2106   1051   526.5   263.25   131.625
    (a) 131.625   (b) 1051
    (c) 4212   (d) 8424
    (e) 263.25

DIRECTIONS (Qs. 31-35) : *Study the graph carefully to answer the following questions.*

Percent Profit Earned by Six Companies During 2014 and 2015
Profit = Income – Expenditure

$$\text{Percent profit} = \frac{\text{Income} - \text{Expenditue}}{\text{Expenditure}}$$

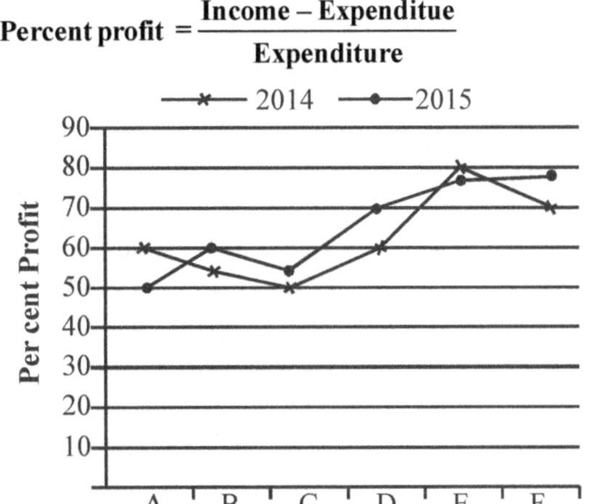

31. If the income of Company A in the year 2015 was ₹45 lakh, what was its expenditure in that year?
    (a) ₹27.621 lakh   (b) ₹23.145 lakh
    (c) ₹29.246 lakh   (d) ₹22.455 lakh
    (e) None of these

32. If the expenditure incurred by Company C in the year 2002 was ₹389 lakh, what was its income in that year?
    (a) ₹62.6 lakh   (b) ₹60.7 lakh
    (c) ₹58.9 lakh   (d) ₹56.4 lakh
    (e) None of these

33. If the total expenditure of companies B and C together in the year 2015 was ₹56 lakh, what was the total income of these two companies in that year?
    (a) ₹87 lakh   (b) ₹72 lakh
    (c) ₹75 lakh   (d) Can't be determined
    (e) None of these

34. Income of company D in the year 2014 was ₹42.5. What was the amount of profit earned?
    (a) ₹23.6 lakh   (b) ₹17.5 lakh
    (c) ₹18.9 lakh   (d) ₹22.5 lakh
    (e) None of these

35. If the expenditure of company E in the year 2002 and 2003 are equal, what was the ratio of its income in the year 2002 to that in 2003?
    (a) 35 : 36   (b) 15 : 16
    (c) 41 : 46   (d) Can't be determined
    (e) None of these

REASONING ABILITY

DIRECTIONS (Qs. 36-40) : *In each question below are two/three statements followed by two conclusions numbered I and II. You have to take the two/three given statements to be true even if they seem to be at variance from commonly known facts and then decide which of the given conclusions logically follows from the given statements disregarding commonly known facts.*

Give answer (a) if only conclusion I follows
Give answer (b) if only conclusion II follows.
Give answer (c) if either conclusion I or conclusion II follows.
Give answer (d) if neither conclusion I nor conclusion II follows.
Give answer (e) if both conclusion I and conclusion II follow.

(Qs. 36-38) :
Statements : All gliders are parachutes.
              No parachute is an airplane.
              All airplanes are helicopters.

36. **Conclusions :** I. No glider is an airplane.
                    II. All gliders being helicopters is a possibility.

37. **Conclusions :** I. No helicopter is a glider.
                    II. All parachutes being helicopters is a possibility.

38. **Statements** : Some mails are chats.
                   All updates are chats.
    Conclusions : I. All mails being updates is a possibility.
                    II. No update is a mail.

(Qs. 39-40) :
Statement : No stone is metal.
             Some metals are papers.
             All papers are glass.

39. **Conclusions :** I. All stones being glass is a possibility.
                    II. No stone is a paper.

40. **Conclusions :** I. No glass is a metal.
                    II. Atleast some glass is metal.

DIRECTIONS (Qs. 41-45): *Study the following information carefully and answer the given questions.*

Nine friends A, B, C, D, E, F, G, H and K are sitting around a circle facing the centre. A sits second to left of D. K sits third to right of F. Neither K nor F is an immediate neighbour of A or D. G and H are immediate neighbours of each other. E sits third to right of H. B is not an immediate neighbor of F.

41. What is the position of F with respect to the position of B ?
    (a) Second to the right   (b) Third to the left
    (c) Second to the left   (d) Third to the right
    (e) Sixth to the right

42. Who amongst the following is an immediate neighbour of H ?
    (a) C   (b) B
    (c) K   (d) F
    (e) A

43. Starting from A, if all the friends are made to sit in the alphabetical order in clockwise direction, the positons of how many (except A) will remain unchanged ?
    (a) None   (b) One
    (c) Two   (d) Three
    (e) Four

44. H is related to C and B is related to E in a certain way. To whom amongst the following is G related following the same pattern ?
    (a) F   (b) H
    (c) C   (d) A
    (e) D

45. What will come in place of the question mark ?
    DC DB DF DA ?
    (a) DG   (b) DE
    (c) DH   (d) DK
    (e) Either DK or DE

DIRECTIONS (Qs. 46-50): *Study the following arrangement carefuully and answer the questions given follow.*

H 3 R % M A δ K 2 P 5 E © N 4 W @ F & Q 1 U V 9 J I D 7 8

46. Which of the following is the sixth to the left of the fourteenth from the left end of the above arrangement?
- (a) 2
- (b) 1
- (c) U
- (d) K
- (e) None of these

47. If all the symbols are dropped from the above arrangement, which of the following will be the eleventh from the right end?
- (a) Q
- (b) F
- (c) N
- (d) 4
- (e) None of these

48. How many such numbers are there in the above arrangement, each of which is immediately preceded by a consonant and also immediately followed by a consonant?
- (a) None
- (b) One
- (c) Two
- (d) Three
- (e) More than three

49. How many such numbers are there in the above arrangement, each of which is immediately preceded by a consonant and immediately followed by a symbol?
- (a) None
- (b) One
- (c) Two
- (d) Three
- (e) More than three

50. What should come next in the following series based on the above arrangement?
3 % M, K P 5, N W @, ?
- (a) *1U
- (b) Q1V
- (c) QUV
- (d) QU9
- (e) None of these

DIRECTIONS (Qs. 51-53): *Use the information given below to answer.*

(i) There is a group of 5 persons A, B, C, D and E

(ii) In the group there is one badminton player, one chess player and one tennis player

(iii) A and D are unmarried ladies and do not play any games

(iv) No lady is a chess player or a badminton player

(v) There is a married couple in the group of which E is the husband

(vi) B is the brother of C and is neither a chess player nor a tennis player

51. Which of the group has only ladies?
- (a) ABC
- (b) BCD
- (c) CDE
- (d) CDA
- (e) None of these

52. Who is the tennis player?
- (a) B
- (b) C
- (c) D
- (d) E
- (e) None of these

53. Who is the wife of E?
- (a) A
- (b) B
- (c) D
- (d) C
- (e) None of these

54. Consider the following statements and answer the question.
M, N, O and P are all different individuals
M is the daughter of N.
N is the son of O
O is the father of P.

Which among the following statements is contradictory to the above premises?
- (a) P is the father of M.
- (b) O has three children.
- (c) M has one brother.
- (d) M is the granddaughter of O.
- (e) None of these

55. In a row of twenty five children Raman is 14th from the right end. Varun is third to the left of Raman. What is Varun's position from the left end of the row?
- (a) Eighth
- (b) Nineth
- (c) Seventh
- (d) Tenth
- (e) None of these

56. A man starts walking in south and walks for 7 km, then turns left and walks for 2 km. Then once again turns led and walks for 12 km, turns left one more time and walks for 2 km. How much distance he has to cover to reach the starting point?
- (a) 7 km
- (b) 12 km
- (c) 4 km
- (d) 5 km
- (e) None of these

57. Pointing to a boy, Mamta said, "he is the only son of my father-in-law's only child." How is the boy related to Mamta?
- (a) Brother
- (b) Daughter
- (c) Son
- (d) Husband
- (e) None of these

DIRECTIONS (Qs. 58-62): *Study the following information to answer the given questions*

Six people C, D, E, F, G and H are standing in a straight line facing North not necessarily in the same order. D is standing second to the right of F.C is standing fourth to the left of H and H is not standing on the extreme end of the line. E is standing second to the right of D.

58. What is the position of G with respect to E?
- (a) Immediate left
- (b) Second to the left
- (c) Third to the left
- (d) Third to the right
- (e) None of these

59. Which of the following pairs represents the people standing at the extreme ends of the line?
- (a) FH
- (b) CE
- (c) DE
- (d) CH
- (e) None of these

60. Who is standing second to the right of C?
- (a) F
- (b) D
- (c) G
- (d) E
- (e) None of these

61. Four of the following five are alike in a certain way based on their positions in the above arrangement and so form a group. Which of the following does not belong to the group?
- (a) CG
- (b) CE
- (c) GH
- (d) DE
- (e) FD

62. If all the people are asked to stand in an alphabetical order from left to right, the positions of how many will remain unchanged?
- (a) One
- (b) Two
- (c) Three
- (d) None
- (e) None of these

63. In a certain code, a number 13479 is written as AQFJL and 2568 is written as DMPN. How is 396824 written in that code?
- (a) QLPNMJ
- (b) QLPNMF
- (c) QLPMNF
- (d) QLPNDF
- (e) None of these

64. In the following sequence or instructions, 1 stands for Run, 2 stands for Stop, 3 stands for Go, 4 stands for Sit and 5 stands for Wait. If the sequence is continued, which instruction will come next ?

    4 4 5 4 5 3 4 5 3 1 4 5 3 1 2 4 5 4 5 3 4 5 3

    (a) Wait   (b) Sit
    (c) Stop   (d) Run
    (e) None of these

65. If the first and second letters in the word DEPRESSION were interchanged, also the third and the fourth letters, the fifth and the sixth letters and so on, which of the following would be the seventh letter from the right ?

    (a) R   (b) O
    (c) S   (d) P
    (e) None of these

DIRECTIONS (Qs. 66-70): *Read the following information carefully to answer the questions that follow.*

There are six teachers A, B, C, D, E and F in a school. Each of the teachers teaches two subjects, one compulsory subject and the other optional subject. D's optional subject is History while three others have it as compulsory subject. E and F have Physics as one of their subjects. F's compulsory subject is Mathematics which is an optional subject of both C and E. History and English are A's subjects but in terms of compulsory and optional subjects, they are reverse of those of D's. Chemistry is an optional subject of any one of them. There is only one female teacher in the school who has English as her compulsory subject.

66. What is C's compulsory subject ?
    (a) History   (b) Physics
    (c) Chemistry   (d) English
    (e) None of these

67. Who is a female member in the group ?
    (a) A   (b) B
    (c) C   (d) D
    (e) None of these

68. Who among the following has same optional subjects as that of the compulsory subject of F ?
    (a) D   (b) B
    (c) A   (d) C
    (e) None of these

69. Disregarding which is compulsory and which is the optional subject, who has the same two subjects combination as F ?
    (a) A   (b) B
    (c) E   (d) D
    (e) None of these

70. Which of the following groups of teachers has History as the compulsory subject ?
    (a) A, C and D   (b) B, C and D
    (c) C and D   (d) A, B and C
    (e) None of these

DIRECTIONS (Qs. 71-80): *Read the following passage carefully and answer the questions given below. There are certain words in the passage printed in bold letters to lead you to find them out easily in order to help you in answering some of the questions.*

Public sector banks are back in focus, not for the **steep** rise in bad loans, but for customer complaints against them. At first glance, the Reserve Bank of India's annual report on the Banking Ombudsman Scheme reveals that customers of PSBs had a litany of grievances, while patrons of private and foreign banks were quite content with the services offered to them. But one reason why PSBs account for about 65 per cent of the complaints is that these banks have a lion's share - about three-fourths - of the loans and deposits in the banking system. If we consider the number of complaints per account or branch, nationalised banks, surprisingly, have fewer complaints than their private and foreign counterparts. Complaints from the rural and semi-urban population have witnessed an increase, implying the wider participation from these segments. But there is a lack of awareness about the ombudsman scheme or lack of access to it in these regions. While they account for about two-thirds of the bank branches in India, less than 30 per cent of the complaints were lodged from here.

Reporting such numbers only scratches the surface of the problem. The ombudsman scheme, which was launched two decades ago to provide a free grievance **redress** system in the face of rising complaints against banks, will now have to use the data to improve its functioning. Both the Centre and the regulator also need to act on **longstanding** grievances. For years now, debit/ credit card operations (21 per cent of complaints) and unfair banking practices (29 per cent) have made up a large **chunk** of the complaints. Customers have had a laundry list of woes regarding failure of withdrawals from ATMs, issue of unsolicited cards and insurance policies, and banks' non-adherence to 'fair practices' or BCSBI (Banking Codes and Standards Board of India) codes. The BCSBI was set up a decade ago to supplement the ombudsman scheme. Hence, the wide non-adherence to these codes on the part of banks is inexcusable. What it highlights is the need for the RBI to follow up more **stringently** on ensuring that banks conform to norms.

Reviewing the scope of the ombudsman scheme and educating customers on the procedures to lodge complaints, will **ensure** that grievances that do find their way into the redressal system get resolved effectively. While the report shows that the scheme disposed 96 per cent of the complaints in 2014-15, rejections were as high as around two-thirds, because the solution to many of the grievances fell outside the jurisdiction of the banking ombudsman. The RBI advisory that banks have an internal redress mechanism to deal with the issue first-hand will work only if the process is streamlined for better results.

71. What could be the best title for the above passage?
    (a) Ombudsman scheme
    (b) RBI's Policies
    (c) Beyond just numbers
    (d) Unfair practices
    (e) Major challenge

72. Which of the following is NOT True according to the passage?
    I.   Rural population is participating more in banking
    II. Banking ombudsman scheme disposed more than 50 percent of the complaints in 2014-2015
    III. Unfair banking practices lead to large number of complaints
    (a) III & I   (b) II & III
    (c) I & II   (d) I, II & III
    (e) None of the above

73. What would be the best way to resolve complaints effectively?
    I.   Debit/credit card operations should be limited
    II. Banks should adhere to fair practices
    III. customers should be educated on the procedures to lodge complaints.
    (a) III only   (b) II & III
    (c) I & II   (d) I, II & III
    (e) None of these

74. Which of the following is TRUE according to the passage?
    (a) Banks have internal banking ombudsman
    (b) BCSBI was set up by RBI a decade ago
    (c) Issuance of unsolicited cards is one of the woes of customers
    (d) PSBs account for less than 65 percent of the complaints
    (e) None of these

DIRECTIONS (Qs. 75-78): *Choose the word which is most SIMILAR in meaning of the word printed in bold as used in the passage.*

75. **Steep**
    (a) gentle   (b) continuous
    (c) abrupt   (d) low
    (e) gadual

76. **Redress**
    (a) same   (b) compensation
    (c) penalty   (d) hurt
    (e) worse

77. **Longstanding**
    (a) strong   (b) high
    (c) long   (d) firm
    (e) abiding

DIRECTIONS (Qs. 78-80): *Choose the word which is most OPPOSITE in meaning of the word printed in bold as used in the passage.*

78. **ensure**
    (a) certify   (b) arrange
    (c) endanger   (d) guard
    (e) sure

79. **stringent**
    (a) inflexible   (b) easy going
    (c) compelling   (d) critical
    (e) bound

80. **chunk**
    (a) block   (b) portion
    (c) large   (d) whole
    (e) part

DIRECTIONS (Qs. 81 - 90): *In the following passage there are blanks each of which has been numbered. These numbers are printed below the passage and against each five words are suggested one of which fits the blank appropriately. Find out the appropriate word in each case.*

The ..81.. of India as an economic superpower is not reflected in the ..82.. of life enjoyed by its 1.2 billion citizens (according to Human Development Index) which ..83... India very low among 182 countries. In our performance-oriented world, measurement issues have taken on ..84.. importance as what we measure affects what we do. In fact, the French President has established an international Commission on the Measurement of Economic Performance and Social Progress, Owing to his ..85.. and that of others with the current state of statistical information about the economy and society.

A big question arises ..86.. the Gross Domestic Product Provides a good measure of living standards. In many cases, GDP statistics seem to ..87.. that the economy is doing far better than most citizens feel it is. Moreover, the focus on GDP creates conflicts- while political leaders are told to maximise it, citizens also demand that ..88.., should be paid to enhancing security, reducing air, water, and noise pollution all of which actually ..89.. GDP growth. Statistics are ..90... to summarize what is going on in our complex society, it is, therefore, an obvious threat that we can't reduce everything to a single number -GDP.

81. (a) pursuit   (b) perception
    (c) conversion   (d) title
    (e) tribute

82. (a) quality   (b) spirit
    (c) span   (d) joy
    (e) loss

83. (a) scored   (b) qualified
    (c) regard   (d) ranked
    (e) counted

84. (a) great   (b) unduly
    (c) trivial   (d) considerably
    (e) negligible

85. (a) confidence   (b) belief
    (c) dissatisfaction   (d) compliance
    (e) obedience

86. (a) unless   (b) because
    (c) against   (d) whether
    (e) that

87. (a) recommend   (b) think
    (c) point   (d) refer
    (e) suggest

88. (a) respect   (b) debt
    (c) attention   (d) expense
    (e) compensation

89. (a) lower   (b) attain
    (c) decline   (d) shrunk
    (e) recover
90. (a) difficult   (b) interpret
    (c) reveal   (d) intended
    (e) inferred

DIRECTIONS (Qs. 91-100): In each of the questions given below a sentence is given which is then divided into five parts out of which last part is correct. There are errors in three out of four remaining parts and therefore only one of the parts (other than the bold one) is correct. You must choose the grammatically correct part as your answer.

91. A Ramayana(A)\ is not just an(B)\ story that probably(C)\ occurs several(D)\ centuries ago(E).
    (a) A   (b) B
    (c) C   (d) D
    (e) None of the above
92. There is no doubting(A)\ that China have(B)\ used their commercial expansion(B)\ to furthering its(D)\ strategic interests(E).
    (a) A   (b) B
    (c) C   (d) D
    (e) None of the above
93. There is an failure(A)\ in story telling(B)\where the death of a(C) language has becomes a(D)\ litany of numbers\(E)
    (a) A   (b) B
    (c) C   (d) D
    (e) None of the above
94. It was only because(A)\ of practice of(B)\ those many years that(C)\ I can prepare myself fast(D)\ for the role that I take up(E).
    (a) A   (b) B
    (c) C   (d) D
    (e) None of the above

95. A democracy that fail (A)\ to being inventive about (B)\ culture eventually becomes (C)\ an nominal, rudimentary (D)\ and standardized world\ (E).
    (a) A   (b) B
    (c) C   (d) D
    (e) None of the above
96. India in many a (A)\ways was an oral(B)\ society that never(C)\ understands the cultures(D)\ of morality(E).
    (a) A   (b) B
    (c) C   (d) D
    (e) None of the above
97. Earn trust is(A)\ a longest term(B)\project and requiring(C) \patience, foresight(D)\and statesmanship(E).
    (a) A   (b) B
    (c) C   (d) D
    (e) None of the above
98. The students alleged(A)\ that shutting down of(B)\ the university is(C)\ a ploy for(D)\ harass them(E).
    (a) A   (b) B
    (c) C   (d) D
    (e) None of the above
99. We will protection the(A)\ biometric of the(B)\ best of ours ability(C)\ and never allow it(D)\ to be compromised(E).
    (a) A   (b) B
    (c) C   (d) D
    (e) None of the above
100. Everyone was happy then, but(A)\ the entire family went(B)\ in grief around midnight(C)\ when they received a call(D)\ about the accident(E).
    (a) A   (b) B
    (c) C   (d) D
    (e) None of the above

Answer Key

1	(b)	11	(c)	21	(e)	31	(e)	41	(d)	51	(d)	61	(b)	71	(c)	81	(b)	91	(c)
2	(b)	12	(d)	22	(a)	32	(c)	42	(d)	52	(b)	62	(e)	72	(e)	82	(a)	92	(e)
3	(c)	13	(a)	23	(c)	33	(d)	43	(b)	53	(d)	63	(d)	73	(a)	83	(d)	93	(c)
4	(b)	14	(c)	24	(b)	34	(b)	44	(a)	54	(a)	64	(d)	74	(c)	84	(a)	94	(d)
5	(b)	15	(c)	25	(c)	35	(a)	45	(c)	55	(b)	65	(d)	75	(c)	85	(c)	95	(c)
6	(b)	16	(b)	26	(e)	36	(a)	46	(d)	56	(d)	66	(a)	76	(b)	86	(d)	96	(e)
7	(c)	17	(c)	27	(d)	37	(b)	47	(b)	57	(c)	67	(d)	77	(e)	87	(e)	97	(d)
8	(b)	18	(a)	28	(c)	38	(d)	48	(e)	58	(c)	68	(d)	78	(c)	88	(c)	98	(a)
9	(e)	19	(d)	29	(d)	39	(a)	49	(a)	59	(b)	69	(c)	79	(b)	89	(a)	99	(d)
10	(d)	20	(c)	30	(b)	40	(b)	50	(c)	60	(c)	70	(d)	80	(d)	90	(d)	100	(b)

HINTS & EXPLANATIONS

1. **(b)** C. P. of 56 kg rice
$$= (26 \times 20 + 30 \times 36)$$
$$= ₹(520 + 1080) = ₹1600$$
S. P. of 56 kg rice $= 56 \times 30 = ₹1680$

Profit % $= \dfrac{80}{1600} \times 100 = 5\%$

2. **(b)** Let P $= ₹x$

$$SI = \frac{x \times 10 \times 10}{100} = x$$
$$A = P + SI$$
$$22500 = x + x$$
$$2x = 22500$$
$$x = 11250$$
∴   He took ₹ 11,250 as loan.

3. **(c)** $6M + 6W \rightarrow 6D$
$15M = ?$ and $9W \rightarrow 10\,D$
So, $(6M + 6W) \times 6 = 90\,W$
$$36\,M + 36\,W = 90\,W$$
$$36\,M = 54\,W$$
$$1W = \frac{2}{3}M$$
$$∴ 9W = 9 \times \frac{2}{3}M = 6\,M$$

Now from $M_1 D_1 = M_2 D_2$, we have $15 \times D_1 = 6 \times 10$
$\Rightarrow D_1 = 4$ Days

4. **(b)** Let C. P. $= x$
Loss $= 19\%$

then S.P. is $\dfrac{119}{100}x$

If profit $= 17\%$ then S. P. $= \dfrac{83}{100}x$

According to question
$$\frac{119x}{100} - 162 = \frac{83x}{100}$$
$$∴ \quad x = 450$$

5. **(b)** Area of towel $= l \times b = 100\,cm \times 50\,cm = 5000\,cm^2$
Now, length decreased by 20% and breadth decreased by 10%
$l' = 100 - 20\%$ of $100 = 80\,cm$
$b' = 50 - 10\%$ of $50 = 45\,cm$
New area $= l' \times b' = 80\,cm \times 45\,cm = 3600\,cm^2$
Change in area $= (5000 - 3600)\,cm^2 = 1400\,cm^2$

% change in area $= \dfrac{1400}{5000} \times 100 = 28\%$

6. **(b)** Let A and B represent the sets of students who passed in English and Mathematics respectively.
If 15% of candidates failed in both, then 85% passed at least one of the exams.
Then, the total number of students passed in one or both subjects
$$= (A \cup B) = n(A) + n(B) - n(A \cap B)$$
$$0.85 = 0.75 + 0.65 - n(A \cap B)$$
$$n(A \cap B) = 1.40 - 0.85 = 0.55$$
0.55% of number of students $= 495$

∴   Number of students $= \dfrac{495}{55} \times 100 = 900$

7. **(c)** Let present age of Ravi be x.
∴   Present age of Ravi's father $= 4x$
According to question,
5 years before,
Ravi's father age $= 7 \times$ Ravi's age
$$4x - 5 = 7(x - 5)$$
$$\Rightarrow 4x - 5 = 7x - 35$$
$$\Rightarrow 3x = 30$$
$$∴ \quad x = 10$$
∴   Ravi's present age $= x = 10$ years
Ravi's father's present age
$= 4 \times 10 = 40$ years

8. (b) Amount = Principal $\left(1 + \dfrac{\text{Rate}}{100}\right)^{\text{Time}}$

$$= 1250\left(1 + \dfrac{4}{100}\right)^2 = 1250 \times \dfrac{26}{25} \times \dfrac{26}{25} = ₹1352$$

9. (e) Money received by M $= \dfrac{3}{8} \times 44352 = ₹16632$

Reamining money $= 44352 - 16632 = ₹27720$

∴ Money received by N $= \dfrac{1}{6} \times 27720 = ₹4620$

Further, remaining money $= 27720 - 4620 = ₹23100$
which was divided between O and P in the ratio of 3:4

Therefore, money received by O $= \dfrac{3}{7} \times 23100 = ₹9900$

10. (d) Required number of ways $= 8! = 40320$

11. (c) Let x and y be the rate of sugar per kg and quantity of sugar.

$$xy = \left(x + \dfrac{20}{100} \times x\right)y'$$

$$xy = \dfrac{6x}{5}y'$$

$$y' = \dfrac{5}{6}y = y - \dfrac{y}{6}$$

Reduction in consumption $= \dfrac{100}{6} = 16\dfrac{2}{3}\%$

12. (d) Speed of cars is $5 : 4 : 6$

Time ratio $= \dfrac{1}{5} : \dfrac{1}{4} : \dfrac{1}{6} = \dfrac{12 : 15 : 10}{60}$

The ratio between the time taken by them to travel the same distance is $12 : 15 : 10$

13. (a) We know,
$31^2 > 920 > 30^2$ i.e., $961 > 920 > 900$
Hence, the required number
$= 961 - 920 = 41$

14. (c) Let the numbers are
$x, x+2, x+4, x+6$ and $x+8$.

$$\text{Average} = \dfrac{x + x + 2 + x + 4 + x + 6 + x + 8}{5}$$

$61 \times 5 = 5x + 20$
$5x = 305 - 20$
$5x = 285$
$x = 57$
First number $= 57$
Last number $= 65$
Required difference $= 65 - 57 = 8$

15. (c) Let the numbers are 3x, 4x and 5x respectively.
According to question $(3x)^2 + (4x)^2 + (5x)^2 = 1250$
$9x^2 + 16x^2 + 25x^2 = 1250$
$50x^2 = 1250$
$x^2 = 25$
$x = 5$
Numbers are 15,20 and 25.
Sum $= 15 + 20 + 25 = 60$

16. (b) $\sqrt{11449} \times \sqrt{6241} - (54)^2 = \sqrt{?} + (74)^2$

$\Rightarrow \quad \sqrt{?} = 107 \times 79 - 2916 - 5476$

$\quad = 8453 - 2916 - 5476 = 61$

∴ $\quad ? = (61)^2 = 3721$

17. (c) $? = \left[\left(3\sqrt{8} + \sqrt{8}\right) \times \left(8\sqrt{8} + 7\sqrt{8}\right)\right] - 98$

$= \left(4\sqrt{8} \times 15\sqrt{8}\right) - 98 = \left(60 \times 8\right) - 98$

$= 480 - 98 = 382$

18. (a) $3463 \times 295 - 18611 = ? + 5883$

∴ $\quad ? = 1021585 - 18611 - 5883 = 997091$

19. (d) $? = \dfrac{28}{65} \times \dfrac{195}{308} \div \dfrac{39}{44} + \dfrac{5}{26} = \dfrac{28}{65} \times \dfrac{195}{308} \times \dfrac{44}{39} + \dfrac{5}{26}$

$= \dfrac{4}{13} + \dfrac{5}{26} = \dfrac{8+5}{26} = \dfrac{13}{26} = \dfrac{1}{2}$

20. (c) $? + 1147.69 = (23.1)^2 + (48.6)^2 - (39.8)^2$
∴ $\quad ? = 533.61 + 2361.96 - 1584.04 - 1147.69 = 163.84$

21. (e) $? - 1128 = 9845 - 3896 + 486$
$\Rightarrow \quad ? - 1128 = 10331 - 3896$
$\Rightarrow \quad ? = 6435 + 1128 = 7563$

22. (a) 55% of 860 + ?% of 450 = 581

$\Rightarrow \quad \dfrac{55}{100} \times 860 + \dfrac{?}{100} \times 450 = 581$

$\Rightarrow \quad 473 + \dfrac{?}{100} \times 450 = 581$

$\Rightarrow \quad \dfrac{?}{100} \times 450 = 581 - 473 = 108$

$\Rightarrow \quad ? = \dfrac{108 \times 100}{450} = 24$

23. (c) Let $\dfrac{10}{11} = \dfrac{110}{x}$. Then, $10x = 11 \times 110$.

∴ $\quad x = \dfrac{11 \times 110}{10} = 121$.

24. (b) Let $\dfrac{20 + 8 \times 0.5}{20 - x} = 12$. Then, $24 = 12(20 - x)$

∴ $12x = 216$ or $x = 18$

25. (c) $? = 16.45 \times 2.8 + 4.5 \times 1.6$
$\Rightarrow \quad ? = 46.06 + 7.20$
$\Rightarrow \quad ? = 53.26$

26. (e) The given number series is based on the following pattern:

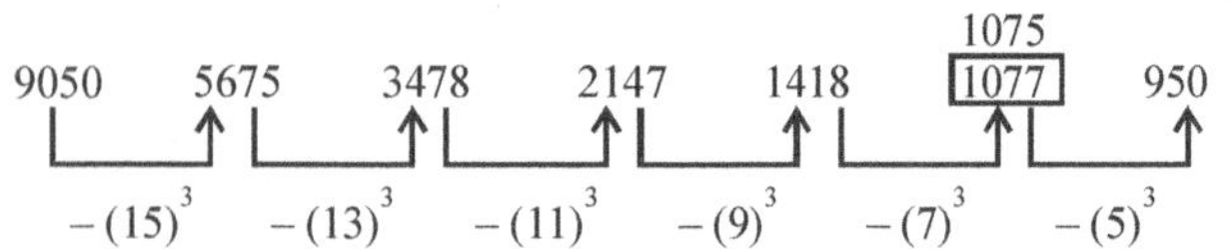

Hence, the number 1077 is wrong and it should be replaced by 1075.

27. (d) The given number series is based on the following pattern :

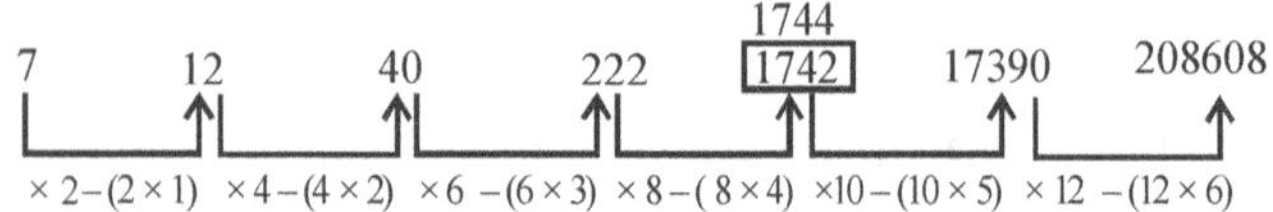

Hence, the number 1742 is wrong and it should be replaced by 1744.

28. (c) The given number series is based on the following pattern:

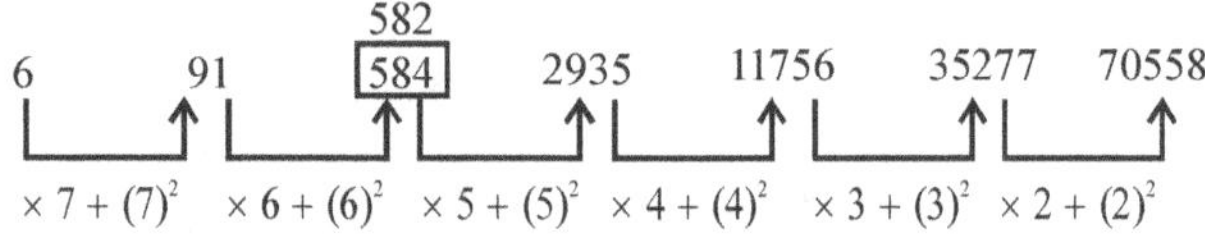

Hence, the number 584 is wrong and it should be replaced by 582.

29. (d) The given number series is based on the following pattern.

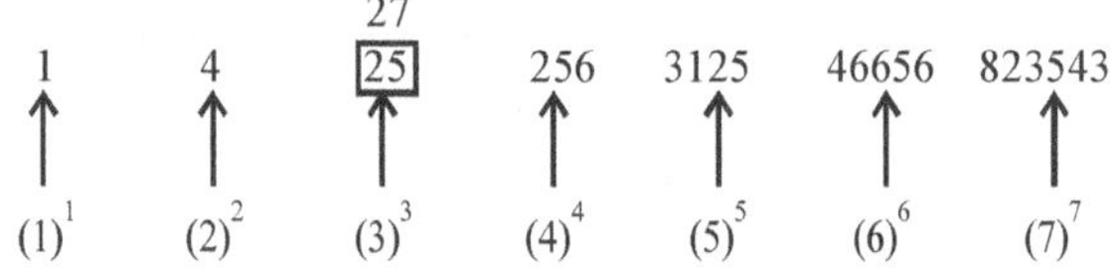

Hence, the number 25 is wrong and it should be replaced by 27.

30. (b) The given number series is based on the following pattern :

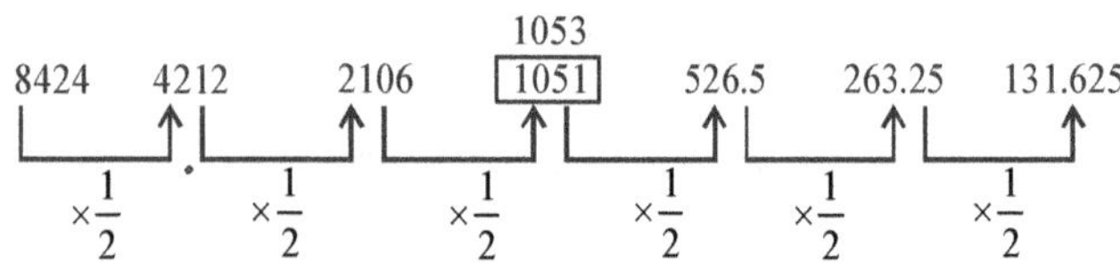

Hence, the number 1051 is wrong and it should be replaced by 1053.

31. (e) Required expenditure

$$= \frac{45 \times 100}{160} = ₹28.125 \text{ lakh}$$

32. (c) Required income $= \dfrac{38 \times 155}{100} = ₹58.9 \text{ lakh}$

33. (d) Can't be determined.

34. (b) The required profit $= \dfrac{42.5}{170} \times 70 = ₹17.5 \text{ lakh}$

35. (a) The required ratio of incomes in the given years $= 175 : 180 = 35 : 36$

Sol. (36 -37) :

According to statements:

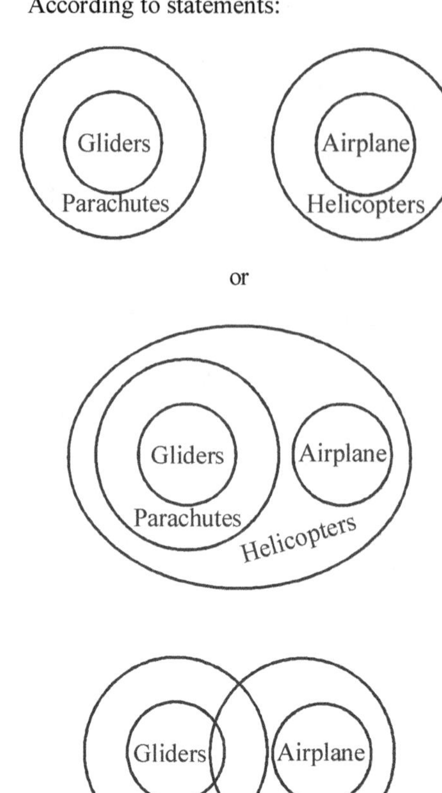

36. (a) Hence, only conclusion I follows.
37. (b) Hence, conclusion II follows.
38. (d) According to statements.

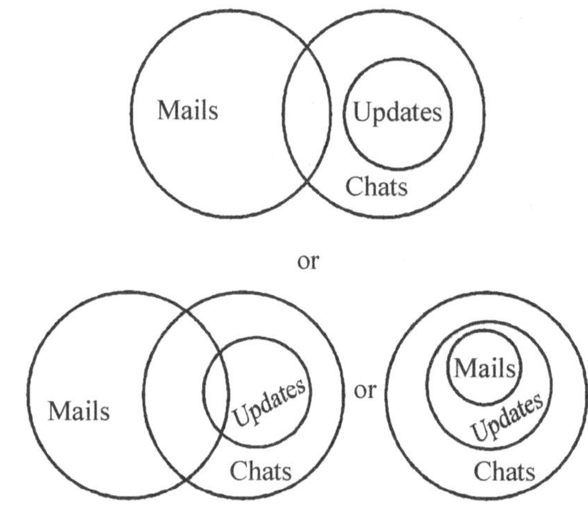

Sol. (39-40) : According to statements

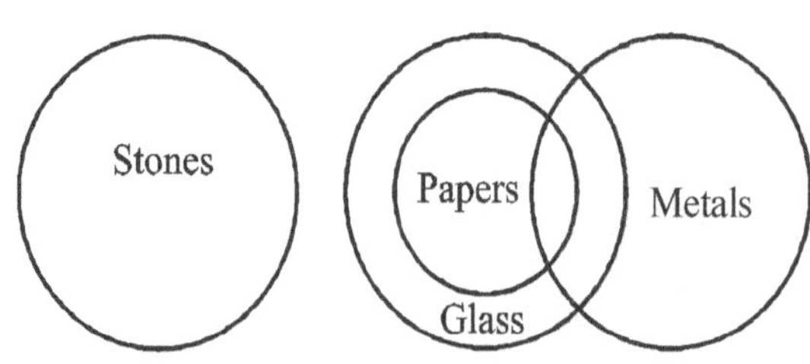

or

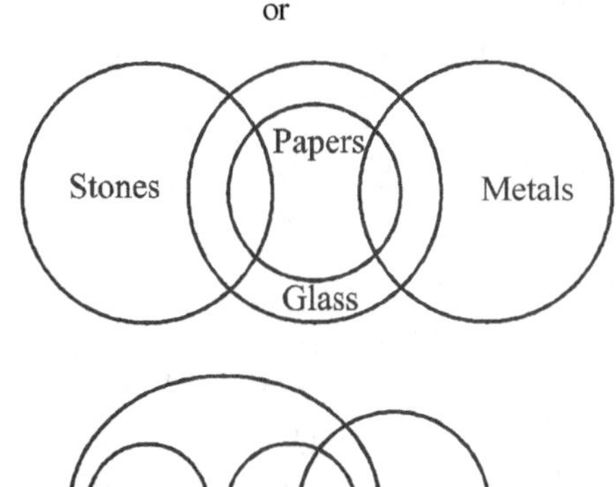

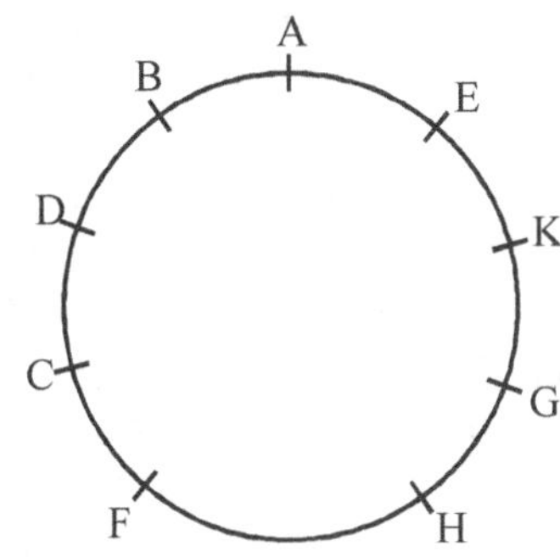

39. (a) Hence, conclusion I follows.
40. (b) Hence, only conclusion II follows.

Sol. (41-45) :

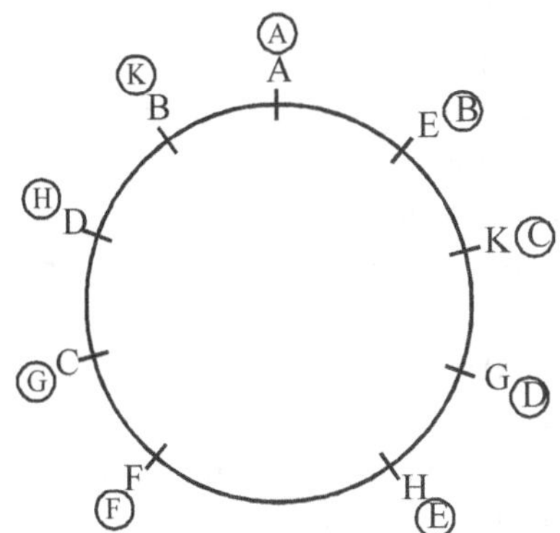

41. (d) F is third to the right of B.
42. (d) F and G are immediate neighbours of H.
43. (b)

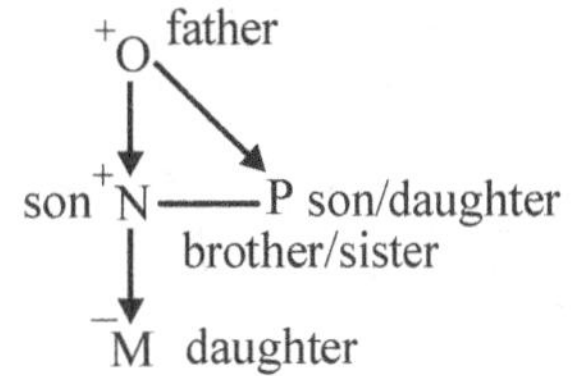

44. (a) H is second to the right of C.
         B is second to the right of E.
         G is second to the right of F.
45. (c) DC, DB $\Rightarrow$ Immediate neighbours of D.
         DF, DA $\Rightarrow$ F is second to the right of D.
         A is second to the right of D.
         Therefore, ? = DH
         H is third to the right of D.

46. (d) $14 - 6 = 8$th $= $ K
47. (b) According to the question, new arrangement

H 3 R M A K 2 P 5 E N 4 W
  F Q 1 U V 9 J I D 7 8

11th from right end

48. (e) Required number in the arrangement = H 3 R, K 2 P, N 4 W, V 9 J
49. (a) Number is none formed.

50. (c)
$$3 \xrightarrow{+6} K \xrightarrow{+6} N \xrightarrow{+6} Q$$
$$\% \xrightarrow{+6} P \xrightarrow{+6} W \xrightarrow{+6} U$$
$$M \xrightarrow{+6} 5 \xrightarrow{+6} @ \xrightarrow{+6} V$$

Sol. (51 -54):

	Badminton	Chess	Tennis	Gender	Marriage status	Relation
A	✗	✗	✗	F	Unmarried	
B	✓	✗	✗	M		Brother of C
C	✗	✗	✓	F	Married with E	
D	✗	✗	✗	F	Unmarried	
E		✓		M		Husband C + E

51. (d) CDA is the group of ladies.
52. (b) It is clear from above table.
53. (d) It is clear from above table.

54. (a)

From above relation diagram, P is the sibling of M's father.

55. (b)

As Raman is 14th from right. So Varun will be 17th from right. So there are 8 people $(25 - 17)$ to the left of Varun. He is the nineth.

56. (d) Aman has taken a rectangular path as is clear from the diagram below.

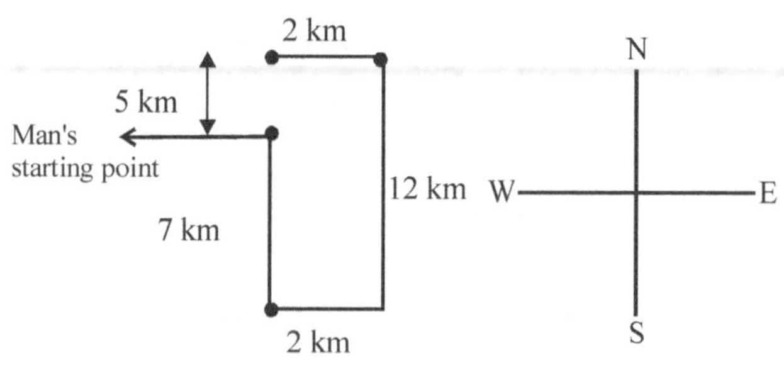

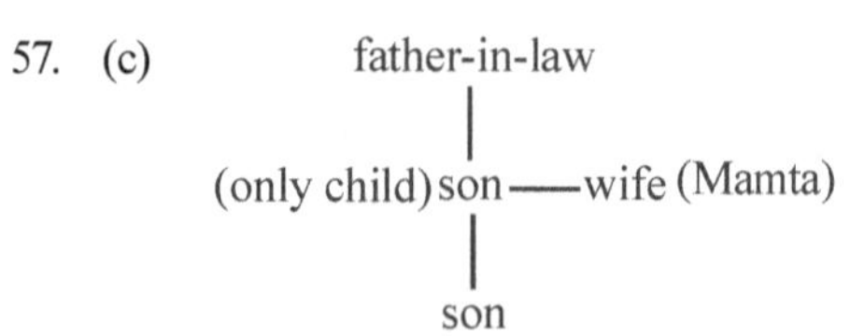

For (Sol. 66 to 70)

The given information is summarised in a table as follows :

Teachers	Subjects	
	Compulsory	Optional
A	History	English
B	History	Chemistry
C	History	Mathematics
D	(Female) English	History
E	Physics	Mathematics
F	Mathematics	Physics

66. (a) History is the compulsory subject of C.

67. (d) D is a female member in the group.

68. (d) The compulsory subject of F (Mathematics) is the optional subject of C.

69. (c) E has physics and Mathematics as his two subjects.

70. (d) A, B and C all have History as the compulsory subjects.

91. (c) Option (c) is the correct option. Option(a) is incorrect as 'the' will be used in place of 'A' as Ramayana is a proper noun. Option(b) is incorrect as 'a' will be used in place of 'an'. Option (d) is incorrect as 'occurred' will be used in place of 'occurs'. The Ramayana has already been written and past tense is to be used.

92. (e) Option(e) is correct as the none of the statements is correct. Option(a) 'doubt' in place of 'doubting'. Option(b) 'has' in place of 'have'. Option(c) 'its' in place of 'their'. Option(d) 'further' in place of 'furthering'.

93. (c) Option(a) use 'a' instead of 'an'. Option(b) 'of' in place of 'in'. Option(d) omit 'has'.

94. (d) Option(a) is incorrect. Use 'is' in place of 'was'. Option(b) Insert 'the' between of and practice. Option(c) Use 'these' in place of 'those'.

95. (c) Option(a) is incorrect. Use 'fails' in place of 'fail'. Option(b) use 'be' in place of 'being'. Option(d) use 'a' in place of 'an'.

96. (e) Option(a) omit "a" Option(b) 'is' in place of 'was' Option(c) omit 'never' Option(d) 'culture' in place of 'cultures'.

97. (d) Option(a) replace 'earn' by 'earning' Option(b) replace 'longest' by 'long' Option(c) omit 'and'.

98. (a) Option(b) remove 'of' Option(c) replace 'is' with 'was' Option(d) replace 'for' with 'to'.

99. (d) Option(a) replace 'protection' with 'protect' Option(b) replace 'of' with 'to' Option(c) replace 'ours' with 'our'.

100. (b) Option(a) remove then Option(c) replace 'in' with 'into' Option(d) replace 'a' with 'the'.

57. (c)

father-in-law
|
(only child) son ——— wife (Mamta)
|
son

Mamta's father-in-law's only child is Mamta's husband and only child's only son is her husband's only son i.e. Mamta's son.

Sol. (58-62)

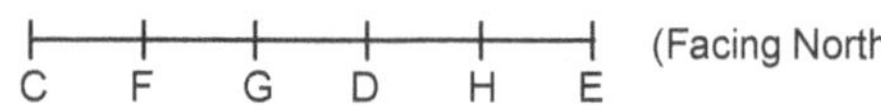

58. (c) G is third to the left of E.

59. (b) C and E are standing at the extreme ends of the line.

60. (c) G is standing second to the right of C.

61. (b) Except G and E, all are having one person between them. While there are two persons (D and H) between G and E.

62. (e) Position of C will remain unchanged on arranging alphabetically.

63. (d)

1	3	4	7	9	2	5	6	8
A	Q	F	J	L	D	M	P	N

Thus,

3	9	6	8	2	4
Q	L	P	N	D	F

64. (d) 4, 45, 453, 4531, 45312, 45, 453, 4531
The next coded digit will be 1. Hence, the instruction Run will come next.

65. (d) The new letter sequence is EDRPSEISNO.
The seventh letter from the right is P.

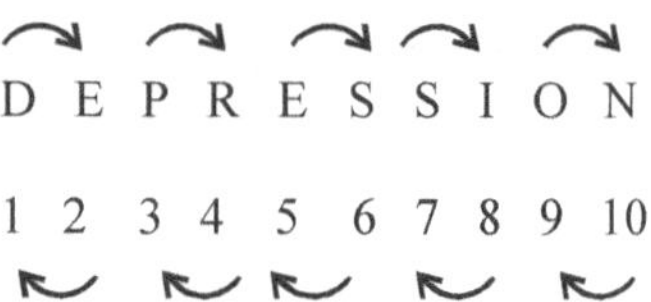

PRACTICE SET 6

Time : 60 Minutes **Max. Marks : 100**

NUMERICAL ABILITY

DIRECTIONS (Qs. 1-5) : *What will come in place of the question mark (?) in the following questions?*

1. $\sqrt[3]{19683} = ? \times 3$
   - (a) $\sqrt{9}$
   - (b) 9
   - (c) 27
   - (d) 18
   - (e) None of these

2. $1515 = ? \div 1515$
   - (a) 2295225
   - (b) 2290225
   - (c) 5115
   - (d) 4485
   - (e) None of these

3. $60 = ?\%$ of 400
   - (a) 15
   - (b) 25
   - (c) 20
   - (d) 6
   - (e) None of these

4. $1400 \times ? = 1050$
   - (a) $\dfrac{2}{5}$
   - (b) $\dfrac{3}{4}$
   - (c) $\dfrac{3}{5}$
   - (d) $\dfrac{2}{3}$
   - (e) None of these

5. 40% of $? = 1.5 = ?$
   - (a) 60
   - (b) 6000
   - (c) 6600
   - (d) 600
   - (e) None of these

DIRECTIONS (Qs. 6-10): *Study the following pie graph carefully and answer the questions given below :*

Cost Estimated by a Family in Renovation of its House

Total Cost Estimated ₹ 120000

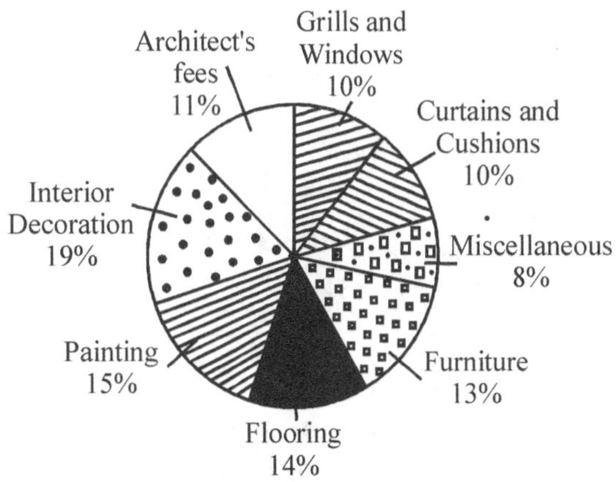

6. The family gets a discount on Furniture and pays 12% less than the estimated cost on Furniture. What is the amount spent on Furniture ?
   - (a) ₹ 13200
   - (b) ₹ 14526
   - (c) ₹ 13526
   - (d) ₹ 13728
   - (e) None of these

7. What is the cost estimated by the family on Painting and Flooring together?
   - (a) ₹ 36500
   - (b) ₹ 34800
   - (c) ₹ 36000
   - (d) ₹ 34500
   - (e) None of these

8. What is the difference in the amount estimated by the family on Interior Decoration and Architect's Fees?
   - (a) ₹ 10000
   - (b) ₹ 9500
   - (c) ₹ 7200
   - (d) ₹ 9000
   - (e) None of these

9. Other than getting the discount of 12% on the estimated cost of Furniture and the actual Miscellaneous expenditure of ₹ 10200 instead of the estimated, the family's estimated cost is correct. What is the total expenditure of the family in renovation of its house?
   - (a) ₹ 116728
   - (b) ₹ 115926
   - (c) ₹ 119500
   - (d) ₹ 116500
   - (e) None of these

10. During the process of renovation, the family actually incurs Miscellaneous expenditure of ₹ 10200. The Miscellaneous expenditure incurred by the family is what percent of the total estimated cost?
    - (a) 9.5
    - (b) 9
    - (c) 8.5
    - (d) 10.5
    - (e) None of these

DIRECTIONS (Qs. 11-15) : *Identify which number is wrong in the given series.*

---

11. 2, 3, 4, 4, 6, 8, 9, 12, 16.
    - (a) 3
    - (b) 9
    - (c) 6
    - (d) 12
    - (e) None of these

12. 3, 4, 10, 32, 136, 685, 41
    - (a) 136
    - (b) 10
    - (c) 4116
    - (d) 32
    - (e) None of these

13. 69, 55, 26, 13, 5
    - (a) 26
    - (b) 13
    - (c) 5
    - (d) 55
    - (e) None of these

14. 24576, 6144, 1536, 386, 96, 24
    - (a) 386
    - (b) 6144
    - (c) 96
    - (d) 1536
    - (e) None of these

15. 11, 5, 20, 12, 40, 26, 74, 54
    - (a) 5
    - (b) 20
    - (c) 40
    - (d) 26
    - (e) None of these

16. A train is moving at a speed of 132 km/h. If the length of the train is 110 metres, how long will it take to cross a railway platform, 165 metres long?
    - (a) 5 s
    - (b) 7.5 s
    - (c) 10 s
    - (d) 15 s
    - (e) None of these

17. If 15 women or 10 men can complete a project in 55 days, in how many days will 5 women and 4 men working together complete the same project?
    - (a) 75
    - (b) 8
    - (c) 9
    - (d) 85
    - (e) None of these

18. Ashu's mother was three times as old as Ashu, 5 years ago. After 5 years, she will be twice as old as Ashu. How old is Ashu at present?
    - (a) 15
    - (b) 20
    - (c) 10
    - (d) 5
    - (e) None of these

19. If the length of a rectangle is increased by 10% and the area is unchanged, then by how much percent does the breadth decrease?
    - (a) 100/11%
    - (b) 100/9%
    - (c) 9%
    - (d) 10%
    - (e) None of these

20. A milkman claims to sell milk at its cost price only, but he is making a profit of 20% since he has mixed some amount of water in the milk. What is the percentage of milk in the mixture?
    - (a) 80%
    - (b) $\dfrac{250}{3}\%$
    - (c) 75%
    - (d) $\dfrac{200}{3}\%$
    - (e) None of these

21. A batsman scores 80 runs in his sixth innings and thus increases his average by 5. What is his average after six innings?`
    - (a) 50
    - (b) 55
    - (c) 60
    - (d) 65
    - (e) None of these

22. A sum was put at simple interest at a certain rate for 2 years. Had it been put at 3% higher rate, it would have fetched ₹ 300 more. Find the sum.
    - (a) ₹ 6000
    - (b) ₹ 8230
    - (c) ₹ 5000
    - (d) ₹ 4600
    - (e) None of these

23. A reduction of 20% in the price of sugar enables a purchaser to obtain $2\dfrac{1}{2}$ kg more for ₹ 160. Find the original price per kg of sugar.
    - (a) ₹ 12
    - (b) ₹ 20
    - (c) ₹ 16
    - (d) ₹ 18
    - (e) None of these

24. Mrs. X spends ₹ 535 in purchasing some shirts and ties for her husband. If shirts cost ₹ 43 each and the ties cost ₹ 21 each, then what is the ratio of the shirts to the ties that are purchased?
    - (a) 1 : 2
    - (b) 2 : 1
    - (c) 2 : 3
    - (d) 3 : 4
    - (e) None of these

25. Anish spends 25% of his salary on house rent, 5% on food, 15% on travel, 10% on clothes and the remaining amount of ₹ 22,500 is saved. What is Anish's salary ?
    - (a) ₹ 40,000
    - (b) ₹ 40,500
    - (c) ₹ 45,500
    - (d) ₹ 50,000
    - (e) None of these

26. If ab = 36, which of the following proportions is correct ?
    - (a) 9 : a = 4 : b
    - (b) a : 18 = b : 3
    - (c) a : 6 = b : 6
    - (d) a : 9 = 4 : b
    - (e) None of these

27. In every 30 min the time of a watch increases by 3 min. After setting the correct time at 5 : 00 am, what time will the watch show after 6 h ?
    - (a) 11 : 48 am
    - (b) 11 : 30 am
    - (c) 11 : 36 am
    - (d) 11 : 42 am
    - (e) 11 : 24 am

28. In how many ways can a group of 5 men and 2 women be made out of a total of 7 men and 3 women ?

    (a) 63   (b) 70
    (c) 36   (d) 56
    (e) None of these

29. A boat covers a distance of 24 km in 10 h downstream. To cover the same distance upstream, the boat takes 2h longer. What is the speed of the boat in still water?
    (a) 2 km/h   (b) 2.8 km/h
    (c) 2.6 km/h   (d) 3.2 km/h
    (e) None of these

30. A tap can fill an empty tank in 12 hours and a leakage can empty the whole tank in 20 hours. If the tap and the leakage are working simultaneously, how long will it take to fill the whole tank?
    (a) 25 hours   (b) 40 hours
    (c) 30 hours   (d) 35 hours
    (e) None of these

DIRECTIONS (Qs. 31-35) : *What approximate value should come in place of the question mark (?) in the following questions ? (You are not expected to calculate the exact value.)*

31. $\sqrt{964} \times \sqrt{348} = ?$
    (a) 575   (b) 570
    (c) 586   (d) 550
    (e) 579

32. $37.35 + 13.064 \times 3.46 = ?$
    (a) 89   (b) 83
    (c) 76   (d) 79
    (e) 85

33. $(4863 + 1174 + 2829) \div 756 = ?$
    (a) 18   (b) 16
    (c) 12   (d) 9
    (e) 22

34. $54 \times 746 \div 32 = ?$
    (a) 1259   (b) 1268
    (c) 1196   (d) 1248
    (e) 1236

35. $[(1.5)^2 \times (3.2)^2] \div 2.3 = ?$
    (a) 6   (b) 4
    (c) 12   (d) 10
    (e) 16

REASONING ABILITY

36. In a certain code '*na pa ka so*' means 'birds fly very high', '*ri so la pa*' means 'birds are very beautiful' and '*ti me ka bo*' means 'the parrots could fly'. Which of the following is the code for 'high' in that language ?
    (a) *na*   (b) *ka*
    (c) *bo*   (d) *so*
    (e) None of these

37. Laxman went 15 km to the west from my house, then turned left and walked 20 km. He then turned East and walked 25 km and finally turning left covered 20 km. How far was he from my house ?
    (a) 5 km   (b) 10 km
    (c) 40 km   (d) 80 km
    (e) None of these

38. A trader in order to code the prices of article used the letters of PSICHOLAZY in the form of '0 to 9' respectively. Which of the following code stands for ₹ 875.50 ?
    (a) AIL.HP   (b) AIL.HS
    (c) ZYA.HO   (d) ZCA.OP
    (e) None of these

39. In a row of girls, Rita and Monika occupy the ninth place from the right end and tenth place from the left end, respectively. If they interchange their places, then Rita and Monika occupy seventeenth place from the right and eighteenth place form the left respectively. How many girls are there in the row?
    (a) 25   (b) 26
    (c) 27   (d) Data inadequate
    (e) None of these

DIRECTIONS (Qs. 40-41) : *Study the following information carefully and answer the question given below.*

Point A is 5 m towards the West of Point B. Point C is 2 m towards the North of point B. Point D is 3 m towards the East of Point C. Point E is 2 m towards the South of Point D.

40. If a person walks 2 m towards the North from Point A, takes a right turn and continues to walk, which of the following points would he reach the first ?
    (a) D   (b) B
    (c) E   (d) C
    (e) Can't be determined

41. Which of the following points are in a straight line ?
    (a) A, B, E   (b) D, C, A
    (c) C, E, D   (d) B, D, A
    (e) A, C, E

DIRECTIONS (Qs. 42-46) : *Study the following information carefully to answer the given questions.*

Eight people M, N, O, P, Q, R, S and T are sitting in a straight line with equal distances between each other, but not necessarily in the same order. Some of them are facing North and some of them are facing south.

- M sits at one of the extreme ends of the line. Only three people sit between M and S. Q sits exactly between M and S.
- T sits third to the right of Q. N is an immediate neighbour of T and faces south. O sits second to the right of R. O is not an immediate neighbour of S.
- Immediate neighbour of S face opposite directions(i.e. if one neighbour faces North then the other neighbour faces south and Voce-Versa)
- M and P face the same direction as Q(i.e if Q faces north then M and P also face North and Vice-Versa). Both the immediate neighbours of Q face south.

42. In the given arrangement, if two people come and sit to the immediate left of Q, how many people will sit between R and O?
    (a) Two   (b) Three
    (c) Four   (d) More than four
    (e) One

43. Who amongst the following sits third to the right of R?
    (a) M
    (b) Q

(c) Other than those given as options
(d) N
(e) S

44. How many people face North as per the given arrangement?
(a) Two (b) Three
(c) Four (d) More than four
(e) One

45. Four of the following five are alike in a certain way based upon their seating arrangement and so form a group. Which of the following does not belong to the group?
(a) QO (b) MR
(c) NR (d) OS
(e) PS

46. Who amongst the following sits at extreme right end of row?
(a) O (b) R
(c) T (d) P
(e) M

DIRECTIONS (Qs. 47-51): *In each question below are three statements followed by three conclusions numbered I, II and III. You have to take the three given statements to be true even if they seem to be at variance from commonly known facts and then decide which of the answers (a), (b), (c), (d) and (e) is the correct answer and indicate it on the answer sheet.*

---

47. **Statements:** Some chairs are tables.
    Some tables are drawers.
    all drawers are shelf.
    Conclusions: **I.** Some shelves are tables.
    II. Some drawers are chairs.
    III. Some shelves are drawers.
    (a) Only I and III follow
    (b) Only I and either II or III follow
    (c) Only II and either I or III follow
    (d) All I, II and III follow
    (e) None of the above

48. **Statements:** All trees are flowers.
    Some flowers are leaves.
    No leaf is bud
    Conclusions: **I.** No bud is a flower.
    II. Some buds are flowers.
    III. Some leaves are trees.
    (a) Only II and III follow
    (b) Only III follows
    (c) Only either I or II follows
    (d) Either I or II and III follow
    (e) None of the above

49. **Statements:** All stones are rocks.
    Some rocks are bricks.
    Some bricks are cement.
    Conclusions: **I.** Some cements are rocks.
    II. Some bricks are stone
    III. Some stones are cement.
    (a) Only I and either II or III follow
    (b) Only either II or III follows
    (c) Only I and II follow
    (d) All follow
    (e) None of the above

50. **Statements:** All flats are buildings.
    All buildings are bungalows.
    All bungalows are apartments.
    Conclusions: **I.** Some apartments are flats.
    II. All flats are bungalows.
    III. Some bungalows are flats.
    (a) None follows
    (b) Only I and II follow
    (c) Only II and III follow
    (d) Only I and III follow
    (e) All I, II and III follow

51. **Statements:** Some spectacles are lenses.
    Some lenses are frames.
    All frames are metals.
    Conclusions: **I.** Some lenses are metals
    II. Some metals are spectacles.
    III. Some frames are spectacles.
    (a) Only III follows
    (b) Only I follows
    (c) Only I and either II or III follow
    (d) Only I and II follow
    (e) None of the above

DIRECTIONS (Qs. 52-56): *Read the following information carefully and answer the questions that follow:*

At a party, A, B, C, D and E are sitting in a circle. The group comprises a professor, an industrialist and a businessman. The businessman is sitting in between the industrialist and his wife D. A, the professor is married to E, who is the sister of B. The industrialist is seated to the right of C. Both the ladies are unemployed.

52. What is A to B ?
    (a) Brother (b) Uncle
    (c) Brother-in-law (d) Can't be determined
    (e) None of these

53. A is sitting to the right of
    (a) the industrialist (b) his wife
    (c) D (d) Can't be determined
    (e) None of these

54. Who is the industrialist ?
    (a) D (b) A
    (c) B (d) Can't be determined
    (e) None of these

55. Who in the group is unmarried?
    (a) Professor (b) Industrialist
    (c) Businessman (d) Can't be determined
    (e) None of these

56. Who among them must be graduate ?
    (a) B (b) A
    (c) C (d) E
    (e) None of these

DIRECTIONS (Qs. 57-61): *Use the following series of elements (alpha-number-symbol) to answer these questions. Every two-digit number (given in brackets) is to be treated as single number.*

2 ★ 8 5 6 B 9 $ Q 3 E 1 7 R D 4 £ (1(c) U ● K (18) A (1(d) P

57. Four of the following five groups of elements are alike in a certain way and so form a group. Which is the one the **does not** belong to that group ?

(a) 2 ★ 8   (b) 5 6 B
(c) Q $ 9   (d) 1 3 E
(e) D R 7

58. If each alphabet has a value of zero, each symbol (i.e., ★, $ and ●) has a value equivalent to the square of the numeral that immediately precedes the symbol or the value of 1 if it is not immediately preceded by a numeral, what will be the sum of the values of the first 10 elements of the series starting from the left end ?
(a) 118   (b) 46
(c) 79   (d) 107
(e) None of these

59. If each of the letters in the above series of elements is given a value equivalent to its serial number in the English alphabet, what will be the difference between the sum of the consonants and the sum of the vowels used in the series ?
(a) 109   (b) 41
(c) 82   (d) 27
(e) None of these

60. Which of the following groups of elements will come in the place of the question-mark in the series of elements given below?
6 8 2 $ B 5 E Q 9   ? £ D 7
(a) ● (1(c) 4   (b) 4 (1(c) ●
(c) U £ D   (d) ● (1(c) £
(e) None of these

61. BQ in the above series is related in ER in a similar way as AP is related to
(a) RD   (b) U ●
(c) KA   (d) Q 3
(e) 6 B

DIRECTIONS (Qs. 62-65) : *Study the set of numbers given below and answer the questions which follow*

427 581 839 275 589

62. Which of the following numbers will be obtained if the second digit of greatest number is subtracted from the second digit of lowest number after adding one to each of the numbers ?
(a) 1   (b) 2
(c) 3   (d) 4
(e) 5

63. If in each number, first and the last digits are interchanged, which of the following will be the third highest number ?
(a) 427   (b) 581
(c) 839   (d) 275
(e) 589

64. If in each number the second and the third digits are interchanged, which will be the second highest number ?
(a) 427   (b) 581
(c) 839   (d) 275
(e) 589

65. If two is subtracted from the first digit of each of the numbers and then the first and the third digits are interchanged, which of the following will be the lowest ?
(a) 427   (b) 581
(c) 839   (d) 275
(e) 589

DIRECTIONS (Qs. 66-70): *Study the following information to answer the given questions:*

A building has seven floors numbered one to seven, in such a way that the ground floor is numbered one, the floor above it, number two and so on such that the topmost floor is numbered seven. One out of seven people viz. A, B, C, D, E, F and G lives on each floor. A lives on fourth floor. E lives on the floor immediately below F's floor. F does not live on the second or the seventh floor.
C live on third floor. B does not live on a floor immediately above or below C's floor. D does not live on the topmost floor. G does not live on any floor below E's floor.

66. Who lives on the topmost floor?
(a) B   (b) C
(c) E   (d) G
(e) Can't be determined

67. Who lives immediately above D's floor?
(a) A   (b) B
(c) C   (d) F
(e) G

68. Four of the following five are alike in a certain way and so form a group. Which is the one that does not belong to that group?
(a) F   (b) E
(c) B   (d) G
(e) C

69. Who lives on floor number 2?
(a) A   (b) C
(c) D   (d) B
(e) E

70. How many people lives between floor F and B?
(a) 3   (b) 4
(c) 6   (d) 7
(e) 5

ENGLISH LANGUAGE

DIRECTIONS (Qs. 71-80): *Read the passage given below and answer the questions that follow based on the information given in the passage.*

Right through history, imperial powers have clung to their possessions to death. Why, then, did Britain in 1947 give up the jewel in its crown, India? For many reasons. The independence struggle exposed the hollowness of the white man's burden. Provincial self-rule since 1935 paved the way for full self-rule. Churchill resisted independence, but the Labour Government of Atlee was anti-imperialist by ideology. Finally, the Royal Indian Navy Mutiny in 1946 raised fears of a second Sepoy Mutiny, and convinced British waverers that it was safer to withdraw gracefully. But politico-military explanations are not enough. The basis of empire was always money. The end of empire had much to do with the fact that British imperialism had ceased to be profitable. World War II left Britain victorious but deeply indebted, needing Marshall Aid and loans from the World Bank. This constituted a strong financial case for ending the no longer-profitable empire.

Empire building is expensive. The US is spending one billion dollar a day in operations in Iraq that fall well short of fullscale

imperialism. Through the centuries, empire building was costly, yet constantly undertaken because it promised high returns. The investment was in armies and conquest. The returns came through plunder and taxes from the conquered. No immorality was attached to imperial loot and plunder. The biggest conquerors were typically revered (hence titles like Alexander the Great, Akbar the Great, and Peter the Great). The bigger and richer the empire, the more the plunderer was admired. This mindset gradually changed with the rise of new ideas about equality and governing for the public good, ideas that culminated in the French and the American Revolutions. Robert Clive was impeached for making a little money on the side, and so was Warren Hastings. The white man's burden came up as a new moral rationale for conquest. It was supposedly for the The Princeton Review CAT sample paper 12 good of the conquered. This led to much muddled **hypocrisy**. On the one hand, the empire needed to be profitable. On the other hand, the white man's burden made brazen loot impossible.

An additional factor deterring loot was the 1857 Sepoy Mutiny. Though crushed, it reminded the British vividly that they were a tiny ethnic group who could not rule a gigantic subcontinent without the support of important locals. After 1857, the British stopped annexing one princely state after another, and instead treated the princes as allies. Land revenue was fixed in absolute terms, partly to prevent local unrest and partly to promote the notion of the white man's burden. The empire **proclaimed** itself to be a protector of the Indian peasant against exploitation by Indian elites. This was denounced as hypocrisy by nationalists like Dadabhai Naoroji in the 19th century, who complained that land taxes led to an enormous drain from India to Britain. Objective calculations by historians like Angus Maddison suggest a drain of perhaps 1.6 percent of Indian Gross National Product in the 19th century.

But land revenue was more or less fixed by the Raj in absolute terms, and so its real value diminished rapidly with inflation in the 20th century. By World War II, India had ceased to be a profit centre for the British Empire. Historically, conquered nations paid taxes to finance **fresh** wars of the conqueror. India itself was asked to pay a large sum at the end of World War I to help repair Britain's finances.

But, as shown by historian Indivar Kamtekar, the independence movement led by Gandhiji changed the political landscape, and made mass-taxation of India increasingly difficult. By World War II, this had become politically impossible. Far from taxing India to pay for World War II, Britain actually began paying India for its contribution of men and goods. Troops from white dominions like Australia, Canada and New Zealand were paid for entirely by these countries, but Indian costs were shared by the British government. Britain paid in the form of non-convertible sterling balances, which mounted swiftly. The conqueror was paying the conquered, undercutting the profitability on which all empire is founded. Churchill opposed this, and wanted to tax India rather than owe it money.

But he was overruled by Indian hands, who said India would resist payment, and paralyze the war effort. Leo Amery, Secretary of State for India, said that when you are driving in a taxi to the station to catch a life-or-death train, you do not loudly announce that you have doubts whether to pay the fare. Thus, World War II converted India from a **debtor** to a creditor with over one billion

pound in sterling balances. Britain, meanwhile, became the biggest debtor in the world. It's not worth ruling over people who are afraid to tax.

71. Which of the following was NOT a reason for the emergence of the 'white man's burden' as a new rationale for empire building in India?
    (a) The emergence of the idea of the public good as an element of governance.
    (b) The decreasing returns from imperial loot and increasing costs of conquest.
    (c) The weakening of the immorality attached to an emperor's looting behaviour.
    (d) A growing awareness of the idea of equality among peoples.
    (e) None of these

72. Which of the following best expresses the main purpose of the author?
    (a) To present the various reasons that can lead to the collapse of an empire and the granting of independence to the subjects of an empire.
    (b) To point out the critical role played by the 'white man's burden' in making a colonizing power give up its claims to native possessions.
    (c) To highlight the contradictory impulse underpinning empire building which is a costly business but very attractive at the same time.
    (d) To illustrate how erosion of the financial basis of an empire supports the granting of independence to an empire's constituents.
    (e) None of these

73. What was the main lesson the British learned from the Sepoy Mutiny of 1857?
    (a) That the local princes were allies, not foes.
    (b) That the land revenue from India would decline dramatically.
    (c) That the British were a small ethnic group.
    (d) That India would be increasingly difficult to rule. The Princeton Review CAT sample paper 13
    (e) None of these

74. Which of the following best captures the meaning of the 'white man's burden', as it is used by the author?
    (a) The British claim to a civilizing mission directed at ensuring the good of the natives.
    (b) The inspiration for the French and the American Revolutions.
    (c) The resource drain that had to be borne by the home country's white population.
    (d) An imperative that made open looting of resources impossible.
    (e) None of these

75. Why didn't Britain tax India to finance its World War II efforts?
    (a) Australia, Canada and New Zealand had offered to pay for the Indian troops.
    (b) India had already paid a sufficiently large sum during World War I.
    (c) It was afraid that if India refused to pay, Britain's war efforts would be jeopardised.

(d) The British empire was built on the premise that the conqueror pays the conquered.

(e) None of these

DIRECTIONS (Qs. 76-78): *Choose the word which is opposite in meaning to the word printed in bold as used in the passage.*

76. **proclaim**
    (a) declare   (b) clarion
    (c) trumpet   (d) predicate
    (e) deny

77. **debtor**
    (a) loanee   (b) drawee
    (c) mortgagor   (d) defaulter
    (e) mortagagee

78. **hypocrisy**
    (a) glibness   (b) phoniness
    (c) honesty   (d) quackery
    (e) deceit

DIRECTIONS (Qs. 79-80): *Choose the word which is most similar in meaning to the word printed in bold as used in the passage*

79. **imperialism**
    (a) developement   (b) quackery
    (c) underprogress   (d) failure
    (e) None of these

80. **fresh**
    (a) new   (b) old
    (c) medium   (d) light
    (e) None of these

DIRECTIONS (Qs. 81-90): *In the following passage, there are blanks, each of which has been numbered. These numbers are printed below the passage and against each, five words are suggested, one of which fits the blank appropriately. Find out the appropriate words without changing the meaning of the passage.*

Does Indian industry need democracy? The Indian economy's sustained growth today is.... (81).... by incomplete democracy. While millions of Indians endure poverty, only a tiny majority ......(82)...... prosperity. On the other hand, many Latin American countries have registered ......(83)...... growth rates under military dictators and today one of the fastest growing economies in the world - china- has an ......(84).........rather than a democracy government. So why does Indian need democracy for sustained growth? To many, democracy ......(85)...... slower decision making with corrupt politicians and red-tapism etc. Industry should, therefore, be ....(86)...... with less, not more, democracy. However, while China ....(87)....... Consumption in order to save and invest more than half its output to produce 10% growth, India ....(88)...... almost two-thirds of its output and manages to achieve 9% growth from one-third of its output. ....(89).......... India's democracy is not inefficient when it comes to making ......(90) ....use of resources.

81.   (a) deprived   (b) hampered
    (c) eliminated   (d) faced
    (e) threaten

82.   (a) pursuit   (b) acquisition
    (c) benefit   (d) enjoy
    (e) value

83.   (a) acceptable   (b) insignificant
    (c) variable   (d) inflated
    (e) affordable

84.   (a) autonomous   (b) economical
    (c) authoritarian   (d) egalitarian
    (e) orthodox

85.   (a) imply   (b) mentions
    (c) attracts   (d) features
    (e) means

86.   (a) gracious   (b) adapted
    (c) fascinated   (d) pleased
    (e) urged

87.   (a) bans   (b) curtails
    (c) regulate   (d) ceases
    (e) discourage

88.   (a) consumes   (b) selects
    (c) indulges   (d) disperse
    (e) hoard

89.   (a) Accordingly   (b) Totally
    (c) Thus   (d) Even
    (e) Likely

90.   (a) ultimately   (b) capably
    (c) modest   (d) secure
    (e) effective

DIRECTIONS (Qs. 91-100): *In each of the questions given below, a sentence is given which is divided into 5 parts. It is then followed by 5 options one of which gives the sequence of the correct parts. Choose the option which gives the correct sequence of the grammatically correct parts.*

91. There was a time when(A)/, like many other aspects of governance(B)/, the critical issue of defence(C)/ preparedness has also hampered(D)/ by policy paralysis(E).
    (a) ABCD   (b) ACDE
    (c) ABCE   (d) BCED
    (e) None of these

92. The Centre have been informed the Delhi High Court(A)/ that it is in the process of issuing guidelines(B)/ to ban the manufacture, import, sale(C)/ and any kind of trade in e-cigarettes(D)/, dubbing it a "new emerging threat"(E).
    (a) ABCD   (b) ACDE
    (c) ABCE   (d) BCDE
    (e) None of these

93. This case dealing with an issue(A)/ of very sensitive nature has caused a lot(B)/ of commotion in the country and(C)/ was also creating anger(D)/, unease and a sense of disharmony(E).
    (a) ABCD   (b) BCDE
    (c) ACDE   (d) ABCE
    (e) None of these

94. The law will not be obstructed by(A)/ the irresponsible actions and statements of a group of people(B)/. Proper procedures are being followed(C)/, investigations are on the fast track(D)/ and justice would have been delivered(E).
    (a) ABCD   (b) BCDE
    (c) ACDE   (d) ABCE
    (e) None of these

95. Tour operators in Mysuru, who had(A)/ come up with the idea of introducing(B)/ the Assembly elections to global

tourists(C)/ who may be keen on seeing(D)/ the democratic exercise unfolding(E).
(a) ABCD   (b) BCDE
(c) ACDE   (d) ABCE
(e) None of these

96. It was said of him that(A)/ when he went out to(B)/ bat you could saw(C)/ the Union Jack fluttering(D)/ on his bat handle(E).
(a) ABCD   (b) BCDE
(c) ACDE   (d) ABCE
(e) ABDE

97. Bedi's bowling action has transcended(A)/ the limits of time and embedding(B)/ itself in the minds of(C)/ even those who never(D)/ saw him play(E).
(a) ABCD   (b) ACDE
(c) BCDE   (d) ABDE
(e) None of these

98. The regulatory framework for the media is not(A)/ a simple manual of dos and don'ts(B)/. It would rather complex and

tries to balance(C)/ free speech and accountability without taking away(D)/ the ability to question those in power(E).
(a) ABCD   (b) BCDE
(c) ABDE   (d) ABCE
(e) ACDE

99. Reasonable restrictions are only a corollary(A)/ to the enabling environment(B)/. It would be disaster if(C)/ restrictions were to take(D)/ precedence over the enabling environment(E).
(a) ABDE   (b) ABCD
(c) BCDE   (d) ACDE
(e) None of these

100. The Guild was right to assume that the(A)/ notification would have been opening(B)/ the door for frivolous complaints(C)/ against journalists(D)/ and news organisations(E).
(a) ABCD   (b) BCDE
(c) ABCE   (d) ABDE
(e) ACDE

Answer Key

1	(b)	11	(b)	21	(b)	31	(e)	41	(a)	51	(b)	61	(c)	71	(b)	81	(b)	91	(c)
2	(a)	12	(d)	22	(c)	32	(b)	42	(b)	52	(c)	62	(c)	72	(d)	82	(d)	92	(d)
3	(a)	13	(c)	23	(c)	33	(c)	43	(a)	53	(d)	63	(a)	73	(c)	83	(a)	93	(d)
4	(b)	14	(a)	24	(b)	34	(a)	44	(c)	54	(c)	64	(e)	74	(a)	84	(c)	94	(a)
5	(d)	15	(c)	25	(d)	35	(d)	45	(a)	55	(d)	65	(b)	75	(c)	85	(e)	95	(b)
6	(d)	16	(b)	26	(d)	36	(a)	46	(d)	56	(b)	66	(d)	76	(e)	86	(d)	96	(e)
7	(b)	17	(a)	27	(c)	37	(b)	47	(a)	57	(d)	67	(c)	77	(e)	87	(b)	97	(b)
8	(e)	18	(a)	28	(a)	38	(e)	48	(c)	58	(a)	68	(a)	78	(c)	88	(a)	98	(c)
9	(e)	19	(a)	29	(e)	39	(b)	49	(e)	59	(b)	69	(c)	79	(a)	89	(c)	99	(a)
10	(c)	20	(b)	30	(c)	40	(d)	50	(e)	60	(e)	70	(e)	80	(a)	90	(e)	100	(e)

HINTS & EXPLANATIONS

1. (b) $\sqrt[3]{19683} = ? \times 3$

$$\therefore \quad ? = \frac{\sqrt[3]{19683}}{3} = \frac{27}{3} = 9$$

2. (a) $1515 = ? \div 1515$

$$\therefore \quad ? = 1515 \times 1515 = (1515)^2$$
$$= 2295225$$

3. (a) $60 = ?\%$ of 400

$$\therefore \ ? = \frac{60 \times 100}{400} = 15$$

4. (b) $1400 \times ? = 1050$

$$\therefore \ ? = \frac{1050}{1400} = \frac{3}{4}$$

5. (d) 40% of $? = 240$

$$\therefore \ ? = \frac{240 \times 100}{40} = 600$$

6. (d) Required amount

$$= 120000 \times \frac{13}{100} \times \frac{(100-12)}{100}$$

$$= 120000 \times \frac{13}{100} \times \frac{88}{100} = ₹13728$$

7. (b) Required cost $= 120000 \times \dfrac{(15+14)}{100}$

$$= 120000 \times \frac{29}{100} = ₹34800$$

8. (e) Required amount

$$= 120000 \times \frac{(19-11)}{100}$$

$$= 120000 \times \frac{8}{100} = ₹9600$$

9. (e) Estimated cost of Furniture

$$= 120000 \times \frac{13}{100} = ₹15600$$

Estimated cost of Miscellaneous items

$$= 120000 \times \frac{8}{100} ₹9600$$

Actual cost of Furniture

$$= ₹15600 \times \frac{88}{100} ₹13728$$

Actural cost of Miscellaneous items $= 10200$

The total expenditure of the family in renovation of house $= ₹\,120000 - ₹\,[(15600 + 9600) - (13728 + 10200)]$
$= ₹120000 - ₹1272 = ₹118728$

10. (c) Required percent

$$= \frac{10200}{120000} \times 100 = 8.5\%$$

11. (b) 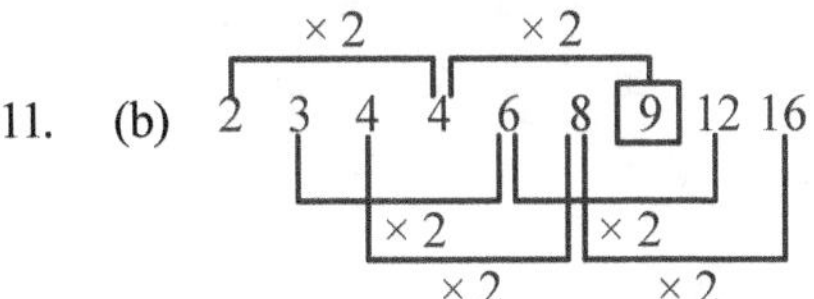

Thus, 9 must be replaced by 8.

12. (d)
$$
\begin{array}{ccccccc}
3 & 4 & 10 & \boxed{32} & 136 & 685 & 4116 \\
\end{array}
$$
$$\times 1 + 1 \quad \times 2 + 2 \quad \times 3 + 3 \quad \times 4 + 4 \quad \times 5 + 5 \quad \times 6 \times 6$$

Thus, 32 is out of place and must be replaced by 33.

13. (c)
$$
\begin{array}{ccccc}
69 & 55 & 26 & 13 & \boxed{5} \\
\end{array}
$$
$$6 \times 9 + 1 \quad 5 \times 5 + 1 \quad 2 \times 6 + 1 \quad 1 \times 3 + 1$$

Thus, 5 does not fit in the series and should be replaced by 4.

14. (a) The succeeding numbers are obtained by dividing the preceding numbers by 4. Therefore, the number 386 does not fit in the series and must be replaced by 384.

15. (c) There are two series in the given series :

$$
\begin{array}{ccccc}
\text{I} & 5 & 12 & 26 & 54 \\
\end{array}
$$
$$\times 2 + 2 \quad \times 2 + 2 \quad \times 2 + 2$$

$$
\begin{array}{ccccc}
\text{II} & 11 & 20 & \boxed{40} & 74 \\
\end{array}
$$
$$\times 2 - 2 \quad \times 2 - 2 \quad \times 2 - 2$$

Hence, the wrong term is 40. It should be replaced by 38.

16. (b) Speed of the train $= 132$ km/h $= \dfrac{132 \times 5}{18}$ m/s

Distance $= (110 + 165) = 275$ m

Time required to cross the railway platform

$$= \frac{275 \times 18}{132 \times 5} = 7.5 \text{ s}$$

17. (a) $15\,W = 10\,M$

Now, $5W + 4M = 5W + \dfrac{4 \times 15}{10}\,W = 5W + 6W$

$$= 11\,W$$

Now, 15 women can complete the project in 55 days, then 11 women can complete the same project in

$$\frac{55 \times 15}{11} = 75 \text{ days}$$

18. (a) Let the present ages of Ashu's mother and that of Ashu be x and y, respectively.

Then, $(x-5) = 3(y-5)$ or $x - 5 = 3y - 15$

or $x - 3y = -10$ ...(i)

and $(x+5) = 2(y+5)$

And $x + 5 = 2y + 10$ or $x - 2y = 5$ ...(ii)

From (i) and (ii), we have $x = 35$ and $y = 15$

Hence, the present age of Ashu = 15 years

19. (a) Area of Rectangle = length × breadth

Here, length is increased by 10%. But area is constant so that breadth is decreased.

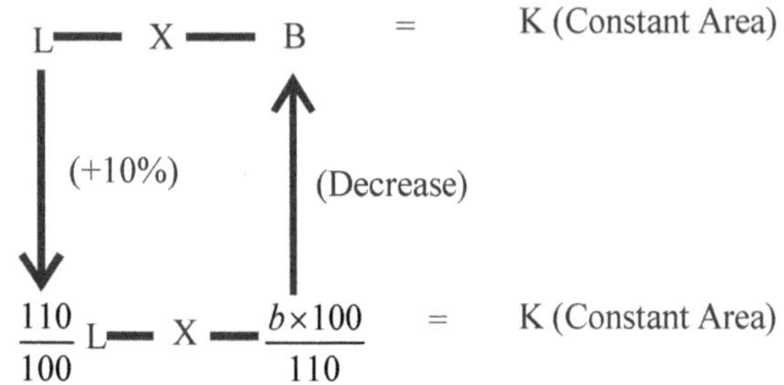

Percentage decrease in breadth $= \dfrac{b - \dfrac{100b}{110}}{b} \times 100 = \dfrac{100}{11}\%$

20. (b) Let milkman buy milk of ₹100.

20% profit, then S. P. = ₹120

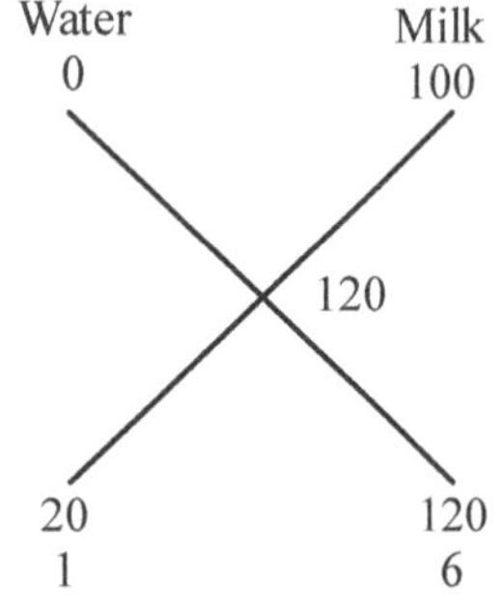

∴ Percentage of milk $= \dfrac{6-1}{6} \times 100 = \dfrac{5}{6} \times 100 = \dfrac{250}{3}\%$

21. (b) Let the average of 5 innings = x

Score in sixth innings = 80

∴ Total of 5 innings = 5x

According to the question,

$$\frac{5x + 80}{6} = x + 5$$

$\Rightarrow 5x + 80 = 6x + 30$

$\Rightarrow x = 80 - 30 = 50$

∴ His average after six innings = 50 + 5 = 55

22. (c) Let the sum = Rs. x and original rate = $y\%$ per annum then, New rate = $(y+3)\%$ per annum

$$\therefore \frac{x \times (y+3) \times 2}{100} - \frac{x \times y \times 2}{100} = 300$$

$xy + 3x - xy = 15000$

∴ $x = 5000$ Thus, the sum = ₹ 5000

23. (c) Total amount used for purchasing = ₹ 160. A reduction of 20% in the price means, now a person gets 5/2 kg for ₹ 32 and this is the present price of the sugar.

∴ Present price per kg $= \dfrac{32}{5} \times 2 = ₹\, 12.8$

Let the original price be ₹ x. Then new price is arrived after reduction of 20% on it.

$\Rightarrow$ x × 0.8 = 12.8 or x = ₹ 16.

24. (b) Mrs. X spends = ₹ 535

∴ Total cost = 43 shirt + 21 ties = 535

By hit and trial, S = 10, T = 5

$\Rightarrow$ Total cost = 43 × 10 + 21 × 5 = 535

Hence, Ratio of shirts to ties = 10 : 5 = 2 : 1

25. (d) Total expense percentage = (25 + 5 + 15 + 10)% = 55%

Savings % = 100 − 55 = 45%

Let Anisha's salary be ₹ x.

45% of x = 22500

$$\therefore x = \frac{22500}{45} \times 100 = ₹\, 50000$$

26. (d) ab = 36

$\Rightarrow$ ab = 4 × 9

$\Rightarrow \dfrac{a}{9} = \dfrac{4}{b} \Rightarrow a:9 = 4:b$

27. (c) In 1 h it increases by 6 min, so in 6h it increases by 36 min. So, the watch will show 11 : 36 am after 6h.

28. (a) The group consists of 7 men and 3 women. We have to select 5 out of 7 men, i.e., $^7C_5$ and 2 out of 3 women, i.e., $^3C_2$. Hence, required number of ways

$= {}^7C_5 \times {}^3C_2$

$= \dfrac{7 \times 6}{2 \times 1} \times \dfrac{3 \times 2}{2 \times 1} = 63$

29. (e) Upstream speed $= \dfrac{24}{12} = 2 \text{ km/h}$

Downstream speed $= \dfrac{24}{10} = 2.4 \text{ km/h}$

∴ Speed of the boat in still water

$= \dfrac{2 + 2.4}{2} = 2.2 \text{ km/h}$

30. (c) Part of the tank filled in an hour

$= \dfrac{1}{12} - \dfrac{1}{20} = \dfrac{5-3}{60} = \dfrac{1}{30}$

Hence, the tank will be filled in 30 hours

31. (e) $? = \sqrt{964} \times \sqrt{348}$

$\approx 31.05 \times 18.6 \approx 579$

32. (b) $? = 37.35 + 13.064 \times 3.46$

$\approx 37.35 + 13 \times 3.5$

$\approx 37.35 + 45.5 \approx 82.85 \approx 83$

33. (c) $? = (4863 + 1174 + 2829) \div 756$
$= 8866 \div 756 = 11.72 \approx 12$

34. (a) $? = \dfrac{54 \times 746}{32} = 1258.87 \approx 1259$

35. (d) $? = [(1.5)^2 \times (3.2)^2] \div 2.3$

$= \dfrac{2.25 \times 10.24}{2.3} \approx 10$

36. (a) na *pa* ka *so* → *birds* fly *very* high
ri *so* la *pa* → *birds* are *very* beautiful
ti me *ka* bo → the parrots could fly
Thus *high* is coded as *na.*

37. (b) 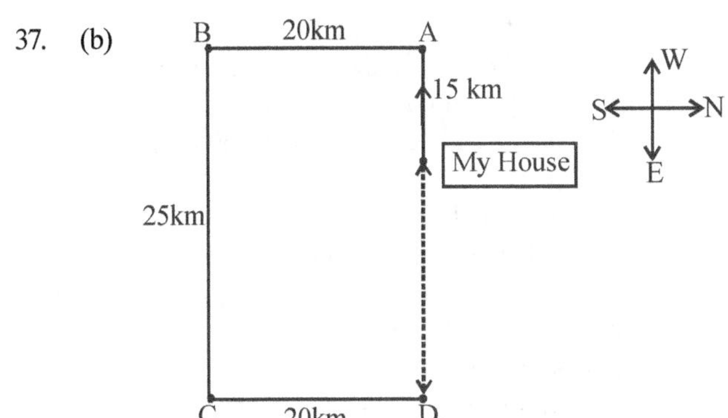

From the above diagram required distance
$= 25 - 15 = 10$ km.

38. (e) P S I C H O L A Z Y
0 1 2 3 4 5 6 7 8 9
875.50 = ZAO.OP

39. (b) Total no. of girls $= 17 + 10 - 1$ or $18 + 9 - 1 = 26$.

(40-41)

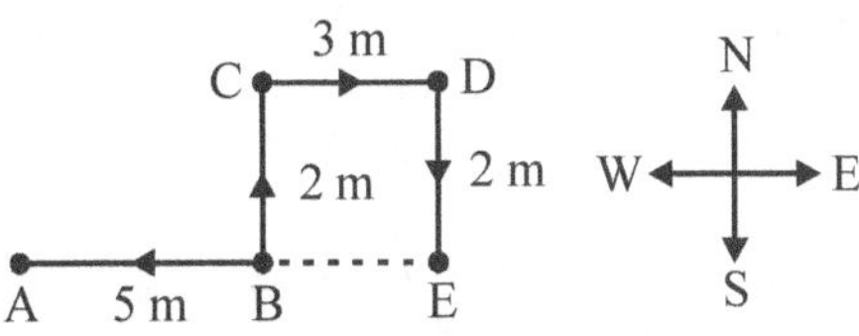

40. (d) Point C will covered by person first.

41. (a) Points A, B and E are in straight line.

(42-46)

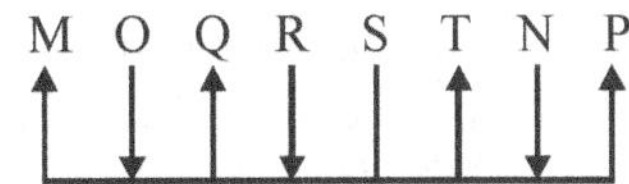

42. (b)
43. (a)
44. (c)
45. (a)
46. (d)

47. (a) 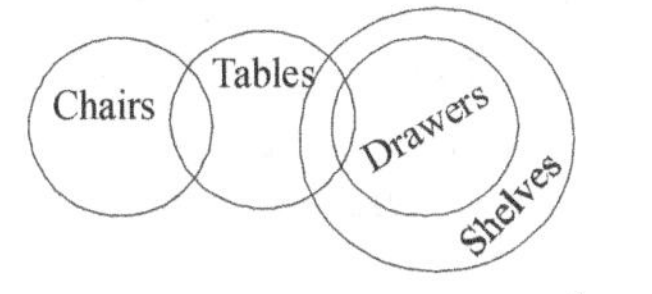

Hence conclusions I. ✓ II. ✗ III. ✓

48. (c) 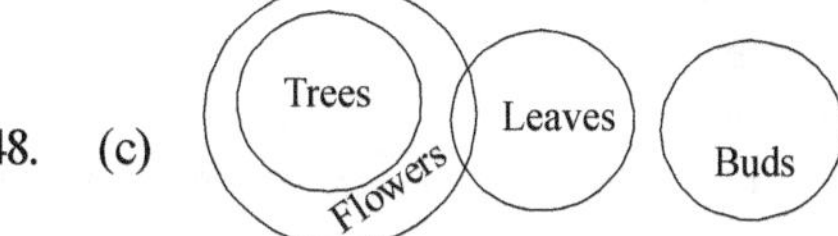

Hence conclusions I. ✗ II. ✗ III. ✗
But I and II are complementary pairs.

49. (e) 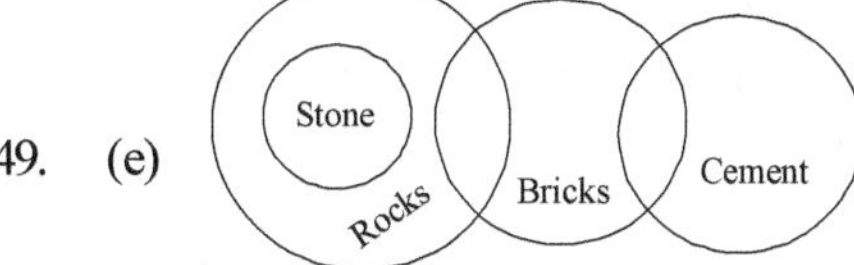

Hence conclusions I. ✗ II. ✗ III. ✗

50. (e) 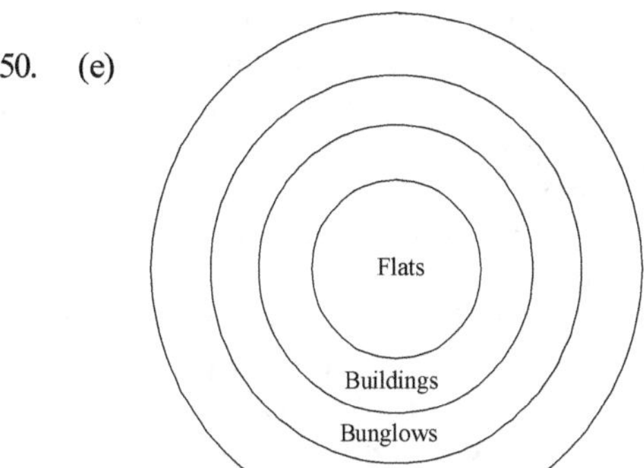

Hence conclusions I. ✓ II. ✓ III. ✓

51. (b) 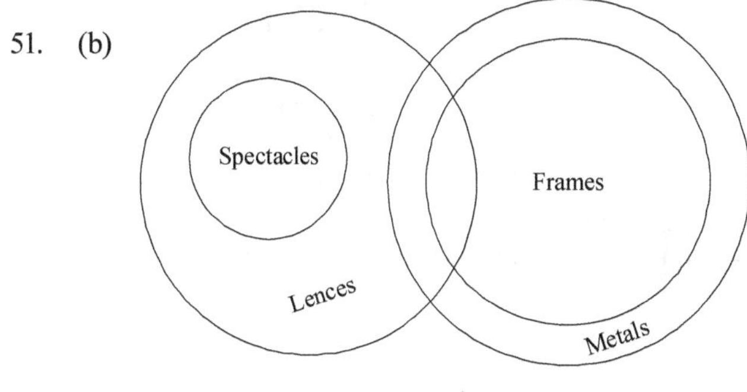

Hence conclusions I. ✓ II. ✗ III. ✗

(52-56)

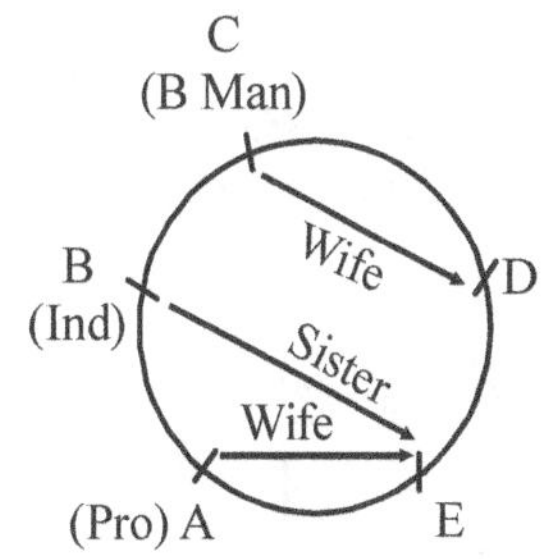

A, the professor is married to E and E is the sister of B.
The wife of the industrialist is D. The industrialist is seated
to the right of C. Thus, A and C cannot be industrialists.
Therefore, B is the industrialist and C is the business man.
Now, we come to the following deductions :

A – Professor   B – Industrialist
C – Businessman   D – Female, hence unemployed
E – Female, hence unemployed

52. (c) A is the husband of E and E is the sister of B. Hence, A is the brother-in-law of B.

53. (d) It cannot be determined, as no information has been provided in the paragraph about the sitting position of A.

54. (c) As deduced earlier, B is the industrialist.

55. (d) It cannot be determined whether the businessman is married or unmarried.

56. (b) As A is a professor, he must be a graduate.

57. (d) Other groups consist of consecutive elements.

58. (a) $2 + 2^2 + 8 + 5 + 6 + 0 + 9 + 9^2 + 0 + 3 = 118$

Where value of alphabet = 0; symbol = square of the previous number; number = the value itself.

59. (b) The letters used in the series are $B\ Q\ E\ R\ D\ U\ K\ A\ P$. Sum of the positions of consonants according to alphabet $= 2 + 17 + 18 + 4 + 11 + 16 = 68$. Similarly, sum of the vowels' positions $= 5 + 21 + 1 = 27$. Hence required difference $= 68 - 27 = 41$.

60. (e) First element of each group follows the order $+ 3, + 3, +3$... and so on.

Middle element and last element also follow the same trend. Hence (?) should be replaced by R 13.

61. (c) Number of elements between B and Q is the same as that between E and R. Similarly, number of elements between A and P is the same as that between K and A.

62. (c) $427 + 1 = 428, 581 + 1 = 582, 839 + 1 = 840$

$275 + 1 = 276, 589 + 1 = 590$

Second digit of the greatest number = 4

Second digit of the lowest number = 7

Subtract is $= 7 - 4 = 3$

63. (a) First and last digits are interchanged

$= 724, 185, 938, 572, 985$

$= 985, 938, 724, 572, 185$

Third highest number is $= 724 \Rightarrow 427$

64. (e) Second and third digits are interchanged

$= 472, 518, 893, 257, 598$

Second highest number is

$= 893, 598, 518, 472, 257$

$= 589$

65. (b) After subtract the numbers are $- 427 \Rightarrow 227$

$581 \Rightarrow 381, 839 \Rightarrow 639, 275 \Rightarrow 075, 589 \Rightarrow 389$

First and the third digits are interchanged

$= 722, 183, 936, 570, 983$

The lowest number is $= 183 \Rightarrow 581$

(66-70) :

Floor	Resident
7	G
6	F
5	E
4	A
3	C
2	D
1	B

66. (d) G is at topmost floor.

67. (c) C is immediately above D's floor.

68. (a) F – 6th floor; E – 5th floor
B – 1st floor; G – 7th floor
C – 3rd floor

69. (c) D lives on floor number 2.

70. (e) 5 people lives between floor F and B.
6th floor is an even digit number.

71. (b) a, c and d are stated in the third paragraph.

72. (d) Refer to the last line of the first paragraph, the second paragraph and the last line of the passage.

73. (c) Refer to the part it reminded the British vividly.

74. (a) Refer to the part it was supposedly for the good of the conquered.

75. (c) Refer to the part India would resist payment, and paralyze the war effort.

81. (b) Hampered - hinder or impede the movement or progress of.

82. (d) Enjoy - fits in the context correctly.

83. (a) Acceptable - fits in the context correctly.

84. (c) Authoritarian - favouring or enforcing strict obedience to authority at the expense of personal freedom.

85. (e) Means- fits in the context correctly.

86. (d) Pleased -fits in the context correctly.

87. (b) Curtail-reduce in extent or quantity; impose a restriction on.

88. (a) Consumes -fits in the context correctly.

89. (c) Thus -fits in the context correctly.

90. (e) Effective-fits in the context correctly.

91. (c) ABCE-'was also hampered' as the sentence is in past tense. Moreover, it's Simple past tense used in the statement.

92. (d) BCDE-'The Centre has informed the Delhi High Court' as in the given sentence 'The Centre'... is a singular subject, and there should be only perfect tense use in that.

93. (d) ABCE-'is also creating anger'-the statement is in present form of tense.

94. (a) ABCD-'justice will be delivered'-the complete sentence is in simple future tense.

95. (b) BCDE-'Tour operators in Mysuru, who have' as the sentence is in present form of tense.

96. (e) ABDE-'bat you could see' as the modal 'could' will take first form of verb after it.

97. (b) ACDE-'the limits of time and embedded' as the preceded part of the statement shows that the sentence is in perfect tense. Hence, the verb used should be in the third form .i.e. 'embedded'

98. (c) ABDE-'It is rather complex and tries to balance' as the whole sentence is in Simple present tense.

99. (a) ABDE-'It would be disastrous' will be the correct usage.

100. (e) ACDE-'notification would have opened' as the sentence is in complete future perfect tense. Thus, there will be no use of writing it in perfect continuous tense.

INSTRUCTIONS

- This Preliminary Exam practice set consists of three sections. Numerical Ability (Qs. 1-35), Reasoning (Qs. 36-70) and English Language (Qs. 71-100).
- All the questions are compulsory.
- Each question has five options, of which only one is correct. The candidates are advised to read all the options thoroughly.
- There is negative marking equivalent to 1/4th of the mark allotted to the specific question for wrong answer.

Time : 60 Minutes   **Max. Marks : 100**

NUMERICAL ABILITY

DIRECTIONS (Qs. 1-10): *What should come in place of the question mark (?) in the following questions?*

1. $8\dfrac{2}{5} \div 10\dfrac{2}{25} = ?$
   - (a) $\dfrac{5}{6}$
   - (b) $\dfrac{5}{7}$
   - (c) $\dfrac{4}{7}$
   - (d) $\dfrac{3}{5}$
   - (e) None of these

2. $6.4 \times ? = 361.6$
   - (a) 53.5
   - (b) 52.5
   - (c) 65.5
   - (d) 56.5
   - (e) None of these

3. 43% of 583 – ?% of 401 = 158.46
   - (a) 22
   - (b) 23
   - (c) 21
   - (d) 24
   - (e) None of these

4. $\dfrac{3}{5}$ of $\dfrac{3}{4}$ of $\dfrac{5}{6}$ of 992 = ?
   - (a) 382
   - (b) 392
   - (c) 372
   - (d) 362
   - (e) None of these

5. $69.2 \times 18.4 \times 4.5 = ?$
   - (a) 5729.76
   - (b) 5772.76
   - (c) 5779.76
   - (d) 5772.76
   - (e) None of these

6. $21.25 + 22.52 + 212.22 = ?$
   - (a) 256.99
   - (b) 245.99
   - (c) 253.99
   - (d) 255.99
   - (e) None of these

7. $123 \div 6 \div 0.8 = ?$
   - (a) 25.625
   - (b) 23.645
   - (c) 27.625
   - (d) 21.665
   - (e) None of these

8. $14^{13} \times 14^3 = ?$
   - (a) 14^{39}
   - (b) 14^7
   - (c) 14^{16}
   - (d) 16
   - (e) None of these

9. 87% of 565 = ?
   - (a) 490.55
   - (b) 491.55
   - (c) 489.55
   - (d) 491.35
   - (e) None of these

10. $1256 \div (32 \times 0.25) = ?$
    - (a) 167
    - (b) 154
    - (c) 165
    - (d) 157
    - (e) None of these

11. If the compound interest on a certain sum of money for 3 years at 10% p.a. be ₹ 993, what would be the simple interest?
    - (a) ₹ 800
    - (b) ₹ 950
    - (c) ₹ 900
    - (d) ₹ 1000
    - (e) None of these

12. Sohan got 54 marks in Hindi, 65 marks in Science, 89 marks in Maths, 69 marks in Social Science and 68 marks in English. The maximum marks of each subject are 100. How much overall percentage of marks did he get?
    - (a) 89
    - (b) 69
    - (c) 68
    - (d) 79
    - (e) None of these

13. How much water must be added to 100 cc of 80% solution of boric acid to reduce it to a 50% solution?
    (a) 20 cc   (b) 40 cc
    (c) 80 cc   (d) 60 cc
    (e) None of these

14. Successive discounts of 20% and 15% are equivalent to a single discount of
    (a) 35%   (b) 32%
    (c) 17.5%   (d) 22.5%
    (e) None of these

15. In how many different ways can the letters of the word FORMULATE be arranged ?
    (a) 81000   (b) 40320
    (c) 362880   (d) 3628280
    (e) None of these

16. Two cars start together in the same direction from the same place. The first goes with a uniform speed of 10 km/h. The second goes at a speed of 8 km/h in the first hour and increases its speed by $\frac{1}{2}$ km with each succeeding hour. After how many hours will the second car overtake the first one, if both go non-stop?
    (a) 9 hours   (b) 5 hours
    (c) 7 hours   (d) 8 hours
    (e) None of these

17. 24 men working 8 hours a day can finish a work in 10 days. Working at the rate of 10 hours a day, the number of men required to finish the same work in 6 days is
    (a) 30   (b) 32
    (c) 34   (d) 36
    (e) None of these

18. The sum of digits of a two digit number is 15. If 9 be added to the number, then the digits are reversed. The number is
    (a) 96   (b) 87
    (c) 78   (d) 69
    (e) None of these

19. Three cubes of a metal are of edges 3 cm, 4 cm and 5 cm. These are melted together and from the melted material, another cube is formed. The edge of this cube is
    (a) 8 cm   (b) 10 cm
    (c) 9 cm   (d) 6 cm
    (e) None of these

20. Yashika got married 8 years ago. Today her age is $1\frac{2}{7}$ times her age at the time of her marriage. At present her daughters age is one-sixth of her age. What was her daughter's age 3 years ago ?
    (a) 2 years   (b) 3 years
    (c) 4 years   (d) 5 years
    (e) None of these

21. Average age of 36 children of the class is 15 years. 12 more children joined whose average age is 16 years. What is the average age of all the 48 children together?
    (a) 15.25 years   (b) 15.5 years
    (c) 15.3 years   (d) 15.4 years
    (e) None of these

22. Profit earned by selling an article of ₹ 1,450 is same as the loss incurred by selling the article for ₹ 1,280. What is the cost price of the article?
    (a) ₹ 1,385   (b) ₹ 1,405
    (c) ₹ 1,355   (d) ₹ 1,365
    (e) None of these

23. Sonia started a business by investing ₹ 60000. Six months later Vivek joined her by investing ₹ 140000. After one year Kirti joined them by investing ₹ 120000. At the end of two years from the commencement of the business, they earn a profit of ₹ 450000. What is Vivek's share in the profit?
    (a) ₹ 195000   (b) ₹ 222500
    (c) ₹ 220000   (d) ₹ 210000
    (e) None of these

24. 6 years hence a father's age will be three times his son's age and three years ago father was nine times as old as his son. What is the present age of father?
    (a) 48 years   (b) 42 years
    (c) 36 years   (d) 30 years
    (e) None of these

25. The total cost of 12 apples and 8 guavas is ₹ 76 and the total cost of 8 apples and 12 guavas is ₹ 64. What is the total cost of one apple and one guava?
    (a) ₹ 5   (b) ₹ 7
    (c) ₹ 8   (d) ₹ 10
    (e) None of these

DIRECTIONS (Qs. 26-30) : *What will come in place of the question mark (?) in the following number series?*

26. 12, 14, 17, 13, 8, 14, 21, 13, 4 ?
    (a) 14   (b) 12
    (c) 16   (d) 20
    (e) None of these

27. 4, 6, 12, 30, 90, 315, ?
    (a) 1180   (b) 1160
    (c) 1260   (d) 1240
    (e) None of these

28. 25, 16, ?, 4, 1
    (a) 3   (b) 6
    (c) 9   (d) 7
    (e) None of these

29. 15, 12, 17, 10, ?, 8, 25, 6
    (a) 27   (b) 23
    (c) 21   (d) 19
    (e) None of these

30. 1, ?, 27, 64, 125
    (a) 8   (b) 10
    (c) 12   (d) 14
    (e) None of these

DIRECTIONS (Qs. 31-35): *Study the following table carefully and answer the questions given below it.*

Number of Students from Various
Schools Playing Various Games

Games	Schools				
	A	B	C	D	E
Football	125	250	100	175	250
Basketball	175	200	195	245	225
Cricket	250	200	225	215	200
Tennis	240	210	200	130	165
Badminton	75	125	55	45	100

31. If 20% of the students playing Football from School A also play Badminton, what would be the total number of students playing Badminton from School A?
    (a) 110   (b) 120
    (c) 95   (d) 100
    (e) None of these

32. The number of students palying Basketball from School C is approximately, what percent of the students playing Basketball from School E?
    (a) 75   (b) 87
    (c) 94   (d) 70
    (e) 81

33. What is the difference between the average number of students playing Cricket from all the schools and the average number of students playing Tennis from all the schools?
    (a) 31   (b) 26
    (c) 29   (d) 33
    (e) None of these

34. The number of students playing Football from School D is what percent of the total number of students playing all the given games from that school? (Rounded off to 2 digits after decimal.)
    (a) 20.61   (b) 21.60
    (c) 22.60   (d) 20.59
    (e) None of these

35. What is the difference between the average number of students palying all the given games from School B and the number of students playing Badminton from that school ?
    (a) 72   (b) 65
    (c) 78   (d) 69
    (e) None of these

REASONING ABILITY

DIRECTION (Qs. 36-37): *Read the following information carefully and answer the questions that follow.*

A, B, C and D live on floors 3 to 6 of the same six storeyed building. A lives on fourth floor. Only one person lives on the floor between A and B. C does not live on a floor above A's floor.

36. Who lives on a floor immediately above B's floor ?
    (a) A   (b) C
    (c) D   (d) A or C
    (e) B lives on top floor

37. Who lives on the fifth floor ?
    (a) A   (b) B
    (c) C   (d) D
    (e) None of these

38. Sunil walks towards the East from point A, turns right at point B and walks the same distance as he walked towards the East. He now turns left, walks the same distance again and finally makes a left turn and stops at point C after walking the same distance. The distance between A and C is how many times as that of A and B?
    (a) Cannot be determined   (b) Two
    (c) Three   (d) Four
    (e) None of these

DIRECTION (Qs. 39–40): *Read the following information carefully and answer the questions, which follow.*

If 'A – B' means 'A is father of B'.
If 'A + B' means 'A is daughter of B'.
If 'A ÷ B' means 'A is son of B'.
If 'A × B' means 'A is wife of B'.

39. In the expression 'P + Q × R' how is R related to P ?
    (a) Daughter   (b) Brother
    (c) Father   (d) Sister
    (e) None of these

40. In the expression 'P ÷ Q – T' how is T related to P?
    (a) Mother   (b) Sister
    (c) Brother   (d) Either brother or sister
    (e) None of these

DIRECTIONS (Qs. 41 - 45): *In each question below, there are three statements followed by two conclusions numbered I and II. You have to take the three given statements to be true even if they seem to be at variance from commonly known facts and then decide which of the given conclusions logically follows from the three statements disregarding commonly known facts.*

Give answer (a) if only conclusion I follows.
Give answer (b) if only conclusion II follows.
Give answer (c) if either I or II follows.
Give answer (d) if neither I nor II follows.
Give answer (e) if both I and II follow.

41. **Statements:** All shoes are pens.
    Some pens are razors.
    Some razors are desks.
    Conclusions:
    I. Some desks are shoes.
    II. Some razors are shoes.

42. **Statements:**
    Some benches are windows.
    Some windows are walls.
    Some walls are trains.
    Conclusions:
    I. Some trains are benches.
    II. No train is bench.

43. **Statements :**
    All brushes are chocolates.
    All chocolates are mirrors.
    All mirrors are tables.
    Conclusions:
    I.   Some tables are brushes
    II. Some mirrors are chocolates.
44. **Statements :**
    Some pencils are knives.
    All knives are papers.
    Some papers are books.
    Conclusions:
    I.   Some books are pencils.
    II. Some papers are pencils.
45. **Statements:**
    Some roofs are figures.
    All figures are lions.
    All lions are goats.
    Conclusions:
    I.   Some goats are roofs.
    II. All goats are figures

DIRECTIONS (Qs. 46-47) : *Study the following information carefully to answer the questions that follow.*

There are six persons A, B, C, D, E and F. C is the sister of F. B is the brother of E's husband. D is the father of A and grandfather of F. There are two fathers, three brothers and a mother in the group.

46. Who is the mother ?
    (a) A   (b) B
    (c) D   (d) E
    (e) None of these
47. Who is E's husband ?
    (a) B   (b) C
    (c) A   (d) F
    (e) None of these

DIRECTIONS (Qs. 48-50) : *These questions are based on five three-digit numbers given below.*

438,   285,   716,   342,   857

48. If '5' is added to each of the above five numbers, which of the following will be the middle digit of the lowest number ?
    (a) 0   (b) 4
    (c) 2   (d) 6
    (e) None of these
49. If '1' is added to the middle digit of each of the above number and '1' is subtracted from the first digit of each of the above numbers, which of the following will be the third digit of the second highest number ?
    (a) 8   (b) 6
    (c) 5   (d) 2
    (e) None of these
50. Which of the following is the sum of the second and the third digits of the highest number ?
    (a) 7   (b) 11
    (c) 12   (d) 13
    (e) None of these

DIRECTIONS (Qs. 51-55) : *Study the following information carefully to answer the given questions.*

Eight people L, M, N, O, P, Q, R and S are sitting around a circular table with equal distance
between each other but not necessarily in the same order. Some of them are facing the centre while some are facing outside.(i.e away from the centre)

*   M sits third to the left of L. Only three people sit between M and S. P sits to the immediate right of S.
*   Immediate neighbours of P face opposite directions(i.e. if one neighbour faces the centre then the other neighbour faces outside and vice-versa.) Only one person sit between P and O.
*   R sits second to the right of O. Both R and N face the same direction as S.(i.e if S faces the centre then R and N also faces the centre and vice-versa.)
*   Immediate neighbours of Q faces opposite directions(i.e if one neighbour faces the centre then the other neighbour faces outside and Vice-versa.)
*   P does not face outside. O faces a direction opposite to that of M.

51. How many people sit between L and Q when counted from the left of Q?
    (a) Five   (b) None
    (c) Four   (d) One
    (e) Two
52. Which of the following statements is true as per the given arrangement?
    (a) Q faces the centre
    (b) Only three people sit between P and L
    (c) R sits to the immediate right of N
    (d) None of the given options is true
    (e) N is an immediate neighbour of O
53. Who amongst the following sits third to the left of P?
    (a) Q   (b) N
    (c) M   (e) L
    (e) R
54. How many people face the centre as per the given arrangement?
    (a) Four   (b) One
    (c) Two   (d) Three
    (e) More than four
55. What will come in place of question mark (?) in the given series based on the positions as given in the arrangement? PS LR MP SM ?
    (a) ON   (b) SO
    (c) NQ   (d) OL
    (e) LS

DIRECTIONS (Qs. 56-60): *Study the following sequence carefully and answer the questions given below:*

M E 5 P B 2 A 7 K N 9 T R U 4 6 I J D F 1 Q 3 W 8 V I S Z

56. How many such numbers are there in the above sequence, each of which is both immediately preceded by and immediately followed by a consonant ?
    (a) None   (b) One
    (c) Two   (d) Three
    (e) More than three
57. If the order of the first twenty letters/numbrs in the above sequence is reversed and the remaining letters/numbers are kept unchanged, which of the following will be the fourteenth letter/number from the right end after the rearrangement?

(a) B (b) 6
(c) 2 (d) 1
(e) None of these

58. Which of the follwing letter/number is the eighth to the left of the nineteenth letter/number from the left end?
(a) N (b) T
(c) 1 (d) D
(e) None of these

59. Four of the following five are alike in a certain way with regard to their position in the above sequence and so form a group. Which is the one that **does not** belong to that group?
(a) WIQ (b) PAE
(c) NR7 (d) 4JR
(e) D16

60. How many such vowels are there in the above sequence, each of which is immediately preceded by a consonant and immediately followed by a vowel?
(a) None (b) One
(c) Two (d) Three
(e) More than three

DIRECTIONS (Qs. 61-65) : *Study the wing information carefully and answer the questions given below:*

A shopkeeper placed eight varieties of cloth pieces of different colours viz. brown, pink, green, white, blue, violet, black and yellow, in a row such that blue cloth is placed fifth from the left end. Green is placed to the extreme right. White cloth is to the second to the left of blue. Violet cloth is exactly in between blue and white. Black is sixth to the left of green and fourth to the left of brown. Pink is not the third to the right of violet.

61. Which colour cloth is placed fifth to the left of yellow?
(a) Violet (b) Brown
(c) Green (d) White
(e) None of these

62. Which of the following is definitely true?
(a) Green cloth is second to the right of yellow.
(b) White cloth is placed fifth to the left of brown.
(c) White cloth is placed exactly in between violet and black.
(d) Pink cloth occupies second position from the left end.
(e) All are true.

63. Which colour cloth is third to the left of Brown ?
(a) Yellow (b) Blue
(c) Green (d) White
(e) Pink

64. Which of the following is the correct position' of Yellow with respect to Pink?
(a) Sixth to the right (b) Sixth to the left
(c) Fifth to the right (d) Fourth to the left
(e) Fifth to the left

65. Which colour cloth is to the immediate right of Pink?
(a) White (b) Blue
(c) Black (d) Brown
(e) Green

DIRECTIONS (Qs. 66-70): Study the following information carefully and answer the questions carefully :

In a Public Sector Undertaking Township, there are five executives - Ambrish, Amit, Rohit, Manu and Tarun and they stay in five different flats, numbered 1 to 5.

1. Two of them play Cricket while the other three play different games viz. Football, Tennis and Chess.
2. One Cricket player and a Chess player stay in the third flat, whereas the other three stay in different flats, i.e. 2nd, 4th and 5th.
3. Two of these five players are mechanical engineers while the other three are quality inspector, design engineer, and power engineer respectively.
4. The chess player is the oldest in age while one of the cricket players, who plays at the national level, is the youngest in age.
5. The age of the other cricket player, who plays at the regional level, lies between the football player and the chess player.
6. Manu is a regional level player and stays in the 3rd flat while Tarun is a quality inspector and stays in the 5th flat.
7. The football player is a design engineer and stays in the 2nd Flat.
8. Amit is a power engineer and plays Chess while Ambrish is the mechanical engineer and plays Cricket at the national level.

66. Who stays in the 4th flat?
(a) Ambrish (b) Amit
(c) Rohit (d) Manu
(e) None of these

67. Which sport does Tarun play?
(a) Chess (b) Football
(c) Cricket (d) Tennis
(e) None of these

68. Who plays football?
(a) Ambrish (b) Amit
(c) Rohit (d) Manu
(e) None of these

69. Who stay in the same flat?
(a) Ambrish and Amit
(b) Maim and Tarun
(c) Amit and Manu
(d) Rohit and Tarun
(e) None of these

70. The Chess player is a:
(a) Power engineer
(b) Mechanical Engineer
(c) Design engineer
(d) Quality inspector
(e) None of these

ENGLISH LANGUAGE

DIRECTIONS (Qs. 71-80): *Read the following passage carefully and answer the questions given after the passage. Certain words/phrases have been printed in bold to help you locate them while answering some of the questions.*

The Global Nutrition Report (GNR) and India Health Report on Nutrition, 2015 (IHR), offer a critical analysis of the state of nutrition in India. The first report, the India Health Report: Nutrition 2015(IHR), provides easy-to-understand, State-wise data dashboards that give a comprehensive view of nutrition and its determinants. It looks at disparities in these outcomes and their multiple determinants across geographical regions, socio-economic classes, and demographic groups to help identify strategic choices for policy-making at the State level.

In turn, GNR assesses progress in reducing malnutrition for all 193 countries. It concludes that while India is on track to meeting only two of the eight global targets on nutrition, it has significantly improved its nutrition performance in the past 10 years. GNR notes that there has been a big increase in the number of countries on track to meet global nutrition targets, and encourages countries, including India, to establish specific and time-bound targets for malnutrition reduction that are consistent with the new Sustainable Development Goals. Together, these reports paint several pictures about India, a data-poor country. They portray one of great progress in improving nutrition across India; stunting among children, a marker of the most **persistent** types of malnutrition, has declined rapidly in the last ten years. And this decline has been faster than in many other countries. But as we dig deeper, there are **diverse** pictures about the life conditions of Indian children — positive stories about children's lives and futures in Goa, Kerala, Manipur and Tamil Nadu, but dismal ones in Bihar, Jharkhand and Uttar Pradesh. What cannot be debated is the reality of deep, systemic inequality; of inequality in the circumstances that children are born into, that they live and grow in. For those of us who are worried about India's economic growth, these are also pictures of inequality that point to how well these children will be able to contribute to India's economic growth and their own prosperity. Their poor nutrition stunts more than their bodies. It stunts their well-being, and, consequentially, that of their home States and their nation. Two other things, both related to inequality, stand out as well in the data. First, the data point to tremendous variability across States in delivering what should be universal, rights-based and already **mandated** health and nutrition services. For example, sample this for intra-State disparity. Food provided by the Integrated Child Development Services reaches barely 1 in 5 children in Uttar Pradesh but over 90 per cent in Odisha. Less than 33 per cent of children in Nagaland are fully immunised; in Goa, it is more than 90 per cent. Close to 80 per cent defecate in the open in Odisha; barely 2 per cent do so in Kerala. Why?

These are disparities across States that operate in the same national framework, and there is, let's face it, no good reason for this other than an inability or an unwillingness to invest in changing ground realities, for everyone and everywhere. This is not an insurmountable challenge and it's certainly an area where States can, if they want it, make dramatic change in short timeframes. Examples abound from within India. The data in the reports show that, clearly, the **imperative** for introspection, and looking within for solutions was never clearer. No child should go without basic health care, food security and things like water and a toilet. Indeed, no adult should either. No society should **condone** such inequalities in the basics. And no society has progressed without addressing these basics.

71. What are the disparities that states are facing in the national framework?
 I. Health and nutirition services
 II. Variable food services
 III. Inequality in education
 (a) III
 (b) II & III
 (c) I & II
 (d) I,II & III
 (e) None of the above

72. The Global Nutrition Report focuses mainly on the
 (a) Sustainable Development Goals
 (b) comprehensive view of nutrition and its determinants
 (c) India's economic growth
 (d) Intra-State variability
 (e) Progress in reducing malnutrition

73. Which of the following would be the suitable title?
 (a) State of nutrition in India
 (b) Global nutrition targets
 (c) Nutrition and its determinants
 (d) Progressive India
 (e) Inequality: A big challenge

74. According to author what is the biggest challenge that India is facing?
 (a) Reducing progress in malnutrition
 (b) Inability to invest in education and health services
 (c) unwillingness and inability to invest in basic facilities
 (d) High global nutrition targets
 (e) None of these

75. What is NOT TRUE according to the above passage?
 I. Food provided by ICDS reaches to only few children in UP.
 II. Nearly 80 percent defecate in the open in West bengal.
 III. Less than 33 percent children in Nagaland are immunised.
 (a) III & II
 (b) I,II & III
 (c) I & II
 (d) I & III
 (e) II only

DIRECTIONS (76-78): *Choose the word which is most OPPOSITE in meaning to the word printed in bold as used in the passage.*

---

76. **Persistent**
 (a) assiduous
 (b) unrelenting
 (c) interrupted
 (d) fixed
 (e) dogged

77. **Diverse**
 (a) varied
 (b) assorted
 (c) separate
 (d) similar
 (e) distant

78. **Mandate**
 (a) edict
 (b) bidding
 (c) order
 (d) abide
 (e) breach

DIRECTIONS (79- 80): *Choose the word which is most SIMILAR in meaning to the word printed in bold as used in the passage.*

---

79. **Imperative**
 (a) trivial
 (b) free
 (c) obligatory
 (d) avoidable
 (e) assured

80. **Condone**
 (a) condemn
 (b) forbid
 (c) regard
 (d) forgive
 (e) censure

DIRECTIONS (81-90): *In the following passage, some of the words have been left out, each of which is indicated by a number. Find the suitable word from the options given against each number and fill up the blanks with appropriate words to make the paragraph meaningfully complete.*

Everyone needs quality sleep every single night, but lifestyle ...(81)... and hurdles make sleep disorders more common than good sleep. This poor sleeping pattern has serious ...(82)... on our health, and the first thing we ...(83)... is unhealthy weight gain or weight loss, low concentration, and mood swings. If you have ...(84)... sleeping ...(85)... every day and this lack of sleep is ...(86)... your day to-day routine, then you may be suffering from one of the many (and most common) sleep disorders. You will be surprised to know that there are many more sleep disorders than just insomnia and sleep apnoea. There are ...(87)... sleep disorders and their ...(88)..., You should take proper ...(89)... before they take a ...(90)... on your life.

81. (a) cozen (b) choices
    (c) abjure (d) deter
    (e) rustic
82. (a) coerce (b) rampage
    (c) repercussions (d) rattle
    (e) assent
83. (a) covert (b) denounce
    (c) bleak (d) notice
    (e) point
84. (a) mutilate (b) trouble
    (c) rear (d) dismay
    (e) cozy
85. (a) utmost (b) in
    (c) for (d) at
    (e) almost
86. (a) glimmering (b) gamut
    (c) fortifying (d) affecting
    (e) cascading
87. (a) bland (b) copious
    (c) various (d) alternate
    (e) growing
88. (a) warning (b) symptoms
    (c) signs (d) indicia
    (e) indication
89. (a) treatment (b) healing
    (c) hubris (d) overt
    (e) regimen
90. (a) abject (b) toll
    (c) barge (d) muse
    (e) poised

DIRECTION (91-100): *In each of the questions given below, a sentence is given which is then divided into five parts out of which last part is correct. There are errors in three out of four remaining parts and therefore only one of the parts (other than the bold one) is correct. You must choose the grammatically correct part as your answer.*

91. Paddy and sugarcane are India's the most water-guzzling crops — using up over half(A)/ of the country's total irrigation water(B)/ resources — but procuring policies and(C)/ water and power subsidies are skews(D)/ **profitability and distorting crop decisions(E).**
    (a) D (b) B
    (c) C (d) A
    (e) None of these

92. As cancer therapy rely on increasing(A)/ the oxidative stress till(B)/ a critical point, the time of(C)/ internal rhythms in reactive-species(D)/ **production is crucial(E).**
    (a) A (b) B
    (c) C (d) D
    (e) None of these

93. By just change (A)/the timing to drug (B)/ administration, the researchers could (C)/ reprogrammed internal rhythms of(D)/ **reactive-species production(E).**
    (a) C (b) D
    (c) A (d) B
    (e) None of these

94. Such trade diversification for relatively less labour-intensive (A)/sectors to value-added industrial products (B)/would in turn leads to(C)/sustaining economic (D)/**growth and employment generation(E).**
    (a) A (b) C
    (c) B (d) D
    (e) None of these

95. Deeper regional integration require(A)/not only the dismantling (B)/ to border tariffs, but also (C)/the elimination to non-tariff (D)/**barriers such as poor infrastructure (E).**
    (a) D (b) A
    (c) B (d) C
    (e) None of these

96. But they could strived harder(A)/ to upheld democratic rights(B)/ and constitutional principles at home(C)/. That is critical in(D)/ **promote sustainable development(E).**
    (a) A (b) C
    (c) D (d) B
    (e) None of these

97. The agreement with Mehta was towards(A)/ 'partial assignment of the rights to made records(B)/ in gramophone and in talkies and no other(C)/ sound produced broadcast device' for a lump sum(D)/ **of Rs. 450 and a royalty of one anna per record sold(E).**
    (a) A (b) B
    (c) C (d) D
    (e) None of these

98. Parliament's recent approval in the redrawn(A)/ electoral constituencies has reinforce(B)/ allegations of gerrymandering (C)/ and unequal sizing to electoral districts(D)/ **to benefit the National Front(E).**
    (a) B (b) D
    (c) A (d) C
    (e) None of these

99. However, the journalistic community which questions(A)/ the wisdom of people who indulged(B)/ in whataboutery cannot taken comfort in(C)/ citing the instances to getting (D)/ **it right when someone points out a shortcoming (E).**
    (a) B (b) A
    (c) D (d) C
    (e) None of these

100. The past shaped the way we are(A)/ today — not only the world we grow out(B)/ in, where we struggled with(C)/ conflicts the seeds of whom(D)/ **were sown long ago(E).**
    (a) B (b) A
    (c) D (d) C
    (e) None of these

Answer Key

1	(a)	11	(c)	21	(a)	31	(d)	41	(d)	51	(c)	61	(e)	71	(c)	81	(b)	91	(b)
2	(d)	12	(b)	22	(d)	32	(b)	42	(c)	52	(a)	62	(c)	72	(e)	82	(c)	92	(d)
3	(b)	13	(d)	23	(d)	33	(c)	43	(e)	53	(c)	63	(d)	73	(a)	83	(d)	93	(a)
4	(c)	14	(b)	24	(d)	34	(b)	44	(b)	54	(d)	64	(a)	74	(c)	84	(b)	94	(c)
5	(a)	15	(c)	25	(b)	35	(a)	45	(a)	55	(a)	65	(c)	75	(e)	85	(e)	95	(c)
6	(d)	16	(a)	26	(a)	36	(e)	46	(d)	56	(e)	66	(a)	76	(c)	86	(d)	96	(b)
7	(a)	17	(b)	27	(c)	37	(c)	47	(c)	57	(a)	67	(d)	77	(d)	87	(c)	97	(a)
8	(c)	18	(c)	28	(c)	38	(b)	48	(e)	58	(e)	68	(c)	78	(e)	88	(b)	98	(d)
9	(b)	19	(d)	29	(c)	39	(c)	49	(b)	59	(e)	69	(c)	79	(c)	89	(a)	99	(b)
10	(d)	20	(b)	30	(a)	40	(d)	50	(c)	60	(a)	70	(a)	80	(d)	90	(b)	100	(b)

HINTS & EXPLANATIONS

1. (a) $? = 8\frac{2}{5} \div 10\frac{2}{25}$

$$= \frac{42}{5} \div \frac{252}{25} = \frac{42}{5} \times \frac{25}{252} = \frac{5}{6}$$

2. (d) $6.4 \times ? = 361.6$

$$\therefore ? = \frac{361.6}{6.4} = 56.5$$

3. (b) $583 \times \frac{43}{100} - 401 \times \frac{?}{100} = 158.46$

$$\Rightarrow 250.69 - 401 \times \frac{?}{100} = 158.46$$

$$\Rightarrow 401 \times \frac{?}{100} = 250.69 - 158.46 = 92.23$$

$$\therefore ? = \frac{92.23 \times 100}{401} = 23$$

4. (c) $? = 992 \times \frac{5}{6} \times \frac{3}{4} \times \frac{3}{5} = 372$

5. (a) $? = 69.2 \times 18.4 \times 4.5 = 5729.76$

6. (d) $? = 21.25 + 22.52 + 212.22 = 255.99$

7. (a) $? = \frac{123}{6 \times 0.8} = 25.625$

8. (c) $? = 14^{13} \times 14^3 = (14)^{13+3} = 14^{16}$

9. (b) $? = 565 \times \frac{87}{100} = 491.55$

10. (d) $? = 1256 \div (32 \times 0.25)$

$$= 1256 \div 8 = \frac{1256}{8} = 157$$

11. (c) Let Principal $= ₹ P$

$$P\left(1 + \frac{10}{100}\right)^3 - P = 993 \Rightarrow \left(\frac{11}{10} \times \frac{11}{10} \times \frac{11}{10} - 1\right)P = 993$$

$$\Rightarrow \left(\frac{1331 - 1000}{1000}\right)P = 993 \text{ or },$$

$$P = \frac{993 \times 1000}{331} = ₹3000$$

$$\therefore \text{ Simple interest} = ₹\left(\frac{3000 \times 3 \times 10}{100}\right) = ₹900$$

12. (b) Sohan's total marks

$$= 54 + 65 + 89 + 69 + 68 = 345$$

$$\therefore \text{ Required percent} = \frac{345}{500} \times 100 = 69$$

13. (d) Concentration of boric acid $= 80\% = 80$ cc
Quantity of water $= 20$ cc
Let x cc of water be added to get the concentration of 50%.

$$\Rightarrow \frac{80}{100 + x} = \frac{50}{100} \text{ or } \frac{80}{100 + x} = \frac{1}{2} \text{ or } x = 60 \text{ cc}$$

14. (b) Successive discounts of 20% and 15% on ₹ 100 yields to
$100 \times 0.8 \times 0.85 = ₹68$

$\therefore$ Single discount $= (100 - 68) = 32\%$

15. (c) The word FORMULATE consists of nine different letters. Hence, the required number of ways $= 9! = 362880$

16. (a) Let the second car overtakes the first car after t hours. Distance covered by the first car = Distance covered by the second car.

$$\Rightarrow 10\,t = 8 + \left(8 + \frac{1}{2}\right) + \left(8 + \frac{2}{2}\right) + \ldots + \left(8 + \frac{t-1}{2}\right)$$

$$\text{or } 10t = 8t + \frac{1}{2}[1 + 2 + \ldots + (t-1)]$$

$$\text{or } 10t = 8t + \frac{1}{2}\frac{t(t-1)}{2} \text{ or } 2t = \frac{1}{4}(t^2 - t)$$

$$\Rightarrow t = 9 \text{ hrs.} \quad [t \neq 0]$$

17. (b) $m_1 \times d_1 \times t_1 \times w_2 = m_2 \times d_2 \times t_2 \times w_1$

$24 \times 10 \times 8 \times 1 = m_2 \times 6 \times 10 \times 1$

$\Rightarrow m_2 = \dfrac{24 \times 10 \times 8}{6 \times 10} = 32 \, \text{men}$

18. (c) Let the two digit number be $10x + y$

We have $x + y = 15$ ....(i)

and $(10x + y) + 9 = (10y + x)$ or $9x - 9y = -9$

or $x - y = -1$ .... (ii)

From (i) and (ii) $x = 7$ and $y = 8$

The number is $10 \times 7 + 8 = 78$

19. (d) Let edge of the new cube $= x$ cm.

Volume of the newly formed figure (cube)

$=$ sum of volume of smaller cubes.

i.e. $(x)^3 = (3)^3 + (4)^3 + (5)^3 = 27 + 64 + 125 = 216 \Rightarrow x = 6 \, \text{cm}$

20. (b) Let present age of Yashika $= x$ years

$\therefore$ Age of Yashika at the time of marriage

$= (x - 8)$ years $\qquad x = \dfrac{9}{7}(x - 8)$

$\Rightarrow 7x = 9x - 72 \qquad \therefore x = \dfrac{72}{2} = 36$ years

$\therefore$ Present age of the daughter $= 36 \times \dfrac{1}{6} = 6$ years

$\therefore$ Her daughter's age 3 years ago $= (6 - 3) = 3$ years

21. (a) Required average age

$= \left(\dfrac{15 \times 36 + 12 \times 16}{36 + 12} \right)$ years $= \left(\dfrac{540 + 192}{48} \right)$ years

$= 15.25$ years.

22. (d) Let the CP of the article be ₹ x.

According to the question,

$1450 - x = x - 1280$

$\Rightarrow 2x = 1450 + 1280 = 2730$

$\Rightarrow x = \dfrac{2730}{2} = ₹ 1365$

23. (d) The ratio of profits of Sonia, Vivek and Kirti is as follows

$\quad$ Sonia $\qquad$ Vivek $\qquad$ Kirti

$60000 \times 24 : 140000 \times 18 : 120000 \times 12$

$\qquad 4 \quad : \quad 7 \quad : \quad 4$

Hence, the required share of Vivek

$= \dfrac{450000 \times 7}{(4 + 7 + 4)} = 30000 \times 7 = ₹ 210000$

24. (d) Let father's present age be x years and son's present age be y years

According to the question,

$(x + 6) = 3(y + 6) \Rightarrow x - 3y = 12$ ... (i)

$(x - 3) = 9(y - 3) \Rightarrow x - 9y = -24$ ... (ii)

Solving (i) and (ii), we get

$x = 30$ and $y = 6$

Hence, father's present age $= 30$ years

25. (b) Let the CP of an apple be ₹ x and that of a guava be ₹ y.

$\therefore 12x + 8y = 76$ ... (i)

$8x + 12y = 64$ ... (ii)

On adding (i) and (ii), we have

$20x + 20y = 140$

$\Rightarrow 20(x + y) = 140$

$\Rightarrow x + y = \dfrac{140}{20} = 7 = ₹ 7$

26. (a) The pattern of number series is as follow

$12 + 2 = 14$

$14 + 3 = 17$

$17 - 4 = 13$

$13 - 5 = 8$

$8 + 6 = 14$

$14 + 7 = 21$

$21 - 8 = 13$

$13 - 9 = 4$

$4 + 10 = \boxed{14}$

27. (c) The pattern of number series is as follow

$4 \times 1.5 = 6$

$6 \times 2 = 12$

$12 \times 2.5 = 30$

$30 \times 3 = 90$

$90 \times 3.5 = 315$

$315 \times 4 = \boxed{1260}$

28. (c) The pattern of number series is as follow

$25 \quad 16 \quad \boxed{9} \quad 4 \quad 1$

$\downarrow \quad \downarrow \quad \downarrow \quad \downarrow$

$5^2 \quad 4^2 \quad 3^2 \quad 2^2 \quad 1^2$

$\therefore \quad ? = 9$

29. (c) The pattern of number series is as follow

$15 - 3 = 12$

$12 + 5 = 17$

$17 - 7 = 10$

$10 + 11 = \boxed{21} \quad 21 - 13 = 8$

$8 + 17 = 25 \quad 25 - 19 = 6$

Note 3, 5, 7, 11, 13, 17 and 19 are consecutive prime numbers.

30. (a) The pattern of number series is as follow

$1 \quad \boxed{8} \quad 27 \quad 64 \quad 125$

$\downarrow \downarrow \downarrow \quad \downarrow \quad \downarrow$

$1^3 \quad 2^3 \quad 3^3 \quad 4^3 \quad 5^3$

$\therefore \quad ? = 2^3 = 8$

31. (d) Total number of students playing Badminton from

School A $= 75 + 125 \times \dfrac{20}{100} = 100$

32. (b) The required percent

$= \dfrac{195 \times 100}{225} = \dfrac{195 \times 4}{9} = 86.67\% \approx 87\%$

33. (c) The required difference

$$(250-240)+(200-210)+(225-200)+$$

$$=\frac{(215-130)+(200-165)}{5}$$

$$=\frac{10-10+25+85+35}{5}=\frac{145}{5}=29$$

34. (b) The required percent

$$=\frac{175}{(175+245+215+130+45)}\times100$$

$$=\frac{175}{810}\times100\approx21.60$$

35. (a) Average number of students palying all the given games from School B

$$=\frac{250+200+200+210+125}{5}=\frac{985}{5}=197$$

The number of students playing Badminton is School B = 125

The required difference = 197 − 125 = 72

Sol. (36-39) :

6	B
5	D
4	A
3	C

36. (e) **37.** (c) **38.** (b)

39. (c) P is daughter of Q.

Q is wife of R.

Thus, R is husband of Q, then P is son of R.

40. (d) P is son of Q

Q is father of T.

Thus, T and P is son or daughter of Q.

41. (d) All shoes are pens. (A-type)

Some pens are razors. (I-type)

A + I ⇒ No Conclusion

42. (c) All the three Premises are Particular Affirmative (I-type).

No Conclusion follows from Particular Premises.

Conclusion I and II from Complementary Pair.

Therefore, either I or II follows

43. (e) All brushes are chocolates. (A-type)

All chocolates are mirrors. (A-type)

A + A ⇒ A-type Conclusion

"All brushes are mirrors"

All biushes are mirrors. (A-type)

All mirrors are tables. (A-type)

"All brushes are tables"

Conclusion I is converse of this Conclusion.

Conclusion II is converse of the second Premise.

44. (b) Some pencils are knives. (I-type)

All knives are papers. (A-type

I + A ⇒ I-type Conclusion

"Some pencils are papers"

Conclusion II is converse of this Conclusion.

45. (a) Some roofs are figure. (I-type)

All figures are lions. (A-type)

I + A ⇒ I-type Conclusion

"Some roofs are lions."

Some roofs are lion. (I-type)

All lions are goats. (A-type)

I + A ⇒ I-(A-type) Conclusion

"Some roofs are goats"

Conclusion I is converse of this Conclusion.

Sol. (46-47) :

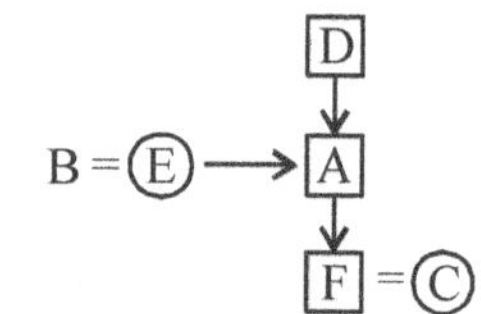

46. (d) A's wife E is the mother.

47. (c) A is the husband of E.

48. (e) On adding 5 to each of the above number.

443 290 721 347 862

∴ The lowest number is 290 where middle digit is 9.

49. (b) 438 → 348,

285 → 195,

716 → 626,

342 → 252,

and 857 → 767

The second highest number is 626 whose third digit is 6.

50. (c) The second and the third digits of 857 are 5 and 7, respectively.

∴ 5 + 7 = 12

(51-55) :

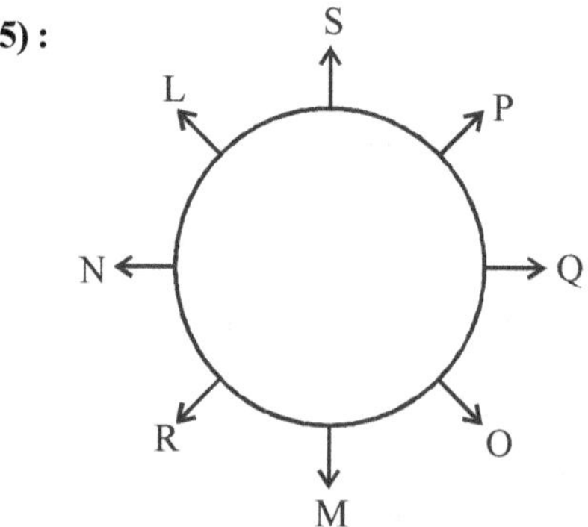

51. (c) **52.** (a) **53.** (c) **54.** (d) **55.** (a)

56. (e) Four

M E 5 P B 2 A 7 K N 9 T R U 4 6 I J D F 1 Q 3 W 8 V I S Z

57. (a) F D J I 6 4 U R T 9 N K 7 A 2 B P 5 E M 1 Q 3 W 8 V I S Z

58. (e) Eighth to the left of the nineteenth letter/number from the left $\Rightarrow$ (19 – 8=) 11th letter/number from left. Hence, required element is 9.

59. (e) Except it second element in each group is third to the right of first element while third element of each group is second to the left of first element of the respective group.

60. (a) There are no such vowels.

Sol. (61-65) :

L E F T	Pink	Black	White	Violet	Blue	Brown	Yellow	Green	R I G H T

61. (e) Black colour cloth is placed fifth to the left of Yellow colour cloth.

62. (c) White cloth is placed exactly in between Violet and Black.

63. (d) White cloth is third to the left of Brown.

64. (a) yellow is sixth to the right of Pink.

65. (c) Black is to the immediate right of Pink.

Sol. (66–70) :

From the above information, we can make a table for this

1. From 7, the football player lives in the second flat and he is a design engineer

2. From 6 and 2, the chess player and cricketer lives in the third flat

3. From 7, Amit is a chess player and a power engineer

4. From 6, Tarun is Quality Inspector

5. As both the cricketers are left (and we have not decided their professions), according to statement three, they both are Mechanical Engineers

6. From 6, Manu and Ambrish are cricketers (regional and national respectively)

7. Lastly, one name of Football player and one game name which is played by Tarun is left. From the information above, the football player's name has to be Rohit and tennis is played by Tarun (these were the only pieces of information missing).

Game	Profession	Name	Flat number
Tenis	Quality Inspector	Tarun	5
Cricketer (National)	Mechanical Engg	Ambrish	4
Chess	Power Engg.	Amit	3
Cricket (regional)	Mechanical Engg.	Manu	3
Football	Design Engg.	Rohit	2

66. (a)
67. (d)
68. (c)
69. (c)
70. (a)
81. (b) 'choices' is correct word.
82. (c) repercussion-an unintended consequence of an event or action, especially an unwelcome one.

83. (d) 'notice' is correct word.
84. (b) 'trouble' is correct word.
85. (e) 'almost' is correct word.
86. (d) 'affecting' is correct word.
87. (c) 'various' is correct word.
88. (b) 'symptoms' is correct word.
89. (a) 'treatment' is correct word.
90. (b) 'toll' is correct word.

91. (b) Paddy and sugarcane are India's most water-guzzling crops—using up over half of the country's total irrigation water resources — but procurement policies and water and power subsidies are skewing profitability and distorting crop decisions.
Part (A): 'the' will be removed as here, we are talking about the India's most water-guzzling crops **Part (C):** noun **'procurement'** will replace the verb **'procuring'** **Part (D): 'skews'** will be replaced by **'skewing'**
Thus, option **(b)** is the correct alternative.

92. (d) As cancer therapy relies on increasing the oxidative stress beyond a critical point, the timing of internal rhythms in reactive-species production is crucial.
Part (A): 'relies' will replace the **'rely'**
Part (B): 'till' will replace the **'beyond'**
Part (C): 'timing' will replace the **'time'**
Thus, option **(d)** is the correct alternative.

93. (a) By just changing the timing of drug administration, the researchers could reprogram internal rhythms of reactive-species production.
Part (A): 'changing' will replace the **'change'**
Part (B): preposition **'to'** will get replaced by **'of'**
Part (D): 'reprogrammed' will replace **'reprogramme'**
Thus, option **(c)** is the correct alternative.

94. (c) Such trade diversification from relatively less labour-intensive sectors to value-added industrial products would in turn lead to sustained economic growth and employment generation. **Part (A): 'from'** will replace **'for'**
Part (C): 'lead' will replace **'leads'**
Part (D): 'sustained' will change to **'sustaining'**
Thus, option **(b)** is the correct alternative.

95. (c) Deeper regional integration requires not only the dismantling of border tariffs, but also the elimination of non-tariff barriers such as poor infrastructure.
Part (A): 'require' will get replaced by **'requires'**
Part (C): 'of' will replace **'to'**
Part (D): 'of' will replace **'to'**
Thus, option **(b)** is the correct alternative.

96. (b) But they could strive harder to uphold democratic rights and constitutional principles at home. That is critical to promote sustainable development.
Part (A): 'strive' will replace **'strived'**
Part (B): 'uphold' will replace **'upheld'**
Part (D): 'to' will replace **'in'**
Thus, option **(c)** is the correct alternative.

97. (a) The agreement with Mehta was towards 'partial assignment of the rights to make records in gramophone and in talkies and any other sound producing broadcast device' for a lump sum of Rs. 450 and a royalty of one anna per record sold.

   Part (B): 'made' will replace **'make'**

   Part (C): 'any' will replace **'no'**

   Part (D): 'producing' will replace **'produced'**

   Thus, option **(a)** is the correct alternative.

98. (d) Parliament's recent approval of the redrawn electoral constituencies has reinforced allegations of gerrymandering and unequal sizing of electoral districts to benefit the National Front.

   Part (A): 'of' will replace **'in'** Part

   (B): 'reinforced' will replace **'reinforce'** Part

   (D): 'of' will replace **'to'**

   Thus, option **(c)** is the correct alternative.

99. (b) However, the journalistic community which questions the wisdom of people who indulge in whataboutery cannot take comfort in citing the instances of getting it right when someone points out a shortcoming.

   Part (B): 'indulge' will replace **'indulge'**

   Part (C): 'take' will replace **'taken'**

   Part (D): 'of' will replace **'to'**

   Thus, option **(a)** is the correct alternative.

100. (b) The past shaped the way we are today — not only the world we grow up in, where we struggle with conflicts the seeds of which were sown long ago.

   Part (B): 'up' will replace **'out'**

   Part (C): 'struggle' will replace **'struggled'**

   Part (D): 'which' will replace **'whom'**

   Thus, option **(a)** is the correct alternative.

PRACTICE SET 8

Time : 60 Minutes   **Max. Marks : 100**

NUMERICAL ABILITY

DIRECTIONS (Qs. 1-5) : *What should come in place of the question mark (?) in the following questions?*

1. $(3158 + 4602 + ?) \div 39 = 347$
   - (a) 5783
   - (b) 5883
   - (c) 5773
   - (d) 5713
   - (e) None of these

2. $(0.08\% \text{ of } 363 + 0.6\% \text{ of } 241) \times 500 = ?$
   - (a) 846.2
   - (b) 868.2
   - (c) 886.2
   - (d) 86.82
   - (e) None of these

3. $555 \times 444 = ?$
   - (a) 246020
   - (b) 246420
   - (c) 248420
   - (d) 242420
   - (e) None of these

4. $\sqrt[3]{328509} = ?$
   - (a) 73
   - (b) 59
   - (c) 63
   - (d) 69
   - (e) None of these

5. $(47045 \div 9.7) + (2035 \div 3.7) = ?$
   - (a) 5400
   - (b) 5800
   - (c) 5600
   - (d) 5900
   - (e) None of these

DIRECTIONS (Qs. 6-10): *What should come in place of the question mark (?) in the following questions ?*

6. $(786 \times 64) \div 48 = ?$
   - (a) 1050
   - (b) 1024
   - (c) 1048
   - (d) 1036
   - (e) None of these

7. $\sqrt[3]{13824} \times \sqrt{?} = 864$
   - (a) 1296
   - (b) 1156
   - (c) 1600
   - (d) 1024
   - (e) None of these

8. $60\% \text{ of } 20\% \text{ of } \dfrac{3}{5} \text{ th of } ? = 450$
   - (a) 6200
   - (b) 6,240
   - (c) 6150
   - (d) 6275
   - (e) None of these

9. $196 \times 948 \div 158 = ?$
   - (a) 1156
   - (b) 1200
   - (c) 1188
   - (d) 1176
   - (e) None of these

10. $3.5 + 11.25 \times 4.5 - 32.5 = ?$
    - (a) 18.275
    - (b) 21.625
    - (c) 32.375
    - (d) 25.45
    - (e) None of these

DIRECTIONS (Qs. 11-15) : *What should come in place of question mark (?) in the following number series?*

11. 121 117 108 92 67 ?
    - (a) 31
    - (b) 29
    - (c) 41
    - (d) 37
    - (e) None of these

12. 50 26 14 ? 5 3.5
    - (a) 6
    - (b) 8
    - (c) 10
    - (d) 12
    - (e) None of these

13. 3 23 43 ? 83 103
    - (a) 33
    - (b) 53
    - (c) 63
    - (d) 73
    - (e) None of these

14. 748 737 715 682 638 ?
    (a) 594   (b) 572
    (c) 581   (d) 563
    (e) None of these

15. 1 9 25 49 81 ? 169
    (a) 100   (b) 64
    (c) 81   (d) 121
    (e) None of these

16. The ratio of ducks and frogs in a pond is 37 : 39 respectively. The average number of ducks and frogs in the pond is 152. What is the number of frogs in the pond?
    (a) 148   (b) 152
    (c) 156   (d) 144
    (e) None of these

17. The number of employees in Companies A, B and C are in a ratio of 4 : 5 : 6 respectively. If the number of employees in the Companies is increased by 25%, 30% and 50% respectively, what will be the new ratio of employees working in Companies A, B and C respectively?
    (a) 13 : 10 : 18   (b) 10 : 13 : 17
    (c) 13 : 15 : 18   (d) Cannot be determined
    (e) None of these

18. The average of five positive numbers is 213. The average of the first two numbers is 233.5 and the average of last two numbers is 271. What is the third number?
    (a) 64   (b) 56
    (c) 106   (d) Cannot be determined
    (e) None of these

19. Ravi borrowed some money at the rate of 4% per annum for the first 3yr, at the rate of 8% per annum for the next 2 yr and at the rate of 9% per annum for the period beyond 5 yr. If he pays a total simple interest of ₹19550 at the end of 7 yr, how much money did he borrow?
    (a) ₹39,500   (b) ₹42,500
    (c) ₹41,500   (d) ₹43,500
    (e) None of these

20. What **approximate** amount of compound interest can be obtained on an amount of ₹ 9, 650 at the rate of 6% p.a. at the end of 3 years?
    (a) ₹1,737   (b) ₹1,920
    (c) ₹1,720   (d) ₹1, 860
    (e) ₹1,843

21. A milkman sells 120 litres of milk for ₹ 3,360 and he sells 240 litres of milk for Rs. 6,120. How much concession does the trader give per litre of milk, when he sells 240 litres of milk?
    (a) ₹2   (b) ₹3.5
    (c) ₹2.5   (d) ₹1.5
    (e) None of these

22. When 3,626 is divided by the square of a number and the answer so obtained is multiplied by 32, the final answer obtained is 2,368. What is the number?
    (a) 7   (b) 36
    (c) 49   (d) 6
    (e) None of these

23. A hall of breadth 4 m and length 6 m is to be renovated by replacing old mosaic tiles. How many square tiles each of 25 cm length and breadth will be required?
    (a) 960   (b) 384
    (c) 320   (d) 480
    (e) None of these

24. A car runs at the speed of 50 kmph, when not serviced and runs at 60 kmph, when serviced. After servicing the car covers a certain distance in 6 hours. How much time will the car take to cover the same distance when not serviced ?
    (a) 8.2 hours   (b) 6.5 hours
    (c) 8 hours   (d) 7.2 hours
    (e) None of these

25. Venkat has some ducks and some sheep. If the total number of animal heads is 81 and the total number of animal feet are 268, how many sheep does Venkat have?
    (a) 28   (b) 53
    (c) 44   (d) Cannot be determined
    (e) None of these

26. 10 years ago, Ram was 5 times as old as Shyam but 20 years later from now he will be only twice as old as Shyam. How many years old is Shyam?
    (a) 20 years   (b) 30 years
    (c) 40 years   (d) 50 years
    (e) None of these

27. 25 shirt pieces of 125 cms. each can be cut from a reel of cloth. After cutting these pieces 90 cms. of cloth remains. What is the length of the reel of cloth in metres?
    (a) 3215 metres   (b) 35.15 metres
    (c) 32.15 metres   (d) 3515 metres
    (e) None of these

28. The profit earned after selling a pair of shoes for ₹ 2,033 is the same as loss incurred after selling the same pair of shoes for ₹ 1,063. What is the cost of the shoes?
    (a) ₹1,650   (b) ₹1,548
    (c) ₹1,532   (d) Cannot be determined
    (e) None of these

29. 56 men can complete a piece of works in 24 days. In how many days can 42 men complete the same piece of work?
    (a) 52   (b) 32
    (c) 42   (d) 48
    (e) None of these

30. An urn contains 4 green and 7 blue marbles. If three marbles are picked at random, what is the proability that only two of them are blue?
    (a) $\dfrac{28}{44}$ (b) $\dfrac{21}{53}$
    (c) $\dfrac{28}{55}$ (d) $\dfrac{11}{28}$
    (e) None of these

DIRECTIONS (Qs. 31-35) : *Study the following graph carefully and answer the questions that follow:*

The graph given below represents the number of users of two broadband services A and B across 5 cities P, Q, R, S and T.

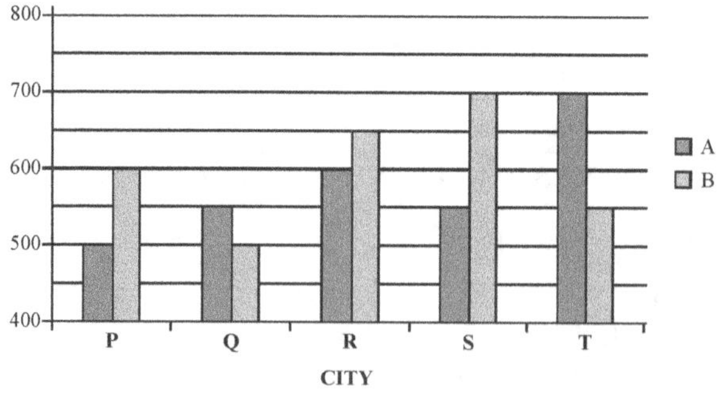

31. What is the total number of users of brand B across all five cities together?
    (a) 2700   (b) 3000
    (c) 3100   (d) 2900
    (e) 3200

32. The number of users of brand A in city T is what percent of the number of users of brand B in City Q?
    (a) 150   (b) 110
    (c) 140   (d) 160
    (e) 120

33. What is the average number of users of brand A across all five cities together?
    (a) 560   (b) 570
    (c) 580   (d) 590
    (e) 550

34. What is the difference between the total number of users of Brand A and B together in city R and the total number of users of brand A and B together in city P?
    (a) 170   (b) 140
    (c) 130   (d) 150
    (e) 160

35. What is the respective ratio of the number of users of brand A in city P to the number of users of brand B in city S?
    (a) 5 : 7   (b) 4 : 7
    (c) 2 : 5   (d) 3 : 4
    (e) 5 : 6

REASONING ABILITY

DIRECTIONS (Qs. 36-40) : *In each of the questions below are given three statements followed by four conclusions numbered I, II, III and IV. You have to take the given statements to be true even if they seem to be at variance with commonly known facts. Read all the conclusions and then decide which of the given conclusions logically follows from the given statements disregarding commonly known facts.*

36. **Statements :** All books are notes.
    Some notes are pencils.
    No pencil is paper.
    Conclusions : I. Some notes are books.
    II. Some pencils are books.
    III. Some books are papers.
    IV. No book is a paper.
    (a) Only I and either III or IV follow
    (b) Either III or IV follows
    (c) Only I and III follow
    (d) Neither II nor III follows
    (e) None of these

37. **Statements :** Some tables are chairs.
    No cupboard is table.
    Some chairs are cupboards.
    Conclusions : I. Some chairs are not tables.
    II. All chairs are either tables or cupboards.
    III. Some chairs are tables.
    IV. All chairs are tables.
    (a) Only I and IV follow
    (b) Only either II or III follows
    (c) Only I and III follows
    (d) Either II or III and I follow
    (e) None of these

38. **Statements :** No table is fruit.
    No fruit is window.
    All windows are chairs.
    Conclusions : I. No window is table.
    II. No chair is fruit.
    III. No chair is table.
    IV. All chairs are windows.
    (a) Either I or III follows   (b) All follow
    (c) Only I and II follow   (d) Only III and IV follow
    (e) None of these

39. **Statements :** No man is sky.
    No sky is road.
    Some men are roads.
    Conclusions : I. No road is man.
    II. No road is sky.
    III. Some skies are men.
    IV. All roads are men.
    (a) Either I or IV follows   (b) Only I follows
    (c) Only I and III follow   (d) Only II follows
    (e) None of these

40. **Statements :** All papers are books.
    All bags are books.
    Some purses are bags.
    Conclusions : I. Some papers are bags.
    II. Some books are papers.
    III. Some books are purses.
    (a) Only I follows
    (b) Only II and III follow
    (c) Only I and III follow
    (d) Only I and II follow
    (e) None of these

DIRECTIONS (41-45): *Study the following information carefully and answer the questions given below:*

Ten persons are sitting in two parallel rows containing five people each, in such a way that there is equal distance between adjacent persons. In row-1, A, B, C, D and E are seated (but not necessarily in the same order) and all of them are facing north. In row-2, L, M, N, O and P are seated (but not necessarily in the same order) and all of them are facing south. Therefore, in the given seating arrangement each member seated in a row faces another member of the other row. B sits second to the right of D. The person facing B sits to the immediate left of N. L sits second to the right of N. Only two persons sit between L and P. E is not an immediate neighbour of D. O does not face E. C neither faces N nor sits at an extreme end of the line.

41. Which of the following statements is **TRUE** regarding O?
    (a) L sits to the immediate left of O.
    (b) Only three persons sit between P and O.
    (c) O sits exactly in the middle of the row.
    (d) O faces one of the immediate neighbours of B.
    (e) None of the given statements is true.

42. Who amongst the following is facing A?
    (a) L   (b) M
    (c) O   (d) P
    (e) N

43. Who amongst the following is facing M?
    (a) E   (b) A
    (c) D   (d) B
    (e) C

44. Four of the following five are alike in a certain way based on the given arrangement and hence form a group. Which is the one that does not belong to the group?
    (a) NO   (b) CE
    (c) AB   (d) PO
    (e) ML

45. What is the position of C with respect to B?
    (a) Second to the left   (b) Third to the left
    (c) Immediate left   (d) Immediate right
    (e) Second to the right

DIRECTIONS (Qs. 46-50): *Study the following information Carefully to answer the given questions*

Eight Children P, Q, R, S, T, U, V and W are playing musical chairs. All of them are sitting on eight different chairs which are kept in a circle and face away from the centre. Four of them are wooden Chairs and four are plastic chairs.
- U sits second to the left of W and both of them sits on different types of chair. V sits second to the left of R and both sit on the same type of chair.
- T is on a wooden chair but opposite to U. Q and S are immediate neighbours of U.
- P does not sits on a wooden chair and the child who sits opposite to P does not sit on the same type of chair.
- The child who is an immediate neighbour of W and T sits on a plastic chair.

46. Who among the following sits opposite to R ?
    (a) R   (b) P
    (c) U   (d) Q
    (e) Can't be determined

47. Who among the following sits third to the right of V ?
    (a) P   (b) Q
    (c) S   (d) U
    (e) None of these

48. Which of the following children sit on the plastic chairs ?
    (a) QSTW   (b) QRTS
    (c) PRUV   (d) PWUT
    (e) None of these

49. Which of the following does not belong to the group ?
    (a) WV   (b) TR
    (c) PV   (d) QU
    (e) None of these

50. If Q is sits between W and U then who among the following sits third to the right of S ?
    (a) U   (b) P
    (c) W   (d) V
    (e) None of these

DIRECTIONS (Qs. 51-55): *Answer these questions referring to the symbol-letter-number sequence given below:*

E G 4 B H 7 5 @ K 8 D N £ Q Z $ W 3 C 1 9 * 1 B 2 S 6

51. How many such consonants are there in the above sequence which are immediately preceded by a symbol and immediately followed by a digit ?

    (a) One   (b) Two
    (c) None   (d) Three
    (e) More than three

52. What should come in place of the question mark (?) in the following sequence ?
    4H@, KDQ, ?, ILS
    (a) ZW1   (b) NQ$
    (c) @8N   (d) $W9
    (e) None of these

53. Which of the following is exactly in the midway between the ninth from left end and the seventh from right end ?
    (a) Q   (b) Z
    (c) $ (d) W
    (e) None of these

54. If the first fifteen elements are written in the reverse order then which of the following will be seventh to the left of twelfth element from right end ?
    (a) 7   (b) @
    (c) 5   (d) K
    (e) None of these

55. How many such digits are there in the above sequence which are immediately preceded as well as followed by digits ?
    (a) None   (b) One
    (c) Two   (d) Three
    (e) None of these

DIRECTIONS (Qs. 56-58) : *Study the following information carefully to answer the given questions.*

Each of the six friends A, B, C, D, E and F scored different marks in an examination. C scored more than only A and E. D scores less than only B. E did not score the least. The one who scores the third highest marks scored 81 marks. E scored 62 marks.

56. Which of the following could possibly be C's score?
    (a) 70   (b) 94
    (c) 86   (d) 61
    (e) 81

57. Which of the following is true with respect to given information?
    (a) D's score was definitely less than 60
    (b) F scored the maximum marks
    (c) Only two people scored more than C
    (d) There is a possibility that B scored 79 marks
    (e) None of these is true

58. The person who scored the maximum, scored 13 marks more than F's marks. Which of the following can be D's score?
    (a) 94   (b) 60
    (c) 89   (d) 78
    (e) 81

DIRECTIONS (Qs. 59-61): *Study the following information carefully to answer the given questions.*

In a certain code 'colours of the sky' is written as 'ki la fa so', 'rainbow colours' is written as 'ro ki' and 'sky high rocker' is written as 'la pe jo' and 'the rocks world' is written as 'pe so ne'.

59. Which of the following is the code for 'colours sky high'?
    (a) ro jo la   (b) fa la jo
    (c) la ki jo   (d) ki jo la
    (e) fa ki fo

60. Which of the following will/may represent 'the'?
    (a) Only fa   (b) Only la
    (c) Only so   (d) Either (a) or (b)
    (e) Either (a) or (c)

61. Which does 'pe' represent in the code?
    (a) colours   (b) sky
    (c) high   (d) rainbow
    (e) rocket

DIRECTIONS (Qs. 62-63): *Read the following information to answer the question.*

'A + B' means 'A is father of B'
'A – B' means 'A is sister of B'
'A × B' means 'A is husband of B'.
'A ÷ B' means 'A is wife of B'

62. Which of the following means S is granddaughter of R?
    (a) R + P + Q + S
    (b) K ÷ R + P × Q – L + S
    (c) K ÷ R + P ÷ Q + S – L
    (d) Can't be determined
    (e) None of these

63. Which of the following means P has a blood relationship with Q?
    (a) R ÷ P + K × L – M + Q
    (b) R ÷ P + K ÷ L + Q – M
    (c) R ÷ P + K – L × M – N + Q
    (d) R ÷ P + K × L – Q
    (e) None of the above

64. A man standing facing north starts walking. After walking for 5 m he took a left turn and walked for 10m. Now he walked for 20 m after turning to his right and again he turned right and finally stopped after walking 10 m. What is the distance from the starting point?
    (a) 18 m
    (b) 20 m
    (c) 15 m
    (d) 25 m
    (e) None of these

65. From a point Sahil starts walking in south-east direction. After walking for 6 m, he turned to west and walks another 10 m. Now he turned towards north-west and walks 6 m and then finally stopped after turning to east and walking 2 m. Find the distance from the starting point.
    (a) 10 m
    (b) 8 m
    (c) 12 m
    (d) 6 m
    (e) None of these

DIRECTIONS (Qs. 66-70): *Study the following information to answer the given questions.*

P, Q, R, S, T, V, X and Y are seated in a straight line facing North. P sits fourth to the left of V. V sits either sixth form the left end of the line or fourth form the right end of the line. S sits second to right of R. R is not an immediate neighbour of V. T and Q are immediate neighbours of each other but neither T nor Q sits between T and X. X does not sit at the extreme end of the line.

66. What is the position of Q with respect to P?
    (a) Fifth to the right
    (b) Immediate neighbour
    (c) Second to right
    (d) Third to left
    (e) None of the above

67. Which of the following represents persons seated at the two extreme ends of the line?
    (a) P, V
    (b) Y, S
    (c) R, V
    (d) Y, P
    (e) R, Y

68. How many persons are seated between R and T?
    (a) One
    (b) Two
    (c) Three
    (d) Four
    (e) None

69. If P is related to Q and S is related to T in a certain way, to which of the following would V be related to following the same pattern?
    (a) Y
    (b) P
    (c) R
    (d) S
    (e) X

70. Who amongst the following sits exactly in the middle of the persons who sit second from the left and the person who sits fifth from the right?

    (a) V
    (b) Q
    (c) T
    (d) S
    (e) P

ENGLISH LANGUAGE

DIRECTIONS (Qs. 71-80): Read the following passages carefully and answer the questions given below it.

We find that today the unity and integrity of the nation is threatened by the divisive forces of regionalism, linguism and communal loyalties which are gaining ascendancy in national life and seeking to tear apart and destroy national integrity. We tend to forget that India is one nation and we are all Indians first and Indians last. It is time we remind ourselves what the great visionary and builder of modern India Jawaharlal Nehru said, "Who dies if India lives, who lives if India dies?" We must realise, and this is unfortunately what many in public life tend to overlook, sometimes out of ignorance of the forces of history and sometimes **deliberately** with a view to promoting their self-interest, that national interest must inevitably and forever prevail over any other considerations **proceeding** from regional, linguistic or communal **attachments.** The history of India over the past centuries bears witness to the fact that India was at no time a single political unit. Even during the reign of the Maurya dynasty, though a large part of the country was under the sovereignty of the Mauryan kings, there were **considerable** portions of the territory which were under the rule of independent kingdoms. So also during the Mughal rule which extended over large parts of the territory of India, there were independent rulers who enjoyed political sovereignty over the territories of their respective kingdoms. It is an interesting fact of history that India was forged into a nation, neither on account of a common language nor on account of the continued existence of a single political regime over its territories but on account of a common culture evolved over the centuries. It is cultural unity—something more fundamental and enduring than any other bond which may unite the people of a country together which has welded this country into a nation. But until the advent of the British rule, it was not constituted into a single political unit. There were, throughout the period of history for which we have fairly authenticated accounts, various kingdoms and principalities which were occasionally engaged in conflict with one another. During the British rule, India became a compact political unit having one single political regime over its entire territories and this led to the evolution of the concept of a nation. This concept of one nation took firm roots in the minds and hearts of the people during the struggle for independence under the leadership of Mahatma Gandhi. He has rightly been called the Father of the Nation because it was he who awakened in the people of this country a sense of national consciousness and instilled in them a high sense of patriotism without which it is not possible to build a country into nationhood. By the time the Constitution of India came to be enacted, insurgent India, breaking a new path of non-violent revolution and fighting to free itself from the shackles of foreign domination, had emerged into nationhood and "the people of India" were inspired by a new enthusiasm, a high and noble spirit of sacrifice and above all, a strong sense of nationalism and in the Constitution which they framed. They set about the task of a strong nation based on certain cherished values for which they had fought.

71. The author has quoted Jawaharlal Nehru to emphasise the point that
    (a) national interest must enjoy supreme importance
    (b) India is going to survive even if the world is under the spell of destruction
    (c) the world will be destroyed if India is on the threshold of destruction
    (d) the survival of the world depends only upon the well being of India
    (e) None of these

72. What, according to the author, is the impact of the divisive forces on our nation?
    (a) They promote a sense of regional pride.
    (b) They help people to form linguistic groups.
    (c) They separate groups of people and create enmity among them.
    (d) They encourage among people the sense of loyalty to their community.
    (e) They remind us of our national pride.
73. "Communal loyalties" have been considered by the author as
    (a) a good quality to be cherished
    (b) of no consequence to the nation
    (c) a very important aspect for nation-building
    (d) a threat to the solidarity of the nation
    (e) None of these
74. Which of the following was instrumental in holding the different people of India together?
    (a) A common national language
    (b) A common cultural heritage
    (c) The endurance level of the people
    (d) Fundamentalist bent of mind of the people
    (e) None of these
75. The passage appears to have been written with the purpose of
    (a) giving a piece of advice to politicians of free India
    (b) assessing the patriotic values and sacrifices made by people for India's freedom
    (c) justifying the teaching of Mahatma Gandhi and its impact on the people
    (d) giving a historical account of how India evolved as a nation
    (e) None of these
76. History shows that India, which was not a political unit earlier, became so
    (a) during the reign of Maurya dynasty
    (b) during the Mughal rule
    (c) after one-national-language policy was adopted
    (d) during the regime of independent rulers
    (e) during the British rule
77. Why do people tend to overlook the paramount importance of national interest?
    (A) Because they are unaware of the imperative need of the day
    (B) Because they give undue importance to their selfish motives
    (C) Because historical events force them to do so
    (a) Only A   (b) Only B
    (c) Only C   (d) A and B only
    (e) B and C only
78. The "people of India", as highlighted by the author in the last sentence of the passage, refer to
    (a) the people of one unified nation
    (b) the subjects of several independent rulers
    (c) the patriots who sacrificed themselves in the freedom struggle
    (d) the people who were instrumental in writing the Constitution
    (e) None of these
79. India's insurgence was for
    (a) breaking the path of non-violence
    (b) having one common national language
    (c) insisting on a unique cultural identity
    (d) several independent sovereign rulers
    (e) None of these

80. Transformation of our country into nationhood was possible because of
    (A) People's spontaneously referring to Mahatma Gandhi as the Father of the Nation
    (B) People's sense of national consciousness
    (C) Generation of a high sense of dedication to the nation among the people
    (a) A and B only   (b) A and C only
    (c) B and C only   (d) All the three
    (e) None of these

DIRECTIONS (Qs.81-90) : *Read each sentence to find out whether there is any grammatical error or idiomatic error in it. The error, if any, will be in one part of the sentence. The number of that part is the answer. If there is no error, the answer is (e). (Ignore errors of punctuation, if any.)*

---

81. His proposal had (a) / to be send to (b) / the President of the company (c) / for her approval (d). No error (e).
82. Each tuesday evening we visited (a) / the farmers in the area (b) / and held a meeting (c) / to discuss the problems they faced (c). No error (e).
83. Though our training facilities (a) / are limited only a (b) / few employees have been (c) / selected for training (d). No error (e).
84. During the interview (a) / the panel asked me (b) / several technical questions (c) / and I answered all of it (d). No error (e).
85. He decided to work for (a) / an NGO, but most of his (b) / classmates opted for high paid (c) / jobs in multinational companies (d). No error (e).
86. It is necessarily to maintain (a)/ a record of all transactions (b) / in case the auditors (c)/ want to see it. (d)/ No error (e).
87. Very few young trainees (a)/ willingly undertake (b)/ a posting to a branch (c)/ located in a rural area (d)/ No error (e).
88. He has travelled (a)/ all over the world (b)/ yet he speaks (c)/ several languages fluently (d)/. No error (e).
89. A successful company is (a)/ any that makes a good (b)/ profit and provides (c)/ high returns to its shareholders (d). No error (e).
90. The agreement on (a)/ which all of us have (b)/ worked so hard will (c)/ be sign tomorrow (d). No error (e).

DIRECTIONS (Qs.91-100) : *In the passage given below, there are blanks each of which has been numbered. These numbers are printed below the passage and against each, five words are suggested, one of which fits the blank appropriately. Find out the appropriate words in each case.*

Today the economies of African countries are growing at 5 per cent every year.

Rich countries usually help poorer ones **(91)** African countries through donations and aid. Their **(92)** are not always successful as loans are **(93)** not used for the projects for which they are **(94)**. China, however, has found a different **(95)** to help Africa - by trading more with the **(96)**. In 2009 China's trade with African countries was $ 90 billion - **(97)** than the U.S., which was $ 86 billion. **(98)** countries have now begun to notice the **(99)** available in Africa. China's attitude has **(100)** the way the world deals with poor countries. "Trade not aid" is the new mantra of African nations.

91. (a) belonging   (b) similarly
    (c) compared   (d) with
    (e) like

92.	(a) efforts	(b) practices			
	(c) challenges	(d) achievements			
	(e) attempt				
93.	(a) given	(b) approved			
	(c) regular	(d) often			
	(e) being				
94.	(a) grant	(b) sanctioned			
	(c) took	(d) hired			
	(e) apply				
95.	(a) goal	(b) fund			
	(c) way	(d) skill			
	(e) dream				

96.	(a) countries	(b) others	
	(c) abroad	(d) neighbours	
	(e) poor		
97.	(a) further	(b) extra	
	(c) more	(d) less	
	(e) high		
98.	(a) Recently	(b) Any	
	(c) Friendly	(d) Many	
	(e) While		
99.	(a) differences	(b) supply	
	(c) quantity	(d) people	
	(e) opportunities		
100.	(a) substitute	(b) changed	
	(c) exchanged	(d) transform	
	(e) convert		

Answer Key

1	(c)	11	(a)	21	(c)	31	(b)	41	(c)	51	(b)	61	(e)	71	(a)	81	(b)	91	(e)
2	(b)	12	(b)	22	(a)	32	(c)	42	(e)	52	(a)	62	(c)	72	(c)	82	(e)	92	(a)
3	(b)	13	(c)	23	(b)	33	(c)	43	(a)	53	(b)	63	(b)	73	(d)	83	(a)	93	(d)
4	(d)	14	(e)	24	(d)	34	(d)	44	(d)	54	(c)	64	(d)	74	(b)	84	(d)	94	(b)
5	(a)	15	(d)	25	(b)	35	(a)	45	(b)	55	(a)	65	(b)	75	(a)	85	(c)	95	(c)
6	(c)	16	(c)	26	(a)	36	(a)	46	(e)	56	(a)	66	(c)	76	(e)	86	(a)	96	(a)
7	(a)	17	(e)	27	(c)	37	(c)	47	(a)	57	(e)	67	(e)	77	(b)	87	(e)	97	(c)
8	(e)	18	(b)	28	(b)	38	(e)	48	(c)	58	(c)	68	(c)	78	(a)	88	(c)	98	(d)
9	(d)	19	(b)	29	(b)	39	(d)	49	(c)	59	(d)	69	(a)	79	(e)	89	(b)	99	(e)
10	(b)	20	(e)	30	(c)	40	(b)	50	(c)	60	(c)	70	(d)	80	(c)	90	(d)	100	(b)

HINTS & EXPLANATIONS

1. (c) $(3158 + 4602 + ?) \div 39 = 347$
$\Rightarrow 3158 + 4602 + ? = 347 \times 39$
$\therefore ? = 13533 - 3158 - 4602 = 5773$

2. (b) $? = (0.08\% \text{ of } 363 + 0.6\% \text{ of } 241) \times 500$
$= (0.2904 + 1.446) \times 500 = 868.2$

3. (b) $? = 555 \times 444 = 246420$

4. (d) $? = \sqrt[3]{328509} = 69$
Go through the given options. First of all look for the digit at the unit's place. Reject (a) and (c) because $3 \times 3 \times 3 = ...7$. Reject (b) because $60^3 = 216000$. Now, check (d).

5. (a) $(47045 \div 9.7) + (2035 \div 3.7) = ?$
$\Rightarrow \quad 4850 + 550 = ?$
$\therefore \quad ? = 5400$

6. (c) $? = \dfrac{786 \times 64}{48} = 1048$

7. (a) $\sqrt[3]{13824} \times \sqrt{?} = 864$
$\sqrt[3]{24 \times 24 \times 24} \times \sqrt{?} = 864$
$\Rightarrow 24 \times \sqrt{?} = 864$
$\Rightarrow \sqrt{?} = \dfrac{864}{24}$
$\therefore ? = 36 \times 36 = 1296$

8. (e) $\dfrac{60}{100} \times \dfrac{20}{100} \times \dfrac{3}{5} \times ? = 450$

$\Rightarrow \dfrac{9}{125} \times ? = 450 \Rightarrow ? = \dfrac{450 \times 125}{9} = 6250$

9. (d) $? = 196 \times 948 \div 158 = \dfrac{196 \times 948}{158} = 1176$

10. (b) $? = 3.5 + 11.25 \times 4.5 - 32.5$
$= 3.5 + 50.625 - 32.5 = 54.125 - 32.5 = 21.625$

11. (a) $121 \quad 117 \quad 108 \quad 92 \quad 67 \quad \boxed{31}$
$\quad -2^2 \quad -3^2 \quad -4^2 \quad -5^2 \quad -6^2$

12. (b) $50 \quad 26 \quad 14 \quad \boxed{8} \quad 5 \quad 3.5$
$\quad \div 2+1 \quad \div 2+1 \quad \div 2+1 \quad \div 2+1 \quad \div 2+1$

13. (c) $3 \quad 23 \quad 43 \quad \boxed{63} \quad 83 \quad 103$
$\quad +20 \quad +20 \quad +20 \quad +20 \quad +20$

14. (e) $748 \quad 737 \quad 715 \quad 682 \quad 638 \quad \boxed{583}$
$\quad -11 \quad -22 \quad -33 \quad -44 \quad -55$

15. (d) $1 \quad 9 \quad 25 \quad 49 \quad 81 \quad \boxed{121} \quad 169$
$\quad 1^2 \quad 3^2 \quad 5^2 \quad 7^2 \quad 9^2 \quad 11^2 \quad 13^2$

16. (c) Let the number of ducks and frogs in the pond be 37x and 39x respectively.

ATQ,

$$\frac{37x + 39x}{2} = 152$$

$$\Rightarrow \quad 38x = 152 \quad \Rightarrow \quad x = \frac{152}{38} = 4$$

$$\therefore \quad \text{Number of frogs} = 39x = 39 \times 4 = 156$$

17. (e) The number of employees in companies A, B and C be $4x$, $5x$ and $6x$ respectively

After increase in the number of employees, required ratio will be

$$= 4x \times \frac{125}{100} : 5x \times \frac{130}{100} : 6x \times \frac{150}{100}$$

$$= 4 \times 25 : 5 \times 26 : 6 \times 30 = 10 : 13 : 18$$

18. (b) According to the question, third number will be
$$= 5 \times 213 - 2 \times 233.5 - 2 \times 271$$
$$= 1065 - 467 - 542 = 56$$

19. (b) Suppose Ravi borrows ₹100 for 7 yr.

The amount of Ravi has to pay as interest for the ₹100
$$= 4 \times 3 + 8 \times 2 + 9 \times 2 = ₹46$$

From the above information it is obvious that Ravi has to pay (as interest) 46% of the total amount. Hence, the amount borrowed by Ravi

$$= \frac{19550}{46} \times 100 = ₹\,42500$$

20. (e) $C.I. = P\left[\left(1 + \frac{r}{100}\right)^t - 1\right] = 9650\left[\left(1 + \frac{6}{100}\right)^3 - 1\right]$

$$= 9650\,(1.191016 - 1)$$
$$= 9650 \times 0.191016 = ₹\,1843$$

21. (c) The rate of milk when milkman sells 120 litres of milk for ₹ 3360

$$\therefore \quad SP = \left(\frac{3360}{120}\right) = ₹\,28$$

The rate of milk when milkman sells 240 litres of milk for ₹ 6120.

$$\therefore \quad SP = \left(\frac{6120}{240}\right) = ₹\,25.5$$

$$\therefore \quad \text{Required discount} = (28 - 25.5) = ₹\,2.5$$

22. (a) Let the number be x.

$$\text{ATQ, } \frac{3626}{x^2} \times 32 = 2368$$

$$\Rightarrow \quad x^2 = \frac{3626 \times 32}{2368} = 49$$

$$\therefore \quad x = \sqrt{49} = 7$$

23. (b) Number of tiles $= \dfrac{400 \times 600}{25 \times 25}$

$$= 16 \times 24 = 384 \text{ tiles}$$

24. (d) After servicing, speed of car = 60 km/h
$\therefore$ Distance covered in 6 hours
$$= (60 \times 6)\text{km} = 360 \text{ km}$$
Before servicing, time taken to cover 360 km

$$\therefore \text{ Time taken } = \frac{360 \text{ km}}{50 \text{ km/h}} = 7.2 \text{ hours}$$

25. (b) Let Venkat has x ducks and y sheep.
$$\therefore \ x + y = 81$$
$$\therefore \ x = 81 - y \qquad \qquad ...(i)$$
and $2x + 4y = 268$
$$\Rightarrow 162 - 2y + 4y = 268$$
$$\Rightarrow 2y = 268 - 162 = 106$$

$$\Rightarrow y = \frac{106}{2} = 53$$

$$\therefore \ \text{Number of sheep} = 53$$

26. (a) Let the age of Shyam and Ram was x and $2x$ years respectively 20 years later from now.

$\therefore$ Present age of Ram $= (2x - 20)$ years
and present age of Shyam $= (x - 20)$ years
10 years ago, the age of Ram $= 2x - 20 - 10$
$$= 2x - 30$$
Age of Shyam $= x - 20 - 10 = (x - 30)$ years
According to the question
$$2x - 30 = 5(x - 30)$$
$$\Rightarrow \quad 2x - 30 = 5x - 150$$
$$\Rightarrow \quad 150 - 30 = 5x - 2x$$
$$\Rightarrow \quad 3x = 120$$

$$\therefore \quad x = \frac{120}{3} = 40$$

$\therefore$ The present age of Shyam $= 40 - 20 = 20$ years.

27. (c) Length of the reel
$$= (25 \times 125 + 90)\,\text{cm} = 3215 \text{ cm} = 32.15 \text{ m}$$

28. (b) Le the CP of the shoes be ₹ x.
$$\therefore \ 2033 - x = x - 1063$$
$$\Rightarrow 2x = 2033 + 1063 = 3096$$

$$\Rightarrow x = \frac{3096}{2} = ₹1548$$

29. (b) Required number of days $= 24\left(\dfrac{56}{42}\right) = 32$

30. (c) The required probability $= \dfrac{{}^{7}C_2 \times {}^{4}C_1}{{}^{11}C_3} = \dfrac{21 \times 4}{165} = \dfrac{28}{55}$

31. (b) Total number of users of brand B across all Five cities
$$= 600 + 500 + 650 + 700 + 550 = 3000$$

32. (c) $700 = x\%$ of 500

$$700 = \frac{x \times 500}{100} \Rightarrow x = \frac{700}{5} = 140$$

33. (c) Required average $= \dfrac{500 + 550 + 600 + 550 + 700}{5}$
$$= 580$$

34. (d) Required difference $= 1250 - 1100 = 150$

35. (a) Required Ratio $= \dfrac{500}{700} = 5:7$

36. (a)

Statements	:	All books are notes.
Conclusions	:	Some books are notes. (Implication) Some notes are books. (conversion) Hence I follows.
Statements	:	Some notes are pencils. No pencil is paper.
Conclusions	:	Some note are not paper. (I + E = O type)
Statements	:	Some notes are pencils.

Conclusions : Some pencils are notes. (conversion)

Statements : No pencil is paper.

Conclusions : Some pencils are not papers. (Implication)
No paper is pencil. (Conversion)

Since III and IV form a complementary I-E pair, either of the two must follow.

37. (c) **Statements** : Some tables are chairs.
Conclusions : Some chairs are tables. (conversion)
Hence, III follows.

Statements : No cupboard is table.
Conclusions : Some cupboards are not table. (Implication)
No table is cupboard. (conversion)

Statements : Some chairs are cupboards.
Conclusions : Some cupboards are chairs. (conversion)
Since, No table is cupboard.
Some cupboards are chairs.

Conclusions : Some chairs are not table.
(E + I = O* type)
Hence, I follows.

38. (e) **Statements** : No table is fruit.
Conclusions : Some tables are not fruit. (Implication)
No fruit is table. (conversion)

Statements : No fruit is window.
Conclusions : Some fruits are not window. (Implication)
No window is fruit. (Conversion)

Statements : No fruit is window
All windows are chairs.
Conclusions : Some chairs are not fruit.
(E + A = O* type)

Statements : All windows are chairs.
Conclusions : Some windows are chairs. (Implication)
Some chairs are windows. (Conversion)
Hence none follows.

39. (d) **Statements** : No man is sky.
Conclusions : Some men are not sky. (Implication)
No sky is man. (conversion)

Statements : No sky is road.
Conclusions : Some skies are not road. (Implication)
No road is sky. (conversion)

40. (b) **Statements** : All papers are books.
Conclusions : Some papers are books. (Implication)
Some books are papers. (conversion)
Hence II follows.

Statements : All bags are books.
Conclusions : Some bags are books. (Implication)
Some books are bags. (conversion)

Statements : Some purses are bags.

Conclusions : Some bags are purses. (conversion)

Statements : Some purses are bags.

All bags are books.

Conclusions : Some purses are books.
(I + A = I-type)
Some books are purses. (conversion)
Hence, III follows.

41. (c) L sits to the immediate right of O. Only one person sits between P and O. O faces one of the immediate neighbours of C or A.

42. (e) N is facing A.

43. (a) E is facing M.

44. (d) Except PO, in all other pairs, the two persons are immediate neighbours of each other. There is one person between O and P.

45. (b) C sits third to the left of B.

(46-50) : Wooden Chairs $\Rightarrow$ W, T, Q, S
Plastic Chairs $\Rightarrow$ P, R, U, V

46. (e) 47. (a) 48. (c) 49. (c) 50. (c)

51. (b) E G 4 B H 7 5 @ <u>K</u> 8 D N £ Q Z $ <u>W</u> 3 C 1 9 * 1 B 2 S 6

52. (a) The first, second and third element of each group is sixth element to the right of the respective element of previous group as given in all in the sequence.

53. (b) There are 27 elements in all in the sequence.
So, $(27 - 9 - 7) = 11$ elements are between the 9th from left and 7th from right.
Hence, $(9 + 6) = 15$th element from the left and will be the required answer.

54. (c) 7th to the left of 12th from right
$= (12 + 7) = 19$th from right
$= (27 - 19 + 1) = 9$th from left
But the first 15 elements are reversed.
$= (15 - 9 + 1) = 7$th from left in the original sequence $= 5$.

55. (a) For the condition to be fulfilled, three digits should be together but it is not so in the given sequence.

(56-58) :

Six friends marks descending order (>) are as follow B > D > F > C > E > A

56. (a) Given, third highest marks $= 81$ and E's marks $= 62$
$\therefore$ C's score marks between 62 and 81.
Hence, C's possible marks $= 70$

57. (e) None is true with respect to the given information.

58. (c) $\therefore$ B scored highest marks.
$\therefore$ B's marks $=$ F's marks $+ 13 = 81 + 13 = 94$
D scored second highest marks.
D scored marks between 81 and 94.
Hence, D's possible marks $= 89$

(59-61) :

colour of the sky = ki la fa so ....(i)
rainbow colour = ro ki ...(ii)
From Eqs. (i) and (ii),
∴ colours = ki
sky high rocker = la pe jo ...(iii)
From Eqs. (i) and (iii), sky = la
the rocket world = pe so ne ...(vi)
From Eqs. (i) and (iv), the = so
From Eqs. (iii) and (iv), rocket = pe

59. (d) colours sky high = ki la jo
60. (c) the represents only so.
61. (e) pe represents rocket.
62. (c) According to the question,

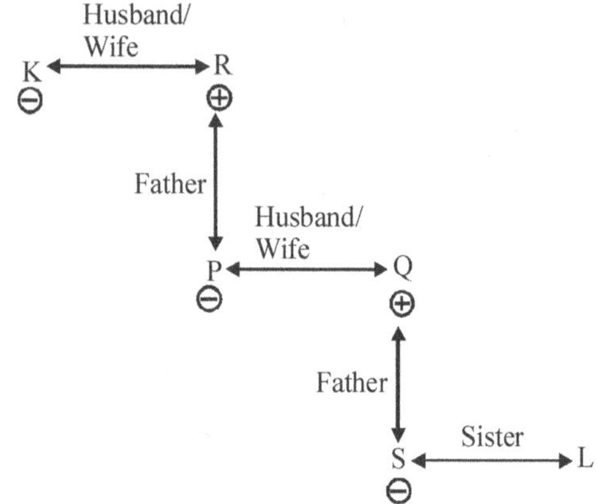

Here, S is daughter of P, Hence, S is granddaughter of R.

63. (b) According to the question,

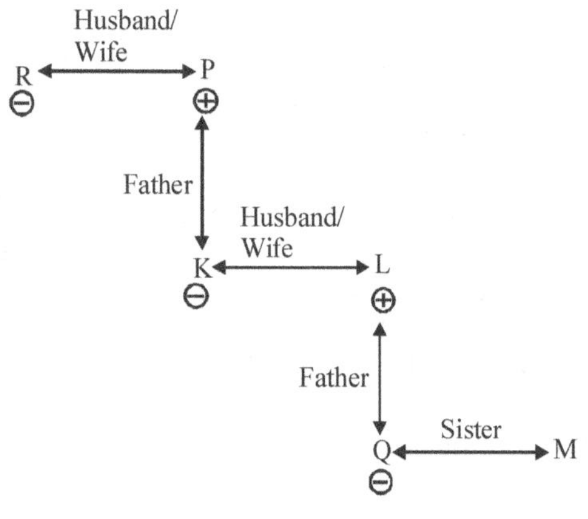

Here, P is the father of Q's mother K. So, P is Q's grandfather which form a blood relation between P and Q.

64. (d)

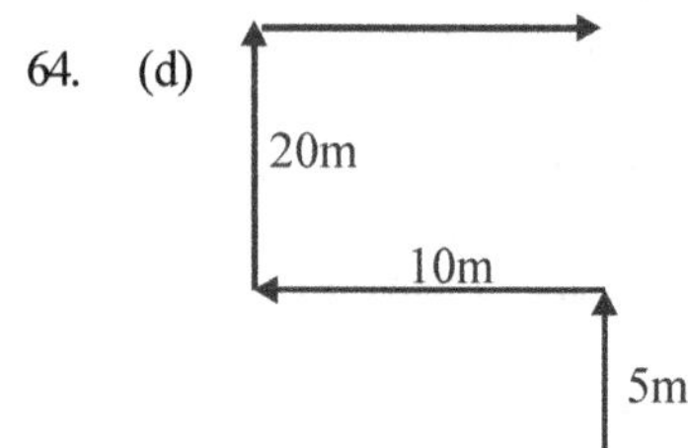

65. (b)

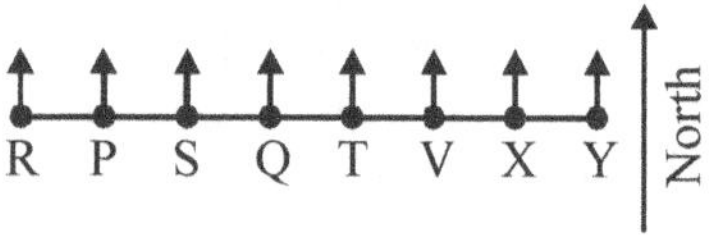

(66-70):

Sitting arrangement of 8 person are as follow

R P S Q T V X Y   North

66. (c) Q is second to right of P.
67. (e) R and Y are seated at the two extreme ends of line.
68. (c) There are three person (P, S and Q) between R and T.
69. (a) Y (Second person seated second to the right of first person)
70. (d) Clearly, S is in middle of person who is second from left (P) and Person who is fifth from right (Q).
72. (c) They are responsible for national disintegration.
73. (d) They are harmful to national integrity.
74. (b) India was forged into a nation on account of a common culture evolved over the centuries.
75. (a) The author wants India to remain as an ideal nation and the passage has certainly a message behind it.
79. (e) India's insurgence stood for gaining freedom by adopting the path of non-violent struggle.
81. (b) 'Sent' is the third form of verb 'send' in passive voice.
83. (a) Replace 'though' by 'As' to express cause and effect in the sentence.
84. (d) Use 'and I answered' properly to express cause and effect in the sentence.
85. (c) Apply the adverb 'highly' before the adjective 'paid'.
86. (a) Replace adverb 'necessarily' by adjective 'necessary'.
87. (e)
88. (c) Use conjunction 'and/therefore' in place of 'yet'.
89. (b) 'Any' shows uncertainty of selection. So, use 'one' instead of 'any'.
90. (d) Use third form of verb 'signed' in passive voice.

PRACTICE SET 9

Time : 60 Minutes **Max. Marks : 100**

NUMERICAL ABILITY

DIRECTIONS (Qs. 1-5) : *In each of these questions a number series is given. In each series only one number is wrong. Find out the wrong number.*

1. 5531 5506 5425 5304 5135 4910 4621
   - (a) 5531
   - (b) 5425
   - (c) 4621
   - (d) 5135
   - (e) 5506

2. 6 7 9 13 26 37 69
   - (a) 7
   - (b) 26
   - (c) 69
   - (d) 37
   - (e) 9

3. 1 3 10 36 152 760 4632
   - (a) 3
   - (b) 36
   - (c) 4632
   - (d) 760
   - (e) 152

4. 7 4 5 9 20 51 160.5
   - (a) 4
   - (b) 5
   - (c) 9
   - (d) 20
   - (e) 51

5. 157.5 45 15 6 3 2 1
   - (a) 1
   - (b) 2
   - (c) 6
   - (d) 157.5
   - (e) 45

6. Sophia invests 25% of her monthly salary in insurance policies. She spends 15% of her monthly salary in shopping and 35% of her salary on household expenses. She saves the remaining amount of ₹ 9,050. What is Sophia's annual income?
   - (a) ₹ 84,500
   - (b) ₹ 5,30,000
   - (c) ₹ 3,25,200
   - (d) ₹ 4,34,400
   - (e) None of these

7. The ages of Vaibhav and Jagat are in the ratio of 12 : 7 respectively. After 6 years the ratio of their ages will be 3 : 2. What is the difference in their ages?
   - (a) 8 years
   - (b) 12 years
   - (c) 9 years
   - (d) 10 years
   - (e) None of these

8. What is the least number to be added to 8008 to make it a perfect square?
   - (a) 273
   - (b) 87
   - (c) 264
   - (d) 92
   - (e) None of these

9. The product of two consecutive odd numbers is 6723. What ais the square root of the smaller number?
   - (a) 9
   - (b) 729
   - (c) 6561
   - (d) 81
   - (e) None of these

10. The owner of a book shop charges his customer 28% more than the cost price. If a customer paid ₹ 1,408 for some books, then what was the cost price of the books?
    - (a) ₹ 1,100
    - (b) ₹ 1,111
    - (c) ₹ 1,110
    - (d) ₹ 1,000
    - (e) None of these

11. The difference between 56% of a number and 39% of the same number is 425. What is 63% of that number?
    - (a) 1525
    - (b) 1650
    - (c) 1700
    - (d) 1575
    - (e) None of these

12. The speed of a boat in still water is 15km/h and its speed upstream is 7km/h. Find the speed of the boat downstream.
    - (a) 23 km/h
    - (b) 25 km/h
    - (c) 35 km/h
    - (d) 33 km/h
    - (e) None of these

13. If a certain sum becomes ₹5375 in 2 yr at compound interest, then what is the rate of interest?
    (a) 10%
    (b) 12%
    (c) 16%
    (d) Can't be determined
    (e) None of the above

14. The perimeter of a rectangle is 54 cm. If the length is twice its breadth, what will be the area (in sq cm) of the rectangle?
    (a) 324
    (b) 205
    (c) 405
    (d) Can't be determined
    (e) None of the above

15. Pure milk costs ₹16 per litre. After adding water the milkman sells the mixture ₹15 per litre and thereby makes a profit of 25%. In what respective ratio does he mix milk with water?
    (a) 3 : 1
    (b) 1 : 3
    (c) 3 : 2
    (d) 4 : 1
    (e) 1 : 4

16. 16 men can complete a piece of work in 8 days. 20 women take 16 days to complete the same piece of work. 12 men and 10 women work together for 6 days. How many more days would 10 women alone require to complete the remaining piece of work?
    (a) 8
    (b) 18
    (c) 12
    (d) 16
    (e) None of these

17. A trader sells 150 metres of cloth for ₹ 6, 600 and he sells 300 metres of cloth for ₹ 12, 750. How much concession does the trader give per metre of cloth, when he sells 300 metres of cloth?
    (a) ₹ 3
    (b) ₹ 2.5
    (c) ₹ 1.5
    (d) ₹ 2
    (e) None of these

18. When 3888 is divided by the square of a number and the answer so obtained is multiplied by 21, the final answer so obtained is 252. What is the number?
    (a) 324
    (b) 16
    (c) 256
    (d) 144
    (e) None of these

19. The sum of the digits of a two digit number is 14. The difference between the first digit and the second digit of the two digit number is 4. What is the two digit number ?
    (a) 86
    (b) 95
    (c) 68
    (d) 77
    (e) None of these

20. A car runs at the speed of 40 when not serviced and runs at 65 kmph. when serviced. After servicing, the car covers a certain distance in 5 hours. How much **approximate** time will the car take to cover the same distance when not serviced?
    (a) 10
    (b) 7
    (c) 12
    (d) 8
    (e) 6

DIRECTIONS (Qs. 21-25) : *What approximate value should come in place of the question mark (?) in the following questions? (You are not expected to calculate the exact value.)*

21. $[(1.3)^2 \times (4.2)^2] \div 2.7 = ?$
    (a) 7
    (b) 21
    (c) 18
    (d) 11
    (e) 16

22. $746 \div 32 \times 15 = ?$
    (a) 350
    (b) 345
    (c) 355
    (d) 340
    (e) 335

23. $\sqrt{834} \times \sqrt{349} = ?$
    (a) 525
    (b) 556
    (c) 534
    (d) 550
    (e) 540

24. $(3986 + 2416 + 3897) \div 754 = ?$
    (a) 18
    (b) 14
    (c) 11
    (d) 9
    (e) 21

25. $41.25 + 11.085 \times 2.75 = ?$
    (a) 63
    (b) 67
    (c) 76
    (d) 72
    (e) 80

DIRECTIONS (Qs. 26-30) : *What will come in place of the question mark (?) in the following questions?*

26. $14.8 \times 12.3 \times 8.6 = ?$
    (a) 1555.444
    (b) 1535.444
    (c) 1545.544
    (d) 1565.544
    (e) None of these

27. 45% of 720 = 30% of ?
    (a) 1008
    (b) 1080
    (c) 1040
    (d) 928
    (e) None of these

28. $3\dfrac{1}{6} + 4\dfrac{2}{3} - 1\dfrac{1}{4} = ?$
    (a) $6\dfrac{4}{7}$
    (b) $6\dfrac{7}{9}$
    (c) $6\dfrac{7}{12}$
    (d) $6\dfrac{3}{7}$
    (e) None of these

29. $63251 + 52894 = ? + 37624$
    (a) 87521
    (b) 67221
    (c) 76821
    (d) 78521
    (e) None of these

30. $7\dfrac{2}{7}$ of $189 + 452 = 2000 - ?$
    (a) 181
    (b) 191
    (c) 170
    (d) 171
    (e) None of these

DIRECTIONS (Qs. 31-35) : *Study the following graph carefully to answer the questions that follow.*

Number of applicants (in lakh) who applied for two different banks during past six years

31. What was the approximate average number of candidates who applied for Bank A over all the years together?
    (a) 4.2 lakh
    (b) 5 lakh
    (c) 3.1 lakh
    (d) 4.5 lakh
    (e) 3.8 lakh

32. Total number of candidates who applied for Bank A overall the years together was approximately what percentage of the total number of candidates who applied for Bank B overall the years together?
    (a) 79
    (b) 66
    (c) 70
    (d) 75
    (e) 60

33. In which years the total number of candidates who applied for both the banks together is exactly equal?
    (a) 2012, 2013, and 2016
    (b) 2012, 2014 and 2015
    (c) 2012, 2015, and 2016
    (d) 2012, 2014 and 2016
    (e) 2014, 2015, and 2016

34. If 20% of candidates who applied for Bank B qualified in the year 2016, then what was the number of candidates who have been disqualified in the same year?
    (a) 7.2 lakh
    (b) 72000
    (c) 6.4 lakh
    (d) 64000
    (e) None of these

35. What was the respective ratio between the total number of candidates who applied for bank A in the year 2014 and 2016 and the total number of candidates who applied for Bank B in the year 2013 and 2016 together?
    (a) 6 : 7
    (b) 4 : 9
    (c) 5 : 12
    (d) 12 : 5
    (e) None of these

REASONING ABILITY

36. A person started walking in south direction. After walking for 40 m he turned to his left and then walked 20 m. Now he turned to north and walked 30 m. In which direction is he now with respect to starting point?
    (a) South-east
    (b) North-east
    (c) North
    (d) South
    (e) North-west

37. Pointing to a photograph Arun said, 'She is the mother of my brother's son's wife's daughter.' How is Arun related to the lady's husband?
    (a) Uncle
    (b) Daughter-in-law
    (c) Cousin
    (d) Brother
    (e) None of these

38. Point A is 7 m west of point B. Point C is 5 m north of point B. A point D on AB 2 m away from point A meets BC at point E with DE = $\sqrt{34}$ m. Find the distance EC.
    (a) 3 m
    (b) 2 m
    (c) 4 m
    (d) Data inadequate
    (e) None of these

DIRECTIONS (Qs. 39-43): *Study the following information Carefully to answer the given questions:*

P, Q, R, S, T, U, V, W and X are sitting in a straight line, facing North. Three of them are not males. Two females sit adjacent to each other. Q is fourth to the left of V, who is second to the right of R, who is not the immediate neighbour of P.
• U is fourth to the right of R and is second to the left of X. S is not an immediate neighbour of either X or Q.
• S is not male. One of the persons sitting on the extreme ends is a female. T is not an immediate neighbour of either V or U.
• No female is an immediate neighbour of U. W does not sit second to the left of P. The immediate neighbour of S are male

39. Which of the following is a group of females ?
    (a) QTS
    (b) TXP
    (c) SVR
    (d) UWX
    (e) None of these

40. Who is sitting to the immediate left of S ?
    (a) V
    (b) Q
    (c) W
    (d) R
    (e) None of these

41. In which of the following combinations is the third person sitting between the first and the second person ?
    (a) PWU
    (b) QTR
    (c) RST
    (d) WUP
    (e) None of these

42. If Q and R, V and U interchange their position then how many persons are sitting between R and V ?
    (a) Four
    (b) Five
    (c) Six
    (d) Two
    (e) None of these

43. Who among the following sits third to the left of P ?
    (a) W
    (b) V
    (c) R
    (d) X
    (e) None of these

DIRECTIONS (Qs. 44-45) : *Read the following information to answer the questions.*

'P # Q' means 'Q, is father of P'
'P ★ Q' means 'Q, is mother of P'
'P £ Q' means 'Q, is brother of P'
'P $ Q' means 'Q, is sister of P'

44. Which of the following means X is grandmother of Y?
    (a) Z $ X ★ K # L £ Y
    (b) Y £ L # K ★ X $ Z
    (c) X * K # L E Y
    (d) Can't be determined
    (e) None of these

45. Which of the following means A is nephew of D ?
    (a) D £ C # B £ A
    (b) A £ B # D £ C
    (c) C £ D # B £ A
    (d) Can't be determined
    (e) None of these

DIRECTIONS (Qs. 46-51) : *In each of the questions below are given three statements followed by the conclusions numbered I, II, III & IV. You have to take the given statements to be true even if they seem to be at variance with commonly known facts and then decide which of the given conclusions logically follow from the given statements. Give answer*

46. **Statements** : Some pots are buckets.
    Some buckets are bags.
    Some bags are purses.
    Conclusions : I. Some purses are buckets.
    II. Some bags are pots.
    III. Some purses are pots.
    IV. Some pots are bags.
    (a) All follow
    (b) None follows
    (c) Only I and III follow
    (d) Only II and IV follow
    (e) None of these

47. Statements : All glasses are roads.

No road is stick.

Some sticks are pens.

Conclusions : I. Some glasses are sticks.

II. Some pens are sticks.

III. Some roads are sticks.

IV. No glass is a stick.

(a) None follows

(b) Only I or IV and II follow

(c) Only either I or II and IV follows

(d) Either I or II follows

(e) None of these

48. Statements : Some ice is ring.

No ring is paint.

Some rings are gold.

Conclusions : I. No gold is paint.

II. No ice is gold.

III. Some rings are paints.

IV. All golds are ring.

(a) None follows   (b) Only I and III follow

(c) Only I and II follow   (d) Only III and IV follow

(e) None of these

49. Statements : No candle is bell.

Some shoes are bells.

All tables are shoes.

Conclusions : I. Some tables are bells.

II. No table is bell.

III. Some shoes are candles.

IV. No flower is fruit.

(a) Only I and IV follow   (b) Only I and II follow

(c) Only III and IV follow   (d) Either II or III follows

(e) None of these

50. Statements : Some cats are rats.

Some rats are ants.

Some ants are flies.

Conclusions : I. Some flies are ants.

II. Some ants are not rats.

III. No rat is fly.

IV. No cat is fly.

(a) Only I and IV follow   (b) Only II follows

(c) Only I and II follow   (d) Only IV follows

(e) None of these

DIRECTIONS (Qs. 51-55) : *Study the following information carefully and answer the questions given below:*

A, B, C, D, E, F, G and H are sitting around a circle facing the centre. D is fourth to the right of H and second to the left of B. F is fourth to the right of B. C is fourth to the right of E who is not an immediate neighbour of B or D. A is not an immediate neighbour of D.

51. Who is to the immediate left of D?

(a) G   (b) C

(c) F   (d) Data inadequate

(e) None of the above

52. Who is third to the right of A?

(a) H   (b) E

(c) F   (d) Data inadequate

(e) None of the above

53. Who is fourth to the left of G?

(a) E   (b) F

(c) A   (d) H

(e) Data inadequate

54. In which of the following combinations is the third person sitting in between the first and the second person?

(a) ABC   (b) GCD

(c) AHE   (d) CBA

(e) EFG

55. What is B's position with respect to G?

(a) Third to the right   (b) Third to the left

(c) Fifth to the right   (d) Fourth to the left

(e) Fourth to the right

DIRECTIONS (Qs. 56-61) : *In each of the questions given below a group of digits is given followed by four combinations of letters/symbols. You have to find out which of the four combinations correctly represents the group of digits based on the letter/symbol codes and the conditions given below. If none of the four combinations represents the group of digits correctly, give (e) i.e. "None of these" as the answer.*

Digit:	3	9	6	2	8	7	5	4	1
Symbol :	K	T	$	F	H	#	%	D	M

Conditions for the coding the group of digits:

1. If the first digit is odd and last digit is even, the codes for the first and the last digits are to be interchanged.
2. If the first as well as the last digit is even, both are to be coded by the code for last digit.
3. If the first as well as the last digit is odd, both are to be coded as 'X'.

56. 564923

(a) %$DTFK   (b) K$DTFK

(c) X$DTFX   (d) K$DTF%

(e) None of these

57. 658247

(a) $%HFD#   (b) #%HFD$

(c) %$HFD#   (d) %#HFD$

(e) None of these

58. 436958

(a) DK$T%D   (b) DK$T%H

(c) HK$T%H   (d) #%$HK#

(e) None of these

59. 756834

(a) #%$HKD   (b) D%$HK#

(c) D%$HKD   (d) #%$HK#

(e) None of these

60. 291378

(a) FTMK#H   (b) XTMK#X

(c) HTMK#F   (d) FTMK#F

(e) None of these

61. 128547

(a) XFH%DX   (b) XFH#DX

(c) MFH%DX   (d) XFH%D#

(e) None of these

DIRECTIONS (Qs. 62 - 63) : Study the following information to answer the given questions:

In a five letter English word (which may or may not be a meaningful English word), there are two letters between L and P. S is not placed immediately next to L. There is only one letter between S and A. S is towards the right of A. S is not placed immediately next to E.

62. Which of the following is correct with respect to the word thus formed?

    (a) E is at one of the extreme ends of the word.

    (b) P is not placed immediately next to A.

    (c) There are two letters between A and E in the word thus formed.

    (d) P is placed second to the right of E.

    (e) None is correct

63. Which of the following words will be formed based on the given conditions?

    (a) SPAEL   (b) PEALS

    (c) LEAPS   (d) SEPAL

    (e) LAPSE

64. How many even numbers are there in the following sequence of numbers which are immediately preceded by an odd number but immediately followed by an even number?

    5 1 4 7 3 9 8 5 7 2 6 3 1 5 8 6 3 8 5 2 3 4 3 4 9 6

    (a) One   (b) Three

    (c) Four   (d) Two

    (e) None of these

65. Pointing to a man in a photograph, Reena said, "His brother's father is the only son of my grandfather." How is Reena related to the man in photograph?

    (a) Mother   (b) Grand Daughter

    (c) Sister   (d) Daughter

    (e) None of these

DIRECTIONS (Qs. 66-70): *Study the information given below to answer these questions.*

(i). A school held competitions for Chess, Table Tennis, Carrom, Kho–kho and Volley Ball during annual sports week form Monday to Saturday, each game on one day, one day being a rest day.

(ii) Carrom competition was held not on the first or on the last day but was held earlier than Table Tennis competition.

(iii) Kho–Kho competition was held on the immediate next day of the Table Tennis competition day.

(iv) Chess competition was held on the immediate previous day of the rest day.

(v) Kho–Kho competition day and Volley Ball competition day had a two days gap between them.

(vi) Volley Ball competition was held on the immediate following day fo the rest day.

66. On which day, the Chess competition was held?

    (a) Thursday   (b) Friday

    (c) Monday   (d) Wednesday

    (e) None of these

67. Which of the following is a wrong statement?

    (a) Carrom competition was held on the immediate previous day of Table Tennis competition

    (b) Kho–Kho competition was held on two days after the day on which Volley Ball competition was held

    (c) There was a gap of three days between the days on which Chess and Table Tennis competitions were held

    (d) There was a two days gap between the rest day and the day on which Carrom competition was held

    (e) None of these

68. Which of the following is the correct statements?

    (a) Kho–Kho competition was held after Table Tennis competition

    (b) Chess competition was held on Thursday

    (c) No competition was held on Wednesday

    (d) Table Tennis competition was held earlier than Chess competition

    (e) None of the above

69. Kho–Kho and Carrom competition days had a gap of how many days between them?

    (a) Nil   (b) Two   (c) Three

    (d) Four   (e) None of these

70. Which of the following was a rest day?

    (a) Wednesday   (b) Tuesday   (c) Friday

    (d) Thursday   (e) None of these

ENGLISH LANGUAGE

DIRECTIONS (Qs. 71-85): *Read the following passage carefully and answer the questions given below it. Certain words/phrases in the passage are printed in bold to help you locate them while answering some of the questions.*

In a country where consumers have traditionally had a raw deal, the Consumer Protection Act was one of the most progressive acts of legislation introduced in 1986. Before this, a shop could get away easily with the line "goods once sold will not be taken back or exchanged" or a car parking contractor with "park at your own risk". It is not that things have changed now but at least a legislation is in place and a forum is available to seek redressal . One of the basic limitations of this act is its mystification and general ignorance. No consumer agency or group has made its provisions general, nor has any redressal commission or **forum**. Restricted as it is by a lack of in frastructure and personnel and great verdicts to encourage consumers. The legislation is comprehensive. It gives consumers the right to redress against defective goods, deficient services and unfair trade practices. Consumer courts must deliver their judgements within 40 days, but rarely is this deadline adhered to. This reviewer had a first-hand experience of the chairman of a consumer court in Delhi who adjourned a case against a foreign airline for two years on the grounds that he did not have staff to type the orders. His replacement found the backlog so shocking that he dismissed several cases without applying his mind, in the process working against the interests of consumers. But what is more important is that the law has it that a consumer can approach court on his own without having to pay legal fees. In practice, this does not happen. The chairperson of the National Commission, who is a sitting judge, is so **attuned** to delivering judgments which can stand scrutiny in a civil court of law that it is insisted upon that a consumer must be represented by a lawyer. If not, cases are

adjourned with **impunity** and set for another day. Girimaji's attempt is creditable in that it is the first of its kind and has addressed almost all possible angles. She has discussed **redressals** in complaints about housing, basic telephony, rail transportation, power supply, life insurance and medical negligence. There are even tips on how to file a complaint. But it is **mired** in the case files of the National/ State Commissions of the Consumer Forum. A useful dimension would have been a comparison with the Law of Torts practised abroad. It is necessary here also, especially in an era of economic liberalisation, when the consumer is likely to be swept off his feet by free-market forces.

71. Why is the consumer likely to be swept off his feet?
    (a) He is easily taken in by the deceptive publicity.
    (b) He is wooed by the charm of foreign brands readily available in the market.
    (c) He is not aware of the Law of Torts as practised abroad.
    (d) He is not aware of the benefits of the consumer rights.
    (e) The Consumer Protection Act has been implemented and he can seek redressal.

72. What does 'lack of... verdicts' imply?
    (a) A lack of the basis of the system, trained staff and decisions based on fact
    (b) A paucity of funds, jury and judgement
    (c) A lack of resources, employees and final decision based on facts
    (d) Not having the required manpower, economy and decisive ruling
    (e) None of these

73. Which of the following statements is/are true?
    A. Girimaji's attempt is comprehensive but could have done with an angle or two more.
    B. Though the Act allows the consumer to approach the court on his own, yet a lawyer to represent him is insisted upon.
    C. Despite the Act, much remains the same.
    (a) Only A and C　　　(b) Only A and B
    (c) Only B and C　　　(d) Only B and D
    (e) None of these

74. What does the author mean by 'mystification of the Act'?
    (a) The mysterious Act is yet to be resolved.
    (b) The consumer is wary of the Act.
    (c) The Act is not easily accessible.
    (d) The consumer remains unaware of his rights and privileges.
    (e) The plight of the consumer is yet to end.

75. Which of the following best describes the judge's replacement?
    (a) He was partial towards the airline as it was a foreign one.
    (b) He never bothered to safeguard the interests of the reviewer.
    (c) He dismissed cases without even giving a second thought to what cases came to him.
    (d) He was apathetic and uninterested about the direction the case might head in.
    (e) He passed irrelevant verdicts indifferently.

76. What does the Act broadly cover?
    (a) It protects the right to redress.
    (b) It is a forum that protects the redresser.
    (c) It shields the consumer from deceptive and unfair trade practices.
    (d) It enables the plaintiff to fight his case free of cost.
    (e) None of these

77. Which of the following is a limitation of the Act?
    (a) It does not cover the international law of torts.
    (b) It is not comprehensive with regard to liberal economy.
    (c) No forum or commission has come forward to bring it to light.
    (d) Its red-tapism
    (e) None of these

78. How has Girimaji's attempt been creditable?
    (a) It has given the Act a new dimension.
    (b) She has brought all the loopholes in the Act to the consumer's notice.
    (c) She has looked at the Act in a very disinterested and impersonal manner.
    (d) She has discussed the law in the most explicit manner.
    (e) Her implicit dialogue with the consumer has made him aware of his rights.

79. What is the functionary role of the chairman of the National Commission?
    (a) To be the titular head of the commission
    (b) To be accountable to the public
    (c) To prevent any dissent arising out of his verdicts and Acts
    (d) To adjourn the cases with impunity
    (e) None of these

DIRECTIONS (Qs. 80-82): *Choose the word which is most SIMILAR in meaning to the word printed in bold as used in the passage.*

80. **Forum**
    (a) Dias　　　　(b) Podium　　　(c) Platform
    (d) Stage　　　(e) None of these

81. **Attuned**
    (a) Brought into harmony
    (b) Adjusted
    (c) Hazardous
    (d) Out of tune
    (e) Malpractice

82. **Adjourned**
    (a) Stopped　　　(b) Postponed　　(c) Decided
    (d) Cleared　　　(e) Pended

DIRECTIONS (Qs. 83-85): *Select the word which is most OPPOSITE in meaning of the word printed in bold as used in the passage.*

83. **Impunity**
    (a) Penalised
    (b) Fine
    (c) Sentence
    (d) Freedom from punishment
    (e) None of these

84. **Mired**
    - (a) Buried (b) Muddy (c) Steeped
    - (d) Free (e) None of these
85. **Redressal**
    - (l) Plea
    - (b) Justice
    - (c) Sue for compensation
    - (d) Not to compensate
    - (e) Put right

DIRECTIONS (86-90): *Read each sentence to find out whether there is any grammatical error or idiomatic error in it. The error if any, will be in one part of the sentence. The number of that part is the answer. If there is no error, the answer is (e). (Ignore errors of punctuations if any.)*

86. Nuclear waste will still being (a)/ radioactive even after twenty thousand years, (b)/ so it must be disposed (c)/ of very carefully. (d)/ No error (e)
87. My friend lived at the top (a)/ of an old house (b)/ which attic had been (c)/ converted into a flat. (d)/ No error (e)
88. A public safety advertising (a)/ campaign in Russia (b)/ hope to draw attention (c)/ of pedestrians crossing the road. (d)/ No error (e)
89. A cash prize was (a)/ award to the most (b)/ successful salesman of the year (c)/ by the President of the company. (d)/ No error (e)
90. The Renaissance was (a)/ a time to 're-awakening' (b)/ in both the arts (c)/ and the sciences. (4)/ No error (e)

DIRECTIONS (91-100): *In the following passage there are blanks, each of which has been numbered. These numbers are printed below the passage, against each, five words are suggested, one of which fits the blank appropriately. Find out the appropriate word in each case.*

Passage - 1

Emperor Akbar was fond of **(91)** tricky questions to Birbal. One day he asked Birbal what he would **(92)** if he were given a choice between justice and a gold coin. "The gold coin," said Birbal. Akbar was **(93)** aback. He had known Birbal for many years and he knew that Birbal was a just person. Then how could he choose the gold coin. "You would prefer a gold coin to justice ?" He asked, incredulously. "Yes," said Birbal. The other courtiers were amazed by Birbal's **(94)** of idiocy. For years they had been trying to discredit Birbal in the emperor's eyes but without success and now the man had gone and **(95)** it himself ! They could not believe their good fortune. "I would have been dismayed if even the lowliest of my servants had said this," continued the emperor. "But coming from you it's shocking - and sad. I did not **(96)** you were so debased ! I never expected this from you. How could you be so shallow ?"

One **(97)** for what one does not have, Your Majesty !" said Birbal, quietly. "You have **(98)** to it that in our country justice is available to everybody. So as justice is already available to me and as I'm always **(99)** of money I said I would choose the gold coin." The emperor laughed. He thought to himself, 'I should have known that Birbal would come up with a witty reply as always.' He was so pleased with Birbal's reply that he gave him **(100)** one but a thousand gold coins.

91. (a) showing (b) asking (c) naming (d) finding (e) telling
92. (a) look (b) said (c) think (d) choose (e) find
93. (a) pushed (b) fallen (c) pulled (d) sent (e) taken
94. (a) idea (b) display (c) reply (d) place (e) showing
95. (a) speak (b) thought (c) done (d) create (e) told
96. (a) felt (b) said (c) know (d) accept (e) saw
97. (a) asks (b) chooses (c) look (d) find (e) wish
98. (a) sure (b) put (c) shown (d) seen (e) made
99. (a) no (b) rich (c) short (d) poor (e) plenty
100. (a) but (b) not (c) and (d) so (e) only

Answer Key

1	(a)	11	(d)	21	(d)	31	(a)	41	(c)	51	(a)	61	(a)	71	(b)	81	(b)	91	(b)
2	(b)	12	(a)	22	(a)	32	(b)	42	(a)	52	(c)	62	(d)	72	(b)	82	(b)	92	(d)
3	(d)	13	(d)	23	(e)	33	(c)	43	(e)	53	(c)	63	(c)	73	(d)	83	(a)	93	(e)
4	(e)	14	(e)	24	(b)	34	(a)	44	(b)	54	(b)	64	(d)	74	(d)	84	(d)	94	(b)
5	(a)	15	(a)	25	(d)	35	(a)	45	(e)	55	(a)	65	(c)	75	(c)	85	(d)	95	(c)
6	(d)	16	(a)	26	(d)	36	(e)	46	(b)	56	(c)	66	(c)	76	(c)	86	(a)	96	(c)
7	(d)	17	(c)	27	(b)	37	(a)	47	(e)	57	(a)	67	(d)	77	(e)	87	(c)	97	(a)
8	(d)	18	(e)	28	(c)	38	(b)	48	(a)	58	(c)	68	(a)	78	(d)	88	(c)	98	(d)
9	(a)	19	(b)	29	(d)	39	(a)	49	(e)	59	(b)	69	(e)	79	(e)	89	(b)	99	(c)
10	(a)	20	(d)	30	(d)	40	(a)	50	(c)	60	(e)	70	(b)	80	(c)	90	(b)	100	(b)

HINTS & EXPLANATIONS

1. (a) The given number series is based on the following pattern:

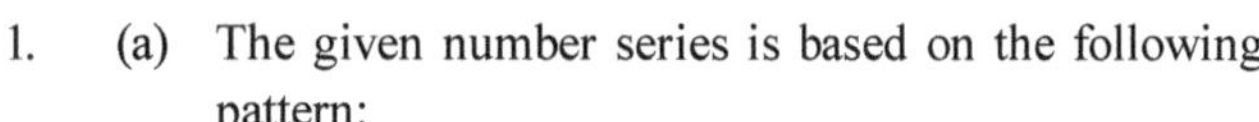

Hence, the number 5531 is wrong and it should be replaced by 5555.

2. (b) The given number series is based on the following pattern:

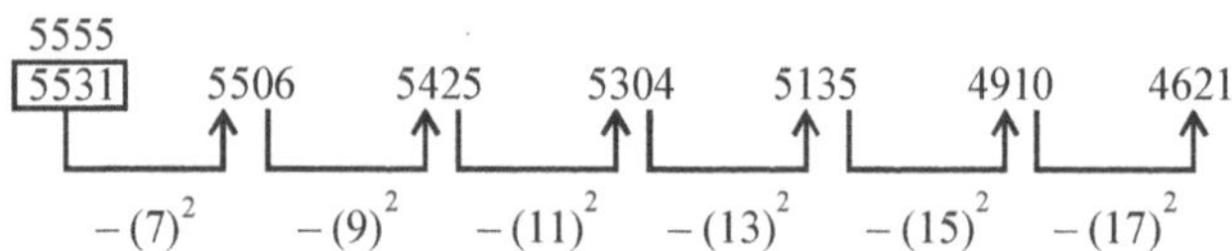

Hence, the number 26 is wrong and it should be replaced by 21.

3. (d) The given number series is based on the following pattern:

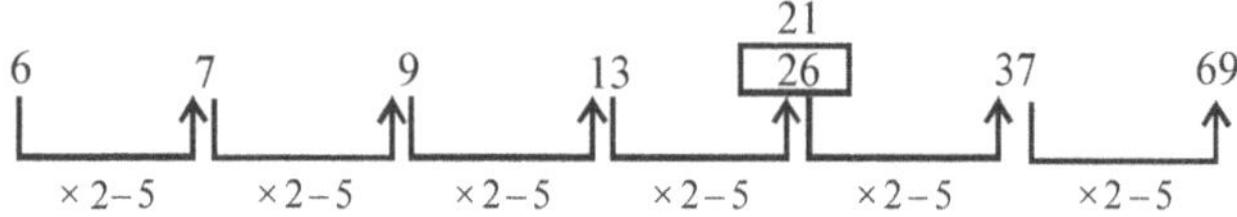

Hence, the number 760 is wrong and it should be replaced by 770.

4. (e) The given number series is based on 8 the following pattern:

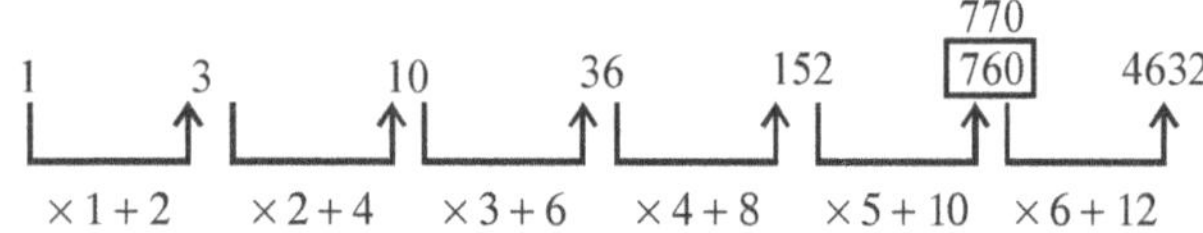

Hence, the number 51 is wrong and it should be replaed by 52.5.

5. (a) The given number series is based on the following pattern:

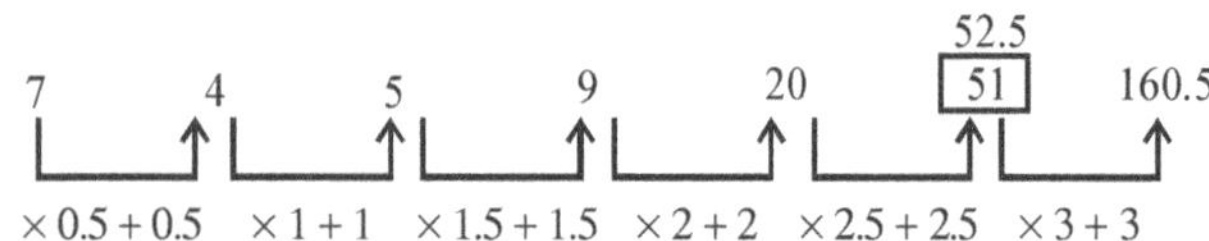

Hence, the number 1 is wrong and it should be replaced by 2.

6. (d) Let Sophia's monthly salary $= ₹\,x$.

ATQ,

Sophia's % monthly expenditure

$= (25 + 15 + 35)\% = 75\%$

Savings % $= 100 - 75 = 25\%$

$\therefore$ 25% of $x = 9050$

$\Rightarrow x = 9050 \times 4 = ₹\,36200$

$\therefore$ Sophia's annual income

$= ₹\,(12 \times 36200) = ₹\,434400$

7. (d) Let the present ages of Vaibhav and Jagat be 12x and 7x years respectively.

According to the question,

$$\frac{12x + 6}{7x + 6} = \frac{3}{2}$$

$\Rightarrow 24x + 12 = 21x + 18$

$\Rightarrow 24x - 21x = 18 - 12 \Rightarrow 3x = 6$

$\Rightarrow x = \dfrac{6}{3} = 2$

$\therefore$ Required difference $= 12x - 7x = 5x$

$= 5 \times 2 = 10$ years

8. (d) $\sqrt{8008} \cong 89.5$

$89^2 = 7921;\ 90^2 = 8100$

$\therefore$ Required number $= 8100 - 8008 = 92$

9. (a) $81 \times 83 = 6723$

$\therefore$ Smaller number $= 81$

Now, $\sqrt{81} = 9$

10. (a) CP of the books

$$= ₹\left(\frac{100}{128} \times 1408\right)$$

$$= ₹1100$$

11. (d) Let the number be x.

According to the question,

$(56 - 39)\%$ of $x = 425$

$$\Rightarrow \frac{x \times 17}{100} = 425$$

$$\Rightarrow x = \frac{425 \times 100}{17} = \frac{42500}{17}$$

$\therefore 63\%$ of x

$$= \frac{42500}{17} \times \frac{63}{100} = 1575$$

12. (a) Speed of boat downstream = Speed of boat in still water + Speed of current $= 15 + (15 - 7) = 23$ km/h

13. (d) Given data is not sufficient to answer the question.

14. (e) Let the breadth of the rectangle be x cm

$\therefore$ Length $= 2x$ cm

Now, $2(x + 2x) = 54$

$\Rightarrow 6x = 54 \Rightarrow x = 9$

$\therefore$ Area of rectangle

$= x \times 2x = 2(9)^2 = 162 \text{cm}^2$

15. (a) $\because$ SP of the mixture $= ₹15$

$\therefore$ CP of the mixture $15 \times \dfrac{100}{125} = ₹12$

Now, by the rule of alligation.

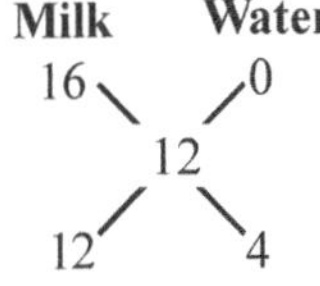

$\therefore$ Ratio of milk and water in the mixture

$= 12 : 4 = 3 : 1$

16. (a) From the first two statements it is obvious that the capacity of 1 man = the capacity of 2.5 women.

And the total work can be finished by 320 women in one day.

Now, 12 men + 10 women $= 12 \times 2.5 + 10 = 40$ women

Hence, during 6 days the work done is equal to the work of 240 women in one day. Hence, the remaining work will be finished in $(320 - 240) \div 10 = 8$ days.

17. (c) SP of 150 metres of cloth $= ₹6600$

$\therefore$ SP of 1 m cloth $= ₹\left[\dfrac{6600}{150}\right] = ₹44$

SP of 300 metres of cloth $= ₹12750$

$\therefore$ SP of 1 m cloth $= ₹\left[\dfrac{12750}{300}\right] = ₹42.5$

$\therefore$ Concession $= ₹(44 - 42.5) = ₹1.5$

18. (e) Let the number $= x$.

ATQ,

$$\frac{3888}{x^2} \times 21 = 252$$

$$\Rightarrow x^2 = \frac{3888}{252} \times 21 = 324$$

$$\therefore x = \sqrt{324} = 18$$

19. (b) Let two digit number $= 10x + y$

ATQ,

$x + y = 14$ ...(i)

$x - y = 4$ ...(ii)

From equation (i) & (ii), we get

$y = 5$

Now, $x + y = 14$

$\therefore \quad x = 14 - 5 = 9$

Thus, required two-digit number

$= 10x + y = 10 \times 9 + 5$

$= 90 + 5 = 95$

20. (d) After servicing, the distance covered in 5 hours $= 65 \times 5 = 325$ km.

Without servicing, speed $= 40$ km/h

$\therefore$ Time $= \dfrac{\text{Distance}}{\text{Speed}} = \dfrac{325}{40} = 8$ hours

21. (d) $? = \dfrac{1.69 \times 17.64}{2.7} = 11.04 \approx 11$

22. (a) $? = 23.31 \times 15 = 350$

23. (e) $? = 28.88 \times 18.68 = 539.52 \approx 540$

24. (b) $? = \dfrac{10299}{754} \approx \dfrac{10300}{750} \approx 14$

25. (d) $? = 41.25 + 30.48 = 71.5 \approx 72$

26. (d) $? = 14.8 \times 12.3 \times 8.6 = 182.04 \times 8.6 = 1565.544$

27. (b) Let $? = x$

45% of $720 = 30\%$ of x

$324 = 30\%$ of x

$$\Rightarrow x \times \frac{30}{100} = 324$$

$$\Rightarrow x = \frac{324 \times 100}{30} = 1080$$

28. (c) $? = 3\dfrac{1}{6} + 4\dfrac{2}{3} - 1\dfrac{1}{4} = \dfrac{19}{6} + \dfrac{14}{3} - \dfrac{5}{4}$

$= \dfrac{38 + 56 - 15}{12} = \dfrac{94 - 15}{12} = \dfrac{79}{12} = 6\dfrac{7}{12}$

29. (d) $63251 + 52894 = ? + 37624$

Let $\quad ? = x$

$\Rightarrow \quad 116145 = x + 37624$

$\Rightarrow \quad x = 116145 - 37624$

$\qquad = 78521$

30. (d) $7\dfrac{2}{7}$ of $189 + 452 = 2000 - ?$

$\Rightarrow \dfrac{51}{7}$ of $189 + 452 = 2000 - ?$

$\Rightarrow \quad \dfrac{51}{7} \times 189 + 452 = 2000?$

$\qquad 51 \times 27 + 452 = 2000 - ?$

$\Rightarrow \qquad 1377 + 452 = 2000 - ?$

$\Rightarrow \qquad 1829 = 2000 - ?$

$\therefore \quad ? = 2000 - 1829 = 171$

31. (a) Required average

$= \left(\dfrac{2 + 3 + 4 + 5 + 4 + 7}{6}\right)$ lakh

$= \left(\dfrac{25}{6}\right)$ lakh $= 4.2$ lakh

32. (b) Number of candidates overall the years

Bank A $\Rightarrow 25$ lakh

Bank B $\Rightarrow (5 + 6 + 5 + 8 + 5 + 9)$

lakh $= 38$ lakh

Required percentage

$= \dfrac{25}{38} \times 100 \approx 66$

33. (c) It is obvious from the graph.

34. (a) Required number of candidates who have been disqualified

$= \left(\dfrac{9 \times 80}{100}\right)$ lakh $= 7.2$ lakh

35. (a) Required ratio $= 12 : 14 = 6 : 7$

36. (e)

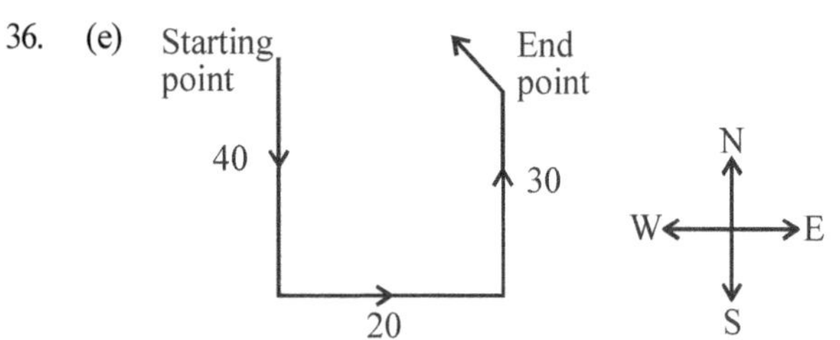

37. (a) One's brother's son's wife's daughter implies paternal grand-daughter of one's brother. Now, the mother of paternal grand-daughter of one's brother implies wife of one's nephew.

Thus, we can conclude that Arun is the paternal uncle of the female's husband.

38. (b)

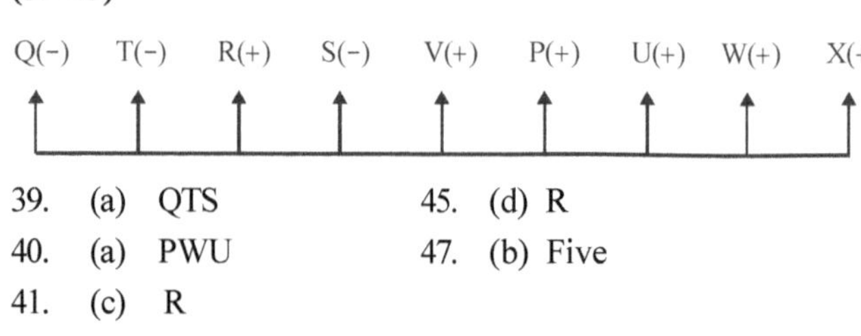

(39-43)

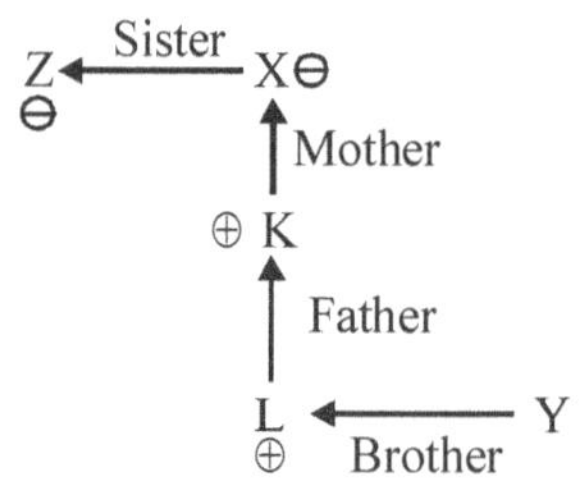

39. (a) QTS

40. (a) PWU

41. (c) R

42. (a) According to the question.

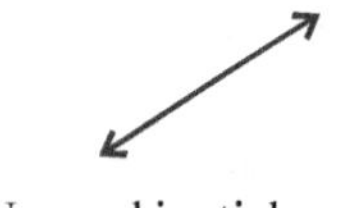

Here, X is mother of Y's fatehr K,

Hence, X is grandmother of Y.

45. (d) R

47. (b) Five

43. (e) Option (b) is wrong as gender of A is not know, (in backward coding, if there is no sign before A, it means gender is unknown).

Option (a) and (c) are worng as A must be before D. (In backward coding, a man of later generation must come earlier in the sequence).

46. (b) **Conclusions :** Some buckets are pots. (conversion)

Some bags are buckets. (conversion)

Some purses are bags. (conversion)

No mediate inference follows.

$\therefore$ No given **Conclusions** follows.

47. (e) **Statements :** All glasses are roads.

No road is stick.

Conclusions : No glass is stick. (A + E = E-type)

Statements : Some sticks is pens.
Conclusions : Pens are not glass. (E + I = O* type)
Statements : No road is stick.

Some sticks are pens.

Conclusions : Some pens are not road.
(E + I = O* type)

Hence only IV follows.

48. (a) **Statements** : Some ice is ring.
Conclusions : Some rings are ice. (conversion)
Statements : Some rings are gold.
Conclusions : Some gold are ring. (conversion)

Statements : No ring is paint.
Conclusions : Some gold are not paint.
(I + E = O-type)
Statements : Some ice is ring.

Noring is paint.
Conclusions : Some ice is not paint.
(I + E = O-type)
Statements : No ring is paint.
Conclusions : No paint is ring. (Implication)

Hence none follows.

49. (e) **Statements** : Some shoes are bells.
Conclusions : Some bells are shoes. (conversion)
Statements : No candle is bell.

Some bells are shoes.

Conclusions : Some shoes are not candle.
(E + I = O*)
Statements : All tables are shoes.
Conclusions : Some tables are shoes. (Implication)
Some shoes are tables. (conversion)
Statements : No candle is bell.
Conclusions : No bell is candle. (conversion)

Hence none follow.

50. (c) **Statements** : Some cats are rats.
Conclusions : Some rats are cats. (conversion)
Statements : Some rats are ants.
Conclusions : Some ants are rats (conversion)

Statements : Some ants are flies.
Conclusions : Some flies are ants. (conversion)
No mediate inference follows.
Hence, only I and II follow.

(51-55):

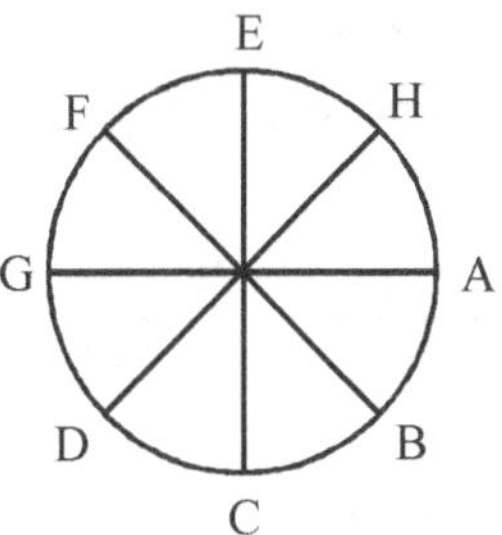

51. (a) G is to the immediate left of D.
52. (c) F is third to the right of A.
53. (c) A is fourth to the left of G.
54. (b) D is sitting between G and C.
55. (a) B is third to the right of G.

(56-61): Simply follow the rules of the codes and do these sums.

56. (c) X$DTFX (Because 1st and last digits are odd.)
56. (a) $%HFD# (No any condition.)
57. (c) HK$T%H (Because 1st and the last digits are even.)
58. (b) D%$HK# (Because 1st digit is odd and the last digit is even.)
59. (e) HTMK#H (Because Ist and the last digits are even.)
60. (a) XFH% D X (Because Ist and last digits are odd)

(62-63):

The meaningful english word 'LEAPS' will be formed.

Left ⊢———L———E———A———P———S———⊣ Right

62. (d) P is placed second to the right of E.
63. (c) The word 'LEAPS' will be formed based on the given conditions.

64. (d) 5 1 4 7 3 9 8 5 7 [2] 6 3 1 5
[8] 6 3 8 5 2 3 4 3 4 9 6

65. (c)
Grand Father
↓ only son
Reena's Father
↓
Reena

Man's Father
↓
Man — Brother

From above two diagram, it is clearly under stood that Reena's father and Man's father is the same. And Reena is sister to that man.

(66-70):

Day	Play
Monday	Chess
Tuesday	—
Wednesday	Volley Ball
Thursday	Carrom
Friday	Table Tennis
Saturday	Kho–Kho

66. (c) Competition on Chess was held on Monday.

67. (d) There is only one day between the rest day and the day on which Carrom competition was held.

68. (a) Kho–Kho competition was held after Table Tennis competition, is definitely correct.

69. (e) There is only one day gap betwen Kho–Kho and Carrom Competition.

70. (b) Tuesday is a rest day.

86. (a) Here, Nuclear waste will still remain/be .... should be used.

87. (c) Here, whose attic had been should be used. Whose is used to say which person or thing you mean.
Look at the sentence :
It is the house whose door is painted red.

88. (c) Here, subject i.e. A public safety advertising campaign is singular. Hence, hopes to draw attention ... should be used here.

89. (b) Look at the structure of the sentence in Passive Voice of Past Simple.
Subject + was/were + V_3 (Past Participle)
Hence, awarded to the most .... should be used.

90. (b) Here, a time of reawakening .... should be used.

PRACTICE SET (10)

INSTRUCTIONS

- This Preliminary Exam practice set consists of three sections. Numerical Ability (Qs. 1-35), Reasoning (Qs. 36-70) and English Language (Qs. 71-100).
- All the questions are compulsory.
- Each question has five options, of which only one is correct. The candidates are advised to read all the options thoroughly.
- There is negative marking equivalent to $1/4^{th}$ of the mark allotted to the specific question for wrong answer.

Time : 60 Minutes   **Max. Marks : 100**

NUMERICAL ABILITY

DIRECTIONS (Qs. 1-5) : *What will come in place of question mark (?) in the following questions ?*

1. $196 \times 948 \div 158 = ?$
   - (a) 1156
   - (b) 1200
   - (c) 1188
   - (d) 1176
   - (e) None of these

2. $3.5 + 11.25 \times 4.5 - 32.5 = ?$
   - (a) 18.275
   - (b) 21.625
   - (c) 32.375
   - (d) 25.45
   - (e) None of these

3. $\dfrac{\sqrt{4096} \times 56}{764 - 652} = ?$
   - (a) 36
   - (b) 48
   - (c) 32
   - (d) 44
   - (e) None of these

4. $(98360 + 25845 - 36540) \div 2500 = ?$
   - (a) 36.585
   - (b) 30.082
   - (c) 32.085
   - (d) 35.066
   - (e) None of these

5. $7414 + 3698 + 1257 + 1869 = ?$
   - (a) 14328
   - (b) 14438
   - (c) 13428
   - (d) 13248
   - (e) None of these

DIRECTIONS (Qs. 6-10): *What should come in place of the question mark (?) in the following questions ?*

6. $\dfrac{\sqrt{4096} \times 56}{764 - 652} = ?$
   - (a) 36
   - (b) 48
   - (c) 32
   - (d) 44
   - (e) None of these

7. $(98360 + 25845 - 36540) \div 2500 = ?$
   - (a) 36.585
   - (b) 30.082
   - (c) 32.085
   - (d) 35.066
   - (e) None of these

8. $7414 + 3698 + 1257 + 1869 = ?$
   - (a) 14328
   - (b) 14438
   - (c) 13428
   - (d) 13248
   - (e) None of these

9. $(91)^2 + (41)^2 - \sqrt{?} = 9858$
   - (a) 11236
   - (b) 10816
   - (c) 10404
   - (d) 9604
   - (e) None of these

10. $(2640 \div 48) \times (2240 \div 35) = ?$
    - (a) 3520
    - (b) 3515
    - (c) 3495
    - (d) 3490
    - (e) None of these

DIRECTIONS (Qs. 11-15) : *Read the following information and answer the question that follows.*

Number of Pages Printed by 6 Printers in Five Different Weeks

Printer Week	A	B	C	D	E	F
1st	664	618	628	552	638	419
2nd	569	441	519	438	621	537
3rd	440	614	503	527	541	742
4th	256	563	347	651	412	321
5th	717	429	598	582	519	693

11. What is the respective ratio between the number of pages printed by Printer B in 2nd week and the number of pages printed by Printer F in 5th week?
    (a) 4 : 9   (b) 11 : 13
    (c) 9 : 13   (d) 7 : 11
    (e) 9 : 11

12. What is the average number of pages printed by all the given printers in 4th week?
    (a) 375   (b) 425
    (c) 415   (d) 430
    (e) 390

13. Which of the following printer printed maximum number of pages in all the given weeks together?
    (a) Printer A   (b) Printer E
    (c) Printer D   (d) Printer C
    (e) Printer F

14. Number of pages printed by Printer A in 3rd week is what percent of the total number of pages printed by Printer D in all the given weeks?
    (a) 22   (b) 18
    (c) 12   (d) 14
    (e) 16

15. What is the difference between the total number of pages printed by Printer E in 1st, 2nd and 4th week together and total number of pages printed by Printer C in all the given weeks together?
    (a) 952   (b) 878
    (c) 924   (d) 934
    (e) 918

DIRECTIONS (Qs. 16-20) : *What will come in place of the question mark (?) in the following number series?*

16. 7 9 12 16 ?
    (a) 22   (b) 19
    (c) 20   (d) 21
    (e) None of these

17. 384 192 96 48 ?
    (a) 36   (b) 28
    (c) 24   (d) 32
    (e) None of these

18. 5 6 14 45 ?
    (a) 183   (b) 185
    (c) 138   (d) 139
    (e) None of these

19. 8 9 13 22 ?
    (a) 30   (b) 31
    (c) 34   (d) 36
    (e) None of these

20. 6 11 21 41 ?
    (a) 81   (b) 61
    (c) 71   (d) 91
    (e) None of these

21. Number of students studying in colleges A and B are in the ratio of 3 : 4 respectively. If 50 more students join college A and there is no change in the number of students in college B, the respective ratio becomes 5 : 6. What is the number of students in college B?
    (a) 450   (b) 500
    (c) 400   (d) 600
    (e) None of these

22. 80% of a number is equal to three-fifth of another number. What is the ratio between the first and the second number respectively?
    (a) 3 : 4   (b) 4 : 3
    (c) 4 : 5   (d) 5 : 4
    (e) None of these

23. A train running at the speed of 60 kmph crosses a 200 m long platform in 27 s. What is the length of the train ?
    (a) 250 m   (b) 200 m
    (c) 240 m   (d) 450 m
    (e) None of these

24. Which of the following has the fractions in ascending order?
    (a) $\dfrac{5}{11}, \dfrac{3}{8}, \dfrac{4}{9}, \dfrac{2}{7}$ (b) $\dfrac{5}{11}, \dfrac{4}{9}, \dfrac{3}{8}, \dfrac{2}{7}$
    (c) $\dfrac{2}{7}, \dfrac{3}{8}, \dfrac{4}{9}, \dfrac{5}{11}$ (d) $\dfrac{2}{7}, \dfrac{4}{9}, \dfrac{3}{8}, \dfrac{5}{11}$
    (e) None of these

25. Sum of the digits of a two digit number is 8 and the digit in the ten's place is three times the digit in the unit's place. What is the number?
    (a) 26   (b) 36
    (c) 71   (d) 62
    (e) None of these

26. 10 men can complete a piece of work in 8 days. In how many days can 16 men complete that work?
    (a) 4 days   (b) 5 days
    (c) 6 days   (d) 3 days
    (e) None of these

27. The sum of the age of a father and the age of a son is 75 years. If the product of their ages before 5 years was 750, then what is the present age of the father?
    (a) 60 years   (b) 55 years
    (c) 52 years   (d) 50 years
    (e) None of these

28. A mixture contains milk and water in the ratio 5 : 1. On adding 5l of water, the ratio of milk and water becomes 5 : 2. What is the quantity of milk in the original mixture?
    (a) 5 l (b) 25 l
    (c) 27.5 l (d) 32.5 l
    (e) None of these

29. A man sold two watches, each for ₹ 495. If he gained 10% on one watch and suffered a loss of 10% on the other, then what is the loss or gain percentage in the transaction?
    (a) 1% gain   (b) 1% loss
    (c) $\dfrac{100}{99}$% loss   (d) No gain no loss
    (e) None of these

30. If $16a + 16b = 48$, what is the average of a and b?
    (a) 3.5   (b) 2.5
    (c) 1.5   (d) 5.5
    (e) None of these
31. P can complete a piece of work in 12 days. P and Q and Q together can complete the same piece of work in 4 days. In how many days can Q alone complete the same piece of work?
    (a) 6   (b) 8
    (c) 9   (d) 10
    (e) None of these
32. The compound interest earned on an amount of ₹15000 at the end of 3yr is ₹3895.68. What is the rate of interest percent per annum?
    (a) 8   (b) 7
    (c) 6   (d) 9
    (e) None of these
33. How many words can be formed form the letters of the word SIGNATURE, so that the vowels always come together?
    (a) 720   (b) 1440
    (c) 17280   (d) 2880
    (e) None of these
34. Suraj started a business investing ₹ 38000. After 5 months, Ajay joined him with a capital of ₹ 55000. At the end of the year the total profit was ₹ 22000. What is the approximate difference between the share of profits of Suraj and Ajay?
    (a) ₹ 1865   (b) ₹ 1856
    (c) ₹ 1800   (d) ₹ 1956
    (e) ₹ 1500
35. In a box there are 8 red, 7 blue and 6 green balls. One ball is picked up randomly. What is the probabillity that it is neither red nor green?

    (a) $\dfrac{7}{19}$ (b) $\dfrac{2}{3}$

    (c) $\dfrac{3}{4}$ (d) $\dfrac{1}{3}$

    (e) None of these

REASONING ABILITY

DIRECTIONS (Qs. 36-37): *Read the following information carefully and answer the questions given below it.*

'A – B' means 'A is the sister of B'
'A × B' means 'A is the husband of B'
'A ÷ B' means 'B is the brother of A'
'A + B' means 'B is the mother of A'

36. If $P + Q - R \div S \times T$, then R is T's
    (a) Brother–in–law   (b) Sister–in–law
    (c) Either (A) or (B)   (d) Can't be determined
    (e) None of these
37. Which of the following shows N is the mother-in-law of K?
    (a) $K \div L \times M + N$ (b) $K \times L - M + N$
    (c) $K - L + M + N$ (d) $K \div L + M + N$
    (e) None of these
38. In a class of 20 students, Alisha'a rank is 15th from the top. Manav is 4th ranks above Alisha. What is Manav's rank from the bottom?

    (a) 10th   (b) 11th
    (c) 9th   (d) 12th
    (e) None of these
39. Mohan walked 30 m towards South, took a left turn and walked 15m. He then took a right turn and walked 20m. He again took a right turn and walked 15 m. How far is he from the starting point?
    (a) 95 m   (b) 50 m
    (c) 70 m   (d) Can't be determined
    (e) None of these
40. In a certain code language, 'how can you go' is written as 'ja da ka pa', 'can you come here' as written as' na ka sa ja' and 'come and go' is written as 'ra pa sa'. How is 'here' written in that code language?
    (a) ja   (b) na
    (c) pa   (d) Data inadequate
    (e) None of these

DIRECTION (Qs. 41-45) : *In each of the questions below are given two or three statements followed by the conclusions numbered I and II. You have to take the given statements to be true even if they seem to be at variance with commonly known facts and then decide which of the given conclusions logically follows from the given statements. Give answer*

(a) if only conclusion I follows.
(b) if only conclusion II follows.
(c) if neither I nor II follows.
(d) if both I and II follow.
(e) None of these

41. **Statements :**   All toys are dolls .
                       All dolls are jokers.
                       Some toys are cars.
    Conclusions : I. Some cars are jockers.
                       II. Some dolls are cars.
42. **Statements :**   All pens are boxes.
                       Some boxes are blades.
                       Some blades are files.
    Conclusions : I. Some blades are pens.
                       II. Some pens are files.
43. **Statements :**   All books are ledgers.
                       All pens are keys.
                       Some pens are books.
    Conclusions : I   Some ledgers are keys.
                       II. Some keys are books.
44. **Statements :**   Some roses are thorns.
                       All thorns are flowers.
                       No flower is a petal.
    Conclusions : I. No petal is a rose.
                       II. Some flowers are roses.
45. **Statements:**   All leaders are good team workers.
                       All good team workers are good orators.
    Conclusions: I. Some good team workers are leaders.
                       II. All good orators are leaders.

DIRECTIONS (Qs. 46- 50) : *Read the following information carefully to answer the questions that follow.*

There are six teachers A, B, C, D, E and F in a school. Each of the teachers teaches two subjects, one compulsory subject and the other optional subject. D's optional subject is History while three others have it as compulsory subject. E and F have Physics as one of their subjects. F's compulsory subject is Mathematics which is an optional subject of both C and E. History and English are A's subjects but in terms of compulsory and optional subjects, they are reverse of those of D's. Chemistry is an optional subject of any one of them. There is only one female teacher in the school who has English as her compulsory subject.

46. What is C's compulsory subject ?
    (a) History   (b) Physics
    (c) Chemistry   (d) English
    (e) None of these

47. Who is a female member in the group ?
    (a) A   (b) B
    (c) C   (d) D
    (e) None of these

48. Who among the following has same optional subjects as that of the compulsory subject of F?
    (a) D   (b) B
    (c) A   (d) C
    (e) None of these

49. Disregarding which is compulsory and which is the optional subject, who has the same two subjects combination as F ?
    (a) A   (b) B
    (c) E   (d) D
    (e) None of these

50. Which of the following groups of teachers has History as the compulsory subject?
    (a) A, C and D   (b) B, C and D
    (c) C and D   (d) A, B and C
    (e) None of these

DIRECTIONS (Qs. 51-55) : *In each questions below is given a group of letters followed by four combinations of digits/symbols numbered (a), (b), (c) and (d). You have to find out which of the combinations correctly represents the group of letters based on the following coding system and conditions that follow and mark the number of that combination as your answer. If none of the combination correctly represents the group of letters, mark (e) i.e. None of these'*

Letter	R	D	E	K	A	F	H	I	U	B	M	Z	W	J
Digit/Symbol Code	7	1	★	2	%	3	8	©	4	@	9	5	6	$

Conditions

(i) If the first and the third letters are vowels, both are to be coded as the code for the third letter.

(ii) If the first and the fourth letters are consonants both are to be coded as the code for the first letter.

(iii) If the first letter is a vowel and the last letter is a consonant, their codes are to be interchanged.

51. EBAJWU
    (a) ★@%$64   (b) 4@%$6★
    (c) ★@★$64   (d) %@%$64
    (e) None of these

52. JBIFMR
    (a) $@©397   (b) 7@©39$
    (c) $@$397   (d) 3@©$97
    (e) None of these

53. DEKRBJ
    (a) 7★@27@$ (b) 17★21@$
    (c) $★27@1   (d) 7★27@$
    (e) None of these

54. UZMKEF
    (a) 3592★4   (b) 4592★3
    (c) 4594★3   (d) 9592★3
    (e) None of these

55. HIREBW
    (a) 8©78@6   (b) 7©7★@6
    (c) 8©7★@6   (d) 6©7★@8
    (e) None of these

DIRECTIONS (Qs. 56-60): *Study the following information carefully and answer the questions given below.*

P, Q, R, S, T, U, V, and W are sitting around a circle facing at the centre. T is second to the left of P and third to the right of V. S is second to the right of W, who is to the immediate right of T. Q is third of the right of U.

56. In which of the following paris is the third person sitting in between the first and the second persons?
    (a) USP   (b) VRU
    (c) TQW   (d) WPS
    (e) None of these

57. Who is to the immediate left of T?
    (a) Q   (b) W
    (c) R   (d) Data inadequate
    (e) None of the above

58. Who is second to the right of P?
    (a) S   (b) V
    (c) U   (d) Q
    (e) Data inadequate

59. What is R's position with respect to W?
    (a) Third to the left   (b) Fourth to the left
    (c) Sixth to the right   (d) Fifth to the left
    (e) None of the above

60. Who is fourth to the left of R?
    (a) U   (b) P
    (c) S   (d) W
    (e) None of these

DIRECTIONS (Qs. 61-65) : *The following questions are based on the five three digit numbers given below*

972   526   487   359   251

61. If the position of the digits of each of the numbers are interchanged such that the first becomes second, second becomes third and third becomes first, which of the following will be the highest?
    (a) 927   (b) 526
    (c) 487   (d) 251
    (e) 359

62. If the digits in each of the above numbers are written in reverse order which will be the second highest number?
    (a) 251   (b) 359
    (c) 487   (d) 526
    (e) 972

63. If 2 is added to the sum of the digits of each of the above numbers how many will be multiples of 5?
    - (a) None
    - (b) One
    - (c) Two
    - (d) Three
    - (e) None of these

64. if the positions of the first and second digits interchanged which of the following will be third if they arranged in ascending order?
    - (a) 359
    - (b) 972
    - (c) 256
    - (d) 487
    - (e) 251

65. If 1 is substracted from the last digit of each of the above numbers then sum of the digits of how many of them are prime numbers?
    - (a) None
    - (b) Two
    - (c) One
    - (d) Three
    - (e) All five

DIRECTIONS (Qs. 66 - 70) : *Study the following information to answer the given questions :*

Six people C, D, E, F, G and H are standing in a straight line facing North not necessarily in the same order. D is standing second to the right of F. C is standing fourth to the left of H and H is not standing on the extreme end of the line. E is standing second to the right of D.

66. What is the position of G with respect to E?
    - (a) Immediate left
    - (b) Second to the left
    - (c) Third to the left
    - (d) Third to the right
    - (e) None of these

67. Which of the following pairs represents the people standing at the extreme ends of the line?
    - (a) FH
    - (b) CE
    - (c) DE
    - (d) CH
    - (e) None of these

68. Who is standing second to the right of C?
    - (a) F
    - (b) D
    - (c) G
    - (d) E
    - (e) None of these

69. Four of the following five are alike in a certain way based on their position in the above arrangement and so form a group. Which of the following does not belong to the group?
    - (a) CG
    - (b) GE
    - (c) GH
    - (d) DE
    - (e) FD

70. If all the people are asked to stand in an alphabetical order from left to right, the position of how many will remain unchanged?
    - (a) One
    - (b) Two
    - (c) Three
    - (d) None
    - (e) None of these

ENGLISH LANGUAGE

DIRECTIONS (Qs. 71-80) : Read the following passages to answer the given question bused on it. Some words/phrases are printed in bold to help you locate them while answering some of the questions.

Political ploys initially hailed as master-strokes often end up as flops. The ₹ 60,000 crore farm loan waiver announced in the budget writes off 100% of overdues of small and marginal farmers holding upto two hectares, and 25% of overdues of larger farmers. While India has enjoyed 8%-9% GDP growth for the past few years, the boom has bypassed many rural areas and farmer distress and suicides have made newspaper headlines. Various attempts to provide relief (employment guarantee scheme, public distribution system) have made little impact, thanks to huge leakages from the government's lousy delivery systems. So, many economists think the loan waiver is a worthwhile alternative to provide relief.

However the poorest rural folk are landless labourers who get neither farm loans nor waivers. Half of the small and marginal farmers get no loans from banks, and depend entirely on moneylenders, and will not benefit. Besides, rural India is full of the family holdings rather than individual holdings and family holdings will typically be much larger than two hectares even for dirt-poor farmers, who will, therefore, be denied the 100% waiver. It will thus fail in both economic and political objectives. IRDP loans to the rural poor in the 1980s demonstrated that crooked bank officials demand bribes amounting to one third the intended benefits. Very few of the intended beneficiaries who merited relief received it. After the last farm loan waiver will similarly slow down fresh loans to deserving farmers. While overdues to co-operatives may be higher, economist Snrjit Bhalla says less then 5% of farmer loans to banks are overdue ie overdues exist for only 2.25 million out of 90 million farmers. If so, then the 95% who have repaid loans will not benefit. They will be angry at being penalised for honesty.

The budget thus grossly overestimates the number of beneficiaries. It also underestimates the negative effects of the waiver encouraging wilful default in the future and discouraging fresh bank lending for some years. Instead of trying to reach the needy, through a plethora of leaky schemes we should transfer cash directly to the needy using new technology like biometric smart cards, which are now being used in many countries, and mobile phones bank accounts. Then benefits can go directly to phone accounts operable only by those with biometric cards, ending the massive leakages of current schemes.

The political benefits of the loan waiver have also been exaggerated since if only a small fraction of farm families benefit, and many of these have to pay bribes to get the actual benefit, will the waiver really be a massive vote-winner? Members of joint families will feel aggrieved that, despite having less than one hectare per head, their family holding is too large to qualify for the 100% waiver. All finance ministers, of central or state governments, give away freebies in their last budgets, hoping to win electoral regards. yet, four-fifth of all incumbent government are voted out. This shows that beneficiaries of favours are not notably grateful, while those not so favoured may feel aggrieved, and vote for the opposition. That seems to be why election budgets constantly fail to win elections in India and the loan waiver will not change that pattern.

71. Why do economists feel that loan waivers will benefit farmers in distress?
    - (a) It will improve the standard of living of those farmers who can afford to repay their loans but are exempted.
    - (b) Other government relief measures have proved ineffective,

  (c) Suicide rates of farmers have declined after the announcement of the waiver.

  (d) Farmers will be motivated to increase the size of their family holdings not individual holdings.

  (e) The government will be forced to re-examine and improve the public distribution system.

72. What message will the loan waiver send to farmers who have repaid loans?

  (a) The Government will readily provide them with loans in the future.

  (b) As opposed to money lenders banks are a safer and more reliable source of credit.

  (c) Honesty is the best policy.

  (d) It is beneficial to take loans from co-operatives since their rates of interest are lower.

  (e) They will be angry at being penalised for honesty.

73. What is the author's suggestion to provide aid to farmers?

  (a) Families should split their joint holding to take advantage of the loan waiver.

  (b) The government should increase the reach of the employment guarantee scheme.

  (c) Loans should be disbursed directly into bank accounts of the farmers using the latest technology.

  (d) Government should ensure that loans waivers can be implemented over the number of years.

  (e) Rural infrastructure can be improved using schemes which were successful abroad.

74. What was the outcome of IRDP loans to the rural poor?

  (a) The percentage of bank loan sanctioned to family owned farms increased.

  (b) The loans· benefited dishonest moneylenders not landless labourers.

  (c) Corrupt bank officials were the unintended beneficiaries of the loans.

  (d) It resulted in tne Government sanctioning thrice the amount for the current loan waiver.

  (e) None of these.

75. What are the terms of the loan waiver?

  (1) One-fourth of the overdue loans of landless labourers will be written off.

  (2) The ₹ 60,000 crore loan waiver has been sanctioned for 2.25 million marginal farmers.

  (3) Any farmer with between 26 per cent to 100 per cent of their loan repayments overdue will be penalised.

  (a) Only (1)   (b) On1y (2)

  (c) Both (2) and (3) (d) All (1), (2) and (3)

  (e) None of these

76. What is the author's view of the loan waiver?

  (a) It will have an adverse psychological impact on those who cannot avail of the waiver.

  (b) It is a justified measure in view of the high suicide rate among landless labourers.

  (c) It makes sound economic and political sense in the existing scenario.

  (d) It will ensure that the benefits of India's high GDP are felt by the rural poor.

  (e) None of these

77. Which of the following **cannot** be said about loan waiver?

  (1) Small and marginal farmers will benefit the most.

  (2) The loan waiver penalises deserving farmers.

  (3) A large percentage ie ninety five per cent of distressed farmers will benefit.

  (a) Only (3)   (b) Both (1) and (3)

  (c) Only (1)   (d) Both (2) and (3)

  (e) None of these

78. Which of the following will definitely be an impact of loan waivers?

  (1) Family holdings will be split into individual holdings not exceeding one hectare.

  (2) The public distributipn system will be revamped.

  (3) Opposition will definitely win the election.

  (a) None   (b) Only (1)

  (c) Both (1) and (2) (d) Only (3)

  (e) All (1), (2) and (3)

79. What impact will the loan waiver have on banks?

  (a) Banks have to bear the entire brunt of the write off.

  (b) Loss of trust in banks by big farmers.

  (c) Corruption among bank staff will increase.

  (d) Farmers will make it a habit to default on loans

  (e) None of these

80. According to the author, what is the government's motive in sanctioning the loan waiver?

  (a) To encourage farmers to opt for bank loans from money lenders.

  (b) To raise 90 million farmers out of indebtedness.

  (c) To provide relief to those marginal farmers who have the means to but have not repaid their loans

  (d) To ensure they will be re-elected

  (e) None of these

DIRECTIONS (Qs. 81-90): *Read each sentence to find out whether there is any grammatical error or idiomatic error in it. The error, if any will be in one part of the sentence. The number of that part is the answer. If there is no error, the answer is (e). (Ignore errors of punctuations, if any)*

81. In times of crisis, (a) / the Bhagavad Gita giv es light (b)/ and guide to the mind tortured by doubt (c)/ and torn by conflict of duties. (d)/ No Error (e)

82. It was not easy for late Raja Ram Mohan Roy (a)/ to root out the custom of sati (b) / because a majority of (c)/ the educated class does not support him. (d) / No Error (e)

83. Deplete of the Ozone layer (a) / and the greenhouse effect (b) / are two long-term effects (c)/of air pollution. (d)/ No Error (e)

84. Most of the people which (a)/ have been victims (b) / of extreme violence (c)/ are too frightened to report it to the police. (d)/ No Error (e)

85. The doctor helps (a)/ to reducing human suffering (b)/by curing diseases (c)/ and improving health. (d)/ No Error (e)

86. The shepherd counted (a) / his sheep and found (b) / that one of (c) / them is missing. (d) / No Error (e)

87. The teacher were (a) / impressed by her performance (b) / and asked her to (c) / participate in the competition. (d) No Error (e)

88. She asked her (a) / son for help her (b) / find a place to bury (c) / the gold ornaments (d) No Error (e)
89. The painter was (a) / ask to paint a (b) / picture of the king, (c) / sitting on his throne (d) No Error (e)
90. The story was (a) / about how an (b) / intelligent man had saving (c) / himself from being robbed (d) No Error (e)

DIRECTIONS (Qs 91-100): *In the passage given below, there are blanks, each of which has been numbered. These numbers are printed below the passage, against each, five words are suggested, one of which fits the blank appropriately. Find out the appropriate word in each case.*

Once upon a time, two friends were **(91)** through the desert. During some point of the **(92)** they had an argument, and one friend slapped the other one in the face. The one who got slapped was **(93)** but without saying anything, he wrote in the sand, "Today my best friend slapped me in the face." They kept on walking **(94)** they found an oasis, where they **(95)** to take a bath. The one, who had been slapped, got **(96)** in the quicksand and started drowning, but the friend saved him. After the friend **(97)** from the near drowning he wrote on a stone, "Today my best friend saved my life." The friend who had slapped and saved his best friend asked him, "After I hurt you, you wrote in the sand and **(98)** you write on a stone, why?" The other friend **(99)**, "When someone hurt us, we should write it down in sand where wind of forgiveness can erase it away. But, when someone does something good for us, we must **(100)** it in stone where no wind can ever erase it."

91. (a) crawling   (b) speaking
    (c) swimming   (d) walking
    (e) dancing

92. (a) journey   (b) sand
    (c) running   (d) border
    (e) hunt

93. (a) dead   (b) captured
    (c) presentable   (d) missing
    (e) hurt

94. (a) as   (b) until
    (c) from   (d) with
    (e) through

95. (a) decided   (b) fell
    (c) made   (d) want
    (e) left

96. (a) home   (b) stuck
    (c) blended   (d) mixed
    (e) sitting

97. (a) separated   (b) leaked
    (c) died   (d) recovered
    (e) saved

98. (a) so   (b) how
    (c) when   (d) tomorrow
    (e) now

99. (a) called   (b) tell
    (c) replied   (d) questioned
    (e) asked

100. (a) talk   (b) push
     (c) engrave   (d) add
     (e) bury

Answer Key

1	(d)	11	(d)	21	(d)	31	(a)	41	(d)	51	(d)	61	(e)	71	(b)	81	(c)	91	(d)
2	(b)	12	(b)	22	(a)	32	(a)	42	(c)	52	(e)	62	(c)	72	(e)	82	(d)	92	(a)
3	(c)	13	(c)	23	(a)	33	(c)	43	(d)	53	(b)	63	(d)	73	(c)	83	(a)	93	(e)
4	(d)	14	(e)	24	(c)	34	(b)	44	(b)	54	(a)	64	(a)	74	(c)	84	(a)	94	(b)
5	(e)	15	(c)	25	(d)	35	(d)	45	(a)	55	(c)	65	(b)	75	(b)	85	(b)	95	(a)
6	(c)	16	(d)	26	(b)	36	(c)	46	(a)	56	(e)	66	(c)	76	(a)	86	(d)	96	(b)
7	(d)	17	(c)	27	(b)	37	(b)	47	(d)	57	(a)	67	(b)	77	(b)	87	(a)	97	(d)
8	(e)	18	(e)	28	(b)	38	(a)	48	(d)	58	(c)	68	(c)	78	(d)	88	(b)	98	(e)
9	(b)	19	(e)	29	(b)	39	(b)	49	(c)	59	(a)	69	(b)	79	(d)	89	(b)	99	(c)
10	(a)	20	(a)	30	(c)	40	(b)	50	(d)	60	(b)	70	(a)	80	(d)	90	(c)	100	(c)

HINTS & EXPLANATIONS

1. (d) $? = 196 \times 948 \div 158 = \dfrac{196 \times 948}{158} = 1176$

2. (b) $? = 3.5 + 11.25 \times 4.5 - 32.5$
$= 3.5 + 50.625 - 32.5 = 54.125 - 32.5 = 21.625$

3. (c) $? = \dfrac{\sqrt{4096} \times 56}{764 - 652} = \dfrac{64 \times 56}{112} = 32$

4. (d) $? = (98360 + 25845 - 36540) \div 2500$
$= 87665 \div 2500 = 35.066$

5. (e) $? = 7414 + 3698 + 1257 + 1869 = 14238$

6. (c) $? = \dfrac{\sqrt{4096} \times 56}{764 - 652} = \dfrac{64 \times 56}{112} = 32$

7. (d) $? = (98360 + 25845 - 36540) \div 2500$
$= 87665 \div 2500 = 35.066$

8. (e) $? = 7414 + 3698 + 1257 + 1869 = 14238$

9. (b) $(91)^2 + (41)^2 - \sqrt{?} = 9858$
$\Rightarrow 8281 + 1681 - \sqrt{?} = 9858$
$\Rightarrow \sqrt{?} = 9962 - 9858 = 104$
$\therefore ? = 104 \times 104 = 10816$

10. (a) $? = (2640 \div 48) \times (2240 \div 35)$
$= 55 \times 64 = 3520$

11. (d) Required ratio =
$$\dfrac{\text{Number of pages Printed by Printer B in 2nd week}}{\text{Number of pages Printed by Printer F in 5th week}}$$
$= \dfrac{441}{693} = \dfrac{49}{77} = 7 : 11$

12. (b) Required average
Number of pages printed by
$$= \dfrac{\text{all the given printers in 4th week}}{6}$$
$$= \dfrac{256 + 563 + 347 + 651 + 412 + 321}{6}$$
$$= \dfrac{2550}{6} = 425$$

13. (c) Total number of pages printed in al the given weeks together by Printer
A $= 664 + 569 + 440 + 256 + 717 = 2646$ by Printer
C $= 628 + 519 + 503 + 347 + 598 = 2695$ by Printer
D $= 552 + 438 + 527 + 651 + 582 = 2750$ by Printer
E $= 638 + 621 + 541 + 412 + 519 = 2750$ by Printer
F $= 419 + 537 + 742 + 321 + 693 = 2712$ by Printer
Thus, Printer D printed the maximum number of pages.

14. (e) Required percentage
$$= \dfrac{\substack{\text{Number of pages printed by} \\ \text{Printer A in 3d week}}}{\substack{\text{Total number of pages printer by} \\ \text{Printer D in all the given weeks}}}$$
$\times 100\% = \dfrac{440}{2750} \times \dfrac{440}{2750} \times 100\% = 16\%$

15. (c) Number of pages printed by Printer E in 1st, 2nd and 4th week together
$= 638 + 621 + 412 = 1671$
Total number of pages printed by Printer C in all the given weeks together $= 2595$
$\therefore$ Required difference $= 1671 \sim 2595 = 924$

16. (d) Pattern of the series would be as follows

$$7 \quad 9 \quad 12 \quad 16 \quad 21$$
$$+2 \quad +3 \quad +4 \quad +5$$

17. (c) Pattern of the series would be as follows

$$384 \quad 192 \quad 96 \quad 48 \quad 24$$
$$\div 2 \quad \div 2 \quad \div 2 \quad \div 2$$

18. (e) Pattern of the series would be as follows
$$5 \times 1 + 1 = 6$$
$$6 \times 2 + 2 = 14$$
$$14 \times 3 + 3 = 45$$
$$\therefore \quad 45 \times 4 + 4 = 184$$

19. (e) Pattern of the series would be as follows

$$8 \quad 9 \quad 13 \quad 22 \quad 38$$
$$+(1)^2 \quad +(2)^2 \quad +(3)^2 \quad +(4)^2$$

20. (a) Pattern of the series would be as follows

$$6 \quad 11 \quad 21 \quad 41 \quad 81$$
$$+5 \quad +10 \quad +20 \quad +40$$

21. (d) Let total number of students in college $A = 3x$
and total number of students in college $B = 4x$
After 50 more students join college A

$$\text{New Ratio} = \frac{3x + 50}{4x} = \frac{5}{6}$$
$$\Rightarrow \quad 18x + 300 = 20x$$
$$\Rightarrow \quad 2x = 300$$
$$\Rightarrow \quad x = \frac{300}{2} = 150$$

Total number of students in college
$B = 4x = 4 \times 150 = 600$

22. (a) Let the first number be x
and the second number be y

Then, 80% of $x = \dfrac{3}{5}$ of y

$$\Rightarrow \quad \frac{80}{100} \times x = \frac{3}{5} \times y$$
$$\Rightarrow \quad \frac{4}{5} \times x = \frac{3}{5} \times y \qquad \Rightarrow \qquad 4x = 3y$$
$$\Rightarrow \quad \frac{x}{y} = \frac{3}{4} = 3 : 4$$

23. (a) Let length of the train be x m

Speed of the train be 60 km/h $= 60 \times \dfrac{5}{18} = \dfrac{50}{3}$ m/s

Then, $\dfrac{x + 200}{\frac{50}{3}} = 27$

$$\Rightarrow \quad \frac{3(x + 200)}{50} = 27$$
$$\Rightarrow \quad 3x + 600 = 1350$$
$$\Rightarrow \quad 3x = 1350 - 600$$
$$\Rightarrow \quad 3x = 750$$
$$\Rightarrow \quad x = \frac{750}{3} = 250 \text{ m}$$

24. (c) Each fractions, decimal value are given below :

$$\frac{5}{11} = 0.454, \ \frac{3}{8} = 0.375, \ \frac{4}{9} = 0.444, \ \frac{2}{7} = 0.286$$

So, ascending order of the fractions is $\dfrac{2}{7}, \dfrac{3}{8}, \dfrac{4}{9}, \dfrac{5}{11}$.

25. (d) Let ten's digit be x and unit's digit be $8 - x$
Then, $x = 3(8 - x)$
$$\Rightarrow \qquad x = 24 - 3x,$$
$$\Rightarrow \qquad 4x = 24$$
$$\Rightarrow \qquad x = \frac{24}{4} = 6$$
$\therefore$ unit's digit $= 8 - x = 8 - 6 = 2$
So, required number $= 62$

26. (b) Suppose 16 men can complete the same work in x days
Then,   Men   days

$$10 \qquad 8$$
$$16 \qquad x$$

$$16 : 10 :: 8 : x$$
$$\Rightarrow \quad 16 \times x = 10 \times 8$$
$$\Rightarrow \quad x = \frac{10 \times 8}{16} = 5 \text{ days}$$

27. (b) Let the present age of father and the son is x years
and $(75 - x)$ years respectively.
5 years ago, age of father $= (x - 5)$ years
and age of son $= 75 - x - 5 = (70 - x)$ years
According to the question,
$$(x - 5)(70 - x) = 750$$
$$\Rightarrow \quad 70x - x^2 - 350 + 5x = 750$$
$$\Rightarrow \quad -x^2 + 75x - 350 = 750$$
$$\Rightarrow \quad x^2 - 55x - 20x + 1100 = 0$$
$$\Rightarrow \quad (x - 55)(x - 20) = 0$$
$$\therefore \quad x = 20, 55$$
$\therefore$ Present age of father $= 55$ years

28. (b) Let quantities of milk and water are $5x$ and x l.
According to the question,

$$\frac{5x}{x + 5} = \frac{5}{2}$$
$$\Rightarrow \quad 10x = 5x + 25$$
$$\Rightarrow \quad 5x = 25$$
$$\therefore \quad x = 5$$
Hence, the quantity of milk in the original mixture
$= 5 \times 5 = 25 \ l$

29. (b) Loss/gain per cent $= \left(10 - 10 - \dfrac{10 \times 10}{100} \right)\% = -1\%$

(– sign indicate that there is a loss of 1%)

30. (c) $16a + 16b = 48 \Rightarrow (a + b) = 48$
$\therefore \quad a + b = 3$
Hence, the required average of a and b

$$= \frac{3}{2} = 1.5$$

31. (a) Required days $= \dfrac{12 \times 4}{12 - 4} = 6$ days

32. (a) Since, the interest obtained ₹3895.68 is around 26% of the sum ₹15000, the rate of interest must be slightly less than $(26 \div 3)$, i.e., 8.6 (approx). Hence, reject the options (2), (3) and (4).

Now, check (1).

$$1500 \times \left(1 + \frac{8}{100}\right)^3 = 15000 \times \left(\frac{108}{100}\right)^3 = 18895.68$$

Now, $18895.68 - 15000 ₹ 3895.68$

Here,

$$15000\left(1 + \frac{r}{100}\right)^3 = 15000 + 3895.68$$

$$\therefore \left(1 + \frac{r}{100}\right)^3 = \frac{18895.68}{15000}$$

$$1 + \frac{r}{100} = \frac{108}{100} \Rightarrow r = 8\%$$

33. (c) The word SIGNATURE consists of nine letters comprising four vowels (A, E, I and U) and five consonants (G, N, R, T and S). When the four vowals are considered as one letter, we have six letters which can be arranged in $^6P_6$ ways i.e., 6! ways. Note that the four vowels can be arranged in 4!

Hence, required number of words = 6! × 4! = 720 × 24 = 17280

34. (b) Ratio of investment

$= 38000 \times 12 : 55000 \times 7$

$= 38 \times 12 : 55 \times 7$

$= 456 : 385 = 45 : 38$

Required difference

$$= \frac{22000}{45 + 38} \times (45 - 38)$$

$$= \frac{22000 \times 7}{83} = \frac{22000}{12}$$

$= 1835 = ₹ 1856$

35. (d) If the drawn ball is neither red nor green, then it must be blue, which can be picked in $^7C_1 = 7$ ways. One ball can be picked from the total $(8 + 7 + 6)$ in $^{21}C_1 = 21$ wasy.

36. (c) According to the questions.

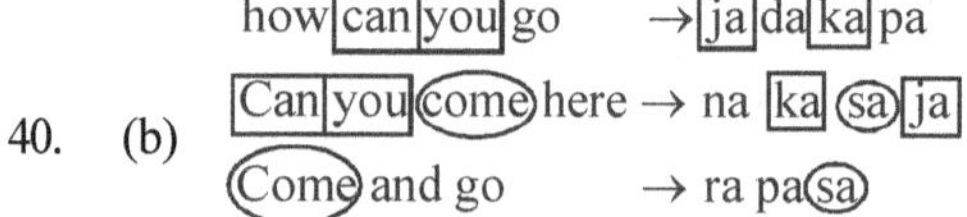

Here, Gender of R is not confirm. While R is either brother or sister of S. Hence, R may be brother-in-law or sister-in-law of T.

37. (b) According to the questions.

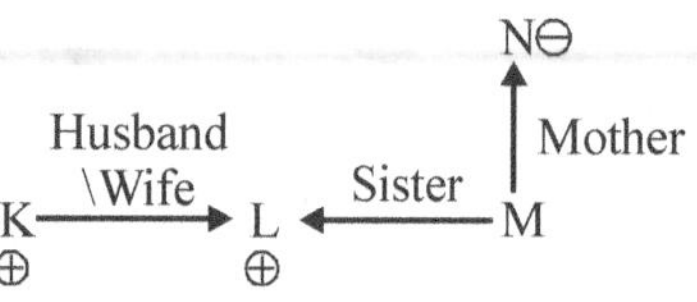

38. (a)

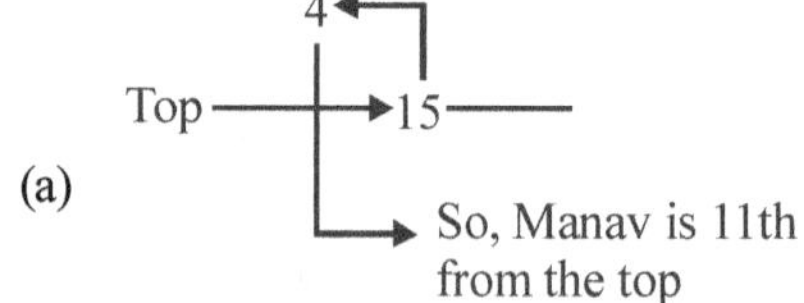

$\therefore$ Manav's rank from the bottom $= (20 - 11) + 1 = 10$th

39. (b)

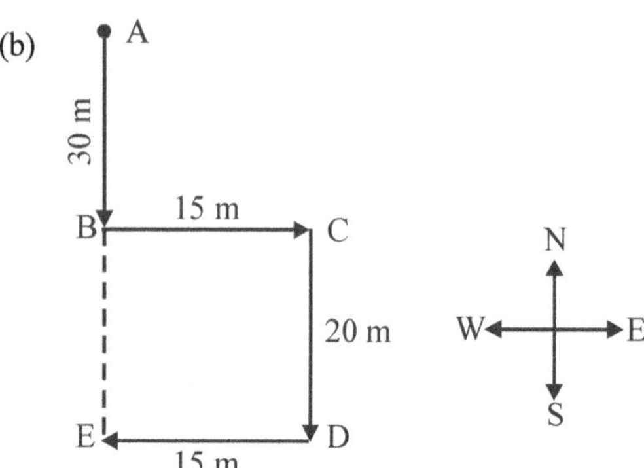

Required distance $= AE = (AB + BE)$

$= (30 + 20) = 50$

40. (b)

Hence, 'here' code is 'na'.

41. (d) **Statements** : All toys are dolls.

All dolls are jokers

Conclusions : All toys are jokers.

[A + A = A-type conclusion]

Statements : Some toys are cars.

Conclusions : Some cars are toys. (Conversion)

Statements : All toys are jokers.

Conclusions : Some cars are jokers.

(I + A = I-type conclusion)

$\therefore$ I follows.

Some cars are toys

Statements : All toys are dolls.

Conclusions : Some cars are dolls.

Some dolls are cars. (Conversion)

$\therefore$ II follows.

42. (c) **Conclusions :** Some pens are boxes.
(Implication of first statement)
Some boxes are pens.
(Conversion of first statement)
Some blades are boxes.
(Conversion of second statement)
Some files are blades.
(Conversion of third statement)
No mediate inference follows. Hence, no given **Conclusions** follows.

43. (d) **Statements :** Some pens are books.
Conclusion : Some books are pens. (conversion)

Statements : All pens are keys.
Some books are keys.
(I + A = I-type conclusion)
Some keys are books. (Conversion)
∴ II follows.
Statements : Some pens are books.

All books are ledgers.
Conclusions : Some pens are ledgers.
(I + A = I-type)
Some ledgers are pens. (conversion)

Statements : All pens are keys.
Conclusions : Some ledgers are keys.
(I + A = I-type)
∴ I follows.

44. (b) **Statements :** Some roses are thorns.

All thorns are flowers.
Conclusions : Some roses are flowers.
(I + A = I-type)
Some flowers are roses. (conversion)
Hence, II follows.
Statements : No flower is petal.
Conclusions : No petal is flower. (conversion)

Some flowers are roses.
Conclusions : Some roses are not petals.
(E + I = O*-type)
Hence, I does not follow.

45. (a) **Statements :** All leaders are good team workers.
Conclusions : Some good team workers are leaders. (Conversion)
Hence, I follows.
Statements : All good team workers are good orators.
Conclusions : Some good orators are good team workers. (conversion)
Hence, II does not follow.

(46 to 50)
The given information is summarised in a table as follows :

Teachers	Subjects	
	Compulsory	**Optional**
A	History	English
B	History	Chemistry
C	History	Mathematics
D	(Female) English	History
E	Physics	Mathematics
F	Mathematics	Physics

46. (a) History is the compulsory subject of C.
47. (d) D is a female member in the group.
48. (d) The compulsory subject of F (mathematics) is the optional subject of C.
49. (c) E has physics and mathematics as his two subjects.
50. (d) A, B and C all have history as the compulsory subjects.

51. (d)

E	B	A	J	W	U
↓	↓	↓	↓	↓	↓
%	@	%	$	6	4

Condition (i) follows.

52. (e)

J	B	I	F	M	R
↓	↓	↓	↓	↓	↓
$	@	©	$	9	7

Condition (ii) follows.

53. (b)

D	E	K	R	B	J
↓	↓	↓	↓	↓	↓
1	★	2	1	@	$

Condition (ii) follows.

54. (a)

U	Z	M	K	E	F
↓	↓	↓	↓	↓	↓
3	5	9	2	★	4

Condition (iii) follows.

55. (c)

H	I	R	E	B	W
↓	↓	↓	↓	↓	↓
8	©	7	★	@	6

None of condition follows.

Sol (56-60) According to given information, sitting arrangment is as follow

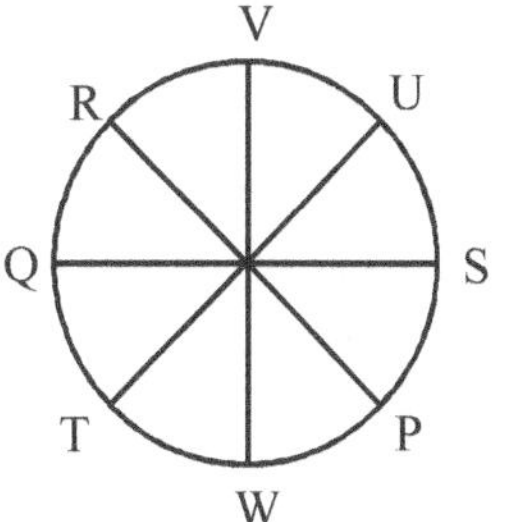

56. (e) There is no such pair given.
57. (a) Q is to the immediate left of T.
58. (c) U is second to the right of P.
59. (a) R is third to the left of W.
60. (b) P is fourth to the left of R.
61. (e) Numbers → 972, 526, 487, 359, 251
According to conditions → 297, 652, 748, 935, 125
so, the highest number = 935 i.e., 359
62. (c) Number → 972, 526, 487, 359, 251
Accoridng to conditions → 279, 625, 784, 953, 152
so, second largest number = 784 i.e., 487
63. (d) Number →

972,	526,	487,	359,	251
↓	↓	↓	↓	↓
9+7+2	5+2+6	4+8+7	3+5+9	2+5+1
18+2	13+2	19+2	17+2	8+2
↓	↓	↓	↓	↓
20	15	21	19	10

Thus, the multiples of 5 are three.
64. (a) Number → 972, 526, 487, 359 251

According to condition → 792, 256, 847, 539 , 521

In ascending order → 847, 792, 559 , 521, 256

So, third number is 539 i.e., 359
65. (b) Number →

972,	526,	487,	359,	251
↓	↓	↓	↓	↓
9+7+	5+2+	4+8+	3+5+9	2+5+1
2−1	6−1	7−1	−1	−1
↓	↓	↓	↓	↓
17	12	18	16	7

So, the sum of digits of two given numbers are prime under given conditions. 17 and 7 are prime numbers.

(66-70) :

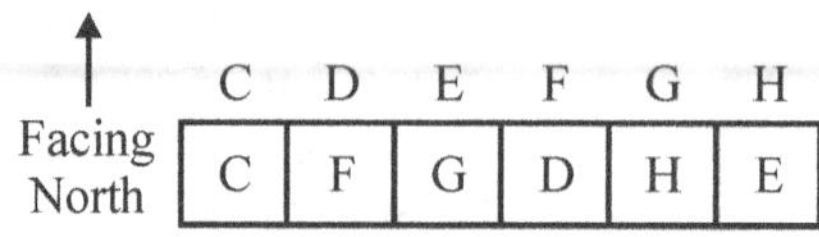

66. (c) Third to the left
67. (b) CE
68. (c) G
69. (b) GE
70. (a) One
81. **(c)** Here, and guidance to the mind tortured by doubt should be used.
Look at the sentence:
All activities take place under the guidance of an experienced tutor.
82. (d) Here, Past Simple i.e. the educated class did not support him .... should be used as the sentence shows past time.
83. (a) Here, Depletion (Noun) of the Ozone layer .... should be used.
84. (a) Here, Most of the people who should be used. Who is used to show which person or people you mean.
Look at the sentence:
The people who called yesterday want to buy the house.
85. (b) Here, in reducing human suffering .... should be used.
86. (d) Since the sentence begins in past tense. It should end in past tense also since it the subject is singular the verb will also be singular. Hence "them *is* missing" should be "them *was* missing".
87. (a) The teacher that is the subject is singular so "were" will be replaced with "was".
88. (b) "Son for help her" should be "son to help her".
89. (b) The verb "ask" will be in the past tense it will become "asked".
90. (c) "Saving" will be replaced with past tense of the verb "Save" that is saved because it is preceded by had.

PRACTICE SET   11

INSTRUCTIONS

- This Preliminary Exam practice set consists of three sections. Numerical Ability (Qs. 1-35), Reasoning (Qs. 36-70) and English Language (Qs. 71-100).
- All the questions are compulsory.
- Each question has five options, of which only one is correct. The candidates are advised to read all the options thoroughly.
- There is negative marking equivalent to 1/4th of the mark allotted to the specific question for wrong answer.

Time : 60 Minutes   **Max. Marks : 100**

NUMERICAL ABILITY

DIRECTIONS (Qs. 1-10) : *What will come in place of question mark (?) in the following questions?*

1. $72.42 + 385.66 + 4976.38 = ?$
   - (a) 5234.46
   - (b) 5434.46
   - (c) 5434.66
   - (d) 5244.66
   - (e) None of these

2. $8\dfrac{5}{9} \times 4\dfrac{3}{5} - 6\dfrac{1}{3} = ?$
   - (a) $32\dfrac{11}{45}$
   - (b) $33\dfrac{11}{45}$
   - (c) $32\dfrac{1}{45}$
   - (d) $33\dfrac{1}{45}$
   - (e) None of these

3. $\dfrac{17 \times 4 + 4^2 \times 2}{90 \div 5 \times 12} = ?$
   - (a) $\dfrac{25}{54}$
   - (b) $\dfrac{22}{57}$
   - (c) $\dfrac{11}{27}$
   - (d) $\dfrac{13}{27}$
   - (e) None of these

4. 16% of $250 + 115\%$ of $480 = ?$
   - (a) 522
   - (b) 588
   - (c) 582
   - (d) 498
   - (e) None of these

5. 55% of $860 + ?\%$ of $450 = 581$
   - (a) 24
   - (b) 28
   - (c) 32
   - (d) 36
   - (e) None of these

6. $16.45 \times 2.8 + 4.5 \times 1.6 = ?$
   - (a) 56.23
   - (b) 56.32
   - (c) 53.26
   - (d) 53.66
   - (e) None of these

7. $8\dfrac{2}{5} \times 5\dfrac{2}{3} + ? = 50\dfrac{1}{5}$
   - (a) $3\dfrac{2}{5}$
   - (b) $2\dfrac{2}{5}$
   - (c) $3\dfrac{3}{5}$
   - (d) $2\dfrac{3}{5}$
   - (e) None of these

8. $2520 \div 14 \div 9 = ?$
   - (a) 22
   - (b) 18
   - (c) 20
   - (d) 16
   - (e) None of these

9. $\dfrac{5}{9}$ of $504 + \dfrac{3}{8}$ of $640 = ?$
   - (a) 520
   - (b) 480
   - (c) 460
   - (d) 540
   - (e) None of these

10. 3.2% of $250 + 1.8\%$ of $400 = ?$
    - (a) 14.8
    - (b) 15.75
    - (c) 14.75
    - (d) 15.2
    - (e) None of these

11. Populations of two villages X and Y are in the ratio of 5 : 7 respectively. If the population of village Y increases by 25000 and the population of village X remains unchanged the respective ratio of their populations becomes 25:36. What is the population of village X?

    (a) 625000   (b) 675000
    (c) 875000   (d) 900000
    (e) None of these

12. The length of a rectangular field is thrice its breadth. If the cost of cultivating the field at ₹ 367.20 per square metre is ₹ 27,540, then what is the perimeter of the rectangle?
    (a) 47 m   (b) 39 m
    (c) 52 m   (d) 40 m
    (e) None of these

13. If the fractions $\dfrac{8}{5}, \dfrac{7}{2}, \dfrac{9}{5}, \dfrac{5}{4}, \dfrac{4}{5}$ are arranged in descending order of their values, which one will be the fourth?
    (a) $\dfrac{4}{5}$ (b) $\dfrac{5}{4}$
    (c) $\dfrac{9}{5}$ (d) $\dfrac{8}{5}$
    (e) $\dfrac{7}{2}$

14. In how many different ways can 4 boys and 3 girls be arranged in a row such that all the boys stand together and all the girls stand together?
    (a) 75   (b) 576
    (c) 288   (d) 24
    (e) None of these

15. Mr. Sharma invested an amount of ₹25000 in fixed deposit @ compound interest 8% per annum for two years. What amount Mr. Sharma will get on maturity ?
    (a) ₹ 28540   (b) ₹ 29160
    (c) ₹ 29240   (d) ₹ 28240
    (e) None of these

16. Beena and Meena started a boutique investing amounts of ₹ 35000 and ₹ 56000 respectively. If Beena's share in the profit earned by them is ₹ 45000, what is the total profit earned?
    (a) ₹ 81000   (b) ₹ 127000
    (c) ₹ 72000   (d) ₹ 117000
    (e) None of the above

17. Nandkishore gives 35% of the money he had to his wife and gave 50% of the money he had to his sons. Remaining amount of ₹ 11250 he kept for himself. What was the total amount of money Nandkishore had?
    (a) ₹ 63750   (b) ₹ 75000
    (c) ₹ 73650   (d) ₹ 72450
    (e) None of these

18. Simple interest accrued on an amount in eight years @ 11% per annum is ₹ 57200. What was the principal amount ?
    (a) ₹ 72000   (b) ₹ 82000
    (c) ₹ 75000   (d) ₹ 65000
    (e) None of these

19. Four-fifth of a number is 10 more than two-third of the same number. What is the number?
    (a) 70   (b) 75
    (c) 69   (d) 85
    (e) None of these

20. A shopkeeper purchased 200 bulbs for ₹ 10 each. However, 5 bulbs were fused and had to be thrown away. The remaining were sold at ₹ 12 each. What will be the percentage profit?
    (a) 25   (b) 15
    (c) 13   (d) 17
    (e) None of these

21. The average monthly income of a family of four earning members was ₹15,130. One of the daughter in the family got married and left home, so the average monthly income of the family came down to ₹ 14,660. What is the monthly income of the married daughter?
    (a) ₹ 15,350   (b) ₹ 12,000
    (c) ₹ 16,540   (d) Cannot be determined
    (e) None of these

22. On a test consisting of 250 questions, Jassi answered 40% of the first 125 questions correctly. What percent of the other 125 question does she need to answer correctly for her grade on the entire exam to be 60%?
    (a) 75   (b) 80
    (c) 60   (d) Cannot be determined
    (e) None of these

23. The ratio between the ages of *A* and *B* is 2 : 5. After 8 years their ages will be in the ratio 1 : 2. What is the difference between their present ages?
    (a) 20 years   (b) 22 years
    (c) 24 years   (d) 25 years
    (e) None of these

24. Excluding the stoppages, the speed of a bus is 64 km/hr and including the stoppage the speed of the bus is 48 km/hr. For how many minutes does the bus stop per hour?
    (a) 12.5 minutes   (b) 15 minutes
    (c) 10 minutes   (d) 18 minutes
    (e) None of these

25. In an army camp ration is available for 100 soldiers for 10 days. After 2 days, 60 soldiers joined. Then, for how many more days will the remaining ration last?
    (a) 7 days   (b) 6 days
    (c) 5 days   (d) 4 days
    (e) None of these

DIRECTIONS (Qs. 26-30): *What should come in place of the question mark (?) in the following number series?*

26. 10000, 2000, 400, 80, 16, 3. 2, ?
    (a) 0.38   (b) 0.45
    (c) 0.64   (d) 0.54
    (e) None of these

27. 2, 10, 42, 170, ?, 2730, 10922
    (a) 588   (b) 658
    (c) 596   (d) 682
    (e) None of these

28. 600, 519, ?, 406, 370, 345, 329
    (a) 435   (b) 455
    (c) 425   (d) 445
    (e) None of these

29. 5, ?, 15, 75, 525, 4725, 51975
    - (a) 5
    - (b) 10
    - (c) 8
    - (d) 6
    - (e) None of these
30. 3, 6, 12, 24, 48, 96, ?
    - (a) 192
    - (b) 182
    - (c) 186
    - (d) 198
    - (e) None of these

DIRECTIONS (Qs. 31-35) : *Study the following graph carefully to answer the questions that follow.*

Number of Students (in hundred) from Two Different Schools who Qualified in an Exam in Six Different Years

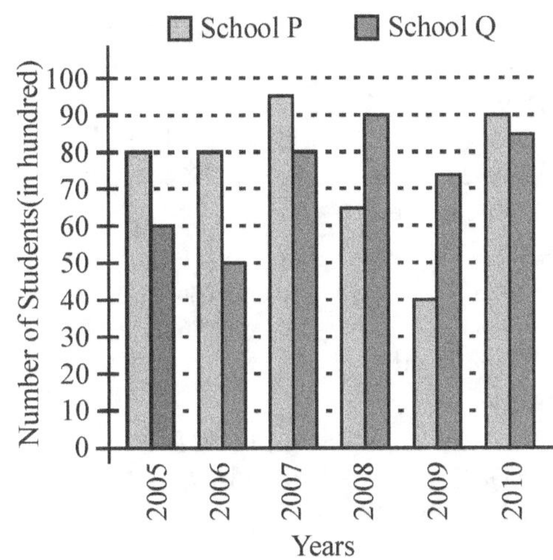

31. What was the approximate percent increase in the number of students who qualified in the exam from School Q in the year 2007 as compared to the previous year?
    - (a) 30
    - (b) 36
    - (c) 60
    - (d) 49
    - (e) 26
32. What was the respective ratio between the number of students who qualified in the exam from School P in the year 2005 and the number of students who qualified in the exam from School Q in the year 2008 ?
    - (a) 13 : 18
    - (b) 8 : 9
    - (c) 9 : 8
    - (d) 13 : 19
    - (e) None of these
33. What was the difference between the total number of students who qualified in the exam in the year 2005 from both the schools together and the total number of students from School Q who qualified in exam over all the years together?
    - (a) 30000
    - (b) 30500
    - (c) 29000
    - (d) 29500
    - (e) None of these
34. Total number of students who qualified in the exam from School P overall the years together was approximately what percentage of total number of students who qualified in the exam from both the schools together in the years 2006 and 2007 together?
    - (a) 143
    - (b) 159
    - (c) 155
    - (d) 165
    - (e) 147

35. If 40% of the total students who qualified in the exam from both the schools together overall the years are females, then what was the total number of males who qualified in the exam overall the years from both the schools together?
    - (a) 51000
    - (b) 54300
    - (c) 53400
    - (d) 52000
    - (e) None of these

DIRECTIONS (Qs. 36-40) : *In each of the questions below are given three statements followed by four conclusions numbered I, II, III and IV. You have to take the given statements to be true even if they seem to be at variance with commonly know facts. Read all the conclusions and then decide which of the given conclusions logically follows from the given statements disregarding commonly known facts.*

36. **Statements :**
    - A. Some boys are rains.
    - B. All rains are clouds.
    - C. Some clouds are cars.

    Conclusions :
    - I. Some clouds are boys.
    - II. Some cars are boys.
    - III. Some cars are rains.
    - IV. Some rains are boys.
    - (a) Only II follows
    - (b) Only IV follows
    - (c) Only I follows
    - (d) Both I and IV follow
    - (e) None of these
37. **Statements :**
    - A. All bricks are flowers.
    - B. Some houses are flowers.
    - C. All pens are houses.

    Conclusions :
    - I. Some houses are bricks.
    - II. Some pens are flowers.
    - III. Some flowers are bricks.
    - IV. No pen is flower.
    - (a) Only either II or IV and III follow
    - (b) Only either II or IV and I follow
    - (c) Only either I or II and IV follow
    - (d) Either II or IV follow
    - (e) None of these
38. **Statements :**
    - A. All lions are ducks.
    - B. No duck is a horse.
    - C. All horses are fruits.

    Conclusions :
    - I. No lion is a horse.
    - II. Some fruits are horses.
    - III. Some ducks are lions.
    - IV. Some lions are horses.
    - (a) All follows
    - (b) Only either I or II and both III and IV follow
    - (c) Only either I or IV and both II and III follow
    - (d) Neither I nor II follow
    - (e) None of these
39. **Statements :**
    - A. Some stones are bricks.
    - B. All plants are stones.
    - C. No flower is a plant.

Conclusions :
- I. No flower is a stone.
- II. Some bricks are plants.
- III. No bricks are plants.

(a) Only I follows   (b) Only II follows

(c) Only III follows   (d) Either II or III follows

(e) None of these

40. **Statements :**
- A. All tigers are jungles.
- B. No jungle is a bird.
- C. Some birds are rains.

Conclusions :
- I. No rain is a jungle.
- II. Some rains are jungles.
- III. No bird is a tiger.

(a) Only either II or III follows

(b) Only I and II follow

(c) Only either I or II and III follow

(d) Neither II nor III follow

(e) None of these

DIRECTIONS (Qs. 41-45) : *Study the following information carefully to answer the given questions.*

Eleven colleagues P, Q, R, S, T, U, V, W, X, Y and Z are sitting in the first row of the table facing the chairman. S who is to the immediate left of U is second to the right of R. P is second to the right of T, who is at one of the ends. Y is an immediate neighbour of P and Q and third to the left of V. W is to the immediate left of S and third to the right of X.

41. Who is sitting in the middle of the row?

(a) Q   (b) V

(c) R   (d) Y

(e) None of these

42. Which of the groups of colleagues is sitting to the right of V?

(a) RVXY   (b) SURX

(c) TQWY   (d) SURW

(e) SUWP

43. Which of the following is true with respect to above arrangement?

(a) T and S are sitting at the extreme ends

(b) X is between S and R

(c) There are two persons between P and X

(d) Z and P are immediate neighbours of Y

(e) None of these

44. If all the members are made to sit in an alphabetical order from left to right, how many of them retain the same position?

(a) none   (b) one

(c) two   (d) three

(e) four

45. Which among the following is sitting third to the left of second from the right end?

(a) V   (b) U

(c) X   (d) Y

(e) Z

DIRECTIONS (Qs. 46-50) : *In each of these questions a group of letters is given followed by four combinations of numbers codes lettered (a), (b), (c) and (d). The group of letters is to be coded with the numbers codes and the condition given below. The 'serial number of the number combination'. Which correctly represents the letter group, is your answer.*

Letters	D	J	K	Q	H	V	N	E	B	A
Numbers Codes	3	9	7	6	4	8	2	1	5	0

Conditions : If the first or the last letter or both in the letter group is /are a vowel then the same is/are to be coded by symbol #.

46. EHNDJV

(a) #42389   (b) 142398

(c) #42398   (d) 14239#

(e) None of these

47. KQDJNH

(a) 763942   (b) 736924

(c) #36924   (d) #63924

(e) None of these

48. AJNVQE

(a) #9286#   (b) 09286#

(c) #92861   (d) 092861

(e) None of these

49. QHJVND

(a) 648923   (b) 649823

(c) #49823   (d) 64892#

(e) None of these

50. JKEDHA

(a) 97#34#   (b) 971340

(c) 971430   (d) 97134#

(e) None of these

DIRECTIONS (Qs. 51-55) : *Study the following arrangement to answer the given questions.*

915   678   435   768   123   576

51. If the position of the 1st letter and the 2nd letter of each number are interchanged, then which of the following number will be the lowest number ?

(a) 213   (b) 951

(c) 768   (d) 195

(e) None

52. Which of the following is the sum of the 1st and 3rd digits of the second highest number ?

(a) 15   (b) 14

(c) 13   (d) 12

(e) None

53. If the position of 1st and 3rd letters are interchanged then what will be the third highest number ?

(a) None   (b) 876

(c) 576   (d) 657

(e) 435

54. If 1 is added to the first digit of the even number and 1 is subtracted from the first digit of an odd number, then What will be the sum of second lowest number ?

(a) 15   (b) 20

(c) 14   (d) 11

(e) None

55. If all the digits of each number is written in increasing order, then two number will be equal, find that number?
    (a) 159   (b) 678
    (c) 567   (d) 321
    (e) None

56. How many meaningful English words can be formed with the letters NCEO using each letter • only once in each word ?
    (a) None   (b) One
    (c) Two   (d) Three
    (e) More than three

57. The positions of first and the fourth letters of the word LIQUID are interchanged, similarly, the positions of second and fifth letters and third and Sixth letters are interchanged. In the new arrangement thus formed, how many letters are there in the English alphabetical series between the alphabets which are at the extreme ends?
    (a) None   (b) Two
    (c) Three   (d) Four
    (e) More than four

58. Vinay goes 30 m North, then turns right and walks 40 m, then again turns right and walks 20 m, then again turns right and walks 40 m. How many metres is he from his original position ?
    (a) 0   (b) 10
    (c) 20   (d) 40
    (e) None of these

DIRECTIONS: (Qs. 59-60): *Read the following information carefully to answer the following questions.*

A * B means A is the sister of B
A ÷ B means A is the brother of B
A + B means A is the father of B
A - B means A is the mother of B

59. What is the relation between Q and R in 'P + Q ÷ R - S'
    (a) Q is the aunt of R   (b) Q is the brother of R
    (c) Q is the mother of R   (d) Q is the father of R
    (e) None of these

60. In P - Q + R ÷ S, what is P to R-
    (a) Grandfather   (b) mother
    (c) grandmother   (d) father
    (e) None of these

DIRECTIONS: (Qs. 61-65): *Study the given information carefully and answer the questions that follow.*

Eight friends - P, Q, R, S, T, U, V and W - are sitting around a circular table facing the centre but not necessarily in the same order. Each of them likes different cricketers - Kohli, Rohit, Dhawan, Smith, Warner, Root, Gayle and Nehra.

• There are two persons between those two persons who like Kohli and Rohit and neither of them sits opposite P. R and V are immediate neighbours and neither of them likes Nehra or Rohit. P, who likes Gayle, sits second to the right of the girl who likes Nehra. Q and T neither like Nehra nor sit adjacent to P. T, who likes Rohit, sits second to the left of V, who likes

Smith. R does not like Kohli.

• The immediate neighbour of T faces R, who sits third to the left of the one who likes Gayle. U does not like Nehra. Both S and W do not like Kohli and Dhawan. Q likes Root while S likes Warner. Q is not an immediate neighbour of P.

61. Which of the following is the favourite cricketer of P?
    (a) Warner   (b) Kohli
    (c) Dhawan   (d) Gayle
    (e) None of these

62. Dhawan is the favourite cricketer of which of the following?
    (a) P   (b) Q
    (c) R   (d) S
    (e) None of these

63. Who among the following is exactly between Q and S?
    (a) R   (b) U
    (c) V   (d) T
    (e) None of these

64. Four of the following five are alike in a certain way based on the given arrangement and thus form a group. Which of the following does not belong to that group?
    (a) V - Smith   (b) P - Gayle
    (c) Q - Kohli   (d) R - Dhawan
    (e) S - Warner

65. Who is sitting opposite to the person who likes Nehra?
    (a) Q   (b) T
    (c) P   (d) R
    (e) None of these

DIRECTIONS (66-68): *Study the following information carefully to answer the questions.*
(a) If the data in statement I alone is sufficient to answer the question.
(b) If the data in statement II alone is sufficient to answer the question.
(c) If the data either in statement I alone or statement II alone are sufficient to answer the question.
(d) If the data given in both I and II together are not sufficient to answer the question.
(e) If the data in both the statements I and II together are necessary to answer the question.

66. Who is sitting in between A and B in a circular arrangement of 5 people?
    I. B is sitting 2nd to the right of C and is immediate neighbor of D.
    II. D is immediate neighbor of C.

67. How many children does Anuradha have?
    I. Preeti is the only sister of Ravi who is grandson of Bhuvan. Anuradha is daughter-in-law of Madhu and sister-in-law of Radhika.
    II. Manish is married to Anuradha and is son of Bhuvan. Ritu, sister of Anuradha is married to Suraj. Ravi is the only brother of Preeti.

68. Which direction is Anu facing?
    I. Shilpi is facing the opposite direction of Anu and also Shipra who is facing east is sitting in left of Shilpi.
    II. Bhavna starts from her home in north direction, goes straight and turns; now she is facing Anu.

DIRECTIONS (69-70): *Study the following information carefully and answer the questions given below.*

A is 15 m to the west of B. C is 13 m to the South of B and 5 m to the east of D. E is 20 m to north of D. E is 10 m to the east of G.

69. If X is 7 m to the west of E, then which of the following will be nearest point of X?
   (a) C   (b) G
   (c) D   (d) B
   (e) A

70. In which direction is G with respect of A?
   (a) South-East   (b) South
   (c) North-West   (d) South-West
   (e) North

ENGLISH LANGUAGE

DIRECTIONS (Q. 71-80): *Read the following passage to answer the given questions based on it, Some words/phrases are printed in bold to help you locate them while answermg some of the questions.*

The e-waste (Management and Handling) Rules, 2011, notified by the Ministry of Environmynt and Forests, have the potential to turn a growing problem into a developmental opportunity. With almost half-a-year to go before the rules take effect, there is enough time to create the necessary infrastructure for collection, dismantling and recycling of electronic waste. The focus must be on sincere and efficient implementation. Only decisive action can reduce the pollution and health costs associated with India's hazardous waste recycling industry. If India can achieve a transformation, it will be creating a whole new-employment sector that provides good wages and working conditions for tens of thousands. The legacy response of the States to even the basic law on urban waste, the Municipal Solid Wastes (Management and Handling) Rules has been one of indifference; many cities continue to simply bum the garbage or dump it in lakes. With the emphasis now on segregation of waste at source and recovery of materials. it should be feasible to implement **both sets of rules** efficiently. A welcome feature of the new e-waste rules is the emphasis on extended producer responsibility. In other words, producers must take responsibility for the disposal of end-of-life products. For this provision to work, they must ensure that consumers who sell scrap get some form of financial incentive.

The e-waste rules, which derive from those pertaining to hazardous waste, are scheduled to come into force on May 1, 2012. Sound as they are, the task of scientifically disposing a few hundred thousand tonnes of trash electronics annually depends heavily on a system of oversight by State Pollutions Control Boards (PCBs). Unfortunately, most PCBs remain unaccountable and often lack the resources for active enforcement. It must be pointed out that, although agencies handling e-waste must obtain environmental clearances and be authorised and registered by the PCBs even under the Hazardous Wastes (Management, Handling and Transboundary Movement) Rules 2008, there has been little practical impact. Over 95 per cent of electronic waste is collected and recycled by the informal sector. The way forward is for the PCBs to be made accountable for enforcement of the e-waste rules and the levy of penalties under environmental laws. Clearly, the first order priority is to create a system that will absorb the 80,000-strong workforce in the informal sector into the proposed scheme for scientific recycling. Facilities must be created to upgrade the skills of these workers through training and their occupational health must be ensured.

Recycling of e-waste is one of the biggest challenges today. In such a time, when globalisation and information technology are growing at a pace **which could only be imagined few years back**, e-waste and its hazards have become more prominent over a period of time and should be given immediate attention.

71. What, according to the passage, is important now for e-waste management?
   (a) Making rules   (b) Reviewing rules
   (c) Implementing rules   (d) Notifying rules
   (e) Amending rules

72. Which of the following can be one ofthe by-products of effective e-waste management?
   (a) India can guide other countries in doing so.
   (b) It will promote international understanding.
   (c) It will promote national integration.
   (d) It will create a new employment sector.
   (e) It will further empowet judiciary.

73. Which of the following rules has not been indicated in the passage?
   (a) e-waste Rules 20 11
   (b) Pollution Check Rules
   (c) Hazardous Wastes Rules, 2008
   (d) Municipal Solid Wastes Rules
   (e) All these have been indicated

74. "Both sets of rules" is being referred to which of the following?
   (a) Solid wastes and hazardous wastes
   (b) e-waste and hazardous waste
   (c) Solid waste and e-waste
   (d) e-waste and e-production
   (e) Solid waste and recycling waste

75. e-waste rules have been derived from those pertaining to
   (a) Hazardous waste   (b) PC waste
   (c) Computer waste   (d) Municipal solid waste
   (d) National waste

76. Which of the following will help implement "both sets of rules"?
   (a) Employment opportunities
   (b) International collaboration
   (c) Financial incentive
   (d) Segregation of waste at source
   (e) Health costs

77. e-waste Rules came/come into force from
   (a) 2008   (b) 2009
   (c) 2010   (d) 2011
   (e) 2012

78. Which of the following best explains the meaning of the phrase "which could only be imagined few years back" as used in the passage?
   (a) It was doomed.

    (b)   It took us few years.
    (c)   It took us back by few years
    (d)   Imagination is better than IT.
    (e)   None of these

79. Which of the following is true in the context of the passage?
    (a)   No city dumps its waste in lakes.
    (b)   Some cities burn garbage.
    (c)   PCBs have adequate resources for'active enforcement.
    (d)   e-waste was a much bigger chajlenge in the past.
    (e)   None of these

80. Which of the following is **not true** 10 the context of the passage?
    (a)   Some fonn offmancial incentive is recommended for the producers.
    (b)   Some financial incentive is recommended for the consumers.
    (c)   e-waste will be a few hundred thousand tonnes.
    (d)   The agencies handling e-waste have to obtain environmental clearances.
    (e)   Those involved in e-waste management would need to upgrade their skills.

DIRECTIONS (Qs. 81-90): *Read each sentence to find out whether there is any grammatical error or idiomatic error in it. The error, if any will be in one part of the sentence. The number of that part in the answer. If there is no error, the answer is (e). (Ignore error of punctuation, if any).*

81. The decline of her moral (a) / was caused by a lot of (b) / factors that were once (c) / fascinating to her. (d) / No Error (e)

82. He took me to a restaurant (a) / and ordered for two cups (b) / of cold coffee (c) / which the waiter brought in an hour. (d) / No Error (e)

83. There are some animals (a) / that can live (b) / both in water an land (c) / without any difficulty. (d) / No Error (e)

84. During his tour (a) / to the south (b) he visited not only to Chennai (c) / but also Karnataka. (d) / No Error (e)

85. The President Mr. Kalam (a) / is much sought after (b) / by school students and (c) / is invited for many functions. (d) / No Error (e)

86. His mother is not well (a) / but he (b) / does not look for her (c) / properly. (d) / No Error (e)

87. We may have to await for (a) / a new political revival (b) / to eradicate the (c) / corruption from our economy. (d) / No Error (e)

88. When she was (a) / in jail (b) / she was debarred to send (c) / a letter even to her son. (d) / No Error (e)

89. Despite of the best efforts (a) / put by the doctors (b) / the condition of the patient (c) / is deteriorating from bad to worse. (d) / No Error (e)

90. The militant yielded for (a)/the temptation and fell (b)/into the trap (c)/of police. (d)/No Error (e)

DIRECTIONS (QS. 91-100): *In the passage given below there are blanks, each of which has been numbered. The numbers are printed below the passage, against each, five words are suggested, one of which fits the blank appropriately. Find the appropriate word in each case.*

The Right of Children to Free and Compulsory Education (RTE) Act, 2009, which came **(91)** effect in April this year, is meant to transform the education sector and take India closer to the goal of universal schooling. But with admissions to the new academic session just **(92)** the corner, it is fast becoming clear that **(93)** well intentioned ideas into **(94)** will take some doing. For a start, the guidelines for admissions under the RTE prohibit schools from conducting any sort of student profiling. The stress on a random yet justifiable admission process means that schools will have to resort to something as quirky as a lottery system. However, leaving admission to a good school to pure **(95)** will only incentivise manipulations, defeating the very essence of RTE.

The main problem facing the education sector is that of a resource crunch. The provisions for ensuring universal access to education are all very well, **(96)** we have the infrastructure in place first. Brick and mortar schools need to precede open admission and not the **(97)** way around. In that sense, legislators' assessment of ground realities is **(98)** target when they endorse the closure of tens of thousands of low-cost private schools for not meeting the minimum standards of land plot, building specifications and playground area as laid out in the RTE Act. Instead of bearing down **(99)** on private schools for failing to conform to abstract bureaucratic criteria, efforts to bring about universal education should focus on upgrading and expanding the existing government school infrastructure to accommodate all. Only then can we ensure the much needed supply-demand **(100)** in the education sector.

91. (a) with   (b) for   (c) on
    (d) into   (e) in

92. (a) around   (b) near   (c) into
    (d) about   (e) reaching

93. (a) forming   (b) translating   (c) having
    (d) taking   (e) framing

94. (a) affect   (b) ideas   (c) practice
    (d) concept   (e) procedure

95. (a) benefit   (b) merit   (c) chance
    (d) basis   (e) method

96. (a) unless   (b) until   (c) executed
    (d) provided   (e) exercised

97. (a) other   (b) any   (c) two
    (d) differ   (e) after

98. (a) on   (b) of   (c) often
    (d) taken   (e) off

99. (a) soft   (b) more   (c) less
    (d) only   (e) hard

100. (a) need   (b) equilibrium
    (c) expectation   (d) attempt
    (e) aspects

Answer Key

1	(b)	11	(a)	21	(c)	31	(c)	41	(e)	51	(b)	61	(d)	71	(c)	81	(a)	91	(d)
2	(d)	12	(d)	22	(b)	32	(b)	42	(d)	52	(a)	62	(c)	72	(d)	82	(b)	92	(a)
3	(a)	13	(b)	23	(c)	33	(a)	43	(c)	53	(c)	63	(d)	73	(b)	83	(c)	93	(b)
4	(e)	14	(c)	24	(b)	34	(e)	44	(b)	54	(d)	64	(c)	74	(e)	84	(c)	94	(c)
5	(a)	15	(b)	25	(c)	35	(c)	45	(a)	55	(b)	65	(b)	75	(a)	85	(d)	95	(c)
6	(c)	16	(d)	26	(c)	36	(e)	46	(c)	56	(c)	66	(d)	76	(d)	86	(c)	96	(d)
7	(d)	17	(b)	27	(d)	37	(a)	47	(e)	57	(c)	67	(d)	77	(e)	87	(a)	97	(a)
8	(c)	18	(d)	28	(b)	38	(c)	48	(a)	58	(b)	68	(a)	78	(e)	88	(c)	98	(e)
9	(a)	19	(b)	29	(a)	39	(d)	49	(b)	59	(b)	69	(b)	79	(b)	89	(a)	99	(e)
10	(d)	20	(d)	30	(a)	40	(c)	50	(d)	60	(c)	70	(e)	80	(a)	90	(a)	100	(b)

HINTS & EXPLANATIONS

1. (b) $? = 72.42 + 385.66 + 4976.38$
$\Rightarrow ? = 5434.46$

2. (d) $? = 8\frac{5}{9} \times 4\frac{3}{5} - 6\frac{1}{3}$

$\Rightarrow ? = \frac{77}{9} \times \frac{23}{5} - \frac{19}{3}$

$\Rightarrow ? = \frac{1771 - 285}{45}$

$\Rightarrow ? = \frac{1486}{45} = 33\frac{1}{45}$

3. (a) $? = \dfrac{17 \times 4 + 4^2 \times 2}{90 \div 5 \times 12}$

$\Rightarrow ? = \dfrac{68 + 16 \times 2}{18 \times 12}$

$\Rightarrow ? = \dfrac{68 + 32}{216}$

$\Rightarrow ? = \dfrac{100}{216} = \dfrac{25}{54}$

4. (e) $? = 16\% \text{ of } 250 + 115\% \text{ of } 480$

$\Rightarrow ? = \dfrac{16}{100} \times 250 + \dfrac{115}{100} \times 480$

$\Rightarrow ? = \dfrac{4000}{100} + \dfrac{55200}{100}$

$\Rightarrow ? = 40 + 552 = 592$

5. (a) $55\% \text{ of } 860 + ?\% \text{ of } 450 = 581$

$\Rightarrow \dfrac{55}{100} \times 860 + \dfrac{?}{100} \times 450 = 581$

$\Rightarrow 473 + \dfrac{?}{100} \times 450 = 581$

$\Rightarrow \dfrac{?}{100} \times 450 = 581 - 473 = 108$

$\Rightarrow ? = \dfrac{108 \times 100}{450} = 24$

6. (c) $? = 16.45 \times 2.8 + 4.5 \times 1.6$
$\Rightarrow ? = 46.06 + 7.20$
$\Rightarrow ? = 53.26$

7. (d) $8\frac{2}{5} \times 5\frac{2}{3} + ? = 50\frac{1}{5}$

$\Rightarrow \dfrac{42}{5} \times \dfrac{17}{3} + ? = \dfrac{251}{5}$

$\Rightarrow \dfrac{238}{5} + ? = \dfrac{251}{5}$

$\Rightarrow ? = \dfrac{251}{5} - \dfrac{238}{5}$

$\Rightarrow ? = \dfrac{13}{5} = 2\frac{3}{5}$

8. (c) $? = 2520 \div 14 \div 9$
$\Rightarrow ? = 180 \div 9 = 20$

9. (a) $? = \dfrac{5}{9} \text{ of } 504 + \dfrac{3}{8} \text{ of } 640$

$\Rightarrow ? = \dfrac{5}{9} \times 504 + \dfrac{3}{8} \times 640$

$\Rightarrow ? = 280 + 240$
$\Rightarrow ? = 520$

10. (d) $? = 3.2\% \text{ of } 250 + 1.8\% \text{ of } 400$

$\Rightarrow ? = \dfrac{3.2}{100} \times 250 + \dfrac{1.8}{100} \times 400$

$\Rightarrow ? = \dfrac{800}{100} + \dfrac{720}{100}$

$\Rightarrow ? = 8 + 7.2 = 15.2$

11. (a) Let the population of village X and Y be $5p$ and $7p$ respectively.
If population of village Y, increases by 25000

the new ratio $\rightarrow \dfrac{5p}{7p+25000} = \dfrac{25}{36}$

$\Rightarrow 180p = 175p + 625000$
$\Rightarrow 5p = 625000$

12. (d) Let the breadth of the rectangle be x metre.
$\therefore$ Length $= 3x$ metre

$\therefore 3x \times x = \dfrac{27540}{367.20} = 75$

$\Rightarrow x^2 = 25$
$\Rightarrow x = 5$

$\therefore$ Perimeter of the rectangle
$= 2(3x + x) = 8x$
$= 8 \times 5 = 40$ metre

13. (b) Decimal equivalent of each fraction :

$\dfrac{8}{5} = 1.6$; $\dfrac{7}{2} = 3.5$

$\dfrac{9}{5} = 1.8$; $\dfrac{5}{4} = 1.25$

$\dfrac{4}{5} = 0.8$

Clearly, $\dfrac{7}{2} > \dfrac{9}{5} > \dfrac{8}{5} > \dfrac{5}{4} > \dfrac{4}{5}$

14. (c) Total number of ways to stand boys and girls together
$= 4! \times 3! \times 2! = 4 \times 3 \times 2 \times 3 \times 2 \times 2 = 288$

15. (b) Required amount $= 25000 \left(1 + \dfrac{8}{100}\right)^2$

$= 25000 \times \dfrac{27}{25} \times \dfrac{27}{25} = ₹29160$

16. (d) Amount ratio between Beena and Meena
$= 35000 : 56000 = 5 : 8$
Let the share of Beena and Meena amount be $5x$ and $8x$ respectively.
Then, $5x = 45000$

$\Rightarrow x = \dfrac{45000}{5} = ₹9000$

$\therefore$ Amount (profit) of Meena $= 8x = 8 \times 9000 = ₹72000$
So, total earned profit $= 45000 + 72000 = ₹117000$

17. (b) Let Nand Kishore's total money was $= ₹x$
After giving some amount to his wife and his sons, remaining amount

$= x - \left(x \times \dfrac{35}{100} + x \times \dfrac{50}{100}\right) = x - \dfrac{85x}{100} = ₹\dfrac{15x}{100}$

Then, $\dfrac{15x}{100} = ₹11250$

$\Rightarrow x = \dfrac{11250 \times 100}{15} = ₹75000$

18. (d) Let principal amount $= x$

Then, $57200 = \dfrac{x \times 11 \times 8}{100}$

$\Rightarrow x = \dfrac{57200 \times 100}{11 \times 8} = ₹65000$

19. (b) Let the number be x.

$\therefore \dfrac{4x}{5} = \dfrac{2}{3}x + 10$

$\Rightarrow \dfrac{4x}{5} - \dfrac{2x}{3} = 10$

$\Rightarrow \dfrac{12x - 10x}{15} = 10$

$\Rightarrow x = \dfrac{10 \times 15}{2} = 75$

20. (d) Total cost price $= 200 \times 10 = ₹2000$
Total selling price $= 12 \times 195 = ₹2340$

$\therefore$ Profit per cent $= \dfrac{2340 - 2000}{2000} \times 100 = 17\%$

21. (c) $\Rightarrow$ Total income of the four-membered family
$= 4 \times 15130 = ₹60520$
$\Rightarrow$ Total income of three family members
$= 3 \times 14660 = ₹43980$
$\Rightarrow$ Monthly income of the married daughter
$= 60520 - 43980 = ₹16540$

22. (b) Total correct questions for getting 60% grade

$= 250 \times \dfrac{60}{100} = 150$

40% of 125 = 50 questions
$\therefore$ x% of 125 = 150 − 50 = 100 questions

$\Rightarrow x = \dfrac{100 \times 100}{125} = 80$

Required percentage = 80%
Note: This can be solved by alligation method quickly. Try it.

23. (c) Let the ages of A and B are $2x$ and $5x$ years.
According to the question,

$\dfrac{2x + 8}{5x + 8} = \dfrac{1}{2}$

$\Rightarrow 4x + 16 = 5x + 8$
$\Rightarrow x = 8$

$\therefore$ Difference between their present ages
$= 5x - 2x = 3x \quad = 3 \times 8 = 24$ years

24. (b) Stoppage time per hour

$= \dfrac{64 - 48}{64} = \dfrac{1}{4} \times 60 = \dfrac{1}{4}$ hr $= 15$ minutes

25. (c)

Soldiers	Days
100 ↑	8 ↓
160	x

$\Rightarrow \dfrac{160}{100} = \dfrac{8}{x}$

$$\therefore \quad x = \frac{8 \times 100}{160} = 5 \text{ days}$$

26. (c) The pattern of number series is as follow

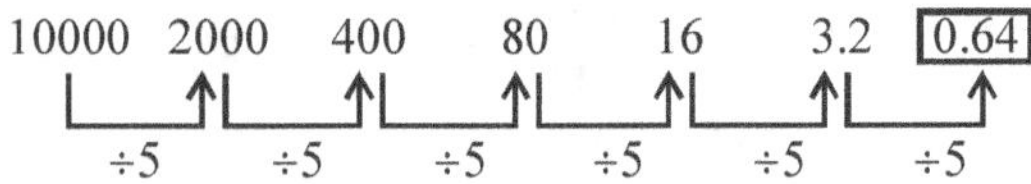

10000 2000   400   80   16   3.2   **0.64**
  ÷5   ÷5   ÷5   ÷5   ÷5   ÷5

27. (d) The pattern of number series is as follow

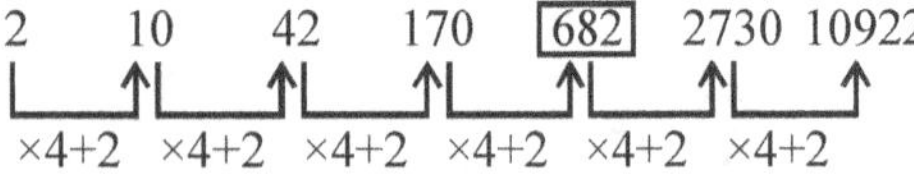

2   10   42   170   **682**   2730 10922
  ×4+2 ×4+2 ×4+2 ×4+2 ×4+2 ×4+2

28. (b) The pattern of number series is as follow

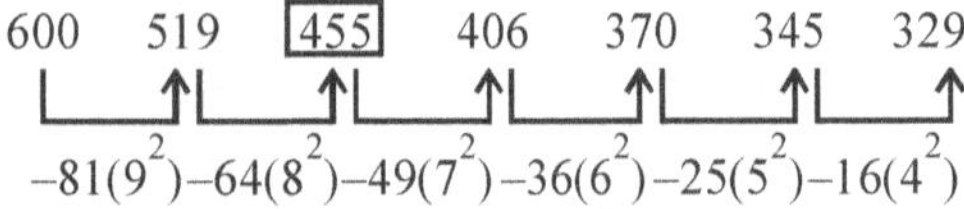

600   519   **455**   406   370   345   329
$-81(9^2) -64(8^2) -49(7^2) -36(6^2) -25(5^2) -16(4^2)$

29. (a) The pattern of number series is as follow

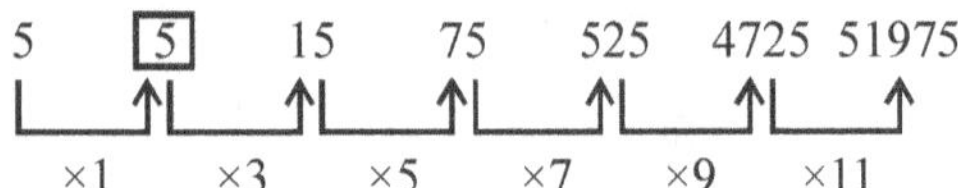

5   **5**   15   75   525   4725 51975
  ×1   ×3   ×5   ×7   ×9   ×11

20. (a) The pattern of number series is as follows

3   6   12   24   48   96   **192**
  ×2   ×2   ×2   ×2   ×2   ×2

31. (c) Percentage increase

$$= \frac{80-50}{50} \times 100$$

$$= \frac{30}{50} \times 100 = 60\%$$

32. (b) Required ratio $= 80 : 90 = 8 : 9$

33. (a) Total number of students from School Q who qualified over the years

$= (60 + 50 + 80 + 90 + 75 + 85) \times 100 = 44000$

$\therefore$ Required difference

$= 44000 - (80 + 60) \times 100$

$= 44000 - 14000 = 30000$

34. (e) Total number of students from School P, who qualified over the years

$= (80 + 80 + 95 + 65 + 40 + 90) \times 100 = 45000$

Total number of students who qualified from both schools in 2006 and 2007

$= (80 + 50 + 95 + 80) \times 100 = 30500$

$\therefore$ Required percent

$$= \frac{45000}{30500} \times 100 \approx 147\%$$

35. (c) Total number of meles who qualified over the years from both the schools together

$= 60\% \text{ of } (45000 + 44000)$

$$= \frac{89000 \times 60}{100} = 53400$$

36. (e)

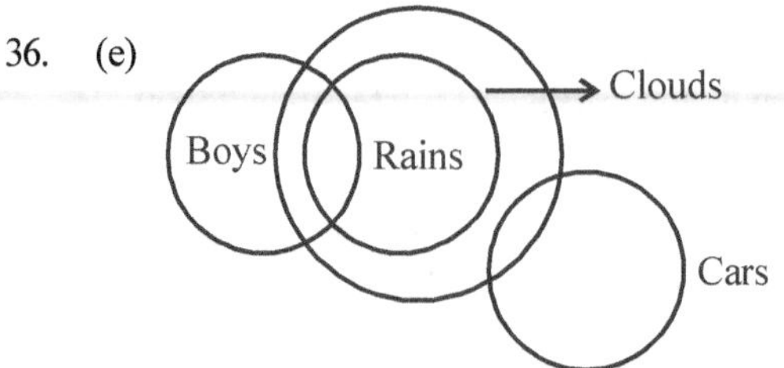

OR   OR

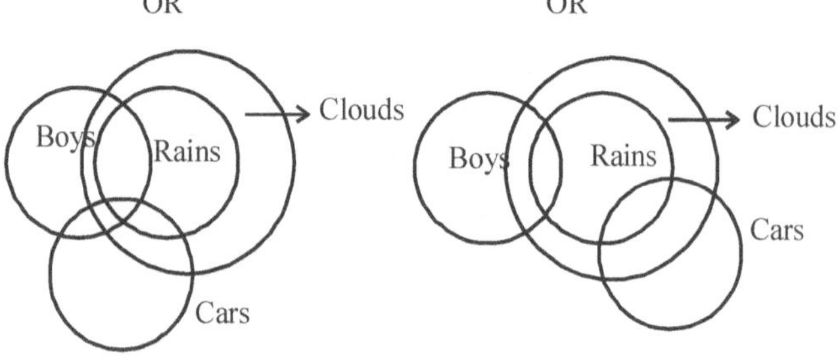

Conclusion - I. ✓
           II. ✓
          III. ✓
          IV. ✓   (Conversion of I Statement)

37. (a)

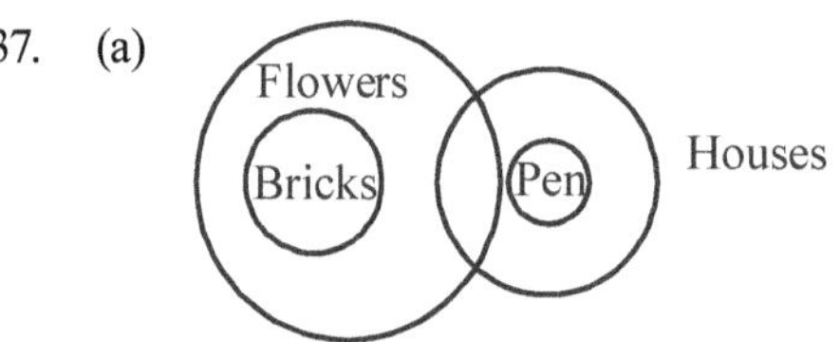

Conclusion - I. ✗
          II. ✗
        III. ✓
        IV. ✗   } Either

38. (c)

Conclusion - I. ✓
          II. ✓
        III. ✓
        IV. ✓   } Either

39. (d)
Statements	:	Some stones are bricks.
Conclusions	:	Some bricks are stone. (conversion)
Statements	:	All plants are stones.
Conclusions	:	Some plants are stones. (Implication)
		Some stones are plants. (conversion)
Statements	:	No flower is plant.
Conclusions	:	Some flowers are not plant.
		(Implication)
		No plant is flower. (Conversion)

	Statements	:	No flower is plant.
			All plants are stones.
	Conclusions	:	Some stones are not flower.
			(E + A = O* type)

Since, II and III form a complementary I-E pair, either of two must follow.

40. (c)

	Statements	:	All tigers are jungles.
	Conclusions	:	Some tigers are jungles. (Implication)
			Some jungles are tigers. (conversion)
	Statements	:	No jungle is bird.
	Conclusions	:	Some jungle are not bird.
			(Implication)
			No bird is jungle. (conversion)
	Statements	:	Some birds are rains.
	Conclusions	:	Some rains are birds. (conversion)
	Statements	:	All tigers are jungles.

No jungle is bird.

| | Conclusions | : | No tiger is bird. (A + E = E-type) |
| | | | No bird is tiger. (conversion) |

Hence III follows.

	Statements	:	No jungle is bird.
			Some birds are rains.
	Conclusions	:	Some rains are not jungle.
			(E + I = O* type)

Since I and II form a complementary E-I pair, either of two must follow.

Sol. (41–45)

```
├──┼──┼──┼──┼──┼──┼──┼──┼──┤
T   Z   P   Y   Q   X   V   R   W   S   U
```

41. (e)   42. (d)   43. (c)   44. (b)   45. (a)

46. (c)

Letter	E	H	N	D	J	V
Code	#	4	2	3	9	8

Condition is applied.

47. (e)

Letter	K	Q	D	J	N	H
Code	7	6	3	9	2	4

48. (a)

Letter	A	J	N	V	Q	E
Code	#	9	2	8	6	#

Condition is applied.

49. (b)

Letter	Q	H	J	V	N	D
Code	6	4	9	8	2	3

50. (d)

Letter	J	K	E	D	H	A
Code	9	7	1	3	4	#

Condition is applied.

51. (b)   195 768 345 678 213 756
195 = 951

52. (a)   768 = second highest number
7 + 8 = 15

53. (c)   519   876   534   867   321   675

54. (d)   815   778   335   868   023   676
3 + 3 + 5 = 11

55. (b)   159   678   345   678   123   567

56. (c)   Meaningful Words ⇒ CON ONCE

57. (c)

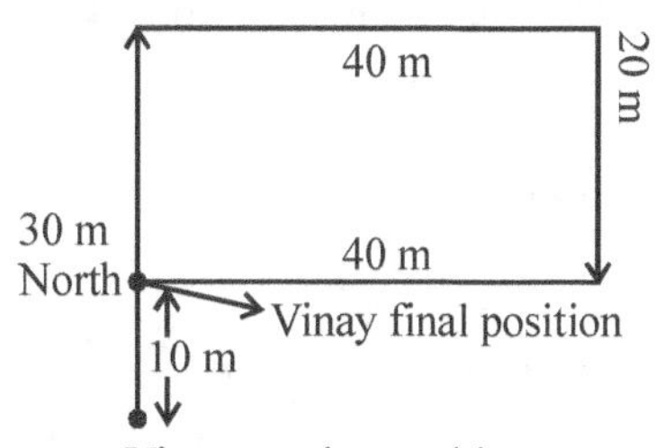

58. (b)

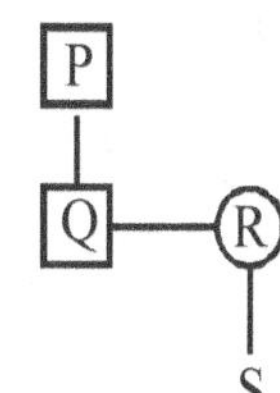

He is 10 m from his original position.

59. (b)

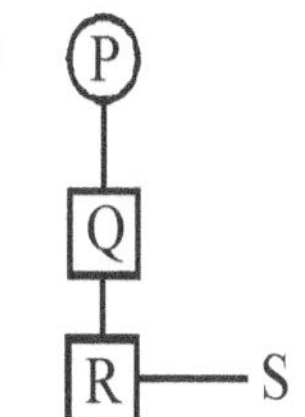

60. (c)

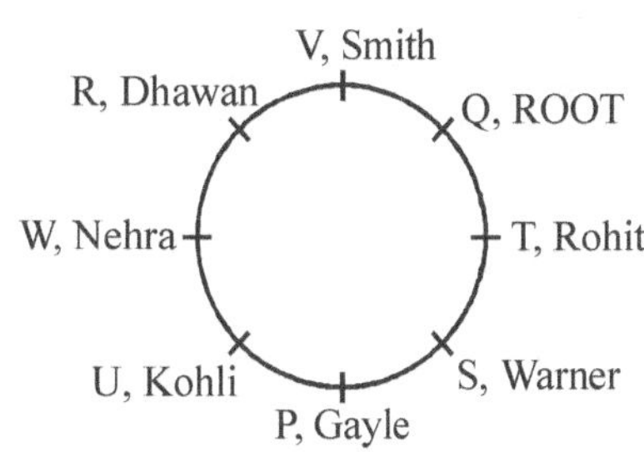

Sol. (61-65)

61. (d)   62. (c)   63. (d)   64. (c)   65. (b)

66. (d)   Since it is not known that who is facing outside or inside circle, cannot be determined by any statement or both.

If the data given in both I and II together are not sufficient to answer the question. So, option (d) is correct.

67. (d) Since it is not known that Bhuvan and Madhu have how many children, it cannot be said that Preeti and Ravi are children of Anuradha and Manish.

If the data given in both I and II together are not sufficient to answer the question. So, options (d) is correct.

68. (a) From I: Shipra is facing east and in left of Shilpi, so Shilpi is facing south, and then Anu north.

From II: Since it is not known that Bhavna turns to which direction, direction of Anu cant be find.

If the data in statement I alone is sufficient to answer the question. So, options (a) is correct.

Sol. (69-70)

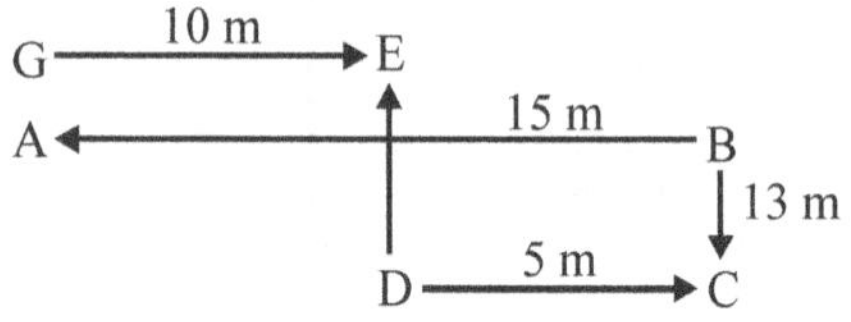

69. (b) G will be nearest point of X.

70. (e) G is in North with respect to A.

71. (c)

72. (d)   73. (b)   74. (e)   75. (a)

76. (d)   77. (e)   78. (e)   79. (b)

80. (a)

81. (a) Change 'decline of' to 'decline in'.

82. (b) Delete 'for' after order.

83. (c) Place on before 'land'.

84. (c) Delete 'to' before Chennai.

85. (d) Replace 'for' by 'to'.

86. (c) Change 'look for' by 'look after'.

87. (a) Delete for after await.

88. (c) debarred from sending is correct.

89. (a) Do not use of with despite. Despite means inspite of.

90. (a) Change it to 'yielded to'

91. (d) into   92. (a) around

93. (b) translating   94. (c) practice

95. (c) chance   96. (d) provided

97. (a) other   98. (e) off

99. (e) hard   100. (b) equilibrium

PRACTICE SET 12

Time : 60 Minutes   **Max. Marks : 100**

NUMERICAL ABILITY

DIRECTIONS (Qs. 1-10): *What will come in place of the question mark (?) in the following questions?*

1. $\dfrac{5}{11}$ of $\dfrac{4}{5}$ of $\dfrac{11}{16}$ of 848=?
   - (a) 216
   - (b) 222
   - (c) 208
   - (d) 212
   - (e) None of these

2. 1.4% of 750 + 2.2% of 480 = ?
   - (a) 21.06
   - (b) 21.16
   - (c) 20.88
   - (d) 21.18
   - (e) None of these

3. $\dfrac{3}{4}$ of 116 − $\dfrac{2}{3}$ of 87=?
   - (a) 31
   - (b) 27
   - (c) 29
   - (d) 26
   - (e) None of these

4. $6.96 \div 1.2 - 18.24 \div 7.6 = ?$
   - (a) 3.4
   - (b) 3.14
   - (c) 3.04
   - (d) 3.24
   - (e) None of these

5. 136% of 250 + ? % of 550 = 670
   - (a) 64
   - (b) 55
   - (c) 56
   - (d) 65
   - (e) None of these

6. $\dfrac{14 \times 25 - 5^3}{24 \times 5 + 8 \times 9} = ?$
   - (a) $1\dfrac{9}{64}$
   - (b) $\dfrac{64}{75}$
   - (c) $1\dfrac{11}{64}$
   - (d) $1\dfrac{11}{75}$
   - (e) None of these

7. $17\dfrac{2}{5} \times 4\dfrac{5}{8} - ? = 46\dfrac{7}{8}$
   - (a) $32\dfrac{3}{5}$
   - (b) $33\dfrac{3}{5}$
   - (c) $33\dfrac{2}{5}$
   - (d) $32\dfrac{2}{5}$
   - (e) None of these

8. $5616 \div 18 \div 8 = ?$
   - (a) 36
   - (b) 76
   - (c) 49
   - (d) 39
   - (e) None of these

9. $22^2 + \sqrt{?} = 516$
   - (a) 1029
   - (b) 1024
   - (c) 1124
   - (d) 1128
   - (e) None of these

10. 45% of 660 + 28% of 450 = ?
    - (a) 413
    - (b) 428
    - (c) 423
    - (d) 418
    - (e) None of these

DIRECTIONS (Qs. 11-15): *In the following number series, a wrong number is given, Find out that wrong number.*

11. 2, 11, 38, 197, 1172, 8227, 65806
    - (a) 11
    - (b) 1172
    - (c) 8227
    - (d) 38
    - (e) 197

12. 16, 19, 21, 30, 46, 71, 107
    - (a) 19
    - (b) 21
    - (c) 71
    - (d) 46
    - (e) 30

13. 8, 27, 125, 342, 1331, 2197
    - (a) 27
    - (b) 125
    - (c) 1331
    - (d) 2197
    - (e) 342

14. 4, 2, 3.5, 7.5, 26.25, 118.125
    (a) 118.125
    (b) 26.25
    (c) 7.5
    (d) 2
    (e) 3.5
15. 16, 4, 2, 1.5, 1.75, 1.875
    (a) 1.875
    (b) 2
    (c) 4
    (d) 1.75
    (e) 1.5
16. If the length of a rectangle is increased by 20% and the breadth is decreased by 10%, what will be the effect on its area?
    (a) 8% increase
    (b) 8% decrease
    (c) 2% increase
    (d) 2% decrease
    (e) None of these
17. Srikant and Vividh started a business investing amounts of ₹ 1,85,000 and ₹ 2,25,000 respectively, If Vividh's share in the profit earned by them is ₹ 9,000, what is the total profit earned by them together?
    (a) ₹ 17,400
    (b) ₹ 16,400
    (c) ₹ 16,800
    (d) ₹ 17,800
    (e) None of these
18. Present ages of father and son are in the ratio of 6 : 1 respectively. After four years the ratio of their ages will become 4 : 1 respectively. What is the son's present age?
    (a) 10 years
    (b) 6 years
    (c) 4 years
    (d) 8 years
    (e) None of these
19. The equivalent discount of successive discounts of 20%, 10% and 5% respectively is
    (a) 36.6%
    (b) 31.6%
    (c) 46.6%
    (d) 35.5%
    (e) None of these
20. The total number of students in a school is 1224. If the number of girls in the school is 600, then what is the respective ratio of the total number of boys to the total number of girls in the school?
    (a) 26 : 25
    (b) 21 : 17
    (c) 18 : 13
    (d) 5 : 4
    (e) None of these
21. A, B and C divide an amount of ₹9861 amongst themselves in the ratio of 3 : 11 : 5 respectively. What is the B's share in the amount?
    (a) ₹4671
    (b) ₹5709
    (c) ₹6228
    (d) ₹7266
    (e) None of these
22. A motorist travels a distance of 10 km at & speed of 50 km/h in the onward journey and 60 km/h while returning. His average speed is
    (a) $54\dfrac{6}{11}$ km / h
    (b) 55 km/h
    (c) $55\dfrac{6}{11}$ km / h
    (d) 54 km/h
    (e) None of these
23. Number of ways of arranging 5 persons in a row is
    (a) 6!
    (b) 5!
    (c) 5
    (d) 25
    (e) None of these
24. In an examination there are 30 questions. 1 mark is given for each correct answer and 0.25 is deducted for every incorrect answer. Ankur attempted all the questions and scored 13.75. How many incorrect answers did he have?

    (a) 10
    (b) 11
    (c) 12
    (d) 15
    (e) None of these
25. Out of the fractions
    $$\frac{9}{31}, \frac{3}{17}, \frac{6}{23}, \frac{4}{11} \text{ and } \frac{7}{25},$$ which is the largest fraction?
    (a) $\dfrac{9}{31}$
    (b) $\dfrac{3}{17}$
    (c) $\dfrac{6}{23}$
    (d) $\dfrac{4}{11}$
    (e) None of these
26. What will come in place of both the question marks (?) in the following question?
    $$\frac{23}{?} = \frac{?}{92}$$
    (a) 56
    (b) 54
    (c) 44
    (d) 46
    (e) None of these
27. The salary of a man increases by 20% every year in the month of January. His salary was ₹ 5,000 in the month of February in year 2009. What will be his salary in the month of February in the year 2011?
    (a) ₹ 7,200
    (b) ₹ 6,200
    (c) ₹ 7,800
    (d) ₹ 6,800
    (e) None of these
28. The simple interest on a certain principal in 5 years at the J dte of 12 p.c. p.a. is ₹ 1,536. What amount of the simple interest would one get if one invests ₹ 1,000 more than the previous principal for 2 years and at the same rate p.c.p.a.?
    (a) ₹ 845.40
    (b) ₹ 614.40
    (c) ₹ 2,136
    (d) ₹ 1,536
    (e) None of these
29. If 3 men or 9 boys can finish a piece of work in 21 days. In how many days can 5 men and 6 boys together do the same piece of work?
    (a) 12 days
    (b) 8 days
    (c) 14 days
    (d) Cannot be determined
    (e) None of these
30. In a test, Rajesh got 112 marks which is 32 more than the passing marks. Sonal got 75% marks which is 70 more than the passing marks. What is the minimum passing percentage of the test?
    (a) 35
    (b) 45
    (c) 40
    (d) 30
    (e) None of these

DIRECTIONS (Qs. 31-35): *Study the following table carefully to answer these questions.*

Percentage Marks Obtained by Six Students in Six Different Subjects.

Student/ Subject	Psy (150)	Socio (120)	Econ (80)	Philosophy (75)	Statistics (125)	Geology (60)
A	72	65	85	65	88	72
B	68	58	74	70	78	54
C	63	73	69	57	68	65
D	56	65	77	61	75	67
E	78	55	82	76	59	74
F	84	70	64	78	82	80

Note : Figures written in bracket under each subject indicate the maximum marks allotted for that subject.

31. What is the difference between the total marks obtained by A in Psychology and Statistics together and the total marks obtained by F in these two subjects together?
    (a) 12.5
    (b) 6
    (c) 10.5
    (d) 11.6
    (e) None of these

32. What is the average percentage of marks obtained by six students in Sociology?
    (a) $77\dfrac{1}{3}$
    (b) $64\dfrac{1}{5}$
    (c) $77\dfrac{1}{5}$
    (d) $64\dfrac{1}{3}$
    (e) None of these

33. What is the total marks obtained by the six students in Philosophy out of 75?
    (a) 58.75
    (b) 50.875
    (c) 67.83
    (d) 65.73
    (e) None of these

34. What is the total marks obtained by A in Psychology, Economics and Geology together?
    (a) 219.2
    (b) 229
    (c) 209.8
    (d) 229.6
    (e) None of these

35. Approximately what is the overall percentage of marks obtained by C in all the subjects together?
    (a) 60
    (b) 56
    (c) 72
    (d) 76
    (e) 66

REASONING ABILITY

DIRECTIONS (Qs. 36-40) : *Study the following information carefully to answer the given questions.*

There are 7 persons P, Q, R, S, T, U and V are sitting in a row facing north. Each of them has a different profession - Executive, Clerk, Professor, Officer, Director, Editor and CA but not necessarily in the same order.

T is not an Editor but sits after the person who immediately follows U. Q is a professor. The one who is an Executive sits second from the right end. The Clerk sits on the immediate left of the Editor. P sits on the immediate right of V and on the immediate left of R. U is fifth from the left end of the row and he is CA. The Director is third from the left end.

36. Who among the following sits on the extreme right end of the row ?
    (a) Clerk
    (b) Officer
    (c) CA
    (d) Editor
    (e) None of these

37. Who among the following is an Executive ?
    (a) Q
    (b) T
    (c) S
    (d) P
    (e) None of these

38. The person sitting on the second left of Q is
    (a) Editor
    (b) Clerk
    (c) CA
    (d) Director
    (e) None of these

39. Which of the following is true ?
    (a) S - Officer
    (b) V - Director
    (c) P - CA
    (d) P - Editor
    (e) None of these

40. Who sits on the centre of the row ?
    (a) Q - Professor
    (b) Q - Editor
    (c) R - CA
    (d) P - Director
    (e) None of these

DIRECTIONS (Qs. 41-45) : *In each of the questions below are given three statements followed by two conclusions numbered I and II. You have to take the given statements to be true even if they seem to be at variance from commonly known facts. Read both of the conclusions and then decide which of the given conclusions logically follows from the given statements disregarding commonly known facts.*

Read the statements and the conclusions which follow it and give answer
(a) If only conclusion I is true.
(b) If only conclusion II is true.
(c) If either conclusion I or conclusion II is true.
(d) If neither conclusion I nor conclusion II is true.
(e) If both conclusions I and II are true.

41. **Statements :**
    All stars are suns.
    Some suns are planets.
    All planets are satellites.
    Conclusions :
    I. Some satellites are stars.
    II. No star is a satellite.

42. **Statements :**
    All curtains are rods.
    Some rods are sheets.
    Some sheets are pillows.
    Conclusions:
    I. Some pillows are rods.
    II. Some rods are curtains.

43. **Statements :**
    All switches are plugs.
    Some plugs are bulbs.
    All bulbs are sockets.
    Conclusions:
    I. Some sockets are plugs.
    II. Some plugs are switches.

44. **Statements :**
    All fishes are birds.
    All birds are rats.
    All rats are cows.
    Conclusions :
    I. All birds are cows.
    II. All rats are fishes.

45. **Statements :**
    Some walls are windows.
    Some windows are doors.
    All doors are roofs.
    Conclusions :
    I. Some doors are walls.
    II. No roof is a window.

DIRECTIONS (Qs. 46-47) : *Read the following information carefully and answer the questions, which follow :*

'A - B' means 'A is father of B'.
'A + B' means 'A is daughter of B'.
'A ÷ B' means 'A is son of B'.
'A × B' means 'A is wife of B'.

46. How is P related to T in the expression 'P + S – T' ?
    (a) Sister   (b) Wife
    (c) Son   (d) Daughter
    (e) None of these

47. In the expression 'P × Q – T' how is T related to P ?
    (a) Daughter   (b) Sister
    (c) Mother   (d) Can't be determined
    (e) None of these

48. If each of the alphabets of the word MIRACLE is arranged in alphabetical order from left to right and then each vowel in the new word thus formed is changed to the next letter in the. English alphabetical series and each consonant is changed to the previous letter in the English alphabetical series which of the followingwill be fifth from the right?
    (a) K   (b) S
    (c) F   (d) E
    (e) J

49. A man walks 1 km towards East and then turns towards South and walks 5 km. Again he turns to East and walks 2 km. After this he turns to North and walks 9 km. Now, how far is he from his starting point ?
    (a) 3 km   (b) 4 km
    (c) 5 km   (d) 7 km
    (e) None of these

50. A girl introduced a boy as the son of the daughter of the father of her uncle. The boy is girl's;
    (a) Cousin   (b) Son
    (c) Uncle   (d) Son-in-law
    (e) None of these

DIRECTIONS (Qs. 51-55) : *Study the following information and answer the questions given below it.*

Seven people – A, B, C, D, E, F and G are sitting in a circle. Five of them are facing the centre while two of them are facing opposite to the centre. C sits third to the left of D and both are facing the centre. E is neither an immediate neighbour of D nor C. The one sitting exactly between D and F is facing opposite to centre. G sits third to the right of A and G is facing the centre. One of B's neighbour is facing opposite to the centre.

51. Which of the following pairs represents persons facing opposite to the centre?
    (a) A and F
    (b) E and F
    (c) A and E
    (d) Can't be determined
    (e) None of the above

52. Who is sitting second to the left of A?
    (a) C   (b) G
    (c) E   (d) B
    (e) None of the

53. Who is sitting to the immediate left of E?
    (a) C   (b) G
    (c) B   (d) A
    (e) None of these

54. What is the position of F with respect to B?
    (a) Fourth to the left   (b) Second to the right
    (c) Third to the right   (d) Second to the left
    (e) None of the above

55. If all the persons are asked to sit in a clockwise direction in an alphabetical order starting from A, the position of how many will remain unchanged, excluding A?
    (a) Three   (b) One
    (c) Two   (d) None
    (e) Four

DIRECTIONS (Qs. 56-60) : *In each question a group of letters is given followed by four combinations of number/symbol numbered (a), (b), (c) and (d). Letters are to be coded as per the scheme and conditions given below. You have to find out the serial number of the combination, which represents the letter group. Serial number of that combination is your answer. If none of the combinations is correct, your answer is (e) i.e. None of these.*

Letters	Q	M	S	I	N	G	D	K	A	L	P	R	B	J	E
Number/Symbol	7	@	4	#	%	$	6	1	2	£	5	*	9	8	3

Conditions :
(i) If the first letter is a consonant and the last a vowel, both are to be coded as the code of the vowel.
(ii) If the first letter is vowel and the last a consonant, the codes for the first and the last are to be interchanged.
(iii) If no vowel is present in the group of letters, the second and the fifth letters are to be coded as ©.

56. **BARNIS**
    (a) 9 2 * % # 4   (b) 9 2 4 # * %
    (c) 9 2 * # % 9   (d) 4 2 * # % 4
    (e) None of these

57. **DMBNIA**
    (a) 6 @ 9 % # 2   (b) 2 @ 9 % # 6
    (c) 2 @ 9 % # 6   (d) 2 @ 9 % # 2
    (e) None of these

58. **IJBRLG**
    (a) # 8 9 * £ $ (b) # 8 9 * £ #
    (c) $ 8 9 * £ #   (d) $ 8 9 * £ $
    (e) None of these

59. **BKGQJN**
    (a) 9 © $ 7 © %   (b) © 9 $ 7 % ©
    (c) 9 1 $ 7 8 %   (d) % 1 $ 7 8 9
    (e) None of these

60. **EGAKRL**
    (a) # £ $ 2 1 *   (b) £ $ 2 1 * 3
    (c) £ $ 2 1 * #   (d) # £ $ 2 1 #
    (e) None of these

DIRECTIONS (Qs. 61-65) : *Study the following arrangement to answer the given questions.*

456   789   145   392   140   653   806

61. Which of the following is the sum of the first and third digit of the third largest number ?
    (a) 14   (b) 9
    (c) 11   (d) 10
    (e) None

62. If the above arrangement are arranged in the ascending order then what will be the middle number ?
    (a) 456   (b) 654
    (c) 653   (d) 789
    (e) None

63. If the position of the first and second digit is interchanged then what will be the second lowest number ?
    (a) 410   (b) 415
    (c) 140   (d) 240
    (e) 415

64. If the position of the first and third is interchanged then what will be the sum of the fourth highest number
    (a) 13   (b) 11
    (c) 6   (d) 9
    (e) 10

65. If an odd number of the first letter is increased by 1 and even number of the first letter is decreased by 1 then what will be the second digit of the second highest number ?
    (a) 0   (b) 9
    (c) 5   (d) 7
    (e) 6

DIRECTIONS (Qs. 66-70) : *Study the following information carefully and answer the given questions.*

One of the seven subjects *viz.* Maths, Zoology, Botany, Chemistry, Physics, English and Statistics is taught on one day in a week starting from Monday and ending on Sunday. Chemistry is taught on Thursday. English is taught the day immediately next to the day when Zoology is taught. English is neither taught on Tuesday nor on Saturday. Only one lecture is held between Chemistry and Botany. Two lectures are scheduled between Maths and Zoology. Statistics is neither taught on Monday nor Sunday.

66. On which of the following days is Physics taught?
    (a) Monday   (b) Tuesday
    (c) Wednesday   (d) Thursday
    (e) Friday

67. How many subjects are taught between Botany and Zoology?
    (a) None   (b) One
    (c) Two   (d) Three
    (e) Four

68. Which of the following subject is taught on Saturday?
    (a) Botany   (b) Statistics
    (c) Zoology   (d) Maths
    (e) Physics

69. On which of the following days is Statistics taught?
    (a) Tuesday   (b) Wednesday
    (c) Thursday   (d) Friday
    (e) Can't be determined

70. If Statistics is related to Zoology and Physics is related to Botany in a certain way, then to which of the following would Chemistry be related to, following the same pattern?
    (a) Maths   (b) Statistics
    (c) Physics   (d) English
    (e) Can't be determined

ENGLISH LANGUAGE

DIRECTIONS (Qs. 71-80): Read each sentence to find out whether there is any error in it. The error, if any, will be in one part of the sentence. The number of this part is the answer. If there is no error, the answer is (e).

71. The banker's association (a) / has submitted a memorandum (b) / for the fulfilment of (c) / their demands. (d) / No Error (e)

72. Five quintals of wooden coal (a) / are (b) / his annual requirement (c) / for the unit. (d) / No Error (e)

73. Dickens have (a) / vehemently criticised (b) / the philosophy (c) in 'Hard Times'. (d) / No Error (e)

74. All his money (a) / is spent (b) / and all his (c) / hopes ruined. (d) / No Error (e)

75. This rule may (a) / and ought to be (b) / disregarded for (c) / the time being. (d) / No Error (e)

76. Why come people don't get (a) / what they deserve (b) / and why others get what they don't deserve (c) / is a matter decided by luck. (d)/No error(e)

77. The committee is thankful to Mr. Roy (a) / for preparing not only the main report (b) / but also for preparing (c) the agenda notes and minutes. (d) / No error (e)

78. In order to save petrol (a) / motorists must have to (b) / be very cautious (c) / while driving along the highways. (d) / No error (e)

79. No country can long endure (a) / if its foundations (b) / were not laid deep (c) / in the material prosperity. (d) / No error (e)

80. Due to certain inevitable circumstances (a) / the scheduled programme had to be (b) / post poned indefinite (c) / but the members could not be informed. (d) / No error (e)

DIRECTIONS (Qs. 81-90) : Read the following passage and answer the questions given below it. Certain words/phrases are given in bold to help you to locate them while answering some of the questions.

We have inherited the tradition of secrecy about the budget from Britain where also the system has been strongly attacked by eminent economists and political scientists including Peter Jay. Sir Richard Clarke, who was the originating genius of nearly every **important** development in the British budgeting techniques during the last two decades, has spoken out about the abuse of budget secrecy: "The problems of long-term tax policy should surely be debated openly with the facts on the table. In my opinion, all governments should have just the same **duty** to publish their expenditure policy. Indeed, this obligation to publish taxation policy is really essential for the control of public expenditure in order to get realistic taxation implications." Realising that democracy **flourishes** best on the principles of open government, more and more democracies are having an open public debate on budget proposals before introducing the appropriate Bill in the legislature. In the United States the budget is conveyed in a message by the President to the Congress, which comes well in advance of the date when the Bill is introduced in the Congress. In Finland the Parliament and the people are already discussing in June the tentative budget proposals which are to be introduced in the Finnish Parliament in September. Every budget contains a cartload of figures in black and white - but the dark figures represent the **myriad** lights and shades of India's life, the contrasting tones of poverty and wealth, and of bread so dear and flesh and blood so cheap, the deep tints of adventure and enterprise and man's ageless struggle for a brighter morning. The Union budget should not be an annual **scourge** but a part of presentation of annual accounts of a partnership between the Government and the people. That partnership would work much better when the nonsensical secrecy is replaced by openness and public consultations, resulting in fair laws and the people's acceptance of their moral duty to pay.

81. How do the British economists and political scientists react to budget secrecy? They are
    (a) in favour of having a mix of secrecy and openness.
    (b) indifferent to the budgeting techniques and taxation policies.
    (c) very critical about maintenance of budget secrecy.
    (d) advocates of not disclosing in advance the budget contents.
    (e) None of these

82. The author thinks that openness in budget is essential as it leads to
    (a) prevention of tax implications
    (b) people's reluctance to accept their moral duties
    (c) exaggerated revelation of the strengths and weaknesses of economy
    (d) making our country on par with Finland
    (e) None of these

83. The author seems to be in favour of
    (a) maintaining secrecy of budget
    (b) judicious blend of secrecy and openness
    (c) transparency in budget proposals
    (d) replacement of public constitution by secrecy
    (e) None of these

84. The secrecy of the budget is maintained by all of the following countries **except**
    A. Finland   B. India
    C. United States
    (a) Only A   (b) Only B
    (c) Only C   (d) A and C
    (e) B and C

85. Which of the following statements is definitely TRUE in the context of the passage?
    (a) The British Government has been religiously maintaining budget secrecy.
    (b) Budget secrecy is likely to lead to corrupt practices.
    (c) Consulting unjustifiable taxes with public helps make them accept those taxes.
    (d) There should be no control on public expenditure in democratic condition.
    (e) None of these

86. Sir Richard Clarke seems to deserve the credit for
    (a) transformation in the British budgetary techniques.
    (b) maintenance of secrecy of the British budget.
    (c) detection of abuse of transparency in budget.
    (d) bringing down the tax load on British people.
    (e) None of these

87. From the contents of the passage, it can be inferred that the author is
    (a) authoritarian in his approach.
    (b) a democratic person.
    (c) unaware of India's recent economic developments.
    (d) a conservative person.
    (e) None of these

88. For making the budget realistic, the Government should
    (a) refrain from making public the proposed provisions before finalisation.
    (b) discuss it secretly within themselves.
    (c) encourage the public to send in their suggestions.
    (d) consult the public, defend their own plans and accept public suggestions.
    (e) None of these

DIRECTIONS (Q. 89) : Choose the word which is most nearly the SAME in meaning to the word printed in bold as used in the passage.

89. **SCOURGE**
    (a) ritual   (b) presentation
    (c) whip   (d) compromise
    (e) remedy

DIRECTIONS (Q. 90) : Choose the word which is most OPPOSITE in meaning to the word printed in bold as used in the passage.

90. **FLOURISHES**
    (a) disappears   (b) degenerates
    (c) vanishes   (d) blooms
    (e) opens

DIRECTIONS (Qs. 91-100) : In the following passage there are blanks, each of which has been numbered. These numbers are printed below the passage and against each, five words are suggested, one of which fills the blank appropriately. Find out the appropriate word in each case.

Fourteen centuries ago when the world was much younger, the ruler of all India, Rajah Balhait, was .....(91).... about his people. A new game of dice, called hard, had ...(92).... the imagination of his subjects, teaching them that chance alone-a-roll of the dice guided the ....(93).... of men. All who played this game of fortune lost their ....(94).... in the virtues of courage, prudence, wisdom and hope. It bred a fatalism that was ....(95).... the spirit of the kingdom.

Raja Balhait commissioned Sissa, an intelligent courter at his court to find an answer to this ...(96).... After much ...(97).... the clever Sissa invented another game. Chaturanga, the exact ...(98).... of hard, in which the four elements of the Indian army were the key pieces. In the game these pieces-chariots, horses, elephants and foot soldiers-joined with a royal ...(99).... to defend their king and ...(100).... the enemy.

91. (a) concerned   (b) confident
    (c) ignorant   (d) indifferent
    (e) partisan

92. (a) propelled   (b) enshrined
    (c) captured   (d) activated
    (e) enhanced

93. (a) communities   (b) ways
    (c) abnormalities   (d) destiny
    (e) groups

94. (a) bravado   (b) interest
    (c) peace   (d) wealth
    (e) faith

95. (a) appalling   (b) crushing
    (c) moistening   (d) promoting
    (e) overwhelming

96. (a) apprehension   (b) risk
    (c) problem   (d) game
    (e) destiny

97. (a) deliberation   (b) absorption
    (c) insight   (d) hesitation
    (e) reluctance

98. (a) nature   (b) equivalent
    (c) picture   (d) opposite
    (e) replica

99. (a) councilor   (b) councillor
    (c) counsilor   (d) counselor
    (e) counsel

100. (a) defeat   (b) protect
     (c) beat   (d) crucify
     (e) overthrow

Answer Key

1	(d)	11	(b)	21	(d)	31	(c)	41	(c)	51	(c)	61	(b)	71	(d)	81	(c)	91	(a)
2	(a)	12	(a)	22	(a)	32	(d)	42	(b)	52	(d)	62	(a)	72	(b)	82	(e)	92	(c)
3	(c)	13	(e)	23	(e)	33	(b)	43	(e)	53	(b)	63	(c)	73	(a)	83	(b)	93	(d)
4	(a)	14	(e)	24	(e)	34	(a)	44	(a)	54	(e)	64	(e)	74	(d)	84	(d)	94	(b)
5	(e)	15	(d)	25	(c)	35	(e)	45	(d)	55	(c)	65	(c)	75	(a)	85	(e)	95	(e)
6	(c)	16	(a)	26	(d)	36	(b)	46	(a)	56	(a)	66	(a)	76	(d)	86	(a)	96	(e)
7	(b)	17	(b)	27	(a)	37	(c)	47	(d)	57	(d)	67	(d)	77	(c)	87	(b)	97	(a)
8	(d)	18	(b)	28	(e)	38	(a)	48	(c)	58	(c)	68	(c)	78	(b)	88	(d)	98	(d)
9	(b)	19	(b)	29	(e)	39	(d)	49	(c)	59	(a)	69	(d)	79	(c)	89	(c)	99	(d)
10	(c)	20	(a)	30	(c)	40	(a)	50	(a)	60	(b)	70	(b)	80	(c)	90	(b)	100	(a)

HINTS & EXPLANATIONS

1. (d) $? = 848 \times \dfrac{11}{16} \times \dfrac{4}{5} \times \dfrac{5}{11} = 212$

2. (a) $? = \dfrac{750 \times 1.4}{100} + \dfrac{480 \times 2.2}{100}$

       $= 10.50 + 10.56 = 21.06$

3. (c) $? = \dfrac{116 \times 3}{4} - \dfrac{87 \times 2}{3}$

       $= 87 - 58 = 29$

4. (a) $? = \dfrac{6.96}{1.2} - \dfrac{18.24}{7.6}$

       $= 5.8 - 2.4 = 3.4$

5. (e) $\dfrac{250 \times 136}{100} + \dfrac{550 \times ?}{100} = 670$

       $\Rightarrow 340 + 5.5 \times ? = 670$

       $\Rightarrow 5.5 \times ? = 670 - 340 = 330$

       $\Rightarrow ? = \dfrac{330}{5.5} = 60$

6. (c) $? = \dfrac{14 \times 25 - 125}{120 + 72} = \dfrac{225}{192}$

       $= \dfrac{75}{64} = 1\dfrac{11}{64}$

7. (b) $\dfrac{87}{5} \times \dfrac{37}{8} - ? = \dfrac{375}{8}$

       $\Rightarrow ? = \dfrac{3219}{40} - \dfrac{375}{8}$

       $= \dfrac{3219 - 1875}{40} = \dfrac{1344}{40}$

       $= \dfrac{168}{5} = 33\dfrac{3}{5}$

8. (d) $? = \dfrac{5616}{18 \times 8} = 39$

9. (b) $484 + \sqrt{?} = 516$

       $\Rightarrow \sqrt{?} = 516 - 484 = 32$

       $\therefore ? = 32 \times 32 = 1024$

10. (c) $? = \dfrac{660 \times 45}{100} + \dfrac{450 \times 28}{100}$

       $= 297 + 126 = 423$

11. (b) The series is

       $\times 3 + 5, \times 4 - 6, \times 5 + 7, \times 6 - 8, \ldots\ldots$

12. (a) The series is $+ 1^2, + 2^2, + 3^2, + 4^2, \ldots$

13. (e) The series is consists of terms which are cubes of consecutive prime numbers starting from 2.

14. (e) The series is

       $\times 0.5, \times 1.5 \times 2.5, \times 3.5, \ldots..$

15. (d) The series is $\times 0.25, \times 0.5, \times 0.75, \times 1, \ldots$

16. (a) Area of rectangle earlier $= lb$

       Area of rectangle after increasing length and decreasing breadth $= (\ell + 0.2\ell)(b - 0.1b) = 1.08\,\ell b$

       $\therefore$ %Effect on area $= \dfrac{(1.08 - 1)\,\ell b}{\ell b} \times 100 = 8\%$ increase

17. (b) Ratio of the profits of Srikant and Vividh

       $= 185000 : 225000 = 37 : 45$

       Sum of the ratios $= 37 + 45 = 82$

       $\therefore$ Total profit earned

       $= \dfrac{82}{45} \times 9000$

       $= ₹\,16400$

18. (b) Father's present age $= 6x$ years

       Son's present age $= x$ years

       After four years

       $\therefore \dfrac{6x + 4}{x + 4} = \dfrac{4}{1}$

       $\Rightarrow 6x + 4 = 4x + 16$

       $\Rightarrow 2x = 12 \Rightarrow x = \dfrac{12}{2} = 6$

       $\therefore$ Son's present age $= 6$ years

19. (b) Equivalent discount

$$= 100 - \frac{(100 - r_1)(100 - r_2)(100 - r_3)}{10000}$$

$$= 100 - \frac{(100 - 20)(100 - 10)(100 - 5)}{10000}$$

$$= 100 - \frac{80 \times 90 \times 95}{10000}$$

$$= 100 - 68.40 = 31.6\%$$

20. (a) Required ratio $= (1224 - 600) : 600 = 624 : 600 = 26 : 25$

21. (b) B's share in the amount $\dfrac{9861 \times 11}{19} = ₹ 5709$

22. (a) When the motorist is in the onward journey, then the time

$$t_1 = \frac{Distance}{Speed}$$

$$t_1 = \frac{10}{50} = 0.2h$$

When the motorist returns, then the time

$$t_2 = \frac{Distance}{Speed}$$

$$= \frac{10}{60} = 01667h$$

So, the average speed $= \dfrac{Total\,distance}{Total\,time}$

$$= \frac{(10 + 10)km}{(0.2 + 0.1667)h} = 54\frac{6}{11} km/h$$

23. (b) No. of ways of arranging 5 persons in a row $= 5! = 120$

24. (e) Suppose correct answer $= x$

$\therefore$ Incorrect answer $= (30 - x)$

Then, $x \times -1 (30 - x) \times 0.25 = 13.75$

$\Rightarrow x - 7.5 + 0.25x = 13.75$

$\Rightarrow 1.25x - 7.5 = 13.75$

$\Rightarrow 1.25x = 21.25 \Rightarrow x = \dfrac{21.25}{1.25} = 17$

$\therefore$ incorrect answer $= 30 - 17 = 13$

25. (d) Decimal equivalent of each fraction :

$$\frac{9}{31} = 0.29 \,;\, \frac{3}{17} = 0.18$$

$$\frac{6}{23} = 0.26 \,;\, \frac{4}{11} = 0.36 \,;\, \frac{7}{25} = 0.28$$

$\therefore$ The largest fraction $= \dfrac{4}{11}$

26. (d) $\dfrac{23}{?} = \dfrac{?}{92}$

$$\Rightarrow ? = 23 \times 92$$

$$\Rightarrow ? = \sqrt{23 \times 23 \times 4}$$

$$= 2 \times 23 = 46$$

27. (a) Tricky Approach

Man's salary in the month of February, 2011

$$= 5000\left(1 + \frac{20}{100}\right)^2 = 5000 \times \frac{6}{5} \times \frac{6}{5}$$

$$= ₹ 7200$$

28. (e) Case I

$$Principal = \frac{S.I.}{Time \times Rate}$$

$$= \frac{1536 \times 100}{5 \times 12} = ₹ 2560$$

Case II

$$S.I. = \frac{Principal \times Time \times Rate}{100}$$

$$= \frac{3560 \times 2 \times 12}{100} = ₹ 854.40$$

29. (e) $\because$ 3 men $\equiv$ 9 boys

$\therefore$ 1 man $\equiv$ 3 boys

$\therefore$ 5 men + 6 boys

$\therefore (5 \times 3 + 6)$ boys $= 21$ boys

$\therefore M_1 D_1 = M_2 D_2$

$$\Rightarrow D_2 = \frac{9 \times 21}{21} = 9\,days$$

30. (c) Let the total marks of the exam be x.

Passing marks $= 112 - 32 = 80$

$$\therefore \frac{x \times 75}{100} = 80 + 70 = 150$$

$$\Rightarrow x = \frac{150 \times 100}{75} = 200$$

If the minimum Pass percentage is y, then

$\therefore$ y% of 200 $= 80 \Rightarrow y = 40$

31. (c) Total marks obtained by A in Psychology and Statistics together

$$\left(= \frac{72 \times 150}{100} + \frac{88 \times 125}{100}\right) = 108 + 110 = 218$$

Total marks obtained by F in these two subjects

$$\left(\frac{84 \times 150}{100} + \frac{82 \times 125}{100}\right) = 126 + 102.5 = 228.5$$

$\therefore$ Difference $= 228.5 - 218 = 10.5$

32. (d) Average percentage of marks obtained by six students in Sociology

$$= \frac{65 + 58 + 73 + 65 + 55 + 70}{6}$$

$$= \frac{386}{6} = 64\frac{1}{3}$$

33. (b) Average marks obtained by 6 students in Philosophy out of 75

$$= \frac{65 + 70 + 57 + 61 + 76 + 78}{6}$$

$$= \frac{407}{6} \times \frac{75}{100} = 50.875$$

34. (a) Required answer

$$= \left(\frac{72 \times 150}{100} + \frac{85 \times 80}{100} + \frac{72 \times 60}{100} \right)$$

$$= 108 + 68 + 43.2 = 219.2$$

35. (e) Percentage of marks obtained by C in all the subjects together

$$\frac{63\% \text{ of } 150 + 73\% \text{ of } 120 + 69\% \text{ of } 80 + 57\% \text{ of } 75 + 68\% \text{ of } 125 + 65\% \text{ of } 60}{150 + 120 + 80 + 75 + 125 + 60}$$

$$= \frac{94.5 + 87.6 + 55.2 + 42.75 + 85 + 39}{610} \times 100 \approx 66\%$$

36. (b)

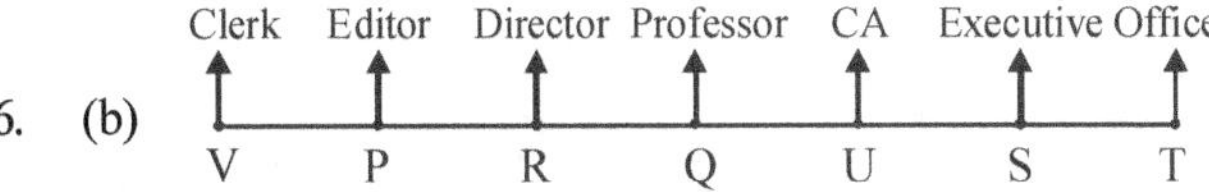

37. (c) S
38. (a) Editor
39. (d) P - Editor
40. (a) Q - Professor
41. (c) Some suns are planets.

All planets are satellites.
(I + A $\Rightarrow$ I-type)
"Some suns are satellites".
Conclusions I and II form Complementary Pair.
Therefore, either I or II follows.

42. (b) All curtains are rods.

Some rods are sheets.
(A + I $\Rightarrow$ No Conclusion)
Some rods are sheets.

Some sheets are pillows
(I + I $\Rightarrow$ No conclusion)
II is the conversion of I statement, so only I follows

43. (e) Some plugs are bulbs

All bulbs are sockets.
(I + A $\Rightarrow$ I-type)
"Some plugs are sockets".
Conclusion I is Converse of second Conclusion.
Conclusion II is Converse of the first Premise.

44. (a) All fishes are birds. (conversion)

All birds are rats.
(A + A $\Rightarrow$ A-type)
"All fishes are rats".
All birds are rats. (conversion)

All rats are cows.
(A + A $\Rightarrow$ A-type)
"All birds are cows".
This is Conclusion I.

45. (d) Some windows are doors.

All doors are roofs.
(I + A $\Rightarrow$ I-type)
"Some windows are roots".

46. (a) P + S $\rightarrow$ P is daughter of S.
S – T $\rightarrow$ S is father of T.
Therefore, P is sister of T.

47. (d) P × Q $\rightarrow$ P is wife of Q.
Q – T $\rightarrow$ Q is father of T.
T is child of P and Q.
The gender of T is not known.
T is either son or daughter of P.

48. (c)

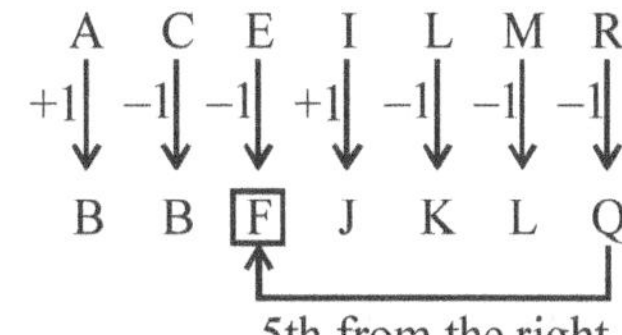

49. (c)

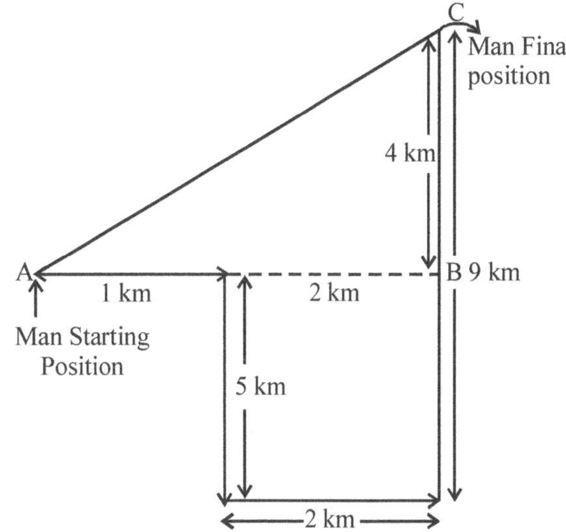

In $\triangle ABC$

$AC^2 = AB^2 + BC^2$

$AC^2 = 3^2 + 4^2 \Rightarrow AC = \sqrt{25} = 5$ km

50. (a) Cousin.

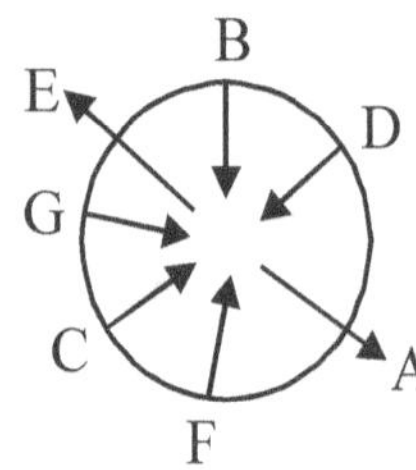

(51-55)

Note A and E are not facing centres rest of all facing centre.

51. (c) A and E persons facing opposite to centre.
52. (d) B, is second to the left of A.
53. (b) G, is to the immediate left of E.
54. (e) F is either third to left or fourth to right of B.
55. (c) Two person (C and E) will remain unchanged.
56. (a) B → 9; A → 2; R → *; N → %; I → #; S → 4
57. (d) D → **2**; M → @; B → 9; N → %; I → #; A → **6**
         Condition (i) is applied.
58. (c) I → **$**; J → 8; B → 9; R → *; L → £; G → #
         Condition (ii) is applied.
59. (a) B → 9; K → ©; G → $; Q → 7; J → ©; N → %
         Condition (iii) is applied.
60. (b) E → **£**; G → $; A → 2; K → 1; R → *; L → **3**
         Condition (ii) is applied.
61. (b) 806   789   653   456   392   145   140
         653 = 6 + 3 = 9
62. (a) 140   145   392   ⓐ456   653   789   806
         456 will be in the middle

63. (c) 546   879   415   932   410   563   086
         410 ⇒ 140
64. (e) 654   987   541   293   041   356   608
         541 = 5 + 4 + 1 = 10
65. (a) 356   889   245   492   240   553   706
         706 ⇒ 0

(66 -70) :

Monday	Physics
Tuesday	Botany
Wednesday	Maths
Thursday	Chemistry
Friday	Statistics
Saturday	Zoology
Sunday	English

66. (a) Physics is taught on Monday.
67. (d) Three subjects (Maths, Chemistry and Statistics.) are taught between Botany and Zoology.
68. (c) Zoology is taught on Saturday.
69. (d) Statistics is taught on Friday.
70. (b) Chemistry will be related to Statistics.
71. (d) Replace 'their' by 'its'. The banker's association – collective noun – so pronoun 'its' singular.
72. (b) Replace 'are' by 'is'. 'five quintals' refers a definite quantity (as collective noun) so verb will be singular.
73. (a) Replace 'have' by 'has'. Dickens is the name of a person.
74. (d) Insert 'are' after 'hopes'. Hopes is plural, so verb will be plural.
75. (a) Place be after may.
76. (d) Remove' a matter'
77. (c) Remove' for preparing'
78. (b) Either' must' or' 'have to' alone should be used
79. (c) Raplace' were' by 'are' .
80. (c) Replace' indefinite' by , indefinitely'.

PRACTICE SET 13

Time : 60 Minutes **Max. Marks : 100**

NUMERICAL ABILITY

DIRECTIONS (Qs. 1-10): *What will come in place of question mark (?) in the following questions?*

1. $\dfrac{3}{5}$ of $\dfrac{4}{7}$ of $\dfrac{5}{12}$ of $1015 = ?$
   (a) 220 (b) 340
   (c) 240 (d) 145
   (e) None of these

2. $1.5 \times 0.025 + (?)^2 = 0.1$
   (a) 0.28 (b) 0.27
   (c) 0.25 (d) 0.235
   (e) None of these

3. $1.5^2 \times \sqrt{0.0225} = ?$
   (a) 0.3375 (b) 3.275
   (c) 32.75 (d) 0.0375
   (e) None of these

4. $\sqrt{0.0289} \times 12 \div 1.5 = ?$
   (a) 1.36 (b) 2.06
   (c) 13.90 (d) 14.80
   (e) None of these

5. 125% of $260 + ?\%$ of $700 = 500$
   (a) 32 (b) 56
   (c) 23 (d) 46
   (e) None of these

6. 45% of $750 - 25\%$ of $480 = ?$
   (a) 216 (b) 217.50
   (c) 245 (d) 236.50
   (e) None of these

7. $75^{8.5} \div 75^{3.8} = 75^?$
   (a) 4.9 (b) 3.6
   (c) 3.3 (d) 4.7
   (e) None of these

8. $5431 + 10500 - 4371 - 1357 = ?$
   (a) 9203 (b) 10003
   (c) 10203 (d) 11203
   (e) None of these

9. $3\dfrac{7}{11} + 7\dfrac{3}{11} \times 1\dfrac{1}{2} = ?$
   (a) $13\dfrac{10}{11}$ (b) $14\dfrac{6}{11}$
   (c) $14\dfrac{9}{11}$ (d) $10\dfrac{17}{22}$
   (e) None of these

10. $1080 \div 12 \div 10 = ?$
    (a) 900 (b) 90
    (c) 120 (d) 12
    (e) None of these

11. The number zero (0) is surrounded by the same 2-digit number on both (left and right) the sides; for example, 25025, 67067, etc. The largest number that always divides such a number is
    (a) 7 (b) 11
    (c) 13 (d) 1001
    (e) None of these

12. If a certain sum of money becomes double at simple interest in 12 years, what would be the rate of interest per annum?
(a) $8\dfrac{1}{3}$
(b) 10
(c) 12
(d) 14
(e) None of these

13. The ratio of the prices of two houses A and B was 4 : 5 last year. This year, the price of A is increased by 25% and that of B by ₹ 50000. If their prices are now in the ratio 9 : 10, the price of A last year was
(a) ₹ 3,60,000
(b) ₹ 4,50,000
(c) ₹ 4,80,000
(d) ₹ 5,00,000
(e) None of these

14. In a mixture of 80 l, the ratio of milk and water is 3 : 1. If the ratio of milk and water is to be 2 : 3 the how much amount of water is to be further added?
(a) 70 l
(b) 80 l
(c) 100 l
(d) 140 l
(e) None of these

15. The age of a mother, two years ago, was eight times the age of her daughter. After 1 year, mother's age will be five times the daughter's age. After how many years from now the mother's age will become three times the daughter's age?
(a) 6 years
(b) 8 years
(c) 10 years
(d) 12 years
(e) None of these

16. The speed of a boat in still water is 11 km/h. It can go 12 km upstream and return downstream to the initial point in 2 h 45 min. What is the speed of stream?
(a) 5 km/h
(b) 4 km/h
(c) 3 km/h
(d) 2 km/h
(e) None of these

17. Three numbers are in the ratio 3 : 2 : 5 and the sum of their squares is 1862. What are the three numbers?
(a) 18, 12, 30
(b) 24, 16, 40
(c) 15, 10, 25
(d) 21, 14, 35
(e) None of these

18. *A* is thrice as efficient as *B* and hence completes a work in 40 days less than the number of days taken by *B*. What will be the number of days taken by both of them when working together?
(a) 22.5 days
(b) 15 days
(c) 20 days
(d) 18 days
(e) None of these

19. A garrison of '*n*' men had enough food to last for 30 days. After 10 days, 50 more men joined them. If the food now lasted for 16 days, what is the value of *n*?
(a) 200
(b) 240
(c) 280
(d) 320
(e) None of these

20. The marked price of a machine is ₹ 18000. By selling it at a discount of 20%, the loss is 4%. What is the cost price of the machine?
(a) ₹ 10000
(b) ₹ 12000
(c) ₹ 14000
(d) ₹ 15000
(e) None of these

21. The average weight of a class of 15 boys and 10 girls is 38.4 kg. If the average weight of the boys is 40 kg, then what is the average weight of the girls?
(a) 36.5 kg
(b) 35 kg
(c) 36 kg
(d) 34.6 kg
(e) None of these

22. The perimeter of a square is 164 m. What is the area of the square?
(a) 1089 sq m
(b) 1764 sq m
(c) 1661 sq m
(d) 1681 sq m
(e) None of these

23. The product of two successive numbers is 1980. Which is the smaller number?
(a) 34
(b) 44
(c) 35
(d) 45
(e) None of these

24. The difference between 55% of a number and 25% of the same number is 11.10. What is 75% of that number?
(a) 27.75
(b) 37
(c) 21.25
(d) 45
(e) None of these

25. A basket contains 3 blue, 2 green and 5 red balls. If four balls are picked at random, what is the probability that two are green and two are blue?
(a) $\dfrac{1}{18}$
(b) $\dfrac{1}{70}$
(c) $\dfrac{3}{5}$
(d) $\dfrac{1}{2}$
(e) None of these

DIRECTIONS (Qs. 26-30) : *Find the next term in the given series in each of the questions below.*

26. 198, 194, 185, 169, (?)
(a) 136
(b) 144
(c) 9
(d) 92
(e) None of these

27. 6, 9, 7, 10, 8, 11, (?)
(a) 12
(b) 13
(c) 9
(d) 14
(e) None of these

28. 7, 11, 19, 35, 67, (?)
(a) 121
(b) 153
(c) 141
(d) 133
(e) None of these

29. 5, 6, 10, 19, 35, (?)
(a) 55
(b) 65
(c) 60
(d) 70
(e) None of these

30. 1, 3, 8, 18, 35, (?)
(a) 61
(b) 72
(c) 67
(d) 52
(e) 71

DIRECTIONS (Qs. 31 - 35) : *Study the following graph carefully and answer the questions given below.*

India's Exports and Imports Over the Years (in million US $)

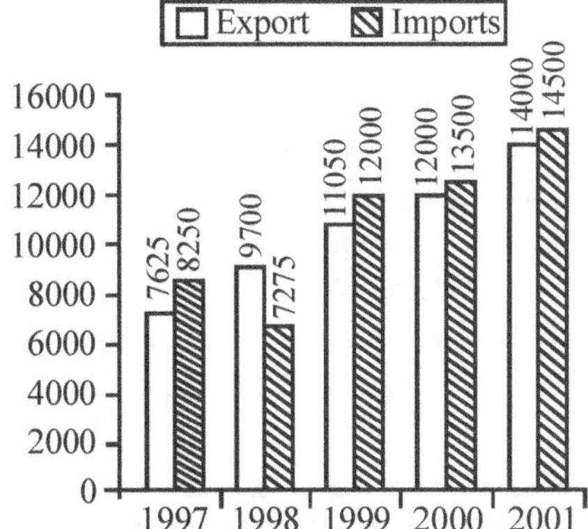

31. What was the difference between the average imports and average exports over the given years ?
    (a) US $ 200 million   (b) US $ 230 million
    (c) US $ 250 million   (d) US $ 275 million
    (e) None of these

32. What was the difference between the exports in 1997 and the average exports over the given years ?
    (a) US $ 2750 million   (b) US $ 3050 million
    (c) US $ 3250 million   (d) US $ 3500 million
    (e) None of these

33. Approximately what was the percentage increase in the imports from 1997 to 2001?
    (a) 62   (b) 66
    (c) 72   (d) 76
    (e) 82

34. In which year differences (absolute) between imports and exports was the maximum?
    (a) 1997   (b) 1998
    (c) 1999   (d) 2000
    (e) 2001

35. In which year percentage of exports over imports of the same year was the minimum?
    (a) 1997   (b) 1998
    (c) 1999   (d) 2000
    (e) 2001

REASONING ABILITY

DIRECTIONS (Qs. 36-40) : *Study the following arrangement carefully and answer the questions given below*

M, D, K, R, T, H, W and A are sitting around a circle facing at the centre. D is second to the right of M who is fifth to the left of T. K is third to the right of R who is second to the right of D. H is second to the right of W.

36. Who is second to the right of A ?
    (a) M   (b) D
    (c) K   (d) Data inadequate
    (e) None of the above

37. Who is third to the left of M ?
    (a) A   (b) T
    (c) H   (d) D
    (e) Data inadequate

38. Who is fourth to the right of H ?
    (a) A   (b) T
    (c) R   (d) K
    (e) None of these

39. In which of the following combinations is the first person sitting between the second and the third person ?
    (a) KMW   (b) MWD
    (c) RHT   (d) TAK
    (e) None of the above

40. If A and W interchange their positions who will be third to the left of R ?
    (a) M   (b) D
    (c) A   (d) K
    (e) None of these

DIRECTIONS (Qs. 41-45) : *In each question below are three statements followed by three conclusions numbered I, II and III. You have to take the three given statements to be true even if they seem to be at variance from commonly known facts and then decide which of the given conclusions logically follows from the three given statements disregarding commonly known facts. Then decide which of the answers (a), (b), (c), (d) and (e) is the correct answer and indicate it on the answer sheet.*

41. **Statements :** Some desks are chairs. All chairs are tables. Some tables are mats.
    Conclusions : I. Some mats are desks.
    II. Some tables are desks.
    III. Some mats are chairs.
    (a) Only I follows   (b) Only II follows
    (c) Only III follows   (d) II and III follow
    (e) None of the above

42. **Statements :** All sweets are fruits. No fruit is pencil. Some pencils are glasses.
    Conclusions : I. Some glasses are sweets.
    II. Some pencils are sweets.
    III. No glass is sweet.
    (a) Only I follows   (b) Only II follows
    (c) Only III follows   (d) either I or III follows
    (e) None of the above

43. **Statements :** Some books are flowers. Some flowers are chains. Some chains are hammers.
    Conclusions : I. Some hammers are flowers.
    II. Some chairs are books.
    III. Some hammers are books.
    (a) None follows   (b) Only I follows
    (c) Only II follows   (d) Only III follows
    (e) II and III follow

44. **Statements :** All roofs are cameras. Some cameras are photographs. Some photographs are stores.
    Conclusions : I. Some stores are cameras.
    II. Some stores are roofs.
    III. Some cameras are roofs.
    (a) Only I follows   (b) Only II follows
    (c) Only III follows   (d) II and III follow
    (e) None of the above

45.   **Statements :** Some nails are horses. All horses are tablets. All tablets are crows.

    Conclusions : I. Some crows are nails.

                    II. Some tablets are nails.

                    III. Some crows are horses.

    (a) Only I follows   (b) I and II follows

    (c) I and III follow   (d) II and III follow

    (e) All I, II and III follow

DIRECTIONS (Qs. 46-48) : *There is family of 6 members P, Q, R, S, T and U in which two are married couples. S is the grandfather of P and father of T. Q is the wife of T and mother of R. P is the granddaughter of S.*

46.   How many males are there in the family?

    (a) two   (b) three

    (c) four   (d) can't be determined

    (e) None of these

47.   What is the relation between U and T?

    (a) U is the father of T

    (b) U is the mother of T

    (c) U is the mother in law of T

    (d) There is no relation between U and T

    (e) None of these

48.   Which among the following is one of the couple?

    (a) TU   (b) SQ

    (c) SU   (d) TP

    (e) None of these

49.   In a certain code language the word PHYSICIAN is written as KSBHRXRZM. How will the word MENDELSON be written in that language ?

    (a) NVMVWOHLM   (b) MVMWVOHLN

    (c) NVMWVOHLM   (d) NVMWVOLKM

    (e) None of these

50.   Alok walked 30 m towards East and took a right turn and walked 40 m. He again took a right turn and walked 50 m. Towards which direction is he from his starting point?

    (a) South   (b) West

    (c) South-West   (d) South-East

    (e) None of these

DIRECTIONS (Qs. 51-55): *Read the following information and answer the questions that follow.*

Ms. Jones is very fussy in watering her flower-pots. She waters pots A, B, C, D, E, F, G, H, I and J on everyday of the week. In going from one pot to another, she strictly adheres to the following rules. The first two pots to be watered everyday must be selected from C, D, E and F, H can't be watered before D and J can't be watered after I. G can be watered only after B. F must be watered before C.

51.   If D is the fourth pot to be watered on a day, which of the following pots can't be fifth on that day ?

    (a) C   (b) F

    (c) E   (d) H

    (e) J

52.   Which of the following is a possible arrangement for the watering of the first five pots ?

    (a) E, H, F, D, C   (b) F, C, H, B, D

    (c) C, D, E, B, H   (d) C, J, E, D, A

    (e) D, F, B, C, A

53.   If D is to be watered immediately after J, then which of the following must be true ?

    (a) F is the first pot to be watered

    (b) Of the first two pots to be watered, one is F

    (c) H is the sixth pot to be watered

    (d) H is either the sixth or seventh pot to be watered

    (e) B is the fourth pot to be watered

54.   If the given condition are reversed, that is first becomes last, before becomes after and so on, which of the following is a possible arrangement for watering the last four pots ?

    (a) G, D, B, H   (b) H, F, C, E

    (c) F, B, C, E   (d) C, B, E, F

    (e) E, F, H, G

55.   If D is the fourth pot to be watered and J the fifth, then which of the following can be the third pot to be watered ?

    (a) A   (b) F

    (c) H   (d) G

    (e) I

DIRECTIONS (Qs. 56-60): *Answer these questions referring to the symbol-letter-number sequence given below:*

E G 4 B H 7 5 @ K 8 D N £ Q Z $ W 3 C 1 9 * 1 B 2 S 6

56.   How many such consonants are threre in the above sequence which are immediately preceded by a symbol and immediately followed by a digit ?

    (a) One   (b) Two

    (c) None   (d) Three

    (e) More than three

57.   What should come in place of the question mark (?) in the following sequence ?

    4H@, KDQ, ?, ILS

    (a) ZW1   (b) NQ$

    (c) @8N   (d) $W9

    (e) None of these

58.   Which of the following is exactly in the midway between the ninth from left end and the seventh from right end ?

    (a) Q   (b) Z

    (c) $ (d) W

    (e) None of these

59.   If the first fifteen elements are written in the reverse order then which of the following will be seventh to the left of twelfth element from right end ?

    (a) 7   (b) @

    (c) 5   (d) K

    (e) None of these

60.   How many such digits are there in the above sequence which are immediately preceded as well as followed by digits ?

    (a) None   (b) One

    (c) Two   (d) Three

    (e) None of these

DIRECTIONS (Qs. 61-63) : *Use the information given below to answer.*

(i) There is a group of 5 persons A, B, C, D and E

(ii) In the group there is one badminton player, one chess player and one tennis player

(iii) A and D are unmarried ladies and do not play any games

(iv) No lady is a chess player or a badminton player

(v) There is a married couple in the group of which E is the husband

(vi) B is the brother of C and is neither a chess player nor a tennis player

61. Which of the group has only ladies?

(a) ABC (b) BCD

(c) CDE (d) CDA

(e) None of these

62. Who is the tennis player?

(a) B (b) C

(c) D (d) E

(e) None of these

63. Who is the wife of E?

(a) A (b) B

(c) D (d) C

(e) None of these

64. When Amir saw Manjeet, he recalled that he is son of the father of the mother of his daughter.

Manjeet is Amir's:

(a) Brother-in-law (b) Brother

(c) Cousin (d) Uncle

(e) None of these

65. In a row of twenty five children Raman is 14th from the right end. Varun is third to the left of Raman. What is Varun's position from the left end of the row?

(a) Eighth (b) Nineth

(c) Seventh (d) Tenth

(e) None of these

66. A man starts walking in south and walks for 7 km, then turns left and walks for 2 km, Then, once again turns left and walks for 12 km, turns left one more time and walks for 2 km. How much distance he has to cover to reach the starting point?

(a) 7 km (b) 12 km

(c) 4 km (d) 5 km

(e) None of these

67. Pointing to a boy, Mamta said, "he is the only son of my father-in-law's only child." How is the boy related to Mamta?

(a) Brother (b) Daughter

(c) Son (d) Husband

(e) None of these

68. It in a certain language CHENNAI is coded as 'DGFMOZJ' how is MUMBAI coded in the same language?

(a) NTNABH (b) LVLCZJ

(c) LTLCBH (d) NVNCBJ

(e) None of these

DIRECTIONS (Qs. 69-70) : *Read the following information carefully and answer the questions which follow.*

Point H is 6 km towards the East of point G. Point R is 8 km North of point G. Point K is 10 km to the SOuth of point Q. Point L is 3 km towards the East from point Q. Point S is exactly midway between point G and point H.

69. What is the distance between Point L and Point S?

(a) 3 km (b) 4 km

(c) 5 km (d) 6 km

(e) Cannot be determined

70. Point L is in which direction from point K?

(a) North (b) South

(c) North-east (d) South-east

(e) None of these

DIRECTIONS (Qs. 71-80) : *Read each sentence to find out whether there is any error in it. The error, if any, will be in one part of the sentence. The number of this part is the answer. If there is no error, the answer is (e).*

71. All three products help wean smokers (a) / from cigarettes by providing small doses (b) / of nicotine designed to replace the basic level (c) / of average smoker's day's nicotine consumption. (d) No error (e)

72. The main lesson is that (a) / the mosquito eradication campaigns (b) / such as the one the French conducted (c) / needs to be followed up. (d) / No error (e)

73. By arresting the local criminals (a) / and encouraging good people, (b) / we can end (c) / hostilities of that area (d) / No error (e)

74. We admired thre way (a) / he had completed all his work (b) / and appreciation the method (c) / adopted by him. (d) / No error

75. I was being astonished (a) / when I heard that (b) / he had left the country (c) / without informing anyone of us . (d) / No. error (e)

76. The Head of the Department, along with his colleagues (a) / are coming to attend (b) / the conference which is (c) / scheduled this afternoon. (d) / No error (e)

77. Govind loved his Guru immensely (a) / and gave him fullest loyalty, (b) / yet he had his own (c) / independent way of thinking (d) / No error (e)

78. In a very harsh tone, (a) / he shouted at his servants (b) / and told them that (c) / he does not neEid their services (d)/ No error (e)

79. This is an important difference in (a) / that it marks the first move towards (b) / an institution for money - earning proposition. (d) / No error (e)

80. The ultimate problem of physics (a)/ is to reduce matter by analysis (b) / to its lowest condition of divisibility (c) / No.error (d)

DIRECTIONS (Qs. 81-90) : *Read the following passage carefully and answer the questions given below it. Certain words/phrases are given in bold to help you to locate them while answering some of the questions.*

In a disarmingly frank talk at the Indian Merchants' Chamber in Mumbai, the Japanese Ambassador in India dwelt at length on issues that exercise the minds of Japanese investors when they consider investment proposals in India.

Raising the question "What comparative advantages does India offer as an investment market ?", he said though labour in India is expensive, wage-levels are offset by productivity level to a large extent.

Acknowledging that the vastness of the Indian market is a great inducement for investment in manufacturing industry, he wondered if it was **justifiable** to provide that overseas remittance of profit in foreign exchange be fully covered by exchange earnings which had been done. Significantly, on the eve of the Prime Minister's visit to Japan, the government delinked profits repatriation from exports in meeting this demand.

The Ambassador said that foreign investors needed to be assured of the continuity and consistency of the liberalisation policy and the fact that new measures which had been put into force by means of administrative notifications without amending government laws acted as a damper.

The Ambassador pleaded for speedy formulation of the exit policy and pointed to the highly restrictive control by the government on disinvestment by foreign partners in joint ventures in India.

While it is all too easy to dismiss critical comment on conditions in India contemptuously, there can be little doubt that if foreign investment is to be wooed assiduously, we will have to meet exacting international standards and cater at least partially to what we may consider the **idiosyncrasies** of our foreign collaborators. The Japanese too have passed through a stage in the fifties when their products were derided as sub-standard and shoddy. That they have come out of that ordeal of fire to emerge as an economic superpower speaks much of their doggedness to pursue goals against all odds to meet acceptable standards.

There is no gainsaying that the past record of Japanese investment is a poor benchmark for future expectations.

81. The author has appreciated the Japanese for their
    - (a) quality of products manufactured in the fifties.
    - (b) passing through an ordeal.
    - (c) perseverance in raising quality of products.
    - (d) future expectations.
    - (e) None of these

82. According to the Japanese Ambassador, which of the following motivates the foreign investors to invest in Indian manufacturing industry? .
    - (a) very large scope of Indian market
    - (b) overseas remittance of profit in foreign exchange
    - (c) assurance of continuity of the liberalisation policy
    - (d) high productivity levels
    - (e) None of these

83. The purpose of the author in writing this passage seems to be to
    - (a) discourage foreign investment in India.
    - (b) critically examine Indian investment environment.
    - (c) paint a rosy picture of India's trade and commerce.
    - (d) criticize government's liberalization policy.
    - (e) raise the expectations of foreign investors.

84. According to the Japanese Ambassador, India offers a comparative advantage to foreign investors in terms of
    - (a) inexpensive labour
    - (b) abysmally low wage levels
    - (c) higher productivity
    - (d) skilled workforce
    - (e) None of these

85. For seeking more and more foreign investment, the author suggests that we should
    - (a) satisfy fully the whims of our foreign collaborators.
    - (b) dismiss all critical comments on Indian conditions.
    - (c) link profit repatriations to exports.
    - (d) raise the quality of product to match international standards.
    - (e) None of these

86. From the passage it can be inferred that the author is
    - (a) a political commentator.
    - (b) a secretary of the Japanese Ambassador.
    - (c) a Japanese investor.
    - (d) an Indian investor.
    - (e) None of these

87. The author attributes Japan's emergence as an economic superpower to
    - A. their ability to overcome any ordeal.
    - B. their tenacity and perserverance despite unfavourable circumstances.
    - C. their ability to improvise and adapt to globally acceptable quality levels.
    - (a) A & B only   8(b) B & C only
    - (c) A & C only   (d) All the three
    - (e) None of these

88. Which of the following statement(s) is/are true about the critical comments on investment conditions in India?
    - A. These comments are difficult to be countered.
    - B. These comments are received from various international quarters.
    - C. These comments are based more on biases than on facts.
    - (a) Only C   (b) Only B
    - (c) Only A   (d) A & B only
    - (e) A & C only

DIRECTIONS (Q. 89): *Choose the word which is most nearly the SAME in meaning to the word printed in capital as used in the passage.*

---

89. **IDIOSYNCRASIES**
    - (a) demands   (b) needs
    - (c) deviations   (d) ideologies
    - (e) identity

DIRECTIONS (Q. 90): *Choose the word which is most OPPOSITE in meaning of the word printed in capital as used in the passage.*

90. **JUSTIFIABLE**

  (a) unreasonable   (b) formidable

  (c) irrevocable   (d) unscrupulous

  (e) inevitable

DIRECTIONS (Qs. 91-100): *In the following passage there are blanks, each of which has been numbered. These numbers are printed below the passage and against each, five words are suggested, one of which fits the blank appropriately. Find out the appropriate word in each case.*

Trust is the basis of human relationships. As trust between people grows, **91** change and interpersonal dynamics are transformed. Diverse skills and abilities become **92** and appreciated as strengths. People begin to **93** one another's attitudes and feelings. They learn to be **94** instead of playing roles. As trust grows the **95** that prevent **96** and openness lessen. People become more expressive, impulsive, frank and **97**. Their communication is efficient and clear. They risk **98** and confrontation, opening the doors to deeper communication, involvement and commitment. Congestion and **99** lessen. The flow of data is open and **100**.

91. (a) motivations   (b) behaviours

  (c) patterns   (d) aspirations

  (e) commitments

92. (a) obvious   (b) necessary

  (c) essential   (d) recognised

  (e) prominent

93. (a) accept   (b) participate

  (c) pronounce   (d) inculcate

  (e) relate

94. (a) advocates   (b) possessed

  (c) exponents   (d) indifferent

  (e) themselves

95. (a) Seriousness   (b) Beliefs

  (c) Barriers   (d) Marks

  (e) Desks

96. (a) snobbery   (b) egoism

  (c) brashness   (d) boasting

  (e) candour

97. (a) projective   (b) Sportaneous

  (c) Plous   (d) Cavaliers

  (e) Calous

98. (a) conflict   (b) persuasiveness

  (c) dedication   (d) propensity

  (e) jealousy

99. (a) pervasiveness   (b) boundaries

  (c) sluggishness   (d) blocking

  (e) enthusiasm

100. (a) unanimous   (b) uncritical

  (c) uninhibited   (d) uncanny

  (e) unusual

Answer Key														
1	(d)	14	(a)	27	(c)	40	(c)	53	(b)	66	(d)	79	(d)	92	(e)
2	(c)	15	(b)	28	(e)	41	(b)	54	(d)	67	(c)	80	(e)	93	(a)
3	(a)	16	(a)	29	(c)	42	(d)	55	(a)	68	(a)	81	(c)	94	(e)
4	(a)	17	(d)	30	(a)	43	(a)	56	(b)	69	(b)	82	(a)	95	(c)
5	(e)	18	(b)	31	(b)	44	(c)	57	(a)	70	(c)	83	(b)	96	(e)
6	(b)	19	(a)	32	(c)	45	(e)	58	(b)	71	(d)	84	(e)	97	(b)
7	(d)	20	(d)	33	(d)	46	(d)	59	(c)	72	(d)	85	(d)	98	(a)
8	(c)	21	(c)	34	(b)	47	(b)	60	(a)	73	(d)	86	(a)	99	(c)
9	(b)	22	(d)	35	(d)	48	(c)	61	(d)	74	(c)	87	(d)	100	(a)
10	(e)	23	(b)	36	(a)	49	(c)	62	(b)	75	(a)	88	(b)		
11	(d)	24	(a)	37	(b)	50	(c)	63	(d)	76	(b)	89	(d)		
12	(a)	25	(b)	38	(d)	51	(b)	64	(a)	77	(d)	90	(a)		
13	(a)	26	(b)	39	(c)	52	(e)	65	(b)	78	(d)	91	(b)		

HINTS & EXPLANATIONS

1. (d) $\dfrac{3}{5}$ of $\dfrac{4}{7}$ of $\dfrac{5}{12}$ of $1015 = \dfrac{3}{5} \times \dfrac{4}{7} \times \dfrac{5}{12} \times 1015 = \dfrac{1015}{7} = 145$

2. (c) $1.5 \times 0.025 + (?)^2 = 0.1 \Rightarrow (?)^2 = 0.1 - 1.5 \times 0.025$

    $\Rightarrow (?)^2 = 0.1 - 0.0375 \Rightarrow ? = \sqrt{.0625} = 0.25$

3. (a) $1.5^2 \times \sqrt{0.0225} = 2.25 \times 0.15 = 0.3375$

4. (a) $\sqrt{0.0289} \times 12 \div 1.5$

    $0.17 \times 8 \Rightarrow 1.36$

5. (e) 125% of $260 + ?\%$ of $700 = 500$

    $\Rightarrow ?\%$ of $700 = 500 - 125\%$ of 260

    $\Rightarrow ?\%$ of $700 = 175$

    $\therefore \quad ? = \dfrac{175 \times 100}{700} = 25$

6. (b) 45% of $750 - 25\%$ of 480

    $= \dfrac{45 \times 750}{100} - \dfrac{25 \times 480}{100} = 337.5 - 120 = 217.5$

7. (d) $75^{8.5} \div 75^{3.8} = 75^{(8.5 - 3.8)} = 75^{4.7}$

8. (c) $5431 + 10500 - 4371 - 1357 = 10203$

9. (b) $3\dfrac{7}{11} + 7\dfrac{3}{11} \times 1\dfrac{1}{2} = \dfrac{40}{11} + \dfrac{80}{11} \times \dfrac{3}{2} = \dfrac{160}{11} = 14\dfrac{6}{11}$

10. (e) $1080 \div 12 \div 10 = \dfrac{1080}{12 \times 10} = 9$

11. (d) First start with the option (d).

    $1001 \times 25 = 25025$

    $1001 \times 67 = 67067$ etc.

    Thus 1001 is the largest number which divides the numbers of the type 25025, 67067 etc.

12. (a) Let the principal be P, then amount after 12 years = 2P

    $\Rightarrow SI = (2P - P) = P$

    Now, $SI = \dfrac{P \times r \times t}{100} \Rightarrow P = \dfrac{P \times r \times 12}{100}$

    or $r = \dfrac{100}{12} = \dfrac{25}{3} = 8\dfrac{1}{3}\%$

13. (a) Let the prices of two houses A and B be ₹$4x$ and ₹$5x$, respectively for the last year.

    Then, the prices of A this year = ₹$(1.25 \times 4x)$ and that of B = ₹$(5x + 50,000)$

    This year, ratio of their prices = 9 : 10

    $\therefore \quad \dfrac{1.25 \times 4x}{5x + 50000} = \dfrac{9}{10}$

    $\Rightarrow 50x - 45x = 450000 \Rightarrow 5x = 450000$

    $\Rightarrow x = 90000$

    Hence, the price of A last year was

    $4x = ₹3,60,000$

14. (a) Volume of mixture of milk and water = 80 l

    Ratio of milk and water = 3 : 1

    $\therefore \quad$ Volume of milk $= \dfrac{3}{3 + 1} \times 80$

    $= \dfrac{3}{4} \times 80 = 60\ l$

    Volume of water = 80 − 60 = 20 l

    Let amount of water added = $x\ l$

    According to given condition,

    $\dfrac{60}{20 + x} = \dfrac{2}{3}$

    $\Rightarrow 40 + 2x = 180$

    $\Rightarrow 2x = 180 - 40$

    $\Rightarrow 2x = 140$

    $\therefore \quad x = 70\ l$

15. (b) Let present age of mother and daughter be x and y.

    2 years ago, $x - 2 = 8(y - 2)$

    $\Rightarrow x - 8y = -14$ ...(i)

    1 year after, $x + 1 = 5(y + 1)$

    $\Rightarrow x - 5y = 4$ ...(ii)

    On solving equations. (i) and (ii), we get

    $y = 6$ years and $x = 34$ years

    Let after z years mother will be three times of her daughter.

    $34 + z = 3(6 + z) \Rightarrow z = 8$ years

16. (a) Let speed of stream = D km/h

Speed of boat in still water = B km/h = 11 km/h.

According to the question

$$B + D = \frac{12}{t_1}$$

$$t_1 = \frac{12}{B + D} \qquad ...(i)$$

$$B - D = \frac{12}{t_2}$$

$$t_2 = \frac{12}{B - D} \qquad ...(ii)$$

Now,

$$t_1 + t_2 = 2 + \frac{45}{60} = \frac{11}{4}$$

$$\Rightarrow \quad \frac{12}{B + D} + \frac{12}{B - D} = \frac{11}{4} \quad \left(\text{Given } B = 11 \text{km/h}\right)$$

$$\Rightarrow \quad \frac{2B}{B^2 - D^2} = \frac{11}{4 \times 12}$$

$$\Rightarrow \quad \frac{2 \times 11}{(11)^2 - D^2} = \frac{11}{4 \times 12}$$

$$\Rightarrow \quad D^2 = 25 \qquad \therefore \ D = 5 \text{ km/h}.$$

17. (d) Let the numbers be $3x$, $2x$ and $5x$.

$$\therefore \quad (3x)^2 + (2x)^2 + (5x)^2 = 1862$$

$$\Rightarrow \quad 9x^2 + 4x^2 + 25x^2 = 1862$$

$$\Rightarrow \quad x^2 = \frac{1862}{38} = 49$$

$$x = 7$$

Hence, the required numbers are 3×7, 2×7 and 5×7. i.e., 21, 14 and 35

18. (b) Let efficiency of B is x

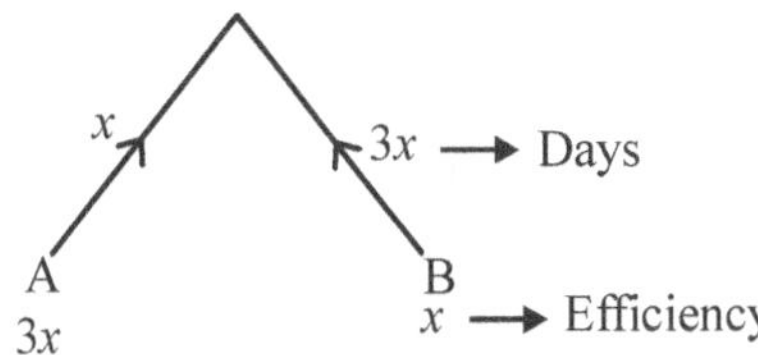

Days are inversely proportional to efficiency.

According to question,

$$\Rightarrow \quad 3x - x = 40$$

$$\Rightarrow \quad 2x = 40$$

$$\therefore \quad x = 20$$

Time taken by A = x days = 20 days

Time taken by B = $3x$ days = 3×20 = 60 days

Time taken by A and B together $= \frac{20 \times 60}{80} = 15$ days

19. (a) $M_1 = n$, $d_1 = 30 - 10 = 20$, $M_2 = (50 + n)$ $d_2 = 16$

By formula,

$$M_1 d_1 = M_2 d_2$$

$$\Rightarrow \quad n \times 20 = (n + 50) \times 16$$

$$\Rightarrow \quad 20n = 16n + 800$$

$$\Rightarrow \quad 4n = 800$$

$$\Rightarrow \quad n = 200$$

20. (d) Given marked price of machine = ₹ 18000

$$\therefore \quad \text{Discount} = \frac{20}{100} \times 18000 = ₹ \ 3600$$

$$\therefore \quad \text{SP} = 18000 - 3600 = ₹ \ 14400$$

If loss of 4%, then

$$\text{CP} = \frac{100 \times \text{SP}}{100 - r} = \frac{100 \times 14400}{100 - 4}$$

$$= \frac{100 \times 14400}{96} = ₹ \ 15000$$

21. (c) Let average weight of girls = x

Total weight of the boys = 40 kg × 15 = 600 kg.

Average weight

$$= \frac{\text{Total weight of boys} + \text{Total weight of girls}}{\text{No. of boys} + \text{No. of girls}}$$

$$\Rightarrow \quad 38.4 = \frac{600 + 10 \times x}{15 + 10}$$

$$\Rightarrow \quad 38.4 = \frac{600 + 10x}{25}$$

$$\Rightarrow \quad 38.4 \times 25 = 600 + 10x$$

$$\therefore \quad x = 36 \text{ kg}$$

22. (d) Area of the square $= \left(\frac{164}{4}\right)^2 = (41)^2$

$$= 1681 \text{ sq m}$$

23. (b) Suppose required small number is x.

$$x \times (x + 1) = 1980$$

$$\Rightarrow \quad x^2 + x - 1980 = 0$$

$$\Rightarrow \quad x^2 + 45x - 44x - 1980 = 0$$

$$\Rightarrow \quad x(x + 45) - 44(x + 45) = 0$$

$$\Rightarrow \quad (x - 44)(x + 45) = 0$$

$$x = 44$$

So, smallest number is 44.

24. (a) Let the number be x.

$$\frac{75}{100}x - \frac{25}{100}x = 11.10 \Rightarrow x = \frac{11.10 \times 100}{30}$$

$$75\% \text{ of } x = \frac{75}{100} \times \frac{11.10 \times 100}{30} = 27.75$$

25. (b) Required probability $= \dfrac{^3C_2 \times ^2C_2}{^{10}C_4} = \dfrac{1}{70}$

$\therefore$ Required probability $= \dfrac{3}{210} = \dfrac{1}{70}$

26. (b)
$$198 \quad 194 \quad 185 \quad 169 \quad \boxed{144}$$
$$\quad -2^2 \quad -3^2 \quad -4^2 \quad -5^2$$

27. (c) The first, third, fifth .... and second, fourth .... terms are groups of consecutive natural numbers.

28. (e) The pattern of the number series is:
$7 \times 2 - 3 = 11$
$11 \times 2 - 3 = 19$
$19 \times 2 - 3 = 35$
$35 \times 2 - 3 = 67$
$67 \times 2 - 3 = 134 - 3 = \boxed{131}$

29. (c) The pattern of the number series is:
$5 + 1^2 = 6$
$6 + 2^2 = 10$
$10 + 3^2 = 19$
$19 + 4^2 = 35$
$35 + 5^2 = 35 + 25 = \boxed{60}$

30. (a) The pattern of the number series is:
$1 + 2 = 3$
$3 + (2 + 3) = 8$
$8 + (2 + 3 + 5) = 18$
$18 + (2 + 3 + 5 + 7) = 35$
$35 + (2 + 3 + 5 + 7 + 9) = \boxed{61}$

31. (b) Required difference $= [(8250 + 7275 + 12000 + 13500 + 14500) - (7625 + 9700 + 11050 + 12000 + 14000)] \div 5$

$= \dfrac{1150}{5} = 230 = $ US $ 230 million

32. (c) Required difference

$= \dfrac{54375}{5} - 7625 = $ US $ 3250 million

33. (d) Required percentage $= \dfrac{14500 - 8250}{8250} \times 100 \approx 76\%$

34. (b) Difference in,
$1997 \Rightarrow 8250 - 7625 = 625$
$1998 \Rightarrow 9700 - 7275 = 2425$
$1999 \Rightarrow 12000 - 11050 = 950$
$2000 \Rightarrow 13500 - 12000 = 1500$
$2001 \Rightarrow 14500 - 14000 = 500$

35. (d) Percentage in,
$1997 \Rightarrow \dfrac{7625}{8250} \times 100 \approx 92.5\%$

$1998 \Rightarrow \dfrac{9700}{7275} \times 100 \approx 133\%$

$1999 \Rightarrow \dfrac{11050}{12000} \times 100 \approx 92\%$

$2000 \Rightarrow \dfrac{12000}{13500} \times 100 \approx 89\%$

$2001 \Rightarrow \dfrac{14000}{14500} \times 100 \approx 97\%$

(36-40) :

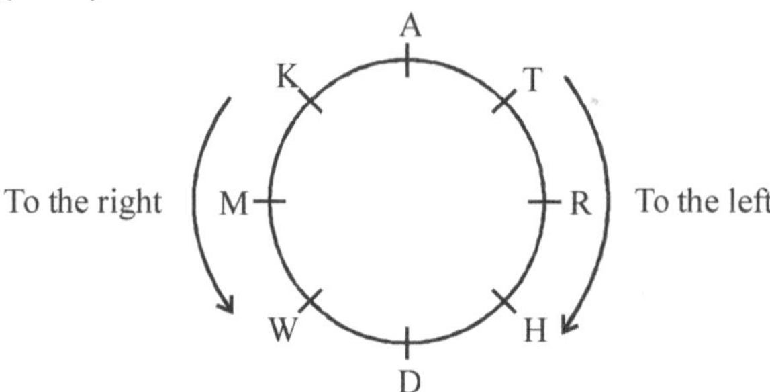

36. (a)   37. (b)   38. (d)   39. (c)
40. (c)

41. (b)

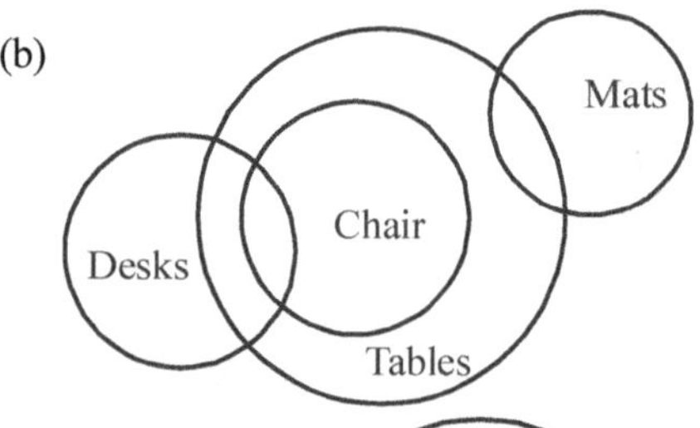

or

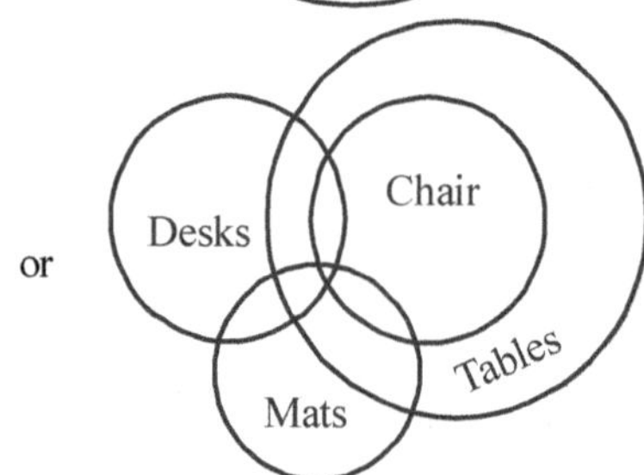

I. False   II. True   III. False

42. (d)

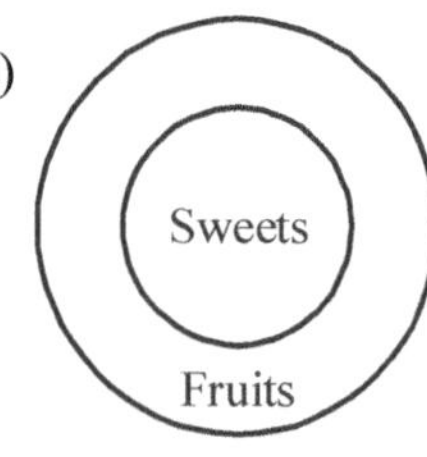

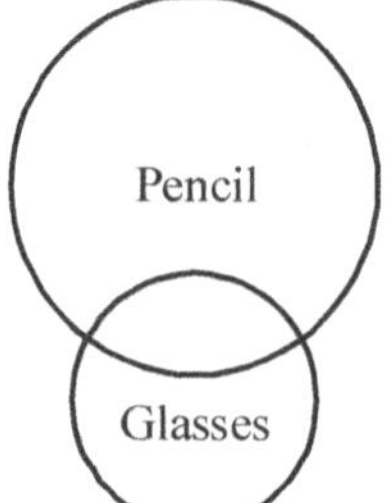

or

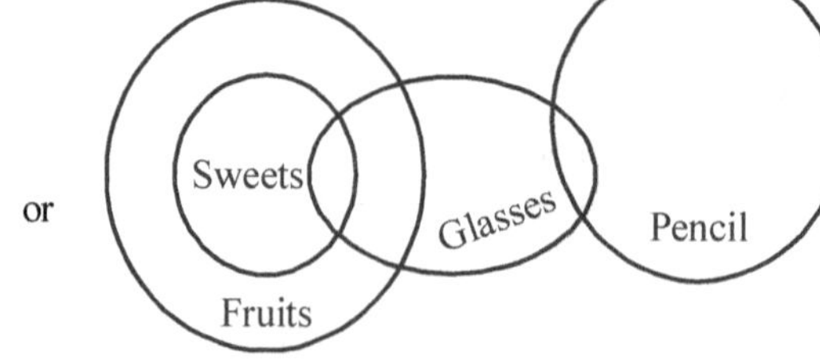

II. False. From both figures it is clear that either I or III follows.

43. (a)

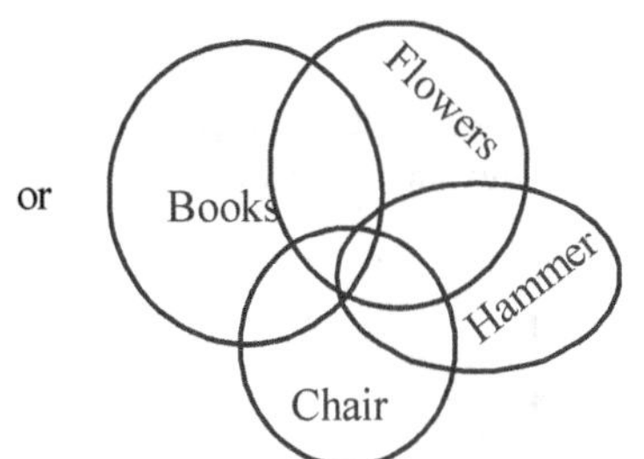

or

I. False   II. False   III. False

44. (c)

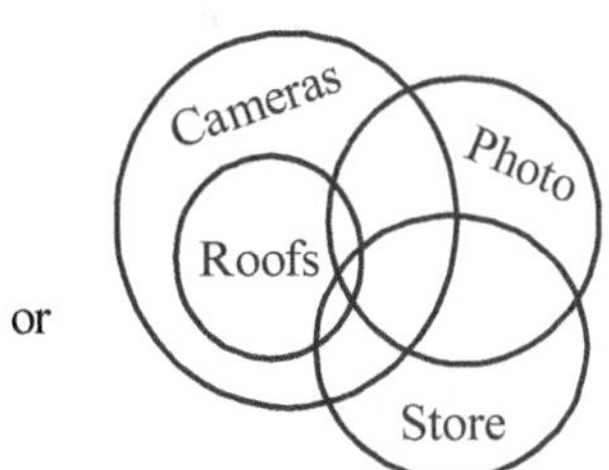

or

I. False   II. False   III. True

45. (e)

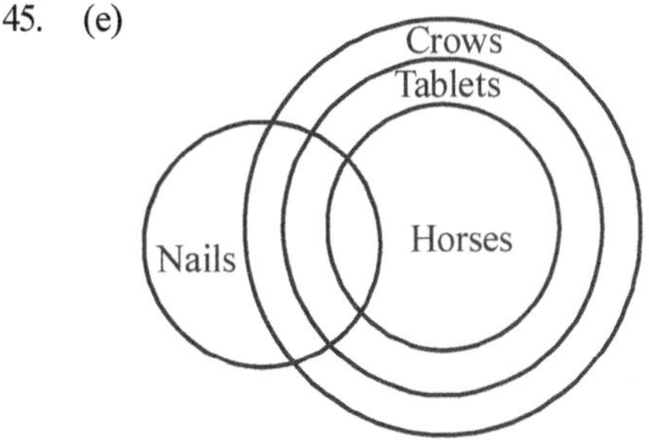

I. True   II. True   III. True

(46-48):

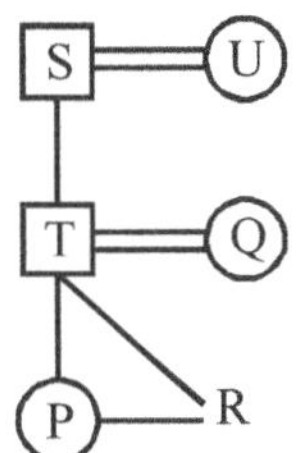

SU and TQ are couples

46. (d) Gender of R is unknown
47. (b)
48. (c)
49. (c) Opposite letters in English alphabet As,

Same as,

Opposite letters in English alphabet

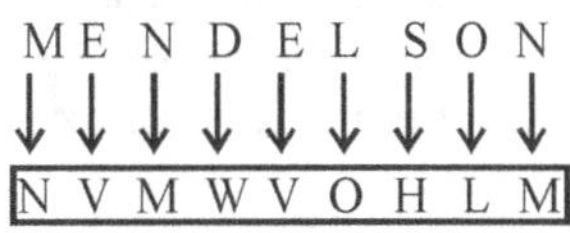

50. (c)

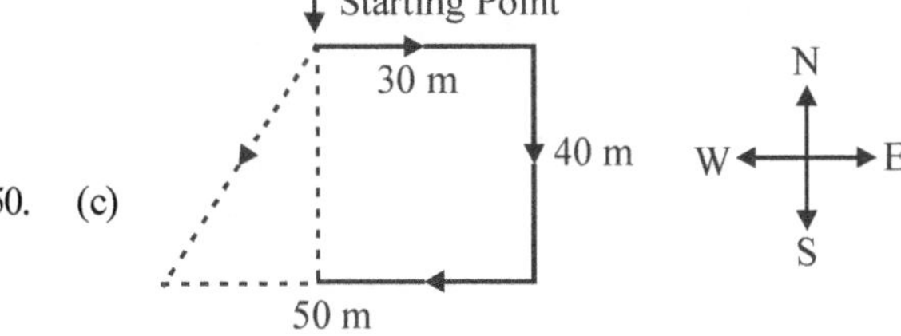

51. (b) If D is the fourth pot and F the fifth, then C and E must be among the first two pots to be watered. Which means C will be watered before F. But this violates the last condition.

52. (e) (a) and (d) are ruled out because the first two pots must include two of the following C, D, E and F, (b) is ruled out because H can't be watered before D. (c) is ruled out because F must be watered before C.

53. (b) If D is to be watered immediately after J, it can't be included among the first two pots. So we are left with C, E and F to select as the first two pots. Now, since F must be watered before C, it must be among the first two pots.

54. (d) The new conditions will read as follows

    (i) Two of the pots C, D, E and F must be among the last two

    (ii) H can't be watered after D.

    (iii) J can't be watered before I.

    (iv) G can be watered only before B.

    (v) F must be watered after C.

    Now, (a) and (e) are ruled out by (i). (b) is ruled out by (ii). (c) is ruled out by (v).

55. (a) Since, D is the fourth pot, F must be among the first two. So, F is ruled out for the third place. H and I are ruled out because H can't be watered before D and J after I. G is ruled out because it can be watered only after B and B, as we known, can't be among the first two.

56. (b) E G 4 B H 7 5 @ K 8 D N £ Q Z $ W 3 C 1 9 * 1 B 2 S 6

57. (a) The first, second and third element of each group is sixth element to the right of the respective element of previous group as given in all in the sequence.

                                                  Practice Set - 13

58. (b) There are 27 elements in all in the sequence.

So, $(27 - 9 - 7 =)$ 11 elements are between the 9th from left and 7th from right.

Hence, $(9 + 6 =)$ 15th element from the left and will be the required answer.

59. (c) 7th to the left of 12th from right

$= (12 + 7 =)$ 19th from right

$= (27 - 19 + 1 =)$ 9th from left

But the first 15 elements are reversed.

$= (15 - 9 + 1 =)$ 7th from left in the original sequence $= 5$.

60. (a) For the condition to be fulfilled, three digits should be together but it is not so in the given sequence.

(61 -63):

	Badminton	Chess	Tennis	Gender	Marriage status	Relation
A	×	×	×	F	Unmarried	
B	✓	×	×	M		Brother of C
C	×	×	✓	F	Married with E	
D	×	×	×	F	Unmarried	
E		✓		M		Husband C + E

61. (d) ACD is the group of ladies.

62. (b) It is clear from above table.

63. (d) It is clear from above table.

64. (a)

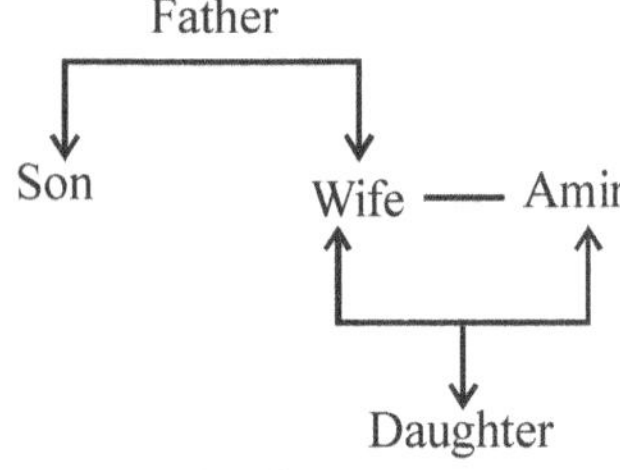

Amir's daughter mother i.e. Amir's wife

Amir's wife's father's son (Manjeet) i.e. brother of Amir's wife hence Manjeet is Amir's brother in law.

65. (b)

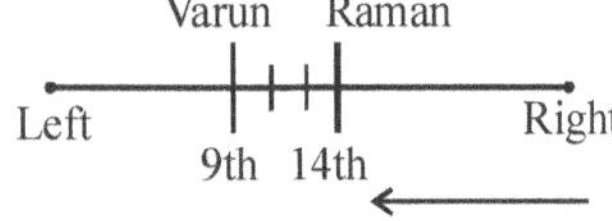

As Raman is 14th from right. So Varun will be 17th from right. So there are 8 people $(25 - 17)$ to the left of Varun. He is the nineth.

66. (d) Aman has taken a rectangular path as is clear from the diagram below.

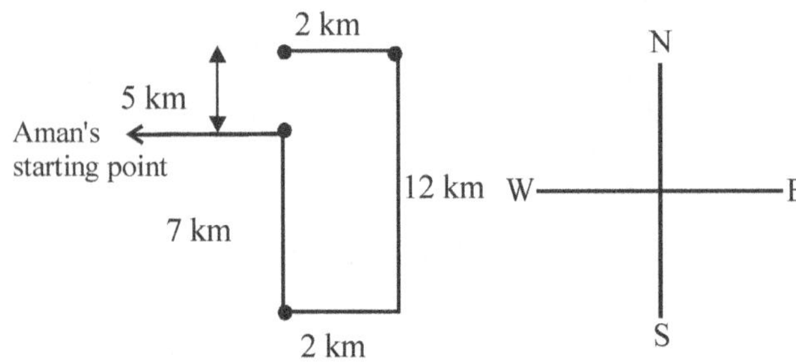

67. (c)

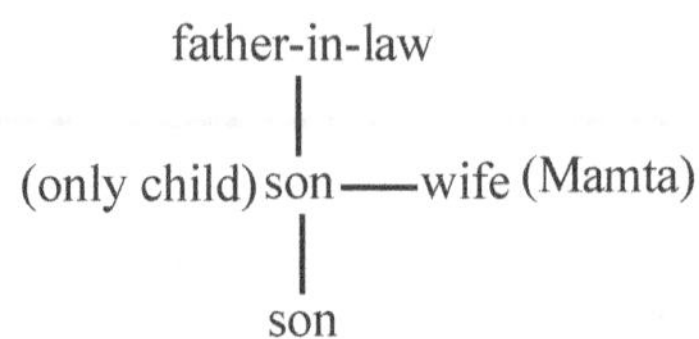

Mamta's father-in-law's only child is Mamta's husband and only child's only son is her husband's only son i.e. Mamta's son.

68. (a) It can be clearly seen that the original word is moved 1 letter forward and backward alternately, such that

$$\begin{array}{ccccccc} C & H & E & N & N & A & I \\ {\scriptstyle +1} & {\scriptstyle -1} & {\scriptstyle +1} & {\scriptstyle -1} & {\scriptstyle +1} & {\scriptstyle -1} & {\scriptstyle +1} \\ D & G & F & M & O & Z & J \end{array}$$

Similarly, in case of the word MUMBAI, the alphabets will also be moved 1 letter forward & backward alternately therefore, options (b) & (c) are ruled out.

$$\begin{array}{cccccc} M & U & M & B & A & I \\ {\scriptstyle +1} & {\scriptstyle -1} & {\scriptstyle +1} & {\scriptstyle -1} & {\scriptstyle +1} & {\scriptstyle -1} \\ N & T & N & A & B & H \end{array}$$

Hence, option (a) is the correct answer.

(69 -70):

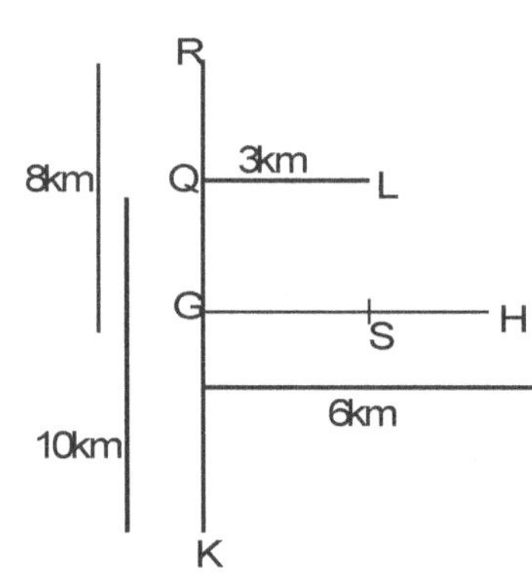

69. (b)　　　　**70.** (c)

71. (d) : Replace' days' by daily' .

72. (d) : Replace' needs' by' need'

73. (d) : Replace' of' by in'

74. (c) : Replace' appreciating' by' appreciated

75. (a) : Remove' being'

76. (b) : Replace 'are' by 'is'

77. (d) : Remove 'independent'

78. (d) : Replace 'does' by 'did'

79. (d) : Replace 'for' by 'of'

80. (e) : No error

PRACTICE SET 14

Time : 60 Minutes | **Max. Marks : 100**

NUMERICAL ABILITY

DIRECTIONS (Qs. 1-10) : *What should come in place of question mark (?) in the following question?*

1. $\dfrac{5.5 \times 6.4}{0.4} = ?$
   - (a) 80
   - (b) 78
   - (c) 88
   - (d) 84
   - (e) None of these

2. $(? - 968) \div 79 \times 4 = 512$
   - (a) 11080
   - (b) 10180
   - (c) 11070
   - (d) 10185
   - (e) None of these

3. $\dfrac{4}{7} \times \dfrac{2}{3} \times ? = 1008$
   - (a) 2688
   - (b) 2604
   - (c) 2666
   - (d) 2646
   - (e) None of these

4. $(764 \times ?) \div 250 = 382$
   - (a) 115
   - (b) 135
   - (c) 145
   - (d) 125
   - (e) None of these

5. $3.7 \times 0.04 + 5.9 = ?$
   - (a) 6.48
   - (b) 6.032
   - (c) 6.048
   - (d) 6.084
   - (e) None of these

6. $\dfrac{1}{4} \times (4856 \times 0.5) \times 12 = ?$
   - (a) 7284
   - (b) 7462
   - (c) 7248
   - (d) 7484
   - (e) None of these

7. $853 + ? \div 17 = 1000$
   - (a) 2500
   - (b) 2482
   - (c) 2499
   - (d) 19399
   - (e) None of these

8. $9643 - 7750 + ? = 4990$
   - (a) 3079
   - (b) 3097
   - (c) 3197
   - (d) 3179
   - (e) None of these

9. $13.15 \times 7.4 + 76.12 = ?$
   - (a) 173.34
   - (b) 94.58
   - (c) 144.43
   - (d) 173.43
   - (e) None of these

10. $6156 \div \sqrt{?} \times 53 = 4028$
    - (a) 6889
    - (b) 6241
    - (c) 6341
    - (d) 6561
    - (e) None of these

11. Which is the smallest of the following numbers?
    - (a) $\sqrt{7}$
    - (b) $\dfrac{1}{\sqrt{7}}$
    - (c) $\dfrac{\sqrt{7}}{7}$
    - (d) $\dfrac{1}{7}$
    - (e) None of these

12. Two equal sums were borrowed at 8% simple interest per annum for 2 years and 3 years, respectively. The difference in the interests was ₹ 56. The difference in the interests was ₹ 56. The sum borrowed were
(a) ₹ 690   (b) ₹ 700
(c) ₹ 740   (d) ₹ 780
(e) None of these

13. A machine is sold at a profit of 10%. Had it been sold for ₹ 80 less, there would have been a loss of 10%. The cost price of the machine is
(a) ₹ 350   (b) ₹ 400
(c) ₹ 450   (d) ₹ 520
(e) None of these

14. A jar of oil was four fifths full. When six bottles of oil were taken out and four bottles of oil were poured into, it was three fourths full. How many bottles of oil were contained by the jar?
(a) 10   (b) 20
(c) 30   (d) 40
(e) None of these

15. During a journey of 80 km, a train covers first 60 km with a speed of 40 km/h and completes the remaining distance with a speed of 20 km/h. What is the average speed of the train during the whole journey?
(a) 30 km/h   (b) 32 km/h
(c) 36 km/h   (d) 40 km/h
(e) None of these

16. An aeroplane takes off 30 minutes later than the scheduled time and in order to reach its destination 1500 km away in time, it has to increase its speed by 250 km/h from its usual speed. Find its usual speed.
(a) 1000 km/h   (b) 750 km/h
(c) 850 km/h   (d) 650 km/h
(e) None of these

17. In an examination, 35% of the candidates failed in one subject and 42% failed in another subject. While 15% failed in both the subjects. If 2500 candidates appeared at the examination, how many students passed in either subject but not in both?
(a) 325   (b) 1175
(c) 2125   (d) 1230
(e) None of these

18. If the length of a certain rectangle is decreased by 4 cm and the width is increased by 3 cm, a square with the same area as the original rectangle would result. The perimeter of the original rectangle (in centimetres) is
(a) 44   (b) 46
(c) 48   (d) 50
(e) None of these

19. Raju decided to marry 3 years after he gets a job. He was 17 years old when he passed class 12th. After passing class 12th', he had completed his graduation course in 3 years and PG Course in 2 years. He got the job exactly 1 year after completing his PG Course. At what age will he get married?
(a) 27 years   (b) 26 years
(c) 28 years   (d) 23 years
(e) None of these

20. The angles of a triangle are in the ratio of 5 : 6 : 7. respectively. What is the sum of the smallest angle and the largest angle together?
(a) 130°   (b) 100°
(c) 110°   (d) 140°
(e) None of these

21. A can do a piece of work in 'x' days and B can do the same work $3x$ days, To finish the work together they take 12 days. What is the value of 'x'?
(a) 8   (b) 10
(c) 12   (d) 16
(e) None of these

22. If the numerator of a fraction is increased by 300% and the denominator is increased by 100%. The resultant fraction is $1\frac{11}{19}$. What was the original fraction?
(a) $\frac{15}{19}$ (b) $\frac{13}{19}$
(c) $\frac{5}{9}$ (d) $\frac{4}{9}$
(e) None of these

23. In how many different ways can the letters of the word 'CASUAL' be arranged?
(a) 36   (b) 720
(c) 240   (d) 360
(e) None of these

24. On a School's Annual Day sweets were to be equally distributed amongst 112 children. But on that particular day, 32 children were absent. Thus, the remaining children got 6 extra sweets. How many sweets was each child originally supposed to get?
(a) 24   (b) 18
(c) 15   (d) Cannot be determined
(e) None of these

25. The sum of the two digits of a number is 15 and the difference between them is 3. What is the product of the two digits of the two digit number?
(a) 56   (b) 63
(c) 42   (d) Cannot be determined
(e) None of these

DIRECTIONS (Qs. 26-30) : *What should come in place of the question mark (?) in the following number series?*

26. 24, ?, 109, 134, 150, 159
(a) 71   (b) 65
(c) 86   (d) 53
(e) None of these

27. 17, 9, 10, ?, 35, 90
(a) 21   (b) 27.5'
(c) 19   (d) 16.5
(e) None of these

28. 3, 20, 78, 332, 1680, ?
(a) 8410   (b) 9836
(c) 10098   (d) 1150
(e) None of these

29. 13, 30, 66, 140, ?, 592
    (a) 210 (b) 290
    (c) 428 (d) 430
    (e) None of these
30. 3, 5, 15, ?, 1125, 84375
    (a) 75 (b) 20
    (c) 45 (d) 80
    (e) None of these

DIRECTIONS (Qs. 31-35) : *Study the following information carefully and answer the given questions.*

Cost of three different fruits (in rupees per kg. in five different cities)

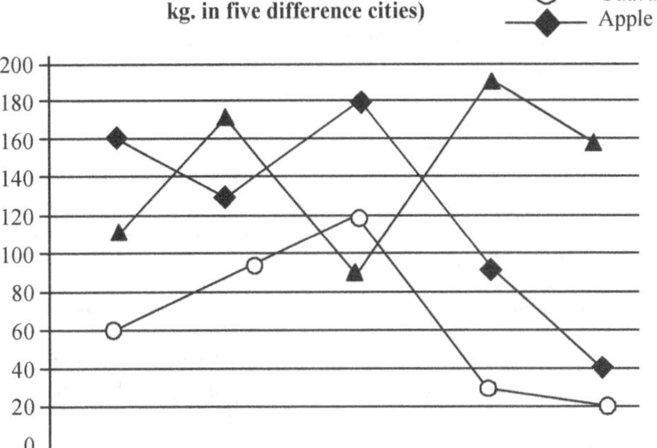

31. In which city is the difference between the cost of one kg of apple and cost of one kg of guava second lowest?
    (a) Jalandhar (b) Delhi
    (c) Chandigarh (d) Hoshiarpur
    (e) Ropar
32. Cost of one kg of guava in Jalandhar is approximately what percent of the cost of two kgs of grapes in Chandigarh?
    (a) 66 (b) 24
    (c) 28 (d) 34
    (e) 58
33. What total amount will Ram pay to the shopkeeper for purchasing 3 kgs of apples and 2 kgs of guavas in Delhi?
    (a) ₹ 530/- (b) ₹ 450/-
    (c) ₹ 570/- (b) ₹ 620/-
    (e) ₹ 490/-
34. Ravinder had to purchase 45 kgs of grapes from Hoshiarpur. Shopkeeper gave him discount of 4% per kg. What amount did he pay to the shopkeeper after the discount?
    (a) ₹ 8,208/- (b) ₹ 8,104/-
    (c) ₹ 8,340/- (b) ₹ 8,550/-
    (e) ₹ 8,410/-

35. What is the respective ratio between the cost of one kg of apples from Ropar and the cost of one kg of grapes from Chandigarh?
    (a) 3 : 2 (b) 2 : 3
    (c) $2^2 : 3^2$ (d) $4^2 : 9^2$
    (e) $9^2 : 4^2$

DIRECTIONS (Qs. 36-37) : *Study the folowing information carefully to answer the given questions*

In a certain code 0 is coded as $ and 1 is * similarly 2 is coded as *$ and 3 is coded as ** and so on....
36. Which of the following will represent 125
    (a) ***$** (b) $*****
    (c) *$**$* (d) **$***
    (e) None of these
37. What is the following number will be represented by *$$$$
    (a) 432 (b) 400
    (c) 421 (d) 401
    (e) None of these

DIRECTIONS (Qs. 38-42) : *Study the given information carefully and answer the given questions.*

Eight people - J, K, L, M, N, O, P and Q are sitting around a circular table facing the centre, not necessarily in the same order. O is sitting third to the right of M. There is only one person sitting between M and J. There are only three people between J and K. P is an immediate neighbour of J. There are only three people between P and L. N is second to the right of P.
38. Which of the following is **true** regarding the given arrangement?
    (a) M is an immediate neighbour of K
    (b) N is an immediate neighbour of J
    (c) P is second to the left of O
    (d) There are four people between N and O.
    (e) None is true
39. Who is sitting second to the left of the one who is sitting second to the left of Q?
    (a) M (b) K
    (c) N (d) L
    (e) J
40. 'Four of the following five are alike in a certain way based on their seating positions in the above arrangement and so form a group. Which one does **not** belong to the group?
    (a) PQ (b) KL
    (c) MN (d) QO
    (e) KO
41. What is N's position with respect to K?
    (a) Second to the left (b) Second to the right
    (c) Third to the left (d) Third to the right
    (e) Fourth to the left
42. How many people are sitting between K and P when counted from the right side of K?
    (a) One (b) Two
    (c) Three (d) None
    (e) More than three

DIRECTIONS (Qs. 43-47): *In each of the questions below, two statements are given followed by two conclusions numbered I and II. You have to take the two statements to be true even if they seem to be at variance from the commonly known facts and then decide which of the given conclusions logically follows from the given statement disregarding the commonly known facts.*

Give answer (a) if **only** concluion **I** follows

Give answer (b) if **only** concluion **II** follows

Give answer (c) if **either** concluion **I** or conclusion **II** follows

Give answer (d) if **neither** conclusion **I** nor conclusion **II** follows

Give answer (e) if **both** conclusions **I and II** follows

43. **Statements :**   Some rings are circles.

                 No circle is a square.

    Conclusions : I.   No ring is a square.

                  II.   All rings are squares.

44. **Statements :**   All rows are lines.

                 All lines are queues.

    Conclusions: I.   All rows are queues.

                 II.   Atleast some queues are lines.

45. **Statements :**   All laptops are computers.

                 Some laptops are notebooks.

    Conclusions: I.   Some notebooks are computers

                 II.   All notebooks are computers.

46. **Statements :**   Some participants are students.

                 Some students are boys.

    Conclusions: I.   No boy is a participant.

                 II.   All boys are participants.

47. **Statements :**   All sparrows are birds.

                 No birds is a reptile.

    Conclusions: I.   No sparrow is a reptile.

                 II.   Some reptiles are sparrows.

DIRECTIONS (Qs. 48-52) : *Study the folowing information carefully to answer the given questions*

12 People are sitting in 2 parallel rows containing 6 people each in such a way that there is an equal distance between adjacent persons. In row 1 - P, Q, R, S, T and V are seated and all of them are facing south. In row 2 - A, B, C, D, E and F are seated all of them are facing north.

A sits 3rd to right of D. Neither A nor D sits at extreme ends. T faces D. V does not face A and V does not sit at any of the extreme ends. V is not an immediate neighbour of T. B sits at on of the extreme ends .Only 2 people sit between B and E. E does not face V. 2 persons sit between R and Q. R is not an immediate neighbour of T. C does not face V. P is not an immediate neighbour of R.

48. Who among the following sits at extreme ends of the rows ?
   (a)   C, A   (b)   P, R
   (c)   C, B   (d)   Both B and C
   (e)   None of these

49. How many persons are seated between T and S ?
   (a)   1   (b)   2
   (c)   3   (d)   More than 3
   (e)   None of these

50. Who among the following faces D ?
   (a)   P   (b)   Q
   (c)   T   (d)   S
   (e)   None of these

51. Who among the following sits between Q and S ?
   (a)   V   (b)   R
   (c)   P   (d)   T
   (e)   None of these

52. Which of the following statement is not true ?
   (a)   Q sits between T and V
   (b)   E is an immediate neighbour of D and F
   (c)   F is immediate left of A
   (d)   2 people sit between T and R
   (e)   None of these

DIRECTIONS (Qs. 53-57) : *Following questions are based on five words given below:*

WIT   BAR   URN   ELF   TOP

(The new words formed after performing the mentioned operations may or may not necessarily be meaningful English words)

53. If in each of the words, all the alphabets are arranged in English alphabetical order within the word, how many words will NOT begin with a vowel ?
   (a)   None   (b)   One
   (c)   Two   (d)   Three
   (e)   More than three

54. How many letters are there in the English alphabetical series between second letter of the word which is second from the right and the third letter of the word which is third from the left of the given words?
   (a)   One   (b)   Two
   (c)   Three   (d)   Four
   (e)   Five

55. If in each of the given words, each of the consonants is changed to previous letter and each vowel is changed to next letter in the English alphabetical series, in how many words thus formed will no vowels appear ?
   (a)   None   (b)   One
   (c)   Two   (d)   Three
   (e)   More than three

56. If the last alphabet in each of the words is changed to the next alphabet in the English alphabetical order, how many words having two vowels (same or different vowels) will be formed ?
   (a)   None   (b)   One
   (c)   Two   (d)   Three
   (e)   Four

57. If the given words are arranged in the order as they would appear in a dictionary from left to right, which of the following will be fourth from the left ?
   (a)   WIT   (b)   BAR
   (c)   URN   (d)   ELF
   (e)   TOP

Digit:	3	9	6	2	8	7	5	4	1
Symbol :	K	T	$	F	H	#	%	D	M

Conditions for the coding the group of digits:

1. If the first digit is odd and last digit is even, the codes for the first and the last digits are to be interchanged.

2. If the first as well as the last digit is even, both are to be coded by the code for last digit.

3. If the first as well as the last digit is odd, both are to be coded as 'X'.

58. **564923**
    - (a) %$DTFK
    - (b) K$DTFK
    - (c) X$DTFX
    - (d) K$DTF%
    - (e) None of these

59. **658247**
    - (a) $%HFD#
    - (b) #%HFD$
    - (c) %$HFD#
    - (d) %#HFD$
    - (e) None of these

60. **436958**
    - (a) DK$T%D
    - (b) DK$T%H
    - (c) HK$T%H
    - (d) #%$HK#
    - (e) None of these

61. **756834**
    - (a) #%$HKD
    - (b) D%$HK#
    - (c) D%$HKD
    - (d) #%$HK#
    - (e) None of these

62. **291378**
    - (a) FTMK#H
    - (b) XTMK#X
    - (c) HTMK#F
    - (d) FTMK#F
    - (e) None of these

63. Which is the third number to the left of the number which is exactly in the middle of the following sequence of numbers?

    1 2 3 4 5 6 7 8 9 2 4 6 8 9 7 5 3 9 8 7 6 4 3 2 1

    - (a) 3
    - (b) 2
    - (c) 5
    - (d) 6
    - (e) None of these

64. If the alphabet is written in the reverse order and every alternate letter starting with Y is dropped, which letter will be exactly in the middle of the remaining letters of the alphabet.
    - (a) M
    - (b) N
    - (c) O
    - (d) M or O
    - (e) None of these

65. In a row of girls, Rita and Monika occupy the ninth place from the right end and tenth place from the left end, respectively. If they interchange their places, then Rita and Monika occupy seventeenth place from the right and eighteenth place form the left respectively. How many girls are there in the row?
    - (a) 25
    - (b) 26
    - (c) 27
    - (d) Data inadequate
    - (e) None of these

DIRECTIONS (Qs. 66-70) : Study the following information carefully to answer these questions.

A group of people has six family members and an advocate. These are L, M, N, O, P, Q and R and having different professions. Each one of them is a journalist, businessman, architect, doctor and pilot but not necessarily in this order. There are three males and three females in the family out of which there are two married couples. M is a businessman and is the father of P. N is a housewife and is daughter-in-law of O. L is neither a pilot nor a journalist. R is an advocate. N is not the mother of P and O is not married to M. No lady is a journalist.

66. Which of the following groups represents the three ladies in the group ?
    - (a) N, P, L
    - (b) P, L, N
    - (c) L, N, O
    - (d) O, P, L
    - (e) None of these

67. Who is married to Q ?
    - (a) N
    - (b) O
    - (c) L
    - (d) Can't be determined
    - (e) None of these

68. Who among the following family members is an architect ?
    - (a) L
    - (b) O
    - (c) P
    - (d) Can't be determined
    - (e) None of these

69. Which of the following is the profession of P ?
    - (a) Architect
    - (b) Pilot
    - (c) Architect or pilot
    - (d) Journalist
    - (e) None of these

70. How is Q related to O ?
    - (a) Father
    - (b) Mother
    - (c) Mother-in- law
    - (d) Son - in - law
    - (e) None of these

ENGLISH LANGUAGE

71. It was astonished (a) / to find that I scarcely had (b) / enough money (c) / to pay the bills. (d) / No error (e)

72. We can not handle (a)./ this complicated case to day (b) / unless full details are not given (c) / to us by now. (d) / No error (e)

73. Even after worked in the office (a) / for as many as fifteen years, (b) / he still does not understand (c) / the basic objectives of the work. (d) / No error (e)

74. Neither the earthquake (a) / nor the subsequent fire (b) / was able to dampen (c) / the spirit of the residents, (d) / No error (e)

75. Our school is making (a) / every possible effort (b) / to provide best facilities (c) / land person attention for each child (d) / No error (e)

76. Our neighbours had repeated (a) / the same illogical sequence of activites (b) / if we had not brought the (c) / facts to their notice. (d) / No error (e)

77. This has forced them to focus at (a) I how to reach and serve their customers, (b) / rather than, say, pumping money (c) / into fancy graphics that look good in management meetings. (d) / No error (e)

78. The loss of forests thus entail (a) / large social and economic costs; (b) the lives of more than one billion people (c) / are already affected by loss of this forest cover (d) / No error (e)

79. Not one of the children (a) / has ever sang (b) / on any occasion (c) / in public before. (d) / No error (e)

80. Reasonable ambition, if supported (a) / at persistent efforts, (b) / is likely to yield (c) / the desied results. (d) / No error (e)

DIRECTIONS (Qs. 81-90) : *Read the following passage carefully and answer the questions given below it. Certain words/phrases are printed in bold to help you to locate them while answering some of the questions.*

Monopolies are bad in national politics and worse in international politics. The unipolar world led by the US is an example of political monopoly. In the language of history and politics, monopolies are discussed in terms of balance of power. What we have today is an imbalance of power. The US-led war against Iraq needs to be seen in the context of this imbalance. There has been much talk about the need for a multipolar world as an ideal solution to the existing anarchy in the international arena. The US – UK combine have been considered to be the perpetrators of the war. They disregarded global public opinion and have gone outside the mandate of the United Nations. This is an indication of US considering itself the only superpower. Its consideration may be justified because it has all the **pervading** might and also the necessary will. Its might is in two domains: one, military, and the other, economic. On every issue of any importance that **confronts** foreign policy-making of any country, US interests become vital. This omnipresence of the US makes it different from any other country. Some political observers argue that this is temporary; that the Russians will be back; that the Germans, Japanese, Europeans are coming; that China is not far away. In short, we occupy a period of **metamorphosis** from a bipolar to a multipolar world, a period that may constitute a unipolar moment but that phase may be over shortly. When will this unipolar moment be over? None has the answer to this question. Most observers view US as somewhere between primacy and dominance, depending on the issue. The main question is how to deal with hegemony, primacy or dominance. In dealing with a big power, a smaller power must choose either balancing or bandwagoning or hiding. In a unipolar world, the general trend of foreign policy will be to **bandwagon**. Middle powers will need to bandwagon less than small powers and on particular issues may be able to balance or hide.

81. For initiating the war, the author of the passage
   (a) appreciates the joint action of the US and the UK
   (b) considers the war as unjustified and blames the US and the UK
   (c) thinks that the United Nations should have admired the US and the UK
   (d) blames the global public opinion
   (e) does not hold any specific viewpoint.

82. According to the author, the world is heading towards
   (a) multipolarity from unipolarity
   (b) unipolarity from bipolarity
   (c) multipolarity from bipolarity
   (d) bipolarity from multipolarity
   (e) not mentioned in the passage

83. What, according to the passage, has made US a super power?
   (a) Its "big-brother" attitude towards other countries
   (b) Its global reach, ambition and might
   (c) Its tactful alignment withUK
   (d) Its war against Iraq for a noble cause
   (e) None of these

84. Which of the following statements is TRUE in the context of the passage?
   (a) The world is heading towards unipolarity.
   (b) The 'multipolarity to unipolarity' transition is certain.
   (c) The unipolarity phase is likely to be short-lived.
   (d) Primacy and dominance are seldom exhibited by the US.
   (e) None of these

85. Which of the following can be inferred from the passage? The author thinks that the US-UK combine should be blamed because they have
   A. converted the world into a bipolar sphere
   B. disregarded anti-war global public opinion
   C. downgraded the esteemed United Nations
   (a) All the three   (b) Only (A) and (C)·
   (c) Only (A) and (B)   (d) Only (B) and (C)
   (e) None of these

86. "Unipolar world" as used in the passage can be best explained by which of the following?
   (a) The world without any independent country and governed by only one superpower
   (b) Existence of only one superpower with all other countries either bandwagoning or hiding
   (c) The world without any geographic or political boundaries
   (d) The unilateral governance with anarchy
   (e) None of these

87. Why do US interests assume importance in deciding foreign policies of any other country?
   (a) US is strong militarily and economically.
   (b) It is hegemonistic and confronts all other small powers.
   (c) It expects others to wag tails before it.
   (d) Other countries are in a multipolar state.
   (e) None of these

88. What is the author's view about middle powers dealing with big powers?
    (a) They can balance, hide or bandwagon, depending upon the issues.
    (b) They can't afford to confront big powers as they might perish.
    (c) They must always shy away from big powers to protect themselves.
    (d) They would like neither to bandwagon nor hide.
    (e) None of these

89. Which of the following is most **OPPOSITE** in meaning of the word pervading given in bold as used in the passage?
    (a) spreading all over
    (b) accommodating the maximum
    (c) with a limited reach
    (d) without influence
    (e) of less importance

90. Choose the word which is most nearly the SAME in meaning to the word **Metamorphosis** given in bold as used in the passage.
    (a) multiples
    (b) agony
    (c) disaster
    (d) lethargy
    (e) transition

DIRECTIONS (Qs. 91–100) : *In the following passage, there are blanks, each of which has been numbered. These numbers are printed below the passage and against each, five words are suggested, one of which fits the blank appropriately. Find out the appropriate word in each case.*

Actually everyday we are engaged in this business of 'reading' people. We do it **91**. We want to figure others out. So we **92** make guesses about what others think, value, want and feel and we do so based on our **93** beliefs and understandings about human nature. We do so because, if we can figure out **94** and intentions of others, the possibility of them **95** or hurting us **96** and this will help us to **97** a lot of unnecessary pain and trouble. We also make second-guesses about what they will do in future, how they will **98** if we make this or that response. Nevertheless, there is a lot of **99** being conducted to **100** the human mind.

91. (a) vehemently
    (b) practically
    (c) actually
    (d) incessantly
    (e) virtually

92. (a) ably
    (b) constantly
    (c) partly
    (d) largely
    (e) positively

93. (a) futuristic
    (b) proactive
    (c) reactive
    (d) decorative
    (e) assumptive

94. (a) manifestations
    (b) expressions
    (c) motives
    (d) hopes
    (e) prospects

95. (a) tricking
    (b) blaming
    (c) furthering
    (d) alarming
    (e) criticising

96. (a) lessens
    (b) happens
    (c) questions
    (d) deepens
    (e) laments

97. (a) approach
    (b) direct
    (c) avoid
    (d) implement
    (e) prepare

98. (a) solve
    (b) apply
    (c) plan
    (d) approach
    (e) respond

99. (a) validation
    (b) derivation
    (c) analysis
    (d) research
    (e) discussion

100. (a) track
     (b) map
     (c) comprehend
     (d) follow
     (e) grasp

Answer Key

1	(c)	11	(d)	21	(d)	31	(b)	41	(c)	51	(a)	61	(b)	71	(c)	81	(b)	91	(d)
2	(a)	12	(b)	22	(a)	32	(d)	42	(b)	52	(d)	62	(e)	72	(c)	82	(c)	92	(b)
3	(d)	13	(b)	23	(d)	33	(c)	43	(d)	53	(b)	63	(b)	73	(a)	83	(b)	93	(e)
4	(d)	14	(d)	24	(c)	34	(a)	44	(e)	54	(e)	64	(b)	74	(c)	84	(c)	94	(c)
5	(c)	15	(b)	25	(e)	35	(c)	45	(a)	55	(c)	65	(b)	75	(d)	85	(d)	95	(a)
6	(a)	16	(b)	26	(e)	36	(d)	46	(d)	56	(c)	66	(b)	76	(a)	86	(b)	96	(a)
7	(c)	17	(b)	27	(d)	37	(b)	47	(a)	57	(c)	67	(a)	77	(c)	87	(a)	97	(c)
8	(b)	18	(d)	28	(c)	38	(b)	48	(d)	58	(c)	68	(d)	78	(a)	88	(a)	98	(e)
9	(d)	19	(b)	29	(b)	39	(a)	49	(b)	59	(a)	69	(a)	79	(b)	89	(c)	99	(d)
10	(d)	20	(e)	30	(a)	40	(e)	50	(c)	60	(c)	70	(a)	80	(b)	90	(e)	100	(b)

HINTS & EXPLANATIONS

1. (c) $? = \dfrac{5.5 \times 6.4}{0.4} = 5.5 \times 16 = 88$

2. (a) Let $? = x, \dfrac{(x - 968)}{79} \times 4 = 512$

$$\Rightarrow x = \dfrac{512 \times 79}{4} + 968 = 11080$$

3. (d) $\dfrac{8}{21} \times ? = 1008 \Rightarrow ? = 1008 \times \dfrac{21}{8}$

$$= 126 \times 21 = 2646$$

4. (d) $? = \dfrac{382 \times 250}{764} = 125$

5. (c) $? = 3.7 \times 0.04 + 5.9$

$? = 0.148 + 5.9 \Rightarrow ? = 6.048$

6. (a) $? = \dfrac{1}{4}(4856 \times 0.5) \times 12$

$$= \left(4856 \times \dfrac{1}{2}\right) \times 3 = 2428 \times 3 = 7284$$

7. (c) $\dfrac{?}{17} = 1000 - 853 = 147 \times 17$

$? = 2499$

8. (b) $? = 4990 - 9643 + 7750 = 3097$

9. (d) $? = 13.15 \times 7.4 + 76.12$

$= 97.31 + 76.12 = 173.43$

10. (d) $\dfrac{6156 \times 53}{\sqrt{?}} = 4028$

$$\Rightarrow \sqrt{?} = 81 \Rightarrow ? = 6561$$

11. (d) Clearly, $\dfrac{1}{7} < \dfrac{1}{\sqrt{7}} = \dfrac{\sqrt{7}}{7} < \sqrt{7}$

$\Rightarrow \dfrac{1}{7}$ is the smallest number.

12. (b) Let the sum be ₹ x

Now, $56 = \dfrac{x \times 8 \times (3 - 2)}{100} \Rightarrow x = ₹ 700$

13. (b) Let the cost price of the machine be ₹ x.

Then, selling price at a profit of 10% = ₹ $\dfrac{11x}{10}$

And the selling price at a loss of 10% = ₹ $\dfrac{9x}{10}$

Consequently, we find that

$$\left(\dfrac{11x}{10} - \dfrac{9x}{10}\right) = 80$$

$$\Rightarrow \dfrac{x}{5} = 80 \Rightarrow x = ₹ 400$$

14. (d) Let the capacity of the jar be of x bottles.
Since 6 bottles were taken out from jar and 4 bottles of oil poured into it
∴ 2 bottles were taken out
Therefore, we have

$$\Rightarrow \dfrac{4}{5}x - 2 = \dfrac{3}{4}x$$

$$\Rightarrow \dfrac{4}{5}x - \dfrac{3}{4}x = 2 \Rightarrow x = 40$$

15. (b) Average speed $= \dfrac{\text{Total distance}}{\text{Total time}} = \dfrac{80}{\dfrac{60}{40} + \dfrac{20}{20}}$

$$= \dfrac{80}{2.5} = 32 \, \text{km/h}$$

16. (b) Let the usual speed of the aeroplane be x km/h.

Then, $\dfrac{1500}{x} - \dfrac{1}{2} = \dfrac{1500}{(x + 250)}$

Solving, we get $x = 750 \, \text{km/h}$

17. (b) Using Venn Diagram

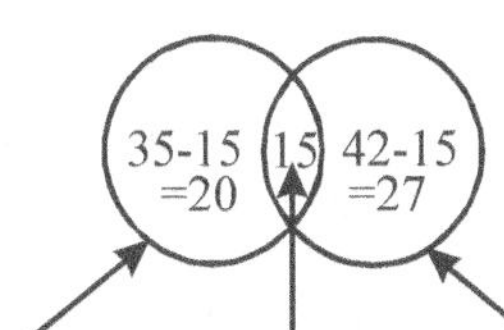

Thus, percentage of students who passed in both subjects
$= 100 - [(35-15) + (42-15) + 15] = 100 - (35+42-15)$
$= 100 - (62) = 38\%$
and percentage of students who failed in both subject $= 15\%$
Therefore, the percentage of students who passed in either subject $= 100 - (38+15) = 100 - 53 = 47\%$
Hence, required no. of students who passed in either subject but not in both $= 2500 \times \dfrac{47}{100} = 1175$

18. (d) Let the length and breadth of the rectangle be x and y cm, respectively.
Then, $(x-4)(y+3) = xy \Rightarrow 3x - 4y = 12$ ... (i)
Also, $(x-4) = (y+3)$ [sides of square]
$\Rightarrow x - y = 7$ ...(ii)
From (i) and (ii),
$x = 16$ and $y = 9$
Perimeter of the original rectangle $= 2(x+y) = 50$ cm

19. (b) Raju's age at the time of marriage
$= 17 + 3 + 2 + 1 + 3 = 26$ years

20. (e) $5x + 6x + 7x = 180°$
$\Rightarrow 18x = 180°$
$\Rightarrow x = \dfrac{180}{18} = 10$
$\therefore$ Sum of the smallest and the largest angles
$= 12x = 12 \times 10 = 120°$

21. (d) 1 day work of $A = \dfrac{1}{x}$
1 day work of $B = \dfrac{1}{3x}$
Both A and B 1 day's work $= \dfrac{1}{x} + \dfrac{1}{3x} = \dfrac{4}{3x}$
1 day work of both A and $B = \dfrac{1}{12}$
$\Rightarrow \dfrac{4}{3x} = \dfrac{1}{12} \Rightarrow 3x = 48$
$\therefore x = 16$

22. (a) Suppose the fraction is $\dfrac{x}{y}$.
$\therefore \dfrac{x + 3x}{y + y} = \dfrac{30}{19}$

$\dfrac{4x}{2y} = \dfrac{30}{19}$
$76x = 60y$
$\dfrac{x}{y} = \dfrac{60}{76} = \dfrac{15}{19}$

23. (d) There are 6 letters in the word CASUAL and 'A' comes two times.
Required number of permutations $= \dfrac{6!}{2!}$
$= \dfrac{6 \times 5 \times 4 \times 3 \times 2!}{2!}$
$= 6 \times 5 \times 4 \times 3 = 360$

24. (c) Suppose each child got x sweets.
$\therefore 112 \times x = (112 - 32) \times (x + 6)$
$112x = 80 \times (x + 6)$
$112x = 80x + 480$
$112x - 80x = 480$
$32x = 480 \Rightarrow x = 15$

24. (e) $x + y = 15$ ...(i)
$x - y = 3$ ...(ii)
Solving Eqs. (i) and (ii), we get
$x = 9, y = 6$
Product of two digits of the number
$= 9 \times 6 = 54$

26. (e) The pattern of number series is as follows:
$24 + 7^2 = \boxed{73}$
$73 + 6^2 = 109$
$109 + 5^2 = 134$
$134 + 4^2 = 150$
$150 + 3^2 = 159$
Hence, the question mark (?) should be replaced by 73.

27. (d) The pattern of number series is as follow:
$17 \times 0.5 + 0.5 = 9$
$9 \times 1 + 1 = 10$
$10 \times 1.5 + 1.5 = \boxed{16.5}$
$16.5 \times 2 + 2 = 35$
$35 \times 2.5 + 2.5 = 90$
Hence, the question mark (?) should be replaced by 16.5.

28. (c) The pattern of number series is as follows:
$3 \times 2 + 14 = 20$
$20 \times 3 + 18 = 78$
$78 \times 4 + 20 = 332$
$332 \times 5 + 20 = 1680$
$1680 \times 6 + 18 = \boxed{10098}$
Hence, the question mark should be replaced by 10098.

29. (b) The pattern of number series is as follow
$13 \times 2 + 4 = 30$
$30 \times 2 + 6 = 66$
$66 \times 2 + 8 = 140$
$140 \times 2 + 10 = \boxed{290}$
$290 \times 2 + 12 = 592$

Hence, the question mark should be replaced by 290.

30. (a) The pattern of number series is as follows
$3 \times 5 = 15$

$5 \times 15 = \boxed{75}$

$15 \times 75 = 1125$

$75 \times 1125 = 84375$

31. (b) Difference between cost of 1 kg apple and cost of 1 kg guava in 5 cities.
J $160 - 60 = 100$
D $130 - 90 = 40$
C $180 - 120 = 60$
H $90 - 30 = 60$
R $40 - 20 = 20$
∴   Cost is second lowest in Delhi.

32. (d) Cost of 1 kg guava in Jalandhar = ₹ 60
Cost of 2 kg grapes in chandigarh = ₹ 90 × 2 = ₹ 180

$\% = \dfrac{60}{180} \times 100 = 33.3 \approx 34\%$

33. (c) Cost of 3 kgs apples for Ram = 3 × 130 = ₹ 390
Cost of 2 kgs guavas for Ram = 2 × 90 = ₹ 180
Total cost that Ram pay = 390 + 180 = ₹ 570

34. (a) Total cost of 45 kgs grapes from Hoshiarpur = 45 × 190
= ₹ 8550

After discount 4% Ravinder paid = $8550 - \dfrac{8550 \times 4}{100}$

= ₹ 8208

35. (c) Cost of 1 kg apples from Ropar :
Cost of 1kg grapes from chandigarh
40 : 90
$4 : 9 \text{ or } 2^2 : 3^2$

36. (d) 0–$
1–*
2–*$
3–**
4–*$$
5–***

37. (b) 4–*$$
0–$
0–$

(38-42)
Formation of fig according to information given

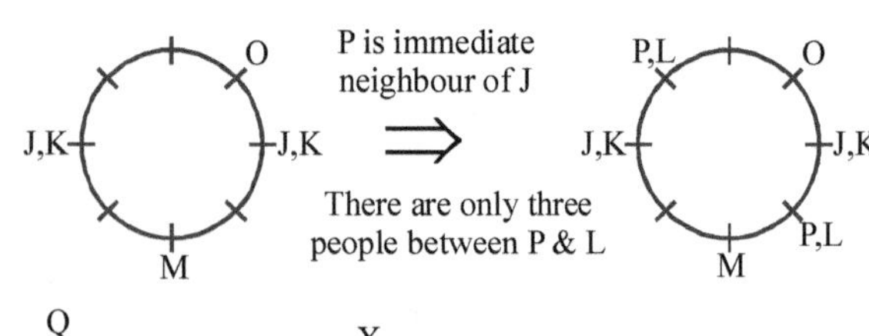

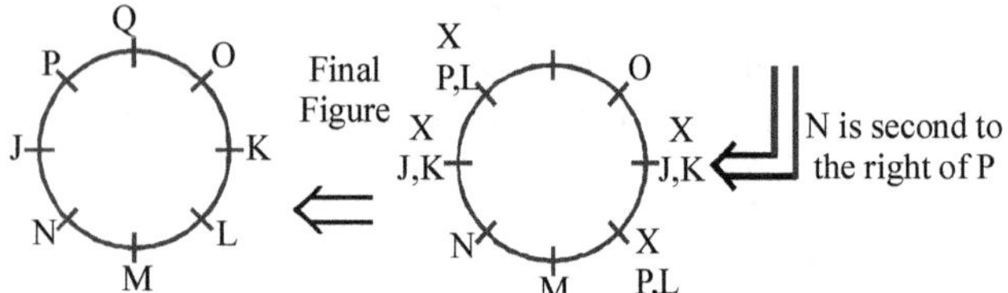

38. (b) N is immediate neighbour of J.
39. (a) 'K' is second to the left of 'Q' and 'M' is second to the left of 'K'.
40. (e) PQ, KL, MN, QO are in clockwise way and KO in anticlockwise way.
41. (c) Third to the left.
42. (b) Only two persons are sitting i.e. 'O' and 'Q'.

43. (d)
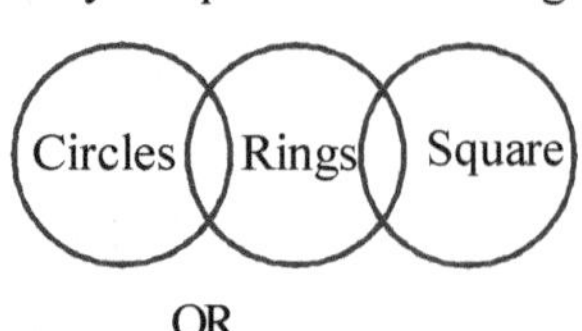

OR

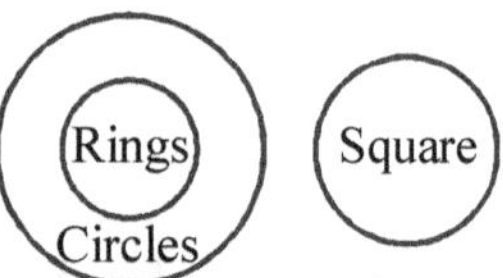

Conclusion-I :   False
Conclusion-II :   False

44. (e)
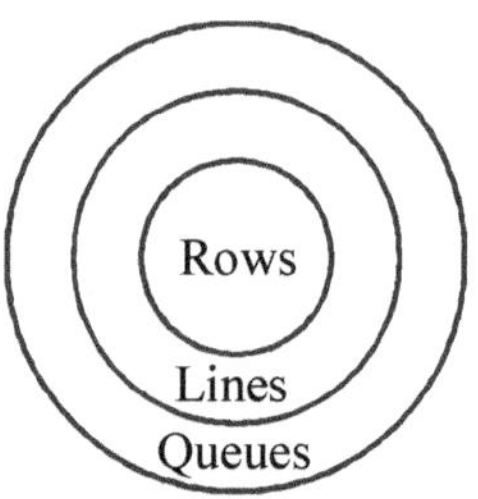

Conclusion-I :   True
Conclusion-II :   True

45. (a)
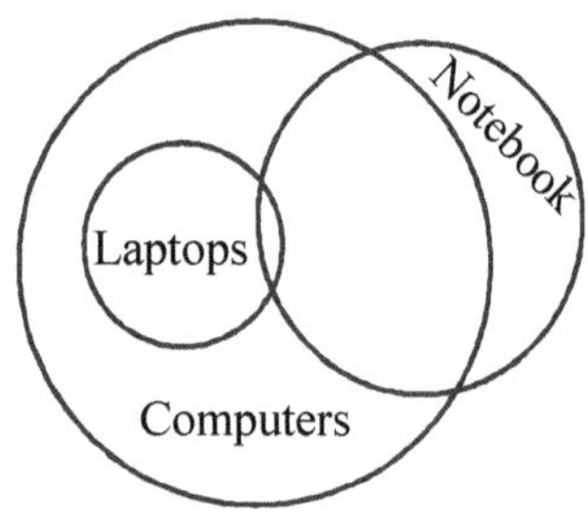

OR

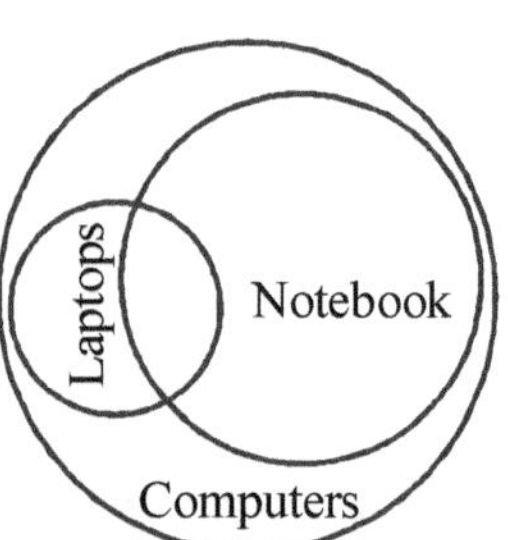

Conclusion-I :   True
Conclusion-II :   False

46. (d)

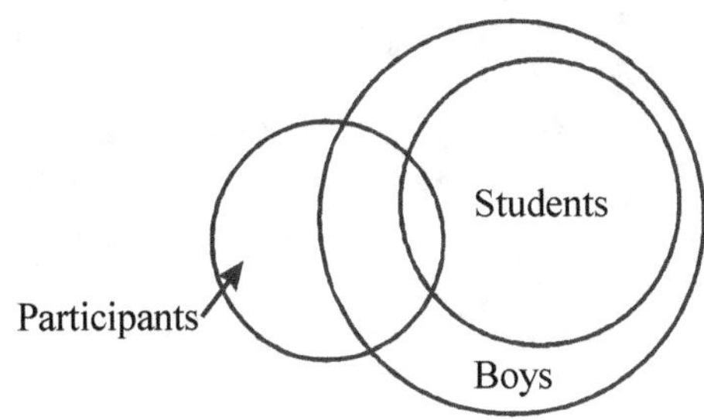

OR

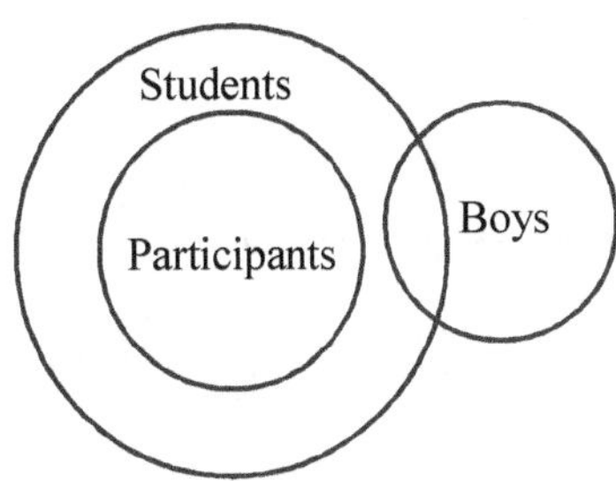

Conclusion-I   False
Conclusion-II   False

47. (a)

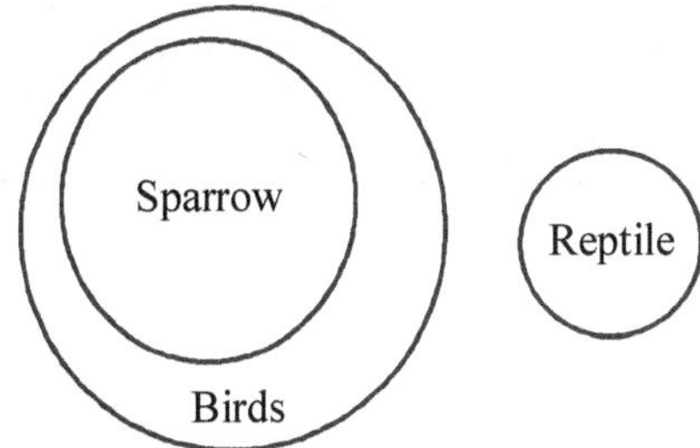

Conclusion-I   True
Conclusion-II   False

(48–52)

48. (d)   **49.** (b)   **50.** (c)   **51.** (a)

52. (d)

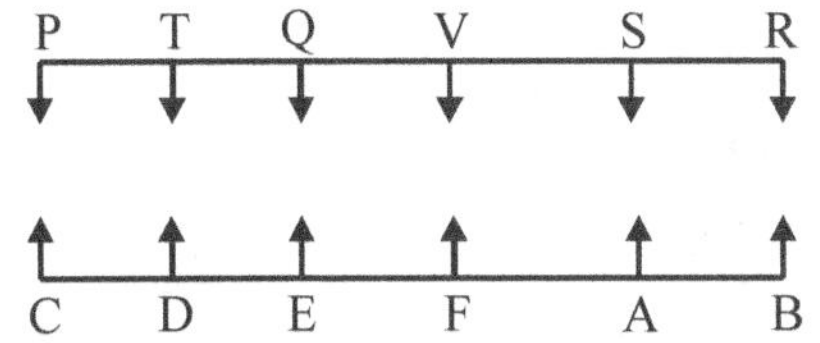

53. (b)   After arranging –

ITW, ABR $\boxed{\text{NRU}}$ EFL OPT

54. (e)

55. (c)

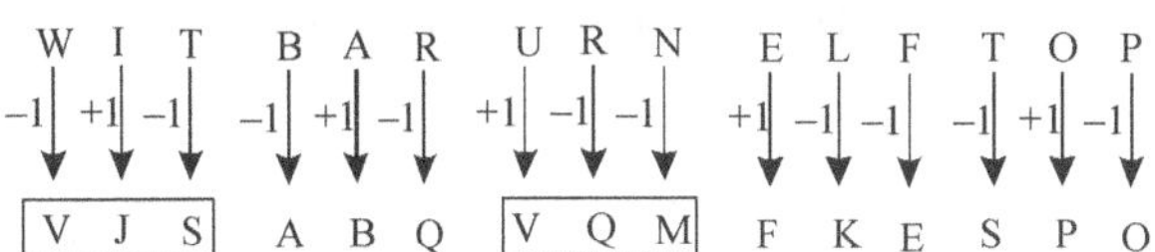

56. (c)   WIT   BAR   URN   ELF   TOP

       ↓ +1   ↓ +1   ↓ +1   ↓   ↓

      $\boxed{\text{WIU}}$ BAS $\boxed{\text{URO}}$ ELG   TOQ

57. (c)   Dictionary order is–

1	2	3	4	5
BAR	ELF	TOP	$\boxed{\text{URN}}$	WIT

(58-62)

Simply follow the rules of the codes and do these sums.

58. (c)   X\$DTFX (Because 1st and last digits are odd.)

59. (a)   \$%HFD# (No condition.)

60. (c)   HK\$T%H (Because 1st and the last digits are even.)

61. (b)   D%\$HK# (Because 1st digit is odd and the last digit is even.)

62. (e)   HTMK#H (Because Ist and the last digits are even.)

63. (b)   There are 25 numbers in the given sequence.
So, middle number = 13th number = 8.
Clearly, the third number to the left of this 8 is 2.

64. (b)   Cancelling every second letter after reversing the alphabet the series becomes.
Z X V T R P N L J H F D B
The middle letter is N.

65. (b)   Total no. of girls = $17 + 10 - 1$ or $18 + 9 - 1 = 26$.

Sol. (66 - 70)

The given information can be tabulated as follows

Person	Sex	Relationship	Profession
L	Female	Wife of M	Architect
M	Male	Father of P.	Businessman
		Husband of L.	
		Son of Q and O.	
N	Female	Daughter-in-law of O and Q.	Housewife
O	Female	Wife of Q	Pilot
P	Male	Son of M and L.	Journalist
Q	Male	Grandfather of P.	Doctor
		Husband of Q.	
		Father of M.	
R	–	–	Advocate

Two married couples : LM and QO.

66. (c)   **67.** (b)   **68.** (a)   **69.** (d)

70. (e)

71. (c) : Replace 'enough' by 'any'

72. (c) : Remove 'not'

73. (a) : Add 'having' after 'after'

74. (c) : Replace 'was able to ' by 'could'

75. (d) : Replace 'for' by 'to'

76. (a) : Replace 'had' by 'would have'

77. (c) : Replace 'pumping' by 'pump'

78. (a) : Replace 'ential' by 'entails'

79. (b) : Replace 'sang' by 'sung'

80. (b) : Replace 'at' by 'with'

PRACTICE SET 15

Time : 60 Minutes **Max. Marks : 100**

NUMERICAL ABILITY

DIRECTIONS (Qs. 1-5) : *What approximate value should come in place of the question mark (?) in the following questions (You are not expected to calculate the exact value).*

1. $623898 \times 99 = ? \times 60000$
   - (a) 1000
   - (b) 1030
   - (c) 1050
   - (d) 1065
   - (e) 1010

2. $\dfrac{4}{5} \times \dfrac{3}{7} \div \dfrac{6}{7} \div \dfrac{5}{9} = ?$
   - (a) $\dfrac{9}{17}$
   - (b) $\dfrac{20}{49}$
   - (c) $\dfrac{18}{25}$
   - (d) $\dfrac{1}{2}$
   - (e) $\dfrac{4}{7}$

3. $399.98^2 = ?$
   - (a) 160000
   - (b) 15999
   - (c) 1600
   - (d) 1599
   - (e) 16000

4. $\sqrt{624.9995} + (4.9989)^2 = ? \div \dfrac{1}{4.9900865}$
   - (a) 6
   - (b) 50
   - (c) 10
   - (d) 125
   - (e) 15

5. $989.001 + 1.00982 \times 76.792 = ?$
   - (a) 1000
   - (b) 1100
   - (c) 1065
   - (d) 110
   - (e) 100

DIRECTIONS (Qs. 6-10) : *What will come in place of question mark (?) in the following questions ?*

6. $784 \div 16 \div 7 = ?$
   - (a) 49
   - (b) 14
   - (c) 21
   - (d) 7
   - (e) None of these

7. $\dfrac{3}{2}$ of $455 + \dfrac{5}{8}$ of $456 = ?$
   - (a) 448
   - (b) 476
   - (c) 480
   - (d) 464
   - (e) None of these

8. $6425 \div 125 \times 8 = ?$
   - (a) 411.2
   - (b) 41.12
   - (c) 64.25
   - (d) 421.25
   - (e) None of these

9. 1.05% of $2500 + 2.5\%$ of $440 = ?$
   - (a) 37.50
   - (b) 37.25
   - (c) 370.25
   - (d) 372.50
   - (e) None of these

10. $4900 \div 28 \times 444 \div 12 = ?$
    - (a) 6575
    - (b) 6475
    - (c) 6455
    - (d) 6745
    - (e) None of these

11. A boy was asked to write $2^5 \times 9^2$ but he wrote 2592. The numerical difference between the two is
    - (a) 0
    - (b) 3
    - (c) 2
    - (d) 9
    - (e) None of these

12. If the two numbers are respectively 20% and 50% of a third number, what is the percentage of the first number to the second?
    - (a) 10
    - (b) 20
    - (c) 30
    - (d) 40
    - (e) None of these

13. A man gains 10% by selling a certain article for a certain price. If he sells it at double the price, then the profit made is
    (a) 120%   (b) 60%
    (c) 100%   (d) 80%
    (e) None of these

14. A, B and C enter into a partnership with investments of ₹3500, ₹4500 and ₹5500, respectively. In the first six months, profit is ₹405. What is A's share in the profit?
    (a) ₹200   (b) ₹105
    (c) ₹250   (d) ₹151
    (e) None of these

15. Pipes A and B can fill a tank in 5 and 6 hours, respectively. Pipe C can empty it in 12 hours. The tank is half full. All the three pipes are in operation simultaneously. After how much time, the tank will be full?
    (a) $3\dfrac{9}{17}$ h   (b) 11 h
    (c) $2\dfrac{8}{11}$ h   (d) $1\dfrac{13}{17}$ h
    (e) None of these

16. If the sum of the digits of an even number is divisible by 9, then that number is always divisible by
    (a) 24   (b) 12
    (c) 18   (d) 27
    (e) None of these

17. A water tank in the form of a cuboid has its base 20 m long, 7 m wide and 10 m deep. Initially, the tank is full but later when water is taken out of it, the level of water in the tank reduces by 2 m. The volume of water left in the tank is
    (a) $1120 \, m^3$ (b) $400 \, m^3$
    (c) $280 \, m^3$ (d) $140 \, m^3$
    (e) None of these

18. The total number of students studying in a college is 4220. If the number of girls studying in the college is 2420, what is the respective ratio of the number of boys to the number of girls studying in the college?
    (a) 90 : 131   (b) 90 : 121
    (c) 121 : 70   (d) 121 : 80
    (e) None of these

19. The cost of 14 kgs. of rice is ₹672, the cost of 12 kgs. of wheat is ₹432 and the cost of 18 kgs. of sugar is ₹504. What is the total cost of 20 kgs. of rice, 15 kgs. of wheat and 16 kgs. of sugar?
    (a) ₹1,898   (b) ₹1,948
    (c) ₹2,020   (d) ₹1,964
    (e) None of these

20. If the compound interest accrued on an amount of ₹14500 in 2yr is ₹4676.25, what is the rate of interest percent per annum?
    (a) 11   (b) 9
    (c) 15   (d) 18
    (e) None of these

21. The average of the ages of 3 friends is 23. Even if the age of the 4th friend is added the average remains 23. What is the age of the 4th friend?
    (a) 32 yr   (b) 21 yr
    (c) 23 yr   (d) Cannot be determined
    (e) None of these

22. Samir drove at the speed of 45 km from home to a resort. Returning over the same route, he got stuck in traffic and took an hour longer, also he could drive only at the speed of 40 km. How many kilometres did he drive each way?
    (a) 250   (b) 300
    (c) 310   (d) 275
    (e) None of these

23. An urn contains 3 red and 4 green marbles. If three marbles are picked at random, what is the probability that two are green and one is red?
    (a) $\dfrac{3}{7}$ (b) $\dfrac{18}{35}$
    (c) $\dfrac{5}{14}$ (d) $\dfrac{4}{21}$

24. The difference between the $\dfrac{3}{4}$th of $\dfrac{4}{5}$th of a number and $\dfrac{1}{6}$th of $\dfrac{2}{5}$th of the same number is 648. What is the number?
    (a) 1110   (b) 1215
    (c) 1325   (d) 1440
    (e) None of these

25. Inside a square plot, a circular garden is developed which exactly fits in the square plot and the diameter of the garden is equal to the side of the square plot which is 28 metres. What is the area of the space left out in the square plot after developing the garden?
    (a) $98 \, m^2$ (b) $146 \, m^2$
    (c) $84 \, m^2$ (d) $168 \, m^2$
    (e) None of these

DIRECTIONS (Qs. 26-30) : *In each of the following questions a number series is given with one wrong number. Find out that wrong number.*

26. 2, 3, 6, 15, 45, 156.5, 630
    (a) 3   (b) 45
    (c) 15   (d) 6
    (e) 156.5

27. 36, 20, 12, 8, 6, 5, 5, 4.5
    (a) 5.5   (b) 6
    (c) 12   (d) 20
    (e) 8

28. 1, 3, 9, 31, 128, 651, 3313
    (a) 651   (b) 128
    (c) 31   (d) 9
    (e) 3

29. 2, 3, 10, 40, 172, 855, 5346
    (a) 3   (b) 855
    (c) 40   (d) 172
    (e) 10

30. 5, 8, 16, 26, 50, 98, 194
    (a) 8   (b) 26
    (c) 50   (d) 16
    (e) 98

DIRECTIONS (31–35) : *Study the pie-charts carefully to answer the questions that follow :*

Percent of employees and women working in different Departments of an Organisation.

Percentage of employees working in different departments

N = 8450 = Total no. of employees

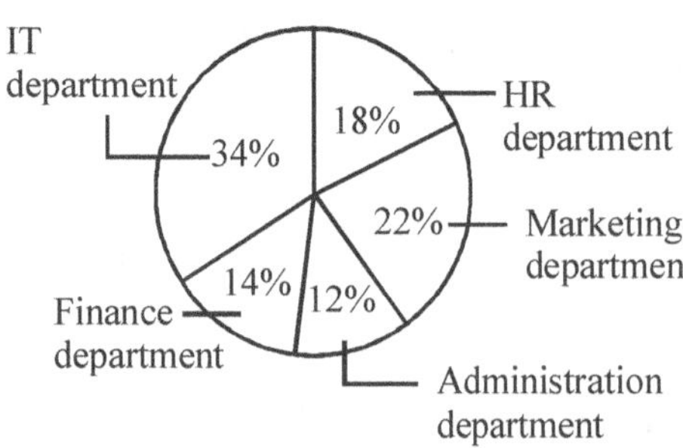

Percentage of women working in different departments
Total no. of women = 3500

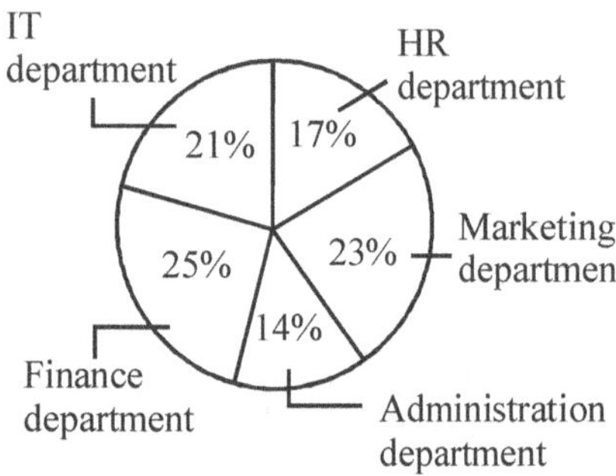

31. Which department has the lowest number of Men working in it?
    (a) HR
    (b) Marketing
    (c) Administration
    (d) Finance
    (e) IT

32. What is the average number of Men working in different departments in the organisation?
    (a) 890
    (b) 900
    (c) 1020
    (d) 780
    (e) None of these

33. What is the respective ratio of number of women working in Administration department to the total number of employees working in that department?
    (a) 6 : 7
    (b) 245 : 507
    (c) 7 : 6
    (d) 243 : 322
    (e) None of these

34. Number of women working in the Finance & IT department together form what per cent of total number of employees in the organisation? (rounded off to two digits after decimal)
    (a) 19.05
    (b) 26.78
    (c) 95.83
    (d) 59.21
    (e) None of these

35. What is the number of men working in the HR department?
    (a) 794
    (b) 823
    (c) 926
    (d) 683
    (e) None of these

DIRECTIONS (Qs. 36-40) : *In each question below are two/ three statements followed by two conclusions numbered I and II. You have to take the two/three given statements to be true even if they seem to be at variance from commonly known facts and then decide which of the given conclusions logically follows from the given statements disregarding commonly known facts.*

Give answer (a) if **only** conclusion I follows.

Give answer (b) if **only** conclusion II follows.

Give answer (c) if **either** conclusion I or conclusion II follows.

Give answer (d) if **neither** conclusion I nor conclusion II follows.

Give answer (e) if **both** conclusion I and conclusion II follow.

36. **Statements** : All kites are birds. All aeroplanes are kites. No bird is a fish.
    Conclusions : I. No fish is a kite.
    II. All aeroplanes are birds.

37. **Statements** : Some wires are fires. All fires are tyres.
    Conclusions : I. Atleast some tyres are wires.
    II. Some fires are definitely not wires.

38. **Statements** : No clip is a pin. All badges are pins.
    Conclusions : I. No badge is a clip.
    II. All pins are badges.

39. **Statements** : No colour is a paint. No paint is a brush.
    Conclusions : I. No colour is a brush.
    II. All brushes are colours.

40. **Statements** : All stars are planets. All planets are galaxies.
    Conclusions : I. All galaxies are planets.
    II. All stares are galaxies.

DIRECTIONS (Qs. 41-45) : *Study the following information to answer the given questions:*

Eight people are sitting in two parallel rows containing four people each, in such a way that there is an equal distance between adjacent persons. In row-1 P, Q, R and S are seated (but not necessarily in the same order) and all of them are facing south. In row-2 A, B, C and D are seated (but not necessarily in the same order) and all of them are facing north. Therefore, in the given seating arrangement each member seated in a row faces another member of the other row.

R sits second to the right of P. A is an immediate neighbour of the person who faces R. Q sits second to left of the person who faces A. Only one person sits between B and C. C does not face P. C does not sit at any of the extreme ends of the line.

41. Four of the following five are alike in a certain way based on the given seating arrangement and thus form a group. Which is the one that does not belong to that group ?
    (a) A
    (b) P
    (c) R
    (d) B
    (e) S

42. Who amongst the following faces B?
    (a) P   (b) Q
    (c) R   (d) S
    (e) Cannot be determined
43. Which of the following is true regarding S?
    (a) S sits exactly between R and P
    (b) S sits second to left of Q
    (c) P is an immediate neighbour of S
    (d) D is an immediate neighbour of the person who faces S
    (e) None is true
44. Who amongst the following faces Q?
    (a) A   (b) B
    (c) C   (d) D
    (e) Cannot be determined
45. Who amongst the following faces the person who sits exactly between B and C?
    (a) P   (b) Q
    (c) R   (d) S
    (e) Cannot be determined

DIRECTIONS (Qs. 46-50) : *In each question below is given a group of letters followed by four combinations of digits/symbols numbered (a), (b), (c) and (d). You have to find out which of the combinations correctly represents the group of letters based on the coding system and the conditions given below and mark the number of that combination as your answer. If none of the combinations correctly represents the group of letters, mark (e) i.e. 'None of these' as your answer.*

Letters	P	M	A	E	J	K	D	R	W	H	I	U	T	F
Digits/symbols Conditions	4	$	1	2	3	#	5	@	©	6	%	δ	7	9

(i) If the first letter is a consonant and the last letter is a vowel, the codes of both these are to be interchanged.
(ii) If both the first and the last letters are consonants both these are to be coded as per the code of the last letter.
(iii) If the first letter is vowel and the last letter is a consonant both these are to be coded as '✶'
    Note: All the remaining letters are to be coded as per their original codes.

46. ERWHKA
    (a) 2@©6#1   (b) 1@©6#2   (c) 1@©6#I
    (d) 2@©6#2   (e) None of these
47. MPEKDU
    (a) $42#5δ   (b) $42#5$ (c) δ42#5δ
    (d) δ425#$ (e) None of these
48. TMEIUF
    (a) 7$2%δ9   (b) 7$2%δ7   (c) 9$2%δ7
    (d) 9$2%δ9   (e) None of these
49. JTAERI
    (a) % 712@3   (b) 3712@3   (c) ✶712@✶
    (d) %712@%   (e) None of these

50. UKTMIH
    (a) ✶#7$%6   (b) 6#7$%δ   (c) ✶#7$%✶
    (d) ✶7#$%6   (e) None of these

DIRECTIONS (Qs. 51-55) : *Study the following information to answer the given questions:*

A, B, C ,D , E, F and H live on eight different floors , Ground floor is no 1, 1st floor is no 2 and so on. There are 2 floors between the floor on which B and H live. D lives on an odd - numbered floor and he does not live immediate below or above F's floor. F lives below H's floor.

D does not live immediately below or above B's floor. A does not live on an even numbered floor. C does not live on the topmost floor. G lives on 6th floor. E does not live below H and B lives on floor no 5.

51. How many floors are there between the floors on which D and H live?
    (a) One   (b) Two
    (c) Three   (d) Four
    (e) None of the above
52. Who among the following lives on the floor no 3?
    (a) A   (b) B
    (c) C   (d) F
    (e) None of the above
53. Four of the following five are alike in a certain way and so form a group. Which does not belong to that group?
    (a) ED   (b) BC
    (c) HF   (d) BA
    (e) None of the above
54. E lives on which of the following floor?
    (a) 4th floor   (b) 8th floor
    (c) 3rd floor   (d) 7th floor
    (e) None of the above
55. Who lives between A and F?
    (a) C   (b) G
    (c) B   (d) H
    (e) None of the above

DIRECTIONS (Qs. 56-57) : A @ B means A is wife of B
A $ B means A is father of B
A # B means A is mother of B
A % B means A is son of B
A © B means A is sister of B

56. How is P related to M in the given expression: M % N © O @ P $ Q?
    (a) Brother   (b) Father
    (c) Aunt   (d) Uncle
    (e) None of the above
57. Which of the following expression represents D is brother of G?
    (a) D @ E $ F $ G   (b) D % E @ F $ G
    (c) G % F @ E $ D   (d) G @ E $ F % D
    (e) None of the above

58. A cat run 20m towards East and Turns to right runs 10m and turns to right runs 9m and again turns to left run 5m and then turns to left runs 12m and finally turns to left and runs 6m .Now which direction cat facing?

   (a) South   (b) West
   (c) North   (d) East
   (e) Cannot be determined

59. In a row of boys, Kapil is eighth from the right and Nikunj is twelfth from the left. When Kapil and Nikunj interchange positions, Nikunj becomes twenty first from the left. Which of the following will be Kapil's position from the right?

   (a) 8th   (b) 17th
   (c) 21st   (d) Canont be determined
   (e) None of these

60. In a certain code ATE is written as 145 and CHAIR is written as 09173 then how TEACHER can be written in that code-

   (a) 4501953   (b) 4510953
   (c) 4310934   (d) 4530943
   (e) None of these

DIRECTIONS (Qs. 61-65) : *Study the following arrangement carefully and answer the questions given below :*

P 1 % T R A 5 # D M 7 K ★ E G 2 8 $ H 3 1 4 V U 6 F ⊕ 9 Z

61. How many such symbols are there in the above arrangment, each of which is immediately preceded by a consonant and also immediately followed by a consonant ?

   (a) None   (b) One
   (c) Two   (d) Three
   (e) More than three

62. Four of the following five are alike in a certain way based on their position in the above arrangement. Which is the one that **does not** belong to that group ?

   (a) V1F   (b) EK8
   (c) R % #   (d) 6V9
   (e) $G3

63. How many such vowels are there in the above arrangement, each of which is immediately preceded by a digit and immediately followed by a consonant ?

   (a) None   (b) One
   (c) Tow   (d) Three
   (e) More than three

64. Which of the following is exactly in the middle between the fifth element from the left end and the seventh element from the right end?

   (a) G   (b) 2
   (c) E   (d) ★
   (e) None of these

65. If the positions of last twelve elements in the above arrangement are reversed, which of the following will be the eigth element to the right of the eleventh element from the left ?

   (a) H   (b) I
   (c) ⊕   (d) 9
   (e) None of these

DIRECTIONS (Qs. 66-70) : *Read the given information carefully and answer the questions :*

Six boxes A, B, C, D, E, and F are placed one above another, also they are occupied with different items i.e. O, P, Q, S, N, and M (but not necessarily in the same order).

Box which is occupied with Q is not placed at top. A is placed either top or bottom, only 2 boxes are placed between A and D, which is occupied with S. Only 1 box is placed between D and F. Box E is not placed just above and below D. Box E is not placed just below the box which is occupied with O. Box which is occupied with M is placed between D and F. The box which is placed just above B is occupied with P. The box which is placed at bottom occupied with N. Box B is not placed above A.

66. Box C is occupied with which of the following item?

   (a) N   (b) P
   (c) S   (d) M
   (e) None of these

67. Which of the following box is placed at top?

   (a) A   (b) F
   (c) C   (d) E
   (e) None of these

68. How many boxes are placed between box F and box E?

   (a) One   (b) Three
   (c) Two   (d) More than three
   (e) None of these

69. Which box is placed just above box B?

   (a) D
   (b) The box which is occupied with P
   (c) F
   (d) Both (b) and (c)
   (e) None of these

70. Box B is occupied with which of the following item?

   (a) N   (b) P
   (c) M   (d) Q
   (e) None of these

ENGLISH LANGUAGE

DIRECTIONS (Qs. 71-80) : *Read each sentence to find out whether there is any error in it. The error, if any will be in one part of the sentence. The number of that part is the answer. If there is no error the answer is (e). (Ignore error of punctuations, if any).*

71. I would have lost (a) / my luggage and other belonging (b) / if I would have left the compartment (c) / and gone out to fetch drinking water. (d) / No errro (e)

72. Whether this happens, and whether the BIFR will (a) / once again reconsiger the Sirmour package (b) / are questions those will be (c) / answered in the comming months. (d) / No error (e)

73. We now look forward for (a) / some great achievements (b) / which to some extent (c) / can restore the country's prestige once again (d) / No error (e)

74. Honesty and integrity are (a) / the qualityes which cannot be (b) / done away with (c) / and hence assume a lot of importance (d) / No error (e)

75. The foreign funds are cheaper than those (a) / available the domestic market and (b) / the company is competent that (c) / it will soon touch its earlier annual turnover, (d) / No error (e)

76. Honesty, integrity and being intelligent (a) / are the qualities which (b) / we look for when (c) / we interview applicants (d) / No error (e)

77. Not only the judges acquitted (a) / him of all the charges (b) / levelled against him, but (c) / also commended all his actions. (d) /No error (e)

78. One of the most effective (a) / solutions is that (b) / she should work on Sunday (c) / and complete the assignment. (d) / No error (e)

79. Our system of assigning (a) I different jobs to different people (b) / should be based on (c) / their strengths and weaknesses (d) / No error (e)

80. There he stood on the dais, (a) / debunked the manner in which the company was run (b) / by the former chairman and managing director, (c) / and promising higher growth and industry. (d) No error (e)

DIRECTIONS (Qs. 81-88): *Read the following passage carefully and answer the questions given below it. Certain words/phrases are printed in **bold** to help you to locate them while answering some of the questions.*

Since July 1991, the Government of India has effectively put the liberalisation policy into practice. The drastic steps even include some administrative reforms for pruning the government agencies. Last year Japanese business circles represented by the Ishikawa Mission called the attention of their Indian counterparts to what they considered to be the major **impediments** in India. However, thanks to the almost revolutionary reforms put into effect by the Indian government, those impediments either have been removed or now are on their way out. This development gives a new hope for the future of economic co-operation between the two countries. At the same time, it should be borne in mind that there is a stiff competition with other countries, notably China and South-East Asian countries, in this regard. The success stories of ASEAN countries welcoming Japanese investments with adequate infrastructure are already known in India but it may be useful if further studies of Japanese joint ventures in ASEAN countries be made by Indian business circles. The coastal areas of China have initiated a very active campaign to welcome foreign economic participation.

Beyond our bilateral relationship, India's more active participation in global economy is needed. India certainly deserves a far bigger share of world trade considering its vast resources. It is strongly hoped that the Indian government's recently initiated effort of enlarging its export market would bear fruit.

India has steadfastly maintained its parliamentary democracy since independence. Considering its size, its population and its internal complexity, the overall maintenance of national integrity and political stability under parliamentary democracy is remarkable and admirable indeed. Here lies the base for the status of India in the world. By effectively implementing its economic reform with the support of public opinion, this democratic polity of India has again demonstrated its viability and **resilience**. At the same time, it gives hope and inspiration to the whole world which faces the difficult problem of North-South confrontation.

81. The Ishikawa Mission during its visit to India emphasized on
    (a) future economic co-operation between Japan and India.
    (b) need for removing policy and/or implementation hurdles.
    (c) need for a stiff competition.
    (d) striking down revolutionary reforms.
    (e) None of these

82. How did the Indian government react to the hurdles in· the way of bilateral trade between India and Japan?
    (a) The government, in principle, agreed for removal of these hurdles.
    (b) Bureaucracy succeeded in maintaining a status quo.
    (c) Government thought it was against liberalisation policy.
    (d) The Japanese delegation could not forcefully argue their case.
    (e) It failed to remove these hurdles.

83. What is the result of Japanese investments in ASEAN nations?
    (a) It could not gather momentum for want of infrastructure.
    (b) The experiment failed because of stiff competition from other countries.
    (c) China and South-East Asian countries objected to Japanese investments.
    (d) The passage does not provide complete information..
    (e) None of these

84. Which of the following is TRUE about the author's view regarding India's participation in world trade?
    (a) India should actively contribute in a big way as it had tremendous resources.
    (b) India's sharing in global economy has already been very fast and beyond its resources.
    (c) India should refrain from making efforts in enlarging its export market.
    (d) India needs to first strengthen its democracy.
    (e) None of these

85. It can be inferred from the content of the passage that the author is a/an
    (a) political analyser   (b) Japanese bureaucrat
    (c) economist   (d) Japanese politician
    (e) Indian Prime Minister

86. The author seems to appreciate India's national integrity and political stability, particularly in view of which of the following ?
    A. the size of the country
    B. India's population
    C. its internal complexity
    (a) None of the three   (b) All the three
    (c) A & B only   (d) B & C only
    (e) A & C only

87. The author feels that India has a better status in the world market because of its
    (a) success in political stability and national integration in democratic set-up.
    (b) vast population.
    (c) giant size.
    (d) effective bilateral relationship with other countries.
    (e) foreign economic participation.

88. Which of the following statements is TRUE in the context of the passage?
    A. India's successful experiment of economic reform has become an inspiration to the world.
    B. Size, population and internal complexity of our country are the barriers in the way of attaining national integrity and political stability.
    C. A few government agencies were not in favour of liberalisation policy at the beginning.
    (a) A only   (b) B only
    (c) C only   (d) All the three
    (e) None of these

DIRECTION (Q. 89) : *Choose the word which is most nearly the SAME in meaning as the word printed in bold as used in the passage.*

89. **Resilience**
    (a) quietening   (b) amplifying
    (c) existence   (d) adaptability
    (e) rejuvenation

DIRECTION (Q. 90):*Choose the word which is most OPPOSITE in meaning of the word printed in bold as used in the passage.*

90. **Impediments**
    (a) exaggeration   (b) compendium
    (c) obstacle   (d) aggravation
    (e) furtherance

DIRECTIONS (Qs. 91 - 100) : *In the following passage there are blanks, each of which has been numbered. These numbers are also printed below the passage and against each five words are suggested, one of which fits the blank appropriately. Find out the appropriate word in each case.*

A good percentage of the population of India is tribal. The tribals live in the hills and forests of the country and have been little **91** by the **92** currents of the plains. Practically all the states of India have their tribal population. The tribes are numerous, computed to about 200, some living in **93** regions in the dense forests, and others on the borders of villages. Some tribes are **94** to a few souls, while others like the Santhals, run into millions and are steadily **95** in numbers. During the British Period some of them were known as 'criminal tribes' for they showed **96** respect for the Indian Panel Code. After independence they have been named Scheduled Tribes. Under modern conditions isolation, however, has become **97** and the hill tribes are getting **98**. The cultural traffic is two-way. Social reformers are taking civilisation to the hills, and the tribes, **99** their old occupations of hunting and **100** farming, are settling in villages, towns and cities as labourers and industrial workers.

91. (a) affected   (b) domiciled
    (c) motivated   (d) deprived
    (e) favoured

92. (a) financial   (b) proud
    (c) cultural   (d) unruly
    (e) swift

93. (a) comfortable   (b) marshy
    (c) wild   (d) unpopulated
    (e) inhospitable

94. (a) devoted   (b) confined
    (c) susceptible   (d) related
    (e) attached

95. (a) constant   (b) deteriorated
    (c) developing   (d) increasing
    (e) decreasing

96. (a) abundant   (b) genuine
    (c) superficial   (d) exorbitant
    (e) scant

97. (a) crucial   (b) convenient
    (c) necessary   (d) indispensable
    (e) difficult

98. (a) civilized   (b) demoralised
    (c) wiped-out   (d) entertained
    (e) reduced

99. (a) escaping   (b) with
    (c) enhancing   (d) leaving
    (e) continuing

100. (a) productive   (b) primitive
     (c) profitable   (d) cultivatable
     (e) scientific

Answer Key

1	(b)	11	(a)	21	(c)	31	(d)	41	(c)	51	(d)	61	(a)	71	(c)	81	(b)	91	(a)
2	(c)	12	(d)	22	(e)	32	(e)	42	(a)	52	(a)	62	(e)	72	(c)	82	(a)	92	(c)
3	(a)	13	(a)	23	(b)	33	(b)	43	(e)	53	(d)	63	(a)	73	(a)	83	(d)	93	(e)
4	(c)	14	(b)	24	(b)	34	(a)	44	(d)	54	(b)	64	(c)	74	(d)	84	(a)	94	(b)
5	(c)	15	(d)	25	(d)	35	(c)	45	(b)	55	(d)	65	(d)	75	(b)	85	(c)	95	(d)
6	(d)	16	(c)	26	(e)	36	(b)	46	(a)	56	(d)	66	(e)	76	(a)	86	(b)	96	(e)
7	(c)	17	(a)	27	(a)	37	(a)	47	(e)	57	(b)	67	(a)	77	(a)	87	(a)	97	(c)
8	(a)	18	(b)	28	(b)	38	(a)	48	(d)	58	(c)	68	(b)	78	(e)	88	(a)	98	(e)
9	(b)	19	(b)	29	(c)	39	(c)	49	(a)	59	(b)	69	(d)	79	(b)	89	(d)	99	(d)
10	(b)	20	(c)	30	(d)	40	(b)	50	(c)	60	(b)	70	(c)	80	(d)	90	(e)	100	(b)

HINTS & EXPLANATIONS

1. (b) We have,
$$623898 \times 99 = ? \times 60000$$
$$\therefore \quad ? = \frac{623898 \times 99}{60000}$$
$$= \frac{623898 \times 100 - 623898}{60000} \approx 1030$$

2. (c) We have,
$$= \frac{4}{5} \times \frac{3}{7} \div \frac{6}{7} \div \frac{5}{9} = \frac{4}{5} \times \frac{3}{7} \times \frac{7}{6} \times \frac{9}{5} = \frac{18}{25}$$

3. (a) $(399.98)2 \approx (400)^2 \approx 160000$

4. (c) We have, $\sqrt{624.9995} + (4.9989)^2 = ? \div \dfrac{1}{4.9900865}$
$$\approx \sqrt{625} + (5)^2 = ? \div \frac{1}{5}$$
$$\therefore \ ? = \frac{1}{5}(25 + 25) = 10$$

5. (c) $989.001 + 1.00982 \times 76.792$
$$\approx 990 + 1 \times 76.8 = 1066.8 \approx 1065$$

6. (d) $? = 784 \div 16 \div 7$
$$\Rightarrow ? = \frac{784}{16} \div 7 \ \Rightarrow \ ? = 49 \div 7 = 7$$

7. (c) $? = \dfrac{3}{7} \text{of } 455 + \dfrac{5}{8} \text{of } 456$
$$\Rightarrow \quad ? = \frac{3}{7} \times 455 + \frac{5}{8} \times 456$$
$$\Rightarrow \quad ? = 195 + 285$$
$$\Rightarrow \quad ? = 480$$

8. (a) $? = 6425 \div 125 \times 8$
$$\Rightarrow \quad ? = 51.4 \times 8$$
$$\Rightarrow \quad ? = 411.2$$

9. (b) $? = 1.05\% \text{ of } 2500 + 2.5\% \text{ of } 440$
$$\Rightarrow \quad ? = \frac{1.05}{100} \times 2500 + \frac{2.5}{100} \times 440$$
$$\Rightarrow \quad ? = \frac{2625}{100} + \frac{1100}{100}$$
$$\Rightarrow \quad ? = \frac{3725}{100} = 37.25$$

10. (b) $? = 4900 \div 28 \times 444 \div 12$
$$\Rightarrow \quad ? = 175 \times 37$$
$$\Rightarrow \quad ? = 6475$$

11. (a) $2^5 \times 9^2 = 32 \times 81 = 2592$
$$\therefore \text{ Difference} = 2^5 \times 9^2 - 2592$$
$$= 2592 - 2592 = 0$$
Hence, the numerical difference is 0.

12. (d) Let the third number be 100. Then, the first and second numbers will be 20 and 50, respectively.
$$\text{Required } \% = \frac{20}{50} \times 100 = 40$$

13. (a) Let the cost price of an article be ₹ 100
then, S.P. = 100 + 10 = ₹ 110
If S.P. = 2 × 110 = ₹ 220
$$\text{then, profit } \% = \frac{(220 - 100)}{100} \times 100 = 120\%$$

14. (b) Ratio of investments of A, B and C
$= 3500 : 4500 : 5500 = 35 : 45 : 55 = 7 : 9 : 11$
Since, Ratio of investment is same as ratio of profit.
∴ Ratio of profit = 7 : 9 : 11
Now, profit = ₹ 405
$$\therefore \ \text{A's share} = \frac{7}{27} \times 405 = ₹ 105$$

15. (d) Part of the tank filled by the three pipes working simultaneously in one hour is $= \dfrac{1}{5} + \dfrac{1}{6} - \dfrac{1}{12} = \dfrac{17}{60}$

i.e. it takes $\dfrac{60}{17}$ hours to fill up the tank completely.

Now, $\dfrac{1}{2}$ of the tank is filled with all the pipes open,

simultaneously together in $\dfrac{60}{17} \times \dfrac{1}{2} = 1\dfrac{13}{17}$ hours

16. (c) Any even number is given by 2n for all n $\in$ Z, where Z is a set of integers. This is divisible by 9 if it form 9 × 2n = 18n, which is divisible by 18.
For example, number 36 is even and sum of digits (3 + 6) is 9, which is divisible by 9. Hence, the number 36 is divisible by 18.

17. (a) Volume of water left in the tank $= \ell \times b \times h$
$= 20 \times 7 \times (10 - 2) = 1120 \, \text{m}^3$

18. (b) Required ratio
$= (4220 - 2420) : 2420$
$= 1800 : 2420$
$= 90 : 121$

19. (b) C.P. of 20 kg of rice
$$= ₹\left(\dfrac{672}{14} \times 20\right)$$
$$= ₹960$$
C.P. of 15 kg of wheat
$$= ₹\left(\dfrac{432}{12} \times 15\right)$$
$$= ₹540$$
C.P. of 16 kg of sugar
$$= ₹\left(\dfrac{504}{18} \times 16\right)$$
$$= ₹448$$
$\therefore$ Total cost price
$= ₹(960 + 540 + 448)$
$= ₹1948$

20. (c) $\text{CI} = P\left[\left(1 + \dfrac{r}{100}\right)^r - 1\right]$

$$467625 = 14500\left[\left(1 + \dfrac{r}{100}\right)^2 - 1\right]$$

$$\Rightarrow \dfrac{467625}{14500} = \left(1 + \dfrac{r}{100}\right)^2 - 1$$

$$\Rightarrow \dfrac{467625}{14500} + 1 = \left(1 + \dfrac{r}{100}\right)^2$$

$$\Rightarrow \dfrac{467625 + 14500}{14500} = \left(1 + \dfrac{r}{100}\right)^2$$

$$\Rightarrow \sqrt{\dfrac{1917625}{14500}} = 1 + \dfrac{r}{100}$$

$$\Rightarrow \sqrt{1.3225} = 1 + \dfrac{r}{100}$$

$$\Rightarrow \sqrt{\dfrac{13225}{10000}} = 1 + \dfrac{r}{100}$$

$$\Rightarrow \dfrac{115}{100} = 1 + \dfrac{r}{100}$$

$$\Rightarrow \dfrac{r}{100} = \dfrac{115}{100} - 1$$

$$\Rightarrow \dfrac{r}{100} = \dfrac{115 - 100}{100}$$

$$\Rightarrow \dfrac{r}{100} = \dfrac{115}{100} \Rightarrow r = 15\%$$

21. (c) $\dfrac{x_1 + x_2 + x_3}{3} = 23 \qquad \text{...(i)}$

ATQ, $\dfrac{x_1 + x_{\frac{3}{2}} + x_3 + x_4}{4} = 23$

$\Rightarrow x_1 + x_2 + x_3 + x_4 = 23 \times 4$

$\Rightarrow \dfrac{x_1 + x_2 + x_3}{3} + \dfrac{x_4}{3} = \dfrac{23 \times 4}{3}$

$\Rightarrow x_4 = 23$

22. (e) Suppose required distance was x km.

$\therefore \quad \dfrac{x}{40} - \dfrac{x}{45} = 1$

$\Rightarrow \dfrac{9x - 8x}{360} = 1 \Rightarrow \dfrac{x}{360} = 1$

$x = 360 \, \text{km}$

23. (b) $n(S)$ = Number of ways to select 3 marbles out of 7 marbles = $^7C_3$

$$= \dfrac{7 \times 6 \times 5}{1 \times 2 \times 3} = 35$$

$n(E)$ = Probability that two are green and one is red

$$= {}^4C_2 \times {}^3C_1 = \dfrac{4 \times 3}{1 \times 2} \times 3 = 18$$

Required probability $= \dfrac{n(E)}{n(S)} = \dfrac{18}{35}$

24. (b) Suppose number is x.

$\therefore \quad x \times \dfrac{4}{5} \times \dfrac{3}{4} - x \times \dfrac{2}{5} \times \dfrac{1}{6} = 648$

$\dfrac{12x}{20} - \dfrac{2x}{30} = 648$

$\Rightarrow \dfrac{36x - 4x}{60} = 648$

$\Rightarrow \dfrac{32x}{60} = 648$

$\Rightarrow x = \dfrac{648 \times 60}{32} = 81 \times 15$

$\Rightarrow x = 1215$

25. (d) 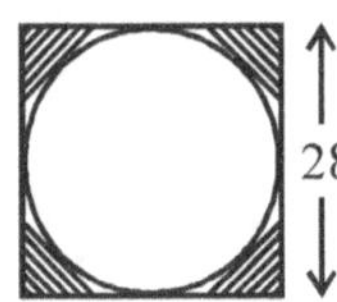

We have to calculate the area of the shaded region which is equal to area of square − Area of the circle

$$\text{Required answer} = (28)^2 - \frac{22}{7} \times 14 \times 14$$

$$= 784 - 616 = 168 \text{ m}^2$$

26. (e) The series is
$\times 1.5, \times 2, \times 2.5, \times 3$
and so on.

27. (a) The series is
$-16, -8, -4, -2, -1, -0.5$
and so on.

28. (b) The series is
$\times 1 + 2, \times 2 + 3, \times 3 + 4$ and so on.

29. (c) The series is
$\times 1 + 1^2, \times 2 + 2^2, \times 3 + 3^2$
and so on.

30. (d) The series is $\times 2 - 2$.

(31–35) :

HR department

$$\text{Total number of employees} = \frac{18}{100} \times 8450 = 1521$$

$$\text{Number of women} = \frac{17}{100} \times 3500 = 595$$

Number of men = 1521 − 595 = 926

Marketing department

$$\text{Total number of employees} = \frac{22}{100} \times 8450 = 1859$$

$$\text{Number of women} = \frac{23}{100} \times 3500 = 805$$

Number of men = 1859 − 805 = 1054

Administration department

$$\text{Total number of employees} = \frac{12}{100} \times 8450 = 1014$$

$$\text{Number of women} = \frac{14}{100} \times 3500 = 490$$

Number of men = 1014 − 490 = 524

Finance department

$$\text{Total number of employees} = \frac{14}{100} \times 8450 = 1183$$

$$\text{Number of women} = \frac{25}{100} \times 3500 = 875$$

Number of men = 1183 − 875 = 308

IT department :

$$\text{Total number of employees} = \frac{34}{100} \times 8450 = 2873$$

$$\text{Number of women} = \frac{21}{100} \times 3500 = 735$$

Number of men = 2873 − 735 = 2138

31. (d) Number of men in finance department = 308

32. (e) Required average = $\dfrac{926 + 1054 + 524 + 308 + 2138}{5}$

$$= \frac{4950}{5} = 990$$

33. (b) Required ratio = 490 : 1014 = 245 : 507

34. (a) Number of women working in the Finance and IT department
= 875 + 735 = 1610
Total number of employees = 8450

$$\text{Required percentage} = \frac{1610}{8450} \times 100 = 19.05$$

35. (c) Number of men working in HR department = 926

36. (b) 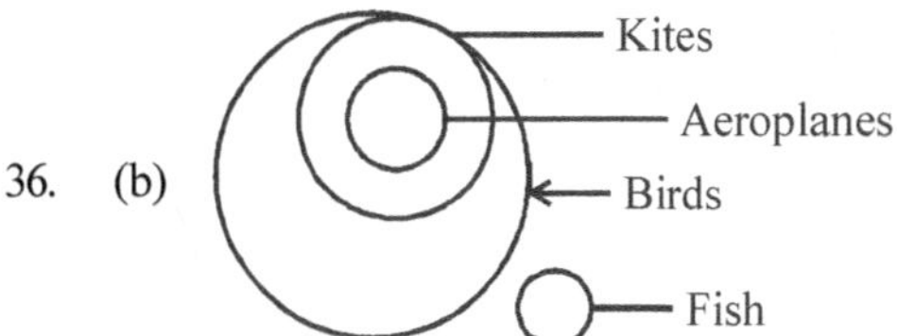

37. (a) 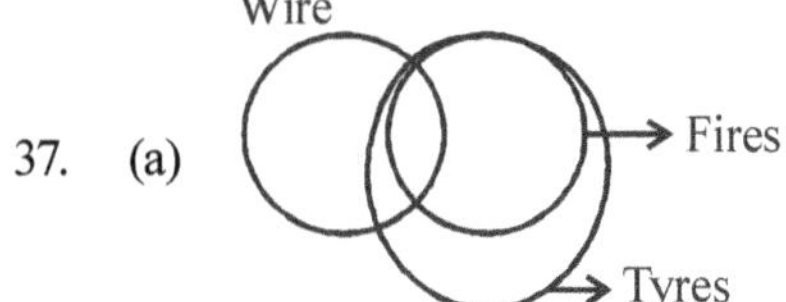

38. (a) 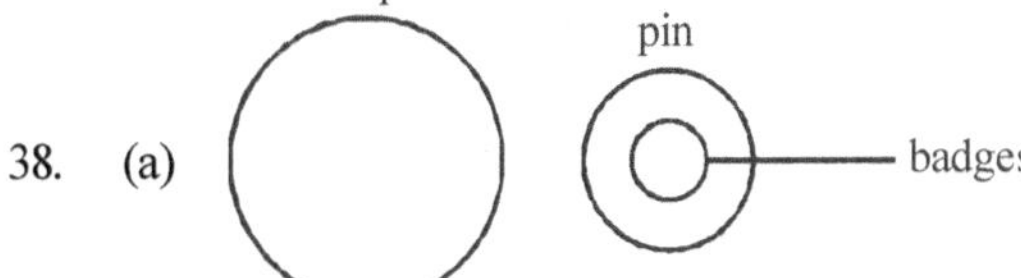

39. (c) 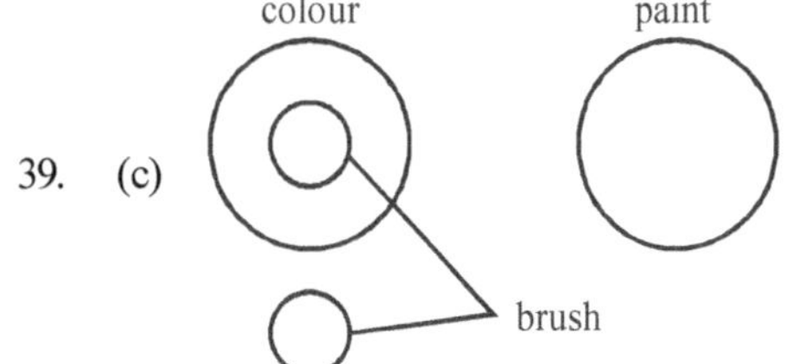

40. (b) 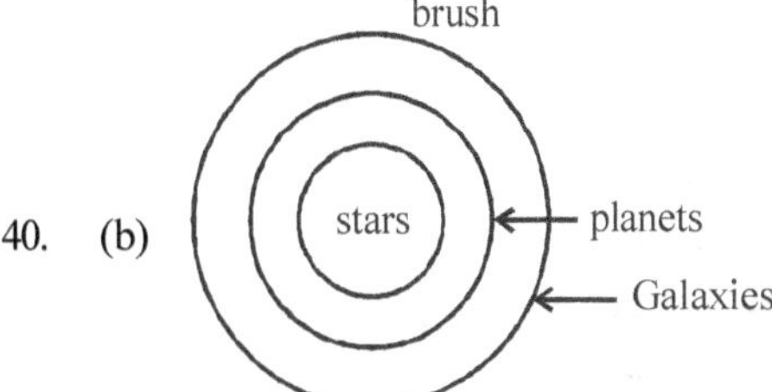

(41-45) 

41. (c)   42. (a)   43. (e)   44. (d)   45. (b)

46. (a)

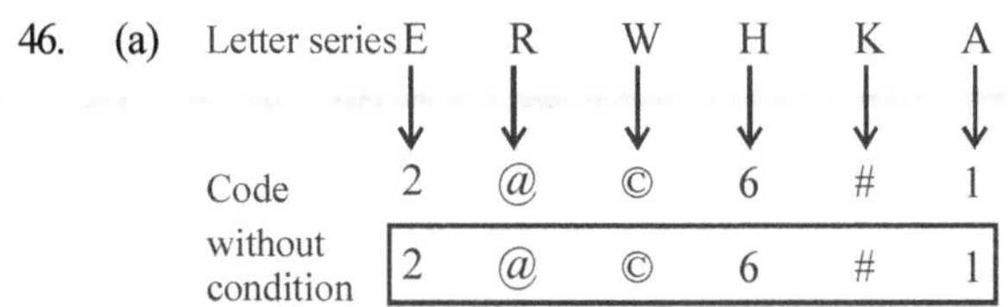

Letter series: E R W H K A

Code: 2 @ © 6 # 1

without condition: 2 @ © 6 # 1

47. (e)

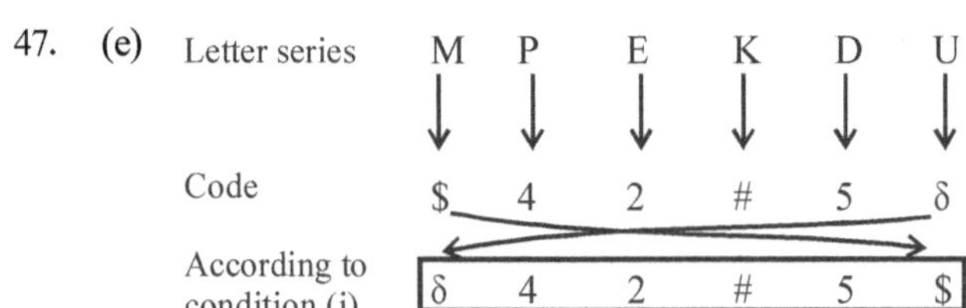

Letter series: M P E K D U

Code: $ 4 2 # 5 δ

According to condition (i): δ 4 2 # 5 $

48. (d)

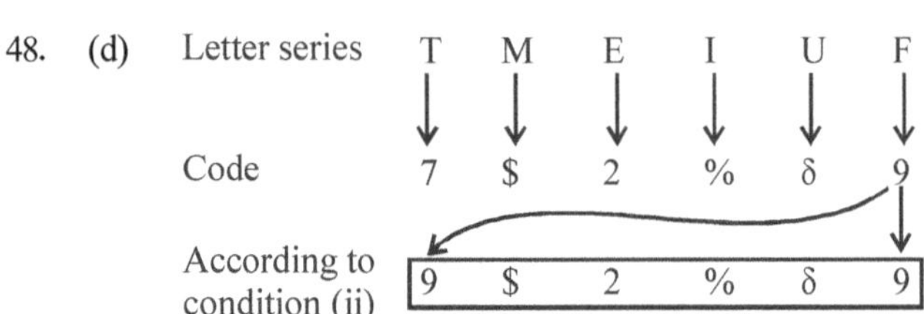

Letter series: T M E I U F

Code: 7 $ 2 % δ 9

According to condition (ii): 9 $ 2 % δ 9

49. (a)

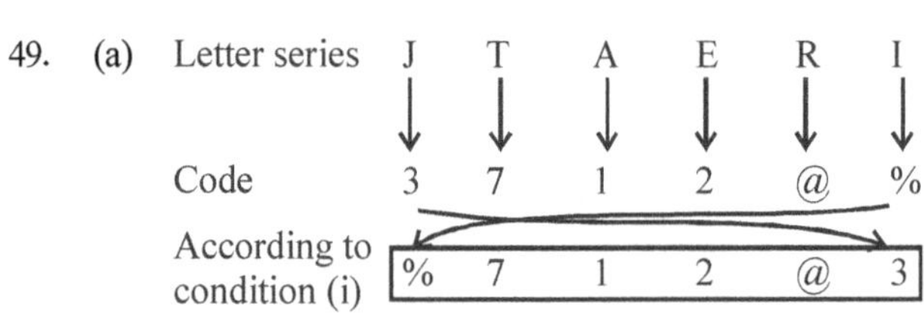

Letter series: J T A E R I

Code: 3 7 1 2 @ %

According to condition (i): % 7 1 2 @ 3

50. (c)

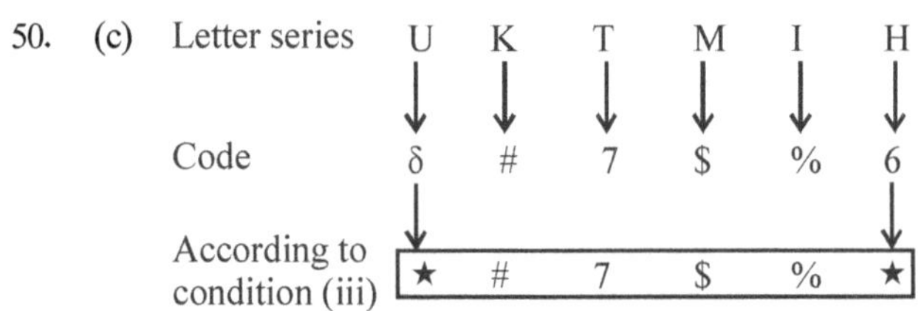

Letter series: U K T M I H

Code: δ # 7 $ % 6

According to condition (iii): ★ # 7 $ % ★

(51-55) :

Floor	Person
8	E
7	D
6	G
5	B
4	C
3	A
2	H
1	F

51. (d)   **52.** (a)   **53.** (d)

54. (b)   **55.** (d)   **56.** (d)

57. (b)

58. (c)

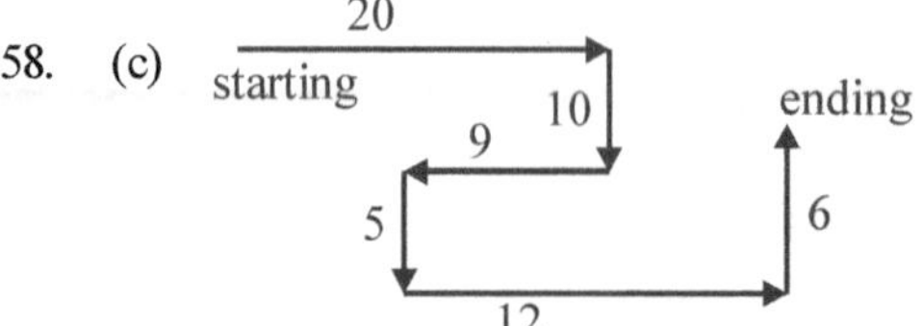

59. (b) Since Kapil and Nikunj interchange places, so Nikunj's new position (21st from left) is the same as Kapil's earlier positon (8th from right).

So, number of boys in the row = (20 + 1 + 7) = 28.

Now, Kapiil's new position is the same as Nikunj's earlier position i.e. 12th from left.

∴ Kapil's position from the right = (28 - 11) = 17th.

60. (b) T = 4, E = 5, A = 1, C = 0, H = 9, E = 5, R = 3 can be decoded directly

61. (a) P 1 % T R A 5 # D M 7 K ★ E G 2 8 $ H 3 1 4 V U 6 F ⧾ 9 Z

In the above series there is no consonant symbol-consonant sequence.

62. (e) Except it in each choice second and third elements are second to the left of first elements and third to the right of first element respectively.

63. (a) We have to look for digit-vowel-consonant sequence in the following series.

P 1 % T R A 5 # D M 7 K ★ E G 2 8 $ H 3 1 4 V U 6 F ⧾ 9 Z

There is no such sequence.

64. (c) E is exactly in the middle between the fifth element from the left end and the seventh element from the right end.

65. (d) After changing the series becomes as follows:

P 1 % T R A 5 # D M 7 K ★ E G 2 8 Z 9 ⧾ F 6 U V 4 1 3 H $

Now, eigth element to the right of eleventh from the left, i.e., 9.

(66-70)

Box	Items
A	O
F	P
B	M
D	S
C	Q
E	N

66. (e)   **67.** (a)   **68.** (b)   **69.** (d)   **70.** (c)

71. (c) Replace 'would have' by 'had'

72. (c) Replace 'those' by 'which'

73. (a) Replace 'for' by 'two'

74. (d) Add 'they' before 'assume'

75. (b) Add 'which are' before 'available'

76. (a) Replace 'being intelligent' by 'intelligence'

77. (a) The correct form is 'The judges not only acquitted

78. (e) No error

79. (b) The correct form is 'different people diferent jobs.'

80. (d) Replace 'promising' by 'promissed'. 366 (c): Replace 'done' by 'made'